Machine Learning for Econometrics

Machine Learning for Econometrics

Christophe Gaillac
Jérémy L'Hour

OXFORD
UNIVERSITY PRESS

OXFORD
UNIVERSITY PRESS

Great Clarendon Street, Oxford, OX2 6DP,
United Kingdom

Oxford University Press is a department of the University of Oxford.
It furthers the University's objective of excellence in research, scholarship,
and education by publishing worldwide. Oxford is a registered trade mark of
Oxford University Press in the UK and in certain other countries

Published in the United States of America by Oxford University Press
198 Madison Avenue, New York, NY 10016, United States of America

British Library Cataloguing in Publication Data

Data available

Library of Congress Control Number: 2025934681

ISBN 9780198918820
ISBN 9780198918837 (pbk.)

DOI: 10.1093/9780198918868.001.0001

Printed and bound by
CPI Group (UK) Ltd, Croydon, CR0 4YY

Jérémy: In loving memory of my mother, Jocelyne L'Hour

Acknowledgments

The authors would like to thank Arthur Charpentier, Laurent Davezies, Emmanuel Flachaire, Gauthier Germain, Yannick Guyonvarch, Elia Lapenta, Franck Malherbet, and Anna Simoni for their valuable feedback throughout its writing process of the French version of the book. We would also like to express our gratitude to Pierre Alquier and Xavier D'Haultfoeuille for encouraging us to teach this course and subsequently write this textbook.

Authors

Christophe GAILLAC is Associate Professor at the University of Geneva, Geneva School of Economics and Management (GSEM), Institute of Economics and Econometrics (IEE), and previously researcher at Oxford University. He received his PhD in Economics from Toulouse School of Economics.

Jérémy L'HOUR is a quantitative researcher at Capital Fund Management (CFM), a Paris-based systematic hedge fund. He received his PhD in Economics from Université Paris-Saclay.

They both are affiliated to the Economics Department of Centre de Recherche en Économie et Statistique (CREST) – Institut Polytechnique de Paris (IP Paris), and taught 'Machine learning for econometrics' as well as numerous courses at ENSAE Paris for several years. They published *Machine learning pour l'économétrie* (Economica, 2023).

Contents

Chapter 1
Introduction

1.1 Econometrics versus machine learning

Econometrics and machine learning (ML) share many statistical tools, as we will see in Chapter 2. However, the philosophies and goals of these two approaches often differ in subtle ways. To draw the contours of the two fields and give the reader an idea of the questions that animate them, we will first exaggerate their differences. We remind the reader that the reality is much more nuanced: the purpose of this textbook is to see how we can harness the forces of one to achieve the goals of the other.

The first point of divergence lies in the purpose of the two approaches. Econometrics, first and foremost, aims to quantify a precisely defined effect. For instance: what is the impact of a minimum wage increase on employment? Are there peer effects among groups of students? What is the average wage gap between women and men? In this sense, the econometrician focuses on one or a few parameters of interest aimed at summarizing the effect they seek to measure. We are particularly interested in statistical inference, i.e., building confidence intervals and testing hypotheses. More specifically, over the last three decades, empirical economics has focused on measuring causal effects, not just correlations (Angrist and Pischke, 2010), an effort crowned by the Nobel Prize awarded to Joshua Angrist, Guido Imbens, and David Card in 2021, as well as the one awarded to Esther Duflo two years earlier. This paradigm is studied in Chapter 3. The crux of most economics articles is to demonstrate the rigor of their *identification strategy*, i.e., to prove that the measured effect is due only to the highlighted causal variable, excluding other parasitic phenomena. Hence, the interest in laboratory, field, or natural experiments, or the search for *exogenous variation* in a particular policy, i.e., generated by a cause independent of the phenomenon of interest.

On the other hand, the goal of ML is to build a model that allows one to obtain the best possible predictive performance for a given problem, often by respecting a computational constraint when calling the model, also called *runtime* or *inference time* performance. Thus, the model must generate predictions within a defined timeframe. ML researchers often talk about *algorithms* rather than *models*, to stress that this process is based on a series of instructions that lead to a prediction, regardless of their nature, rather than on a single statistical model. ML is therefore used to respond to different problems than those of econometrics, such as constructing song or movie recommendation systems, matching job-seekers to firms, translating

Machine Learning for Econometrics. Christophe Gaillac and Jérémy L'Hour, Oxford University Press.
 DOI: 10.1093/9780198918868.003.0001

documents, predicting the next data point in a time series, categorizing products, recognizing patterns in images, retrieving documents based on their content, etc. The term *artificial intelligence* (AI) is often used as a synonym for machine learning. This term underlines that a machine replaces the human in performing a cognitive task and that its implementation can be carried out on a very large scale at a very small marginal cost – the main fixed costs consisting of *training* the algorithm and then making it available. As an aside, these costs are far from negligible, so much so that training large language models (LLMs) like the one that powers ChatGPT from scratch can run to well over a few million dollars.

Machine learning is an area in which computer science is ubiquitous, and comparing ML algorithms with traditional algorithms can help to understand the paradigm differences. Traditional algorithms consist of fixed rules, established a priori by a human, that the machine simply executes; whereas training an ML algorithm consists of using datasets that correctly associate *inputs* with *outputs* to teach the computer the implicit rules underlying these associations, regardless of the exact nature of these rules, as long as they produce relevant responses for the (human) end-user. In the case of analyzing text data, this is the difference between using a regular expression (Chapter 12) and a modern language model (Chapter 14).

It is noteworthy that machine learning, and *deep learning* in particular, have achieved their most impressive successes in well-defined tasks characterized by a favorable signal-to-noise ratio. Such tasks are those that most humans are capable of performing: recognizing an object in an image, finding the synonym of a word, recommending a movie that a friend will enjoy, etc. However, two main roadblocks hinder their automation on a large scale: on the one hand, they are greedy in cognitive resources, and on the other hand, they are challenging to reformulate as standard predictive tasks due to the unstructured nature of the input data. The lack of structure in the input data makes it challenging to create *features* (explanatory variables) or to integrate them into conventional statistical frameworks because they do not neatly fit into a table, as opposed to *tabular data* social scientists are used to tackling. This is the case for images, for example, which are characterized by integer tensors representing pixels, but each pixel taken separately does not contain any information. Text is another case of unstructured data which can be represented as a sequence of integers that are uniquely mapped to *tokens* (pieces of words), which cannot be easily represented in a table because documents vary in length and word occurrences do not follow an auto-regressive process. Therefore, the capability to scale a task achievable by humans and to incorporate unstructured and highly complex data into a mathematical model fuels the current enthusiasm around ML. Its performance on tasks difficult to perform by a human being, because they might suffer from too high a level of noise or flagrant non-stationarities such as the prediction of macroeconomic series or stock prices, is yet to be demonstrated.

To nuance this first difference between the two fields, we recall that forecasting is a well-known econometric subfield whose similarities with machine learning are very easy to see (Chapter 11). Nevertheless, econometric forecasting, because it often deals with complex phenomena, imposes a heavier structure on the data *via* a more constrained model. The goal is to counteract an unfavorable signal-to-noise ratio by injecting theoretical priors into models.

These differences in objectives usually lead to a second point of divergence: the approach to building models. The gist of econometrics is to summarize the information contained in the data to measure a precise quantity. One is concerned only with a particular causal relationship, and not with fully predicting a phenomenon (Chapter 3). Econometric models are therefore preferably simpler, with an emphasis on linearity, and their structure is usually motivated by a theory of the underlying causal relationship or of individual behavior. They are often based on certain assumptions that are not falsifiable, or difficult to verify using statistical tests. A significant example is the exogeneity condition when employing an instrumental variable technique (Section 3.4).

In ML, if we were to paint with a broad brush, prediction performance is the only criterion for selecting a model. Therefore, there is less reluctance to use a black-box approach provided it is effective (e.g., using deep neural networks, Section 2.8). A standard set of metrics is traditionally used to evaluate the performance of a model, and since they are part of the ML background, we must introduce them now. Let's take a binary classification problem where one wants to predict a random variable $Y \in \{0, 1\}$ (also called a *label*). For example: will a customer purchase my product (or click on the link)? Will the price of this asset go up or down next week? Is this product review positive or negative? Notice that this is a *supervised learning* task i.e., one where the ground truth is observed in the data, as opposed to an *unsupervised learning* task for which the "correct answer" is not known with certainty. Suppose we have an algorithm giving a prediction $\widehat{Y}$ for a given input. For a given data point, if $\widehat{Y} = 1$ it is said to be "positive," and if $\widehat{Y} = 0$ it is said to be "negative." Algorithm performance is evaluated by calculating various metrics. The first is the *accuracy*:

$$\mathbb{P}\left(\widehat{Y} = Y\right),$$

which estimates the probability that a prediction is correct. Notice that if a problem is highly imbalanced (one label is much more present than the other in the data), achieving a high accuracy is trivial: it suffices to always predict the most frequent label. That is not to say that ML algorithms are useless in this case, but more so that it is important to establish a baseline level of success. The second is the *precision*:

$$\mathbb{P}(Y = y|\widehat{Y} = y), \text{ for } y \in \{0, 1\}.$$

This quantity measures the proportion of elements correctly labeled by the algorithm among all elements labeled as such. It answers the question: "if the algorithm declares an element to be y, what is the probability that it is correct?" The third is the *recall*:

$$\mathbb{P}(\widehat{Y} = y|Y = y), \text{ for } y \in \{0, 1\}.$$

The recall estimates the proportion of properly labeled items among all elements actually in the category in question in the population. It answers the question: "if an element belongs to category y, what is the probability that the algorithm will detect it?" The F1 score is a synthesis of these two frequently used metrics. Its formula is $2 \times$ precision $\times$ recall /(precision + recall). The *receiver operating characteristic* (ROC) curve, an example of which is shown in Figure 1.1, is another way to measure the performance of a model when it outputs a continuous score instead of simply the predicted label. This curve indicates the trade-off that a model can achieve between false positive and true positive rates (i.e., the recall), the idea being that achieving a higher true positive rate requires classifying more elements as positive, at the risk of being wrong and thus leading to a higher false positive rate. The degree of variation in this false positive rate – i.e., the slope of the ROC curve – measures the marginal "price to pay" to improve the true positive rate. If the classifier is as good as random (but not better), this curvature has a slope of 1: each percentage point gained on the recall results in an equivalent increase in the false positive rate. Conversely, the higher the slope, the lower the rate of false positives reacts to an increase in recall, signaling that the model offers a favorable trade-off. The precise measure of this trade-off is given by the *area under the curve* (AUC), the surface under the ROC curve, which is therefore between 0 and 1.

The use case will determine the choice of the metric to optimize when selecting the model. For example, if the goal is to design a tool to detect tax fraud, an algorithm that offers high precision will be preferred, because the resources to carry out checks are limited and one would like to find an actual case of fraud when human resources

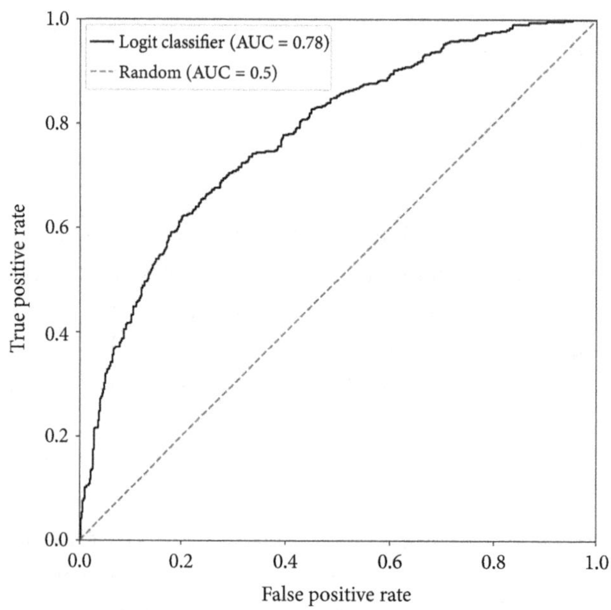

Figure 1.1 Example of a ROC curve that measures the trade-off between the true positive and the false positive rates.

are deployed. On the other hand, if the aim is to build an assistant for detecting cancer in patients, a model with high recall will be preferred because a false positive can always be eliminated by subsequent medical judgment.

Finally, data plays a different role in the two fields. In econometrics, a model is generally limited to one dataset, for the sole purpose of conducting a study or writing an article. The model is not intended to be used on another dataset. At best, a similar study will be carried out on similar data, but with a model whose parameters will be different: the econometrician is interested in summarizing the information contained in the data via a parameter of specific interest. Different datasets, therefore, will yield different parameter estimates. The theoretical guarantees of being able to optimally extract information from a finite number of data points is therefore of primary importance for an econometrician.

As far as machine learning is concerned, models are developed to be *deployed in production*, i.e., used repeatedly, as soon as new data is collected. It is therefore of primary importance to ensure that the algorithm does not suffer from *overfitting*, i.e., misleadingly high performance on the data on which the parameters were optimized, without resulting in a similar performance on a newly collected dataset. This usually means that the predictor has a small bias, but a great variance, because it interpolates between the in-sample data points. It should be noted that the model may also suffer from *underfitting* if its bias is too large and its variance is too small: this problem can be solved by adopting a more complex model. To limit these biases, it is important to separate between a *training* dataset and a *test* dataset: the former is used to optimize the value of the parameters or to select a model, and the latter to evaluate the performance of the model. The test dataset allows to compute an unbiased estimate of the production performance of the model (Chapter 7 in Hastie et al., 2009). The goal is to obtain a model that does not suffer from too large a generalization error. In recent years, the adoption of neural networks containing north of hundreds of millions of parameters has challenged the relevance of the standard bias-variance trade-off that assumes the existence of a "Goldilocks" model (i.e., neither too simple nor too complex), replacing it with models that aggressively interpolate training data but show impressive out-of-sample performance, a phenomenon known as the "double descent" (Belkin et al., 2019).

In addition, in the case of data whose distribution may change over time (e.g., as in the case of time series), it is important not to use future information when training the algorithm, i.e., not to use the information available from a date t to predict a variable observed at the date $t - 1$. This ensures that the training process follows a methodology known as "*point in time*", where only the information available in the present is used to predict the future. For example, when building an automatic trading strategy, it is important to use only information that is available when deciding the position to take in a particular asset, otherwise, the strategy will not be usable in practice.

Before we close this section, let us add a few nuances. First, one can demand that ML algorithms be more than black boxes that return a prediction like a magician pulling a rabbit out of a hat. In recent years, several scandals involving the use of algorithms have highlighted the need to be able to explain their predictions (so called *explainability*), to study and correct their biases (see the *fairness* and *bias mitigation* literature), and to be more cautious when their use directly affects the fate of citizens. A seminal example is the criticism of the COMPAS algorithm in the US, which was used to predict whether criminals would reoffend, and which assigned higher "risk" scores to African Americans who did not reoffend than to white defendants who did not, raising important fairness questions. We can also mention the various scandals and the recurrent suspicions about the impact of social networks in the dissemination of false information and the manipulation of public opinion, the use of certain algorithms for unspeakable purposes such as detecting the sexual orientation of individuals from a photo, gender biases that affect language models (making "homemaker" the feminine equivalent of "computer programmer"; Sun et al., 2019), etc.

On the other hand, "p-hacking" (i.e., the practice of embarking on a specification search to obtain significant results), or more generally the replicability crisis in scientific studies, which also affects empirical economics, can be seen as a problem of overfitting. Several solutions have been considered, such as the introduction of a pre-analysis plan to constraint the parameter space that the researcher is allowed to investigate (Olken, 2015). However, separating the data into an estimation sample and a validation sample, as in machine learning, seems to be an interesting solution (e.g., Wu and Gagnon-Bartsch, 2018; Chernozhukov et al., 2017).

1.2 What is this book about?

The core chapters of this book are divided into four main parts. Chapters 2 and 3 introduce the base statistical and causal inference tools that the core chapters rely upon. Chapter 15 provides a set of problems to test your knowledge.

1.2.1 High dimension and variable selection

Empirical economics involves crucial choices, such as the functional form of the equation to be estimated (e.g., linear or quadratic, the distribution of error terms, the number and identity of control variables, or the choice of instruments). These choices give way to arbitrariness and, more dangerously, to making these choices to get results that match the researcher's prior beliefs about them, which is a form of "p-hacking." In any case, without safeguards, these choices may cast doubt on the credibility of the results. The increasing availability of large datasets and advances in machine learning have both made this problem even more acute – there are now more factors one can control for and traditional methods are not working in this context – while providing potential solutions. In Part II, we focus on high-dimensional methods, which can handle a large number of covariates and instrumental variables, and on certain machine learning techniques with the purpose of performing causal inference in mind.

Let us now briefly describe the problems we will address: the focus is primarily on policy evaluation and causal inference, although these tools apply more broadly. The tools presented in this part must be selected according to the parameter of interest. They can be defined using the potential outcome model of Rubin (1974). $Y_i(0)$ is the potential outcome for individual i if not treated and $Y_i(1)$ is the potential outcome if treated. We only observe the state of treatment $D_i \in \{0, 1\}$ and the realized outcome Y_i defined by:

$$Y_i = Y_i(D_i) = \begin{cases} Y_i(0) & \text{if } D_i = 0, \\ Y_i(1) & \text{if } D_i = 1. \end{cases}$$

One interesting quantity is the average treatment effect $\tau_0 := \mathbb{E}[Y_i(1) - Y_i(0)]$, representing the average impact of the intervention on the study population. If treatment assignment is random when conditioning on observables (i.e., assuming that $\mathbb{E}[\varepsilon_i|D_i, X_i] = 0$ in the model below) and there are only a limited number of significant covariates (sparsity), Chapter 4 provides the tools to estimate τ_0 in the model:

$$Y_i = D_i\tau_0 + X_i'\beta_0 + \varepsilon_i, \text{ with } \mathbb{E}[\varepsilon_i] = 0 \text{ and } \mathbb{E}[\varepsilon_i|D_i, X_i] = 0,$$

where X_i is a vector of p exogenous control variables, p being potentially larger than the number of observations. The large dimension of X_i, combined with the assumption of sparsity, opens the door to the use of selection methods such as the Lasso, which this chapter examines in detail. Chapter 5 extends the insights of the previous chapter, presents a more general framework, and introduces *sample-splitting*, a crucial device when using non-standard tools such as estimators resulting from machine learning procedures.

Chapter 6 then explains how to adapt these tools when the exogeneity assumption possibly no longer holds, i.e., it is assumed that $\mathbb{E}[\varepsilon_i|D_i, X_i] \neq 0$, but there exist a (possibly large) number of instrumental variables Z_i, all satisfying the exogeneity assumption $\mathbb{E}[\varepsilon_i|Z_i] = 0$. We introduce tools to a priori select the ones that are providing the more precise inference. We show that this problem can be reformulated using tools from the previous chapters. To go further, Chapter 7 develops the theoretical refinements of the tools presented so far, with the aim of using weaker assumptions. It deals specifically with non-Gaussian errors, *sample-splitting*, confidence regions for a group of coefficients based on a correction of the Lasso, and panel data.

1.2.2 Estimation of heterogeneous effects

The *average* treatment effect (τ_0 above) does not describe the heterogeneity of responses to an intervention – some people may benefit greatly from it, while others may not be affected or may even be worse off. Chapter 8 is therefore concerned with a more complex parameter of interest, which is the average treatment effect conditional on certain (observed) variables $\tau : x \mapsto \mathbb{E}[Y_i(1)-Y_i(0)|X_i = x]$. Causal random forests are tools adapted from machine learning particularly suited for inference on the function $\tau(\cdot)$, i.e., to test the significance of the effect conditional on covariates taking the value x. However, the theory requires strong assumptions to obtain such tests. The end of the Chapter 8 lowers our requirements to make inference only on certain *characteristics* of the conditional average treatment effect, while ensuring better theoretical guarantees. This makes it possible to use ML methods with few assumptions to test for the heterogeneity of the treatment or to obtain information about its form.

Chapter 9 presents the tools for estimating optimal policies in the context of randomized experiments. The optimal policy obtained directly from using the tools for estimating the heterogeneity in Chapter 8 leads to policies that may be complex or impossible to implement in practice. The methods presented in Chapter 9 therefore allow the optimal policy to be estimated under the constraint that it has limited complexity.

1.2.3 Aggregate data and macroeconomic forecasting

Part IV deals specifically with data that has a temporal structure, often taking a more aggregated form in economics.

In particular, Chapter 10 presents the synthetic control method, an intrinsically high-dimensional method particularly useful for policy evaluation with aggregated data, when micro-data are not available or not relevant to answer the question. It also introduces permutation inference. The synthetic control method offers a data-driven procedure for selecting a comparison unit, called the "synthetic unit" in comparative case studies. The synthetic unit is constructed as a weighted combination of control units, also known as the "donor pool." It aims to best replicate the behavior of the treated unit during the pre-treatment period.

Chapter 11 presents high-dimensional estimation methods in a context where the data is not identically distributed and potentially has heavy tails, as is the case with macroeconomic and financial data. The aim of the chapter is to show how to adapt the tools developed in the previous chapters to that of predicting macroeconomic variables, in the context where one wishes to select without prior from a large number of explanatory variables. The limitations of sparse methods in this context are also underlined and links to factor models, which are "dense" models, are made. We give an example of real-time GDP prediction using "traditional" data as well as text data, which are also available in real time and can thus provide useful information for prediction.

1.2.4 Text data

Finally, Part V deals with the analysis of text data, which are unstructured data sources that can play a key role in empirical economics. However, the use of such data in a statistical model is not straightforward: unlike tabular data (i.e., data from surveys or administrative registers that comes in a table form), textual documents are not calibrated to fit properly into binary or continuous representations, as required for the application of traditional statistical methods.

A key step is therefore to extract a numerical representation of texts, as well as to model the language. Chapter 12 contains a simple introduction to the numerical representation of documents for latter use in standard statistical models: it involves transforming text data into tabular data, and then applying conventional methods such as linear regression. A detour will be made through language modeling, including the unigram model, which forms the basis for a number of simple but useful language models. This chapter will also present several applications that address economic or social topics such as the impact of racism on elections or the definition of markets for goods and services.

Chapter 13 introduces one of the fundamental concepts of modern natural language processing (NLP): word embeddings. We will see that these sophisticated vector representations of words allow to transcribe relationships reflecting the structure of the language. The progressive complexification of the type of embeddings used is the guiding thread of the chapter: from a rudimentary binary representation to a much smaller *distributed* representation, leading to representations from ad hoc models such as the famous `word2vec`. Then, we will see generalizations of the concept of embeddings beyond textual data, still experimental in empirical economics, but identified as promising for the future.

Finally, Chapter 14 is an in-depth presentation of modern language models that use the transformer architecture that gained traction around 2017. Unlike the first parts of this book, the approach is resolutely closer to pure machine learning methods than to the current practice of empirical economics. The idea is to equip the economist with these powerful models, from the training of tokenizers, to the transformer architecture using `BERT` as an example and the different strategies that are used to train these models. The chapter concludes by illustrating the application of these models in building embeddings through Siamese networks.

To help the reader navigate this textbook, Figure 1.2 provides the link between each chapter designated by its number. An edge from one circle to another indicates that the parent chapter is a prerequisite for understanding the child chapter. In addition to Chapters 2 and 3, which are not part of the core of the material, the reader may start with Chapters 4, 8, 12 which are the first chapters of Parts II, III and V respectively, or with one of the two chapters of Part IV.

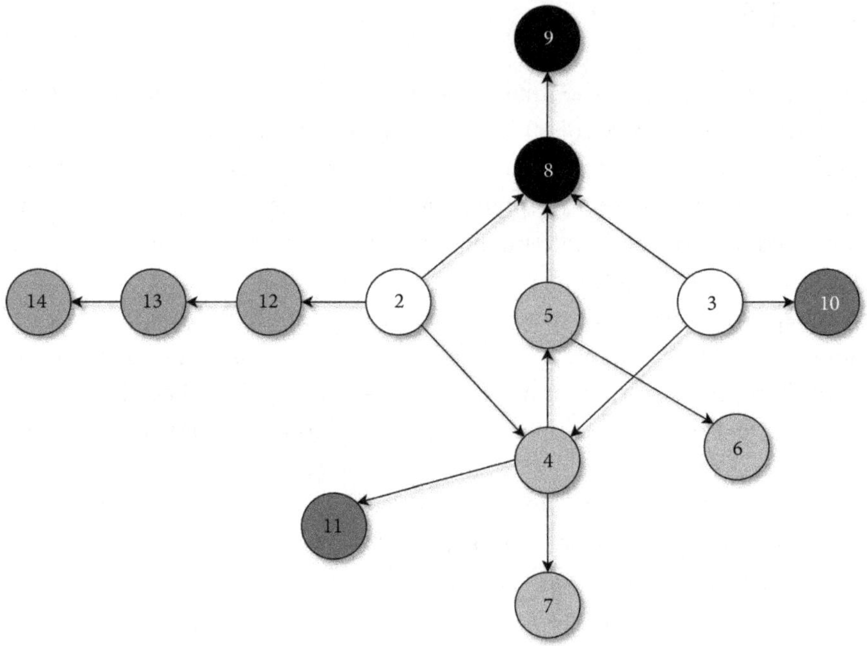

Figure 1.2 Graph depicting the relationships between each chapter.

1.3 Framework and notations

In this book we use boxes according to the following code:

Remark 1.1 A remark

Remarks highlighting some key points are specified in numbered boxes "remark."

Additional references

Additional readings and essential references are given in a box "additional readings."

Code and data

Links to open source shared code repositories are given in the "code and data" boxes.

Key concepts

At the end of the chapter, the list of key words and concepts appears in a box "key concepts."

Questions

At the end of the chapter, questions to test your knowledge can be found in a box "questions."

Unless otherwise specified, n is the sample size and p is the number of variables. As far as possible, the index variable i is used to denote an observation $i \in \{1, \ldots, n\}$; the index variable j is used to denote an explanatory variable $j \in \{1, \ldots, p\}$; the variable t is used to denote an observation in a sequence (i.e., it indexes a set of observations on which there is an order, usually temporal). In general, in the main text, the individual index i will be omitted e.g., Y_i, D_i, X_i in favor of the simplification Y, D, X where this does not lead to confusion.

For a random variable X, the symbol $X \sim \mathcal{L}$ means that it follows the distribution $\mathcal{L}$. $\mathbb{P}(A)$ is the probability of occurrence of event A. $\mathbb{E}[X]$ refers to the expectation of the random variable X, and $\text{Var}(X)$ refers to its variance. φ, Φ, and Φ^{-1} refer respectively to the density function, cumulative distribution function (cdf), and quantile function of the standard Gaussian distribution. $X_n \xrightarrow{p} X$ refers to the convergence in probability of the random variable X_n to the random variable X when $n \to \infty$, while $X_n \xrightarrow{d} \mathcal{L}$ refers to the convergence of the distribution of the variable X_n to the distribution $\mathcal{L}$.

The parameter that is being estimated usually subscripted by 0 and an estimator of this quantity is superscripted with a hat, thus e.g., θ_0 and $\widehat{\theta}$.

The notation $a \lesssim b$ means that $a \leq cb$ for a certain constant $c > 0$ that does not depend on sample size n.

For $x \in \mathbb{R}^p$, the norms $\|x\|_0 := \text{Card}\{1 \leq j \leq p, x_j \neq 0\}$, $\|x\|_1 := \sum_{j=1}^p |x_j|$, $\|x\|_2 := \sqrt{\sum_{j=1}^p x_j^2}$, $\|x\|_\infty := \max_{j=1,\ldots,p} |x_j|$ are defined. For a matrix $\boldsymbol{M}$, $\boldsymbol{M}'$ means its transpose. $\mathbb{I}_p$ means the identity matrix of dimension p. A vector is considered to be a matrix with a second dimension equal to 1. The m-sparse norm of the (square) matrix $\boldsymbol{M}$ is defined as follows:

$$\|\boldsymbol{M}\|_{sp(m)} := \sup_{\substack{\|x\|_0 \leq m \\ \|x\|_2 > 0}} \frac{\sqrt{x'\boldsymbol{M}x}}{\|x\|_2}.$$

The scalar product between two x and y vectors of dimension p is denoted by $x \cdot y = x'y = \sum_{j=1}^p x_j y_j$. $\odot$ means element-wise multiplication. For example, $x \odot y = (x_j y_j)_{j=1,\ldots,p}$. Abbreviations used include: CLT = Central Limit Theorem,

LLN = Law of Large Numbers, CMT = Continuous Mapping Theorem, OLS = Ordinary Least Squares, iid = independent and identically distributed, a.s. = almost surely.

1.4 Additional resources

This book has been designed to be self-contained. However, it is useful to mention related bibliographic resources, which allow to deepen the concepts or to consolidate fundamentals, and which form the basics for this textbook. Indeed, this book is the result of a second-year master's course titled first "High-dimensional Econometrics" and then "Machine Learning for Econometrics", taught at ENSAE Paris as well as at Institut Polytechnique de Paris. It was therefore designed for an audience already familiar with the statistical models and intuitions that are second nature to empirical economists. Although we have written this book with the objective of reducing the cost of adopting these techniques, we are not immune to the use of shortcuts that obscure the understanding. Gaillac and L'Hour (2023) is the French version of this book.

Additional references

The most commonly used econometric tools in this book are developed in two of the reference textbooks: Wooldridge (2002) and Hansen (2022). With regard to causal inference, we can cite the standard references of Angrist and Pischke (2009) and Imbens and Rubin (2015), and the more recent Chernozhukov et al. (2024), focusing on the use of ML methods. A competing causal framework of Rubin (1974), known as Directed Acyclic Graphs (DAG), is developed in Pearl (2000). In addition to the reminders and references given in Chapter 2, Hastie et al. (2009) is a reference for machine learning methods, while Goodfellow et al. (2016) covers neural networks. More generally, the online course "Full-stack Deep Learning" (fullstackdeeplearning.com) is a comprehensive and highly applied reference for the implementation of systems using machine learning algorithms.

Code and data

A GitHub repository is available at the address github.com/jeremylhour/ml4econometrics. It contains scripts in R and Python, which reproduce some of the applications of this work, as well as elements to answer the questions and exercises presented in Part VI.

PART I
STATISTICS AND ECONOMETRICS PREREQUISITES

Chapter 2
Statistical tools

This chapter is a refresher on a number of statistical tools and techniques that will be used throughout this book. The aim is to give a short overview of these methods, but not to provide the keys for a complete mastery. At the end of each section, further references are suggested.

2.1 Linear regression

The linear regression model is the bread and butter of the empirical economist. Let us begin with a refresher on its definition, as well as some properties and examples of its use. Assume we observe a sample of independent and identically distributed random variables $(Y_i, X_i)_{i=1,...,n}$ of size n. Y_i is a scalar. It is the dependent variable, the one we are trying to model. X_i is a vector of dimension p. This is the vector of the explanatory variables, the ones that will be used to explain the dependent variable. That is, we have:

$$X_i = \begin{pmatrix} X_{i1} \\ X_{i2} \\ \vdots \\ X_{ip} \end{pmatrix},$$

where possibly $X_{i1} = 1$ is the intercept. We assume here that $p < n$: we have more observations than explanatory variables, meaning that we are in a small-dimensional case. This assumption will be relaxed in the next section. The linear model is written as:

$$Y_i = X_i'\beta_0 + \varepsilon_i = X_{i1}\beta_{01} + \ldots + X_{ip}\beta_{0p} + \varepsilon_i,$$

where X_i' is the transpose of X_i, β_0 is the parameter vector of dimension p, and ε_i is an error term, which is a random variable that includes the terms that influence Y_i but are not observed. Since the sample is comprised of independent and identically distributed (i.i.d.) random variables at the unit observation level i (individual or "cluster" in the panel data setup), the index i is frequently omitted to streamline notation: $Y = X'\beta_0 + \varepsilon$. This model assumes that the dependent variable is the sum of a linear combination of the explanatory variables and an unobserved error term. The latter is subject to specific assumptions that are necessary to study the properties of the estimator for β_0 that we will compute.

Machine Learning for Econometrics. Christophe Gaillac and Jérémy L'Hour, Oxford University Press.
 DOI: 10.1093/9780198918868.003.0002

At this stage, it is important to distinguish between two concepts: the model and the data-generating process (DGP). The model is the set of assumptions, i.e., the intellectual structure imposed on the data in order to extract meaning from it. By definition, a model is a necessary restriction of reality in order to extract information from it. The data-generating process refers to the process or law that governs the formation of the measured variables – it is unknown by definition, except in the case of computer simulations. It is somewhat the "true" model. Therefore, a linear model can be estimated even if the underlying probabilistic process that generated the sample $(Y_i, X_i)_{i=1,...,n}$ is not linear – the relevance of the abstraction that the linear model represents can then be evaluated theoretically under various assumptions affecting the DGP.

The ordinary least squares (OLS) estimator solves:

$$\widehat{\beta} = \arg\min_{\beta \in \mathbb{R}^p} \frac{1}{n} \sum_{i=1}^{n} (Y_i - X_i'\beta)^2, \tag{2.1}$$

which is the sample analog of the best linear prediction (BLP) problem:

$$\arg\min_{\beta \in \mathbb{R}^p} \mathbb{E}\left[(Y_i - X_i'\beta)^2\right]. \tag{2.2}$$

The program (2.1) is strictly convex if and only if the matrix $\sum_{i=1}^{n} X_i X_i'$ is non-singular. Then, $\widehat{\beta}$ is the value that satisfies the first order conditions, i.e., that makes the gradient of the objective function equal to zero:

$$-\frac{2}{n} \sum_{i=1}^{n} X_i \left(Y_i - X_i'\widehat{\beta}\right) = 0. \tag{2.3}$$

It is a system of p dimension equations that is also referred to as "normal equations." It has a simple analytical solution, provided the square matrix of dimension p, $\sum_{i=1}^{n} X_i X_i'$, is invertible. In this case:

$$\widehat{\beta} = \left(\sum_{i=1}^{n} X_i X_i'\right)^{-1} \left(\sum_{i=1}^{n} X_i Y_i\right).$$

You can also write:

$$\widehat{\beta} = \left(\frac{1}{n}\sum_{i=1}^{n} X_i X_i'\right)^{-1} \left(\frac{1}{n}\sum_{i=1}^{n} X_i Y_i\right), \tag{2.4}$$

which is the empirical counterpart of the theoretical value of the regression coefficient, that is, $\beta_0 = \mathbb{E}[XX']^{-1}\,\mathbb{E}[XY]$. The following remark summarizes the multiple ways in which OLS can be defined.

Remark 2.1 Three ways to define OLS

1. As empirical counterpart to one or more moments (2.4). This approach, often the first one taught in statistics, is called the method of moments.
2. As a solution to the empirical counterpart of an estimating equation, (2.3). Here, $\widehat{\beta}$ is the value that ensures the estimated residuals are orthogonal to the regressors. This approach underlies the generalized method of moments (GMM), see Section 2.5.
3. By minimizing the empirical quadratic risk (2.1), earning the name "least squares." This philosophy of minimizing a loss function is also the underlying principle of maximum likelihood estimation, or empirical risk minimization methods in machine learning.

This estimator has several desirable properties under the following assumption:

Assumption 2.1 (Linear model). *Consider the iid sequence of random variables* $(Y_i, X_i)_{i=1,...,n}$ *such that:*

$$Y_i = X_i'\beta_0 + \varepsilon_i,$$

where $\mathbb{E}[\varepsilon_i|X_i] = 0$, $\mathbb{E}[X_iX_i']$ *exists and is non-singular (or equivalently:* $\mathbb{E}[X_iX_i']$ *is of rank p). Also assume that* $\mathbb{E}[\|\varepsilon_iX_i\|_2^2] < \infty$.

Theorem 2.1 (Asymptotic distribution of the OLS estimator) *Under Assumption 2.1:*

$$\sqrt{n}\left(\widehat{\beta} - \beta_0\right) \xrightarrow{d} \mathcal{N}\left(0, \mathbb{E}[XX']^{-1}\mathbb{E}[\varepsilon^2XX']\mathbb{E}[XX']^{-1}\right), \ as\ n \to \infty.$$

This theorem indicates that as the sample size increases, the ordinary least squares estimator approaches the true value β_0 at a rate proportional to the square root of the sample size. This is good news: the more observations we have, the closer our estimator gets to the true value β_0. However, the marginal information value provided by a new observation decreases at a rate proportional to $n^{-1/2}$. This result also implies that the estimator converges in probability to β_0.

Note that we can further simplify the asymptotic variance of Theorem 2.1 by assuming that $\mathbb{E}[\varepsilon^2XX'] = \mathbb{E}[\varepsilon^2]\mathbb{E}[XX']$ (or $\mathbb{E}[\varepsilon^2|X] = \sigma^2$). This assumption is known as *homoscedasticity*. In this case, two of the matrices in the variance formula cancel out, and we obtain the following asymptotic variance: $\mathbb{E}[\varepsilon^2]\mathbb{E}[XX']^{-1}$. However, this assumption is often unnecessary, so we often prefer to stick to the formula given by Theorem 2.1. In this case, this variance can be estimated using the *heteroskedasticity-robust* or *sandwich* formula:

$$\widehat{V} := \left[\frac{1}{n}\sum_{i=1}^{n} X_i X_i'\right]^{-1} \left[\frac{1}{n}\sum_{i=1}^{n} \widehat{\varepsilon}_i^2 X_i X_i'\right]\left[\frac{1}{n}\sum_{i=1}^{n} X_i X_i'\right]^{-1},$$

where $\widehat{\varepsilon}_i = Y_i - X_i'\widehat{\beta}$.

Theorem 2.1 is useful because it allows to approximate the distribution of $\widehat{\beta}$ when n is large enough, and therefore to build tests as well as confidence intervals. For example, a bilateral asymptotic confidence interval of level $1 - \alpha$ for the j-th element of β_0 is given by:

$$CI_{1-\alpha} = \left[\widehat{\beta}_j \pm \sqrt{\frac{\widehat{V}_{j,j}}{n}}\Phi\left(1 - \frac{\alpha}{2}\right)\right],$$

where $\Phi(.)$ is the cdf of $\mathcal{N}(0,1)$. Note that, thanks to Theorem 2.1,

$$\mathbb{P}\left[\beta_{0,j} \in IC_{1-\alpha}\right] \to 1 - \alpha, \text{ as } n \to \infty.$$

In other words: for sufficiently large n, the true value $\beta_{0,j}$ will be contained in this interval with probability $1 - \alpha$. Likewise, an asymptotic level α test of the null hypothesis H_0: $\beta_{0,j} = c$, for a real number c, is given by:

$$\mathbf{1}\left\{\left|\frac{\sqrt{n}\left(\widehat{\beta}_j - c\right)}{\sqrt{\widehat{V}_{j,j}}}\right| > \Phi\left(1 - \frac{\alpha}{2}\right)\right\}.$$

Additional references

Wooldridge (2002) is an important reference for linear econometrics.

2.2 Singular value decomposition

Before discussing the limitations of OLS, we introduce a useful mathematical tool for analyzing matrices called *singular value decomposition* (SVD). It will come in handy several times in this book.

The rank of a $n \times p$ matrix $\mathbf{X}$, which is denoted by $\mathrm{r}(\mathbf{X}) \leq \min(n,p)$, is the dimension of the vector space spanned by its column vectors. An important mathematical result is that any real such matrix possesses the following SVD:

$$\mathbf{X} = \mathbf{U}\mathbf{S}\mathbf{V}', \tag{2.5}$$

where $\mathbf{U}$ and $\mathbf{V}$ are square matrices of dimension n and p respectively such that $\mathbf{U}'\mathbf{U} = \mathbb{I}_n$ and $\mathbf{V}'\mathbf{V} = \mathbb{I}_p$. $\mathbf{S}$ is a rectangular diagonal matrix, i.e., any entry $s_{i,j}$ of

$\boldsymbol{S}$ such that $j \neq i$ is equal to 0. The diagonal entries of $\boldsymbol{S}$, denoted s_i are known as *singular values* and they are unique and positive. The convention is to sort them in descending order: $s_1 \geq s_2 \geq \cdots \geq 0$. They are strictly positive until the $\mathrm{r}(\boldsymbol{X})$-th after which they become equal to zero. This implies that Equation (2.5) can also be rewritten with $\boldsymbol{S}$ a square matrix of dimension $\mathrm{r}(\boldsymbol{X})$ and the second dimension of both $\boldsymbol{U}$ and $\boldsymbol{V}$ also changed to $\mathrm{r}(\boldsymbol{X})$:

$$\boldsymbol{X} = \sum_{j=1}^{\mathrm{r}(\boldsymbol{X})} s_j u_j v_j',$$

where u_j and v_j are the j-th rows of $\boldsymbol{U}$ and $\boldsymbol{V}$ respectively. So in this case, $\boldsymbol{X}$ can be seen as a sum of matrices of rank 1.

The SVD is a multi-purpose tool. First, it can help detecting multicollinearity or anticipate numerical problems when inverting the Gram matrix. Indeed, notice that if $s_j = 0$ for $j \leq p$, then $\boldsymbol{X}'\boldsymbol{X}$ is singular and the OLS estimator cannot be computed. Or even if $s_p > 0$ but it is very close to zero, it might result in numerical instabilities when inverting $\boldsymbol{X}'\boldsymbol{X}$. Notice here the connection with principal component analysis (PCA): since $\boldsymbol{X}'\boldsymbol{X} = \boldsymbol{V}\boldsymbol{S}'\boldsymbol{S}\boldsymbol{V}'$ and $\boldsymbol{V}'\boldsymbol{V} = \mathbb{I}_p$, s_j^2 is the j-st largest eigenvalue of $\boldsymbol{X}'\boldsymbol{X}$. As a consequence:

$$\boldsymbol{X}'\boldsymbol{X} = \sum_{j=1}^{\mathrm{r}(\boldsymbol{X})} s_j^2 v_j v_j',$$

and v_1 is the first principal component (or *mode*) of $\boldsymbol{X}'\boldsymbol{X}$, associated with the highest variance.

A second purpose is to compute the pseudo-inverse of a square matrix, also called the Moore-Penrose inverse. A direct application in econometrics is when considering the covariance matrix of the features, $\boldsymbol{X}'\boldsymbol{X}$. Indeed, since a non-singular Gram matrix means that $\mathrm{r}(\boldsymbol{X}) < p$ or equivalently that $s_j^2 = 0$ for some $j \leq p$, it also yields that the OLS solution using $\boldsymbol{X}$ as a feature matrix cannot be computed. A generalized inverse of $\boldsymbol{X}'\boldsymbol{X}$ (or pseudoinverse), called the Moore-Penrose inverse, is then naturally defined from the SVD by taking the inverse of the positive eigenvalues:

$$[\boldsymbol{X}'\boldsymbol{X}]^+ := \sum_{j=1}^{\mathrm{r}(\boldsymbol{X})} s_j^{-2} v_j v_j'.$$

Third, the SVD can be a tool for dimension reduction by producing a low-rank approximation of $\boldsymbol{X}$, as we will exploit later when doing factor analysis (2.17). From (2.5), a natural way to approximate $\boldsymbol{X}$ is to truncate its representation to the first $K \leq \mathrm{r}(\boldsymbol{X})$ components:

$$\hat{\boldsymbol{X}} = \sum_{j=1}^{K} s_j u_j v_j'.$$

This decomposition is optimal in the sense that it allows to explain the maximum variance among all possible approximations of K components.

2.3 High dimension and penalized regressions

2.3.1 When OLS fail

Let us continue with the simple linear regression from Section 2.1. X_i is a random vector of dimension p with $p < n$ – we are therefore in a case of low dimension – and we denote $X_{i,j}$ as the j-th component of X_i. The estimator (2.1) has a unique analytical solution in the form given by Equation (2.4) provided that the matrix $\sum_{i=1}^{n} X_i X_i'/n$ (the Gram matrix) is invertible, which requires, in particular, that the columns of the $n \times p$ matrix $(X_i')_{i=1,...,n}$ be linearly independent.

In the aforementioned context, we define *high dimension* as having a large number of regressors, i.e., $p > n$ or simply when p is proportional to n. Two problems then arise: (i) the accuracy of the estimator (2.1) deteriorates (increased variance) due to multicollinearity, and (ii) it becomes impossible to calculate (if the Gram matrix $\sum_{i=1}^{n} X_i X_i'/n$ is no longer invertible). The so-called "high-dimensional" statistics has developed a whole range of techniques to address this issue, and this is what we will introduce in this section.

2.3.2 Ridge regression

For a penalty level $\lambda \geq 0$, the Ridge estimator is defined as the solution to the minimization program:

$$\widehat{\beta}^R(\lambda) = \underset{\beta \in \mathbb{R}^p}{\arg\min} \frac{1}{n} \sum_{i=1}^{n} (Y_i - X_i'\beta)^2 + \lambda \|\beta\|_2^2, \tag{2.6}$$

where $\|\beta\|_2 = \sqrt{\sum_{j=1}^{p} \beta_j^2}$. This program adds an ℓ_2 penalty to the standard OLS objective function. Solving the previous program, we find:

$$\widehat{\beta}^R(\lambda) = \left[\frac{1}{n}\sum_{i=1}^{n} X_i X_i' + \lambda \mathbb{I}_p\right]^{-1} \frac{1}{n}\sum_{i=1}^{n} X_i Y_i.$$

Through the analytical solution, we can see that the penalization by the ℓ_2 norm leads to the additional term $\lambda \mathbb{I}_p$, which makes the $\sum_{i=1}^{n} X_i X_i'/n + \lambda \mathbb{I}_p$ matrix non-singular when $\lambda > 0$ even if $\sum_{i=1}^{n} X_i X_i'/n$ is not of full rank. From the previous section on the SVD, we can check that the extra term in the sum shifts the eigenvalues of the new matrix away from zero by λ, allowing to compute its inverse. The larger λ, the more the Ridge estimator will shrink the OLS towards the null vector. If $\lambda \to \infty$, $\widehat{\beta}^R(\lambda) \to 0$. Conversely, if $\lambda = 0$, it becomes the OLS solution when it exists. If the OLS solution does not exist, we can rely on the following lemma to study the behavior of the Ridge estimator as λ approaches zero from the right:

Lemma 2.1 (Ridge-less regression). *When $\lambda \to 0$, the solution of (2.6) becomes the OLS using the pseudo-inverse of the covariance matrix:*

$$\widehat{\beta}^R(\lambda) \to \left[\frac{1}{n}\sum_{i=1}^{n} X_i X_i'\right]^+ \frac{1}{n}\sum_{i=1}^{n} X_i Y_i,$$

where $\left[\sum_{i=1}^{n} X_i X_i'/n\right]^+$ means the Moore-Penrose inverse of $\sum_{i=1}^{n} X_i X_i'/n$.

A proof, which is a simple application of Section 2.2, can be found at the end of the chapter.

In practice, it is important to note that the solution is sensitive to the scale of the regressors. It is therefore preferable to normalize them, for example by dividing them by their standard deviation or by scaling them to the $[0, 1]$ interval using the transform $x \to (x - \min(x))/(\max(x) - \min(x))$. It is also possible to penalize each element of β differently or not to penalize them all. Typically, we don't penalize the intercept, so we solve instead:

$$\min_{\beta \in \mathbb{R}^p} \frac{1}{n}\sum_{i=1}^{n} \left(Y_i - \beta_1 - X_{i,-1}' \, \beta_{-1}\right)^2 + \lambda \sum_{j=2}^{p} \beta_j^2,$$

where for a vector x of dimension p, x_{-1} means the vector x where its first component is removed.

2.3.3 Lasso regression

For a penalty level $\lambda > 0$, the Lasso estimator is defined as the solution of the following minimization program:

$$\widehat{\beta}^L(\lambda) \in \arg\min_{\beta \in \mathbb{R}^p} \frac{1}{n}\sum_{i=1}^{n} \left(Y_i - X_i'\beta\right)^2 + \lambda \, \|\beta\|_1, \tag{2.7}$$

where $\|\beta\|_1 = \sum_{j=1}^{p} |\beta_j|$. Just like in the case of the Ridge estimator, λ defines the penalty level. Note that $\widehat{\beta}^L(\lambda)$ may not be unique and that the Lasso does not have a closed-form solution in general. However, at a fixed value of λ, the prediction $X_i'\widehat{\beta}^L(\lambda)$ is unique across the observations $i = 1, \ldots, n$. There are efficient algorithms to solve this optimization program, such as the Fast Iterative

Shrinkage-Thresholding Algorithm (FISTA) by Beck and Teboulle (2014). Due to the non-differentiability at zero of the ℓ_1 norm penalty, the obtained solution is frequently *sparse* in the sense that a number of elements of $\widehat{\beta}^L(\lambda)$ will be exactly equal to zero. This property makes the Lasso a commonly used tool for selecting variables. The theoretical properties of the Lasso are discussed in greater detail in Sections 4.2 and 4.3.

Importantly, the Lasso suffers from a finite distance bias due to the penalization, as even the non-zero coefficients are shrunk towards zero. In order to reduce this bias, a second step called "Post-Lasso" (Belloni and Chernozhukov, 2013) can be implemented by re-estimating β_0 using ordinary least squares, having previously selected only the regressors corresponding to a non-zero coefficient in $\widehat{\beta}^L(\lambda)$.

$$\widehat{\beta}^{PL}(\lambda) = \underset{\beta \in \mathbb{R}^p:\ \beta_j = 0 \text{ if } \widehat{\beta}_j^L(\lambda)=0}{\arg\min} \frac{1}{n}\sum_{i=1}^{n}\left(Y_i - X_i'\beta\right)^2. \tag{2.8}$$

2.3.4 Ridge or Lasso?

The choice of penalization between Ridge and Lasso is not trivial and leads to solutions of different natures, reflecting different a priori assumptions on the underlying parameter β_0. In the case of Ridge regression, the solution is considered *dense* in the sense that the elements of $\widehat{\beta}^R(\lambda)$ are small but never exactly zero. In the case of Lasso regression, the solution is said to be *sparse* in the sense that typically $\widehat{\beta}^L(\lambda)$ is a vector for which many elements are exactly zero, for sufficiently large λ. Thus, only Lasso allows for variable selection. It is worth noting that Lasso can be seen as a convexification of the ℓ_0 norm penalization, which counts the number of non-zero coefficients $\|\beta\|_0$. Nevertheless, this latter program with an ℓ_0 penalization:

$$\min_{\beta \in \mathbb{R}^p} \frac{1}{n}\sum_{i=1}^{n}\left(Y_i - X_i'\beta\right)^2 + \lambda \|\beta\|_0 ,$$

is said "NP-hard,"meaning that it cannot be solved in polynomial time, since it is necessary to evaluate 2^p submodels and will not be tractable for large p.

In practice, the Ridge regression implicitly assumes that all the variables exert a weak influence on the outcome. Conversely, the Lasso is employed for variable selection, assuming that only a limited number of entries in β_0 differ from zero or when seeking an easily interpretable regression function. Thus, when Sala-I-Martin (1997) wants to identify the determinant of economic growth, the Lasso should be used, while Ferrara and Simoni (2019) use Ridge regression to reflect the fact that each feature contains relevant information useful to predict macroeconomic variables such as GDP.

This choice can also be interpreted from a Bayesian perspective. Both Ridge and Lasso can each be seen as Maximum A Posteriori (MAP) estimates coming from different *prior* distributions of β_0.

Lemma 2.2 (Bayesian interpretation). *In the model* $Y_i = X_i'\beta_0 + \varepsilon_i$ *where* $\varepsilon_i \sim \mathcal{N}(0, \sigma^2)$*:*

- *The Ridge Estimator is the MAP resulting from prior* $\beta_0 \sim \mathcal{N}_p\left(0, (\sigma^2/\lambda)\mathbb{I}_p\right)$,
- *The Lasso estimator is the MAP resulting from the prior* $\beta_0 \sim \mathcal{L}(1/\lambda)^{\otimes p}$, *where* $\mathcal{L}(1/\lambda)$ *is a notation for the Laplace distribution of parameter* $1/\lambda$, *characterized by density* $x \mapsto (\lambda/2)e^{-\lambda|x|}$.

These distributions imply that β_0 tends to concentrate around the null vector, given that $\mathbb{E}[\beta_0] = 0$. Note that the variance of the *prior* distribution varies inversely proportional to the penalty λ: the greater λ, the more the prior distribution will be concentrated around the null vector. To see why, remember that the variance of a Laplace distribution of parameter $1/\lambda$ is $2/\lambda^2$.

Finally, for $\alpha \in [0, 1]$ and $\lambda > 0$, the *elastic net* combines these two types of penalizations:

$$\widehat{\beta}^E(\lambda, \alpha) = \arg\min_{\beta \in \mathbb{R}^p} \frac{1}{n} \sum_{i=1}^{n} \left(Y_i - X_i'\beta\right)^2 + \lambda(\alpha \|\beta\|_1 + (1 - \alpha)\|\beta\|_2^2), \qquad (2.9)$$

where of course $\widehat{\beta}^E(\lambda, 1) = \widehat{\beta}^L(\lambda)$ and $\widehat{\beta}^E(\lambda, 0) = \widehat{\beta}^R(\lambda)$. As soon as $\alpha > 0$, the proposed solution will be sparse, like for the Lasso.

There are other types of more sophisticated penalizations, reflecting some prior on the sparsity patterns, such as the Group-Lasso (Lounici et al., 2011). The Group-Lasso defines groups of variables that are assumed to be non-zero all together, but assumes that there is sparsity at the group level. This may be the case, for example, when considering baseline regressors interacted with sociodemographic categories. In this context, it can reasonably be assumed that if one of the coefficients is different from zero for a given category, it will also be relevant for other categories. For example, it may be assumed that the same variables explain wages for men and for women (e.g., experience, level of education) even if they do so to different extents.

More formally, let $\mathcal{G} = \{G_1, \ldots, G_G\}$ be a partition of $\{1, \ldots, p\}$ into G groups and β_{G_g} be the vector β whose entries outside of G_g are equal to 0. The Group-Lasso is defined by:

$$\widehat{\beta}^{GL}(\lambda, w_1, \ldots, w_G) \in \arg\min_{\beta \in \mathbb{R}^p} \frac{1}{n} \sum_{i=1}^{n} \left(Y_i - X_i'\beta\right)^2 + \lambda \sum_{g=1}^{G} w_g \left\|\beta_{G_g}\right\|_2, \qquad (2.10)$$

where w_g is the penalty specific to group g, which is usually set in proportion to the square-root of the number of variables in group g, $\sqrt{\text{Card}(G_g)}$.

These considerations are important for estimation tasks. In prediction tasks, selecting between various penalties is based on comparing average losses on a test sample or out-of-sample data.

2.3.5 Choosing λ by cross-validation

The consistency guarantees for the Lasso estimator are based on theoretical penalization choices and are in most cases unfeasible because they depend on unknown quantities (see Section 4.3). Some authors have developed algorithms to achieve asymptotically optimal level of penalization (for estimation) that work well in practice (see Chapter 7 for more details and e.g., Belloni et al., 2014, available in the package `hdm` written in R).

However, in the vast majority of cases, especially when it comes to prediction tasks, an empirical procedure called *cross-validation* is used to select the parameter λ. The idea is to split the data into two disjoint folds, one in which we will compute the estimator for a given λ, and the other in which we will optimize this λ to minimize the out-of-sample (OOS) error. The goal of this procedure is to avoid overfitting, i.e., to avoid fitting too closely to the training data and obtaining an estimator of β_0 that performs poorly on a sample that was not used for its computation. To convince ourselves of the usefulness of this procedure, it is sufficient to note, for example, that $\lambda = 0$ is a solution of:

$$\min_{\lambda \geq 0} \frac{1}{n} \sum_{i=1}^{n} \left(Y_i - X_i' \widehat{\beta}^L(\lambda) \right)^2,$$

because $\widehat{\beta}^L(0) = \widehat{\beta}$ is a solution to Equation (2.1). However, this does not guarantee that the estimator (2.1) will necessarily be the one that produces the minimal mean squared error on a sample not used to compute it. To choose λ, it is therefore necessary to use a different sample than the one used to compute $\widehat{\beta}^L(\lambda)$ at a given λ.

The procedure is as follows. To simplify the notations, it is assumed that $n = K \times n_0$ for two integers K and n_0.

1. For an integer K, randomly draw a partition of $1, \ldots, n$ into K groups of equal sizes n_0 (*folds*). Let $G_i \in 1, \ldots, K$, be the group to which observation i belongs.
2. For each $k = 1, \ldots, K$, using only the data not belonging to group k, compute the Lasso or Ridge estimator:

$$\widehat{\beta}_k^R(\lambda) = \arg\min_{\beta \in \mathbb{R}^p} \frac{1}{(K-1)n_0} \sum_{i:\ G_i \neq k} (Y_i - X_i'\beta)^2 + \lambda \|\beta\|_2^2,$$

$$\widehat{\beta}_k^L(\lambda) = \arg\min_{\beta \in \mathbb{R}^p} \frac{1}{(K-1)n_0} \sum_{i:\ G_i \neq k} (Y_i - X_i'\beta)^2 + \lambda \|\beta\|_1.$$

3. For each $k = 1, \ldots, K$, compute the error on group k:

$$\frac{1}{n_0} \sum_{i:\ G_i=k} \left(Y_i - X_i'\widehat{\beta}_k^R(\lambda)\right)^2,$$

$$\frac{1}{n_0} \sum_{i:\ G_i=k} \left(Y_i - X_i'\widehat{\beta}_k^L(\lambda)\right)^2.$$

4. Aggregate the errors from the previous step and then minimize with respect to λ:

$$\widehat{\lambda}^R = \arg\min_{\lambda \geq 0} \frac{1}{K} \sum_{k=1}^{K} \frac{1}{n_0} \sum_{i:\ G_i=k} \left(Y_i - X_i'\widehat{\beta}_k^R(\lambda)\right)^2,$$

$$\widehat{\lambda}^L = \arg\min_{\lambda \geq 0} \frac{1}{K} \sum_{k=1}^{K} \frac{1}{n_0} \sum_{i:\ G_i=k} \left(Y_i - X_i'\widehat{\beta}_k^L(\lambda)\right)^2.$$

In practice, values like $K = 5$ or $K = 10$ are commonly used. For example, Kohavi (1995) suggests that a value of $K = 10$ provides the best trade-off between bias and variance for a certain number of datasets. Cross-validation is a procedure whose scope is broader: it aims to select relevant hyperparameters that govern the computation of an estimator and can be applied to any model that depends on such hyperparameters.

Additional references

Penalized regressions and cross-validation are detailed in Hastie et al. (2009). Recently, Chetverikov and Sørensen (2022) provide a theoretical justification for using cross-validation with the ℓ_1 penalization.

2.4 Maximum likelihood

2.4.1 General principle

The maximum likelihood method is very general but relies on strong distributional assumptions. Under these assumptions, the obtained results are very powerful (consistency, asymptotic normality, asymptotic efficiency in the sense that it reaches the Cramér-Rao bound).

The principle is as follows: suppose we want to model the relationship between explanatory variables X_i and an outcome variable Y_i, and that we are willing to make an assumption about the conditional distribution of Y_i given X_i with an unknown parameter θ_0 that we want to estimate. For example, we can assume that $Y_i|X_i \sim f(\cdot|X_i;\theta_0)$ for a conditional density $f(\cdot|x;\theta)$. The maximum likelihood method defines the maximum likelihood estimator (MLE) as the quantity that maximizes the joint conditional density with respect to the unknown parameter:

$$\widehat{\theta}^{MLE} = \arg\max_{\theta} \prod_{i=1}^{n} f(Y_i|X_i;\theta).$$

In short, we look for the value of θ that maximizes the probability of observing the sample that was actually collected. In general, for computational reasons – the product of a large number of terms between zero and one quickly becomes very close to zero – it is preferable to minimize the negative log-likelihood:

$$\widehat{\theta}^{MLE} = \arg\min_{\theta} \frac{1}{n}\sum_{i=1}^{n} -\log f(Y_i|X_i;\theta).$$

We can then note that $\widehat{\theta}^{MLE}$ satisfies the following first-order condition:

$$\frac{1}{n}\sum_{i=1}^{n} \partial_\theta \log f(Y_i|X_i;\theta) = 0,$$

which is nothing but the empirical counterpart of the equation:

$$\mathbb{E}\left[\partial_\theta \log f(Y|X;\theta)\right] = 0.$$

It can be shown that the expectation of the score function, $\partial_\theta \log f(Y|X;\theta)$, vanishes at the true value of the parameter $\mathbb{E}\left[\partial_\theta \log f(Y|X;\theta_0)\right] = 0$. The MLE is therefore a specific case of the GMM, which will be presented in Section 2.5. From this observation, it follows that it is often possible to dispense with distributional assumptions to adopt what is called the pseudomaximum likelihood method (Gourieroux et al., 1984).

Let us apply this method to the linear model given in Assumption (2.1). We further assume that $\varepsilon_i \sim \mathcal{N}(0,\sigma^2)$. Denoting the parameters by $\theta := (\beta,\sigma)$, this implies that the conditional distribution of Y_i given X_i is given by:

$$f(y|x;\theta) = \frac{1}{\sqrt{2\pi\sigma^2}}\exp\left[-\frac{1}{2}\left(\frac{y-X'\beta}{\sigma}\right)^2\right],$$

A simple calculation shows that:

$$\widehat{\beta}^{MLE} = \arg\min_{\beta\in\mathbb{R}^p} \frac{1}{n}\sum_{i=1}^{n}\left(Y_i - X_i'\beta\right)^2,$$

$$\widehat{\sigma}^{2,MLE} = \frac{1}{n}\sum_{i=1}^{n}\left(Y_i - X_i'\widehat{\beta}^{MLE}\right)^2,$$

which is nothing but ... the least squares estimator for β_0! For σ^2, the least squares estimator is generally defined as $\widehat{\sigma}^{2MLE} \times n/(n-1)$ because it is an unbiased estimator. However, it should be noted that defining this estimator within the framework of maximum likelihood is more restrictive as it imposes the additional parametric assumption $\varepsilon_i \sim \mathcal{N}(0,\sigma^2)$, instead of assuming only homoscedasticity, $\text{Var}[\varepsilon_i|X_i] = \sigma^2$.

2.4.2 Examples and penalized versions

The penalized approach seen in Section 2.3 is not limited to the quadratic loss (linear regression model), but can also be adapted to any estimator that minimizes a risk or maximizes a likelihood. To convince ourselves, here are some examples.

Example 2.1 (Logistic regression) *In this case, the target variable is binary, $Y_i \in \{0,1\}$, and we assume the following link function:*

$$P[Y_i = 1|X_i] = \frac{\exp(X_i'\theta_0)}{1+\exp(X_i'\theta_0)},$$

or equivalently, $P[Y_i = y|X_i] = \exp(yX_i'\theta_0)/(1+\exp(X_i'\theta_0))$ for $y \in \{0,1\}$. The individual contribution to the likelihood is given by $\exp(Y_iX_i'\theta)/(1+\exp(X_i'\theta))$. Thus, we have the standard estimator of the maximum likelihood of θ_0:

$$\widehat{\theta}^{MLE} = \underset{\theta\in\mathbb{R}^p}{\arg\min}\ \frac{1}{n}\sum_{i=1}^{n} \ln\left(1+\exp\left(X_i'\theta\right)\right) - Y_iX_i'\theta. \quad (2.11)$$

A popular penalized version of (2.11) is (2.12) (e.g., Van de Geer, 2008):

$$\widehat{\theta}^{L}(\lambda) = \underset{\theta\in\mathbb{R}^p}{\arg\min}\ \frac{1}{n}\left[\sum_{i=1}^{n} \ln\left(1+\exp\left(X_i'\theta\right)\right) - Y_iX_i'\theta\right] + \lambda\,\|\theta\|_1. \quad (2.12)$$

We can alternatively use a ℓ_2 norm penalty, and the concepts developed in Section 2.3 (cross-validation, etc.) apply to it as well.

Example 2.2 (Duration model with censoring) *Suppose we are interested in the lifespan of an individual (e.g., a human being, a car, etc.) denoted by $T_i \geq 0$. However, for individuals still alive at the time of the study, we only observe a lower bound on this duration, denoted by C_i. We denote the observed variable by $Y_i = \min(T_i, C_i)$ and $D_i = \mathbb{1}\{T_i < C_i\}$. We assume $T_i \perp\!\!\!\perp C_i|X_i$ and T_i follows an exponential distribution $T_i \sim \mathcal{E}(\exp(X_i'\theta_0))$. The maximum likelihood estimator of θ_0 is:*

$$\begin{aligned}\widehat{\theta}^{MLE} &= \arg\min_{\theta\in\mathbb{R}^p} \frac{1}{n}\sum_{i=1}^{n} D_i\left(\exp(X_i'\theta)Y_i - X_i'\theta\right) + (1-D_i)\exp(X_i'\theta)Y_i,\\ &= \arg\min_{\theta\in\mathbb{R}^p} \frac{1}{n}\sum_{i=1}^{n} \exp(X_i'\theta)Y_i - D_iX_i'\theta.\end{aligned}$$

We may prefer a penalized version of this estimator:

$$\widehat{\theta}^{R}(\lambda) = \arg\min_{\theta\in\mathbb{R}^p} \frac{1}{n}\sum_{i=1}^{n} \exp(X_i'\theta)Y_i - D_iX_i'\theta + \lambda\,\|\theta\|_2^2 .$$

Additional references

The maximum likelihood method is detailed in most good textbooks on mathematical statistics. A classic reference is Wasserman (2010).

2.5 Generalized method of moments

The GMM is a generalization of the definition of the OLS by Equation (2.3). Indeed, in the linear model, the assumption that $\mathbb{E}[\varepsilon|X] = 0$ involves the following orthogonality equation:

$$\mathbb{E}\left[X(Y - X'\beta_0)\right] = 0,$$

which can be used to derive the estimator of the OLS by taking its empirical counterpart, since $\widehat{\beta}$ solves the following equation of which β is the unknown:

$$\frac{1}{n}\sum_{i=1}^{n}\left(Y_i - X_i'\beta\right)X_i = 0.$$

In a more general way, one may want to define a model from a vector of random variables U, a vector of coefficients θ, and moments M that we want to set to zero:

$$M(\theta) := \mathbb{E}\left[\psi(U,\theta)\right] = 0.$$

For example, in the standard linear model above, $U := (Y, X)$ and $\theta := \beta$. Let us denote the empirical counterpart of this vector of moments by:

$$\widehat{M}(\theta) := \frac{1}{n}\sum_{i=1}^{n}\psi(U_i,\theta).$$

The GMM $\hat{\theta}_n$ estimator of the parameter θ_0 is then obtained by minimizing the Euclidean norm of this vector $\|\widehat{M}(\theta)\|_2^2 := \widehat{M}(\theta)'\widehat{M}(\theta)$, which corresponds to the following optimization program:

$$\hat{\theta}_n := \arg\max_{\theta\in\Theta} - \left\|\widehat{M}(\theta)\right\|_2^2. \tag{2.13}$$

The set of Assumptions 2.2 described below implies that $M(\theta)$ takes value 0 only at the value θ_0: $\forall\theta \in \Theta,\ M(\theta) = 0 \implies \theta = \theta_0$, and therefore the parameter θ_0 is identified in the set Θ. These assumptions allow us to prove the asymptotic normality of the GMM estimator $\hat{\theta}_n$. Denote by $G := \mathbb{E}\left[\nabla_\theta\psi(U, \theta_0)\right]$.

Assumption 2.2 (Regularity condition for asymptotic normality of $\hat{\boldsymbol{\theta}}_{\mathbf{n}}$). *Assume that:*

1. *θ_0 is an inner point of Θ, which is a compact set;*
2. *$\psi(u, \cdot)$ is continuously differentiable in a neighborhood $\mathcal{N}$ of θ_0 with a probability close to 1;*
3. *$\mathbb{E}[\|\psi(U, \theta_0)\|^2]$ and $\mathbb{E}[\sup_{\theta\in\mathcal{N}} \|\nabla_\theta\psi(U, \theta)\|]$ are finite quantities;*
4. *The matrix $G'G$ is non-singular.*

Under Assumption 2.2, we obtain the following properties:

1. The objective function of the problem (2.13) converges in probability to

$$-\widehat{M}(\theta)'\widehat{M}(\theta) \xrightarrow{p} -\mathbb{E}[\psi(U, \theta)']\mathbb{E}\left[\psi(U, \theta)\right],$$

a quantity which has a single maximum at $\theta = \theta_0$;

2. The estimator $\hat{\theta}_n$ converges in probability to θ_0 : $\hat{\theta}_n \xrightarrow{p} \theta_0$.
3. The estimator $\hat{\theta}_n$ is asymptotically normal and we have

$$\sqrt{n}\left(\hat{\theta}_n - \theta_0\right) \xrightarrow{d} \mathcal{N}\left(0, (G'G)^{-1}G'\Sigma G((G'G)^{-1})'\right). \tag{2.14}$$

Here, we recall the useful arguments to prove the asymptotic normality under Assumption 2.2. We consider the first-order condition of (2.13),

$$\nabla_\theta\widehat{M}(\hat{\theta}_n)'\widehat{M}(\hat{\theta}_n) = 0,$$

which is satisfied with probability close to 1. Then, using Taylor's theorem at the second order for $\widehat{M}(\hat{\theta}_n)$ and θ_0, we obtain that there exists $\overline{\theta} \in [\theta_0, \hat{\theta}_n]$ such that:

$$\nabla_\theta\widehat{M}(\hat{\theta}_n)'\widehat{M}(\hat{\theta}_n) = \nabla_\theta\widehat{M}(\hat{\theta}_n)'\widehat{M}(\theta_0) + \nabla_\theta\widehat{M}(\hat{\theta}_n)'\nabla_\theta\widehat{M}(\overline{\theta})(\hat{\theta}_n - \theta_0),$$

So we have, with high probability:

$$\sqrt{n}\left(\hat{\theta}_n - \theta_0\right) = \left(\nabla_\theta \widehat{M}(\hat{\theta}_n)' \nabla_\theta \widehat{M}(\overline{\theta})\right)^{-1} \left(-\nabla_\theta \widehat{M}(\hat{\theta}_n)' \left(\sqrt{n}\widehat{M}(\theta_0)\right)\right).$$

Then, using condition (3), we get

$$\nabla_\theta \widehat{M}\left(\overline{\theta}\right) \xrightarrow{p} G \text{ and } \nabla_\theta \widehat{M}(\hat{\theta}_n) \xrightarrow{p} G.$$

Using condition (4), $\sqrt{n}\widehat{M}(\theta_0) \xrightarrow{d} \mathcal{N}(0, \Sigma)$, where $\Sigma = \mathbb{E}[\psi(U, \theta_0)\psi(U, \theta_0)']$, and using Slutsky's theorem, we get (2.14). Thus, in (2.14), the asymptotic variance simplifies to $G^{-1}\Sigma(G^{-1})'$ and takes a specific form

$$V := G^{-1}\mathbb{E}\left[\psi(U, \theta_0)\psi(U, \theta_0)'\right]\left(G^{-1}\right)'. \tag{2.15}$$

Additional references

Theoretical aspects of the GMM, particularly regarding asymptotic theory, are studied in Newey and McFadden (1994).

2.6 Factor models

Factor models are a dimension reduction technique that assumes that the dependence between explanatory variables can be well approximated by a common underlying (or latent) structure of lower dimension (e.g., Stock and Watson, 2002; Bai, 2003; Bai and Ng, 2006; or Chapter 11.13 in Hansen, 2022). We recall the analogy with PCA and the estimation procedure for the resulting factors. In this section, we consider static factor models, and refer to Stock and Watson (2011) for a description of the estimation of dynamic factor models. We work in a time series framework, as it is a framework where factor models are particularly well-suited, as we will see in Chapter 11.

Consider a random vector x_t of p, the approximation by a factor model (*approximate factor model*) assumes that

$$x_t = \mathbf{\Lambda} f_t + \varepsilon_t, \quad t = 1, \ldots, T, \tag{2.16}$$

where Λ is a factor loading matrix of size $p \times r$ and f_t is a vector of factors of size $r \times 1$. The component Λf_t is common to the p variables, while ε_t is an idiosyncratic component. The vector ε_t is assumed to have zero mean, to be uncorrelated with the factors f_t, $E(f_t\varepsilon_t') = 0$, and $E(\varepsilon_t\varepsilon_t')$ is assumed to be positive definite. In many economic contexts, it is reasonable to think that there exist unobserved factors linking the components of the considered x_t – for example, the results in different subjects on an exam can be explained by underlying skills in analytical abilities, oral fluency, patience, creativity, etc.

We can concatenate (2.16) at each date to obtain the following matrix form:

$$\underset{T\times p}{\boldsymbol{X}} = \underset{T\times r}{\boldsymbol{F}}\ \underset{r\times p}{\boldsymbol{\Lambda}'} + \underset{T\times p}{\boldsymbol{E}}, \tag{2.17}$$

where $\boldsymbol{X} = (x_1, \ldots, x_T)'$, $\boldsymbol{F} = (f_1, \ldots, f_T)'$, and $\boldsymbol{E} = (\varepsilon_1, \ldots, \varepsilon_T)'$. This matrix formulation is the starting point for the connection with PCA, which allows for the estimation of the factors.

One way to estimate the factors in (2.17) is to use the least squares, then considering the minimization in $(\boldsymbol{\Lambda}, \boldsymbol{F})$ of the criterion

$$\sum_{t=1}^{T}(x_t - \Lambda f_t)'(x_t - \Lambda f_t) = \|\boldsymbol{X} - \boldsymbol{F}\Lambda\|_{\mathbb{F}}^2, \tag{2.18}$$

where $\|\boldsymbol{A}\|_{\mathbb{F}} = \sqrt{\sum_{t=1}^{T}\sum_{k=1}^{K}\boldsymbol{A}_{k,t}^2}$ is the Frobenius norm of matrix $\boldsymbol{A}$. In order to identify $(\boldsymbol{\Lambda}, \boldsymbol{F})$, however, standardizations must be imposed because, for any matrix $\boldsymbol{A}$ orthogonal size $r \times r$, considering $\boldsymbol{\Lambda A}$ and $\boldsymbol{A}^{-1}f_t$ instead of $\boldsymbol{\Lambda}$ and f_t leaves the product $\boldsymbol{A}f_t$ unchanged. The most appropriate normalization in terms of computational cost depends on the order of p and T: if $T < p$, it is preferable to use the normalization (N1) $\boldsymbol{F}'\boldsymbol{F}/T = \boldsymbol{I}_r$ (i.e., the factors are uncorrelated); if $T > p$, it is preferable to use the normalization (N2) $\boldsymbol{\Lambda}'\boldsymbol{\Lambda} = \boldsymbol{I}_r$. Let us give the intuition of the solution when using (N2). For a fixed $\boldsymbol{\Lambda}$, $\widehat{\boldsymbol{F}}$ is solution of the ordinary least squares, thus

$$\widehat{f}_t(\boldsymbol{\Lambda}) = (\boldsymbol{\Lambda}'\boldsymbol{\Lambda})^{-1}\boldsymbol{\Lambda}'x_t = \boldsymbol{\Lambda}'x_t. \tag{2.19}$$

By substituting this expression (2.19) of $\widehat{f}_t$ into the ordinary least squares objective function (2.18), we obtain

$$\frac{1}{T}\sum_{t=1}^{T}(x_t - \boldsymbol{\Lambda\Lambda}'x_t)'(x_t - \boldsymbol{\Lambda\Lambda}'x_t) = \frac{1}{T}\sum_{t=1}^{T}(x_t'x_t - x_t'\boldsymbol{\Lambda\Lambda}'x_t)$$
$$= \operatorname{tr}\left(\widehat{\boldsymbol{\Sigma}}\right) - \operatorname{tr}\left(\boldsymbol{\Lambda}'\widehat{\boldsymbol{\Sigma}}\boldsymbol{\Lambda}\right),$$

where $\widehat{\boldsymbol{\Sigma}} = \sum_t x_t x_t'/T$ is the empirical covariance matrix. This matrix $\widehat{\boldsymbol{\Sigma}}$ is a real symmetric matrix with eigenvectors denoted by $\theta_1, \ldots, \theta_K$ and associated with ordered eigenvalues, $s_1, \ldots, s_K$. Using the properties of real symmetric matrices, we have:

$$\max_{(N2):\ \boldsymbol{\Lambda}'\boldsymbol{\Lambda}=I_r} \operatorname{tr}\left(\boldsymbol{\Lambda}'\widehat{\boldsymbol{\Sigma}}\boldsymbol{\Lambda}\right) = \sum_{k=1}^{r} s_k. \tag{2.20}$$

The maximum of this problem (2.20) is attained at $\widehat{\mathbf{\Lambda}} = [\theta_1, \ldots, \theta_r]$. This matrix $\widehat{\mathbf{\Lambda}}$ is the matrix composed of the first r eigenvectors θ_k of the empirical covariance matrix of size $p \times p$. We can deduce the factors $\widehat{f}_t = \widehat{f}_t(\widehat{\mathbf{\Lambda}})$ using (2.19). By imposing (N1), we obtain $\widehat{\boldsymbol{F}}$ equal to T times the matrix formed by the eigenvectors of the matrix $\boldsymbol{XX}'$ of size $T \times T$, and $\widehat{\mathbf{\Lambda}}' = (\widehat{\boldsymbol{F}}'\widehat{\boldsymbol{F}})^{-1}\widehat{\boldsymbol{F}}'\boldsymbol{X} = \widehat{\boldsymbol{F}}'\boldsymbol{X}/T$.

This shows that the least squares estimator can be obtained using the eigendecomposition of the empirical covariance matrix, hence the name "principal component method" for this approach. Bai (2003) shows asymptotic convergence results for the factors and weights when both T and p tend to infinity.

To determine the number of components, r, in this decomposition, we introduce the eigenvalue ratio method (e.g., Bai and Ng, 2002; Lam and Yao, 2012; Ahn and Horenstein, 2013). This method simply consists of selecting r as the value that maximizes the decrease between two consecutive eigenvalues $s_k(\widehat{\Sigma})$ of the empirical covariance matrix $\widehat{\Sigma}$:

$$\widehat{r} = \arg\max_{r \leq r_{\max}} \frac{s_k(\widehat{\Sigma})}{s_{k+1}(\widehat{\Sigma})},$$

where $r_{\max}$ is a fixed upper bound a priori. This strong decrease after $\widehat{r}$ indicates that adding the $\widehat{r} + 1$ component will only bring little information to our approximation compared to what is already retained.

Finally, let us describe how to use this lower-dimensional representation of the explanatory variables in a regression (factor augmented regression). Consider the observation of an i.i.d. sample $(x_t, y_t, z_t)_{t=1}^{T}$ satisfying the model

$$y_t = f_t'\gamma + z_t'\beta + \varepsilon_t, \tag{2.21}$$

$$x_t = \Lambda f_t + v_t, \tag{2.22}$$

$$\mathbb{E}(f_t\varepsilon_t) = \mathbb{E}(z_t\varepsilon_t) = \mathbb{E}(f_t v_t') = \mathbb{E}(v_t\varepsilon_t) = 0, \tag{2.23}$$

where Λ is a $p \times r$ matrix of factor weights, and f_t is an $r \times 1$ factor vector. In this model, x_t impacts y_t only through the latent factors. These factors often serve as controls in the equation aimed at estimating the effect of z on y, which is the parameter of interest. The estimation then proceeds in two steps. The first step involves estimating the factors, and the second step involves regressing y on z and the estimated factors. In the case where $T, r \to \infty$ jointly, Bai (2003) shows, among other things, that this factor-augmented regression is consistent if T and p, the dimension of x, are large.

2.7 Random forests

2.7.1 Single sample trees

First, we describe how to grow a decision tree to estimate the conditional expectation $\mu(x) = \mathbb{E}[Y|X = x]$ from an iid sample $(U_i)_{i=1,...,n} = (Y_i, X_i)_{i=1,...,n}$ using *recursive partitioning.* A decision tree estimates the conditional expectation of Y given X by a piecewise constant function on a partition defined by the data. The construction method of a decision tree produces an adaptive weighting $\alpha_i(x)$ to quantify the importance of the i-th training sample W_i at the evaluation point X:

$$\hat{\mu}(x) = \sum_{i=1}^{n} \alpha_i(x)Y_i, \text{ with } \alpha_i(x) := \frac{1\{X_i \in L(x)\}}{|\{i : X_i \in L(x)\}|}, \qquad (2.24)$$

where $L(x)$ is the "leaf" in which the point x falls. In other words, (2.24) is a locally weighted average of the $\alpha_i(x)$ of all Y_i corresponding to an X_i falling in a neighborhood (in the same leaf) of the point x. The leaves constitute a *partition* of the feature space $\mathcal{X}$. This partition maximizes a global segmentation criterion.

More specifically, given a set $A \in \mathcal{X}$, each node of the tree partitions the feature space into two child nodes A_1, A_2. For a *random-split* tree, this is done as follows: (a) draw a variable $j \in \{1, \ldots, p\}$ according to a certain distribution (b) use a *segmentation test* of the type $X_j \geq s$ where s is chosen to maximize heterogeneity between the two child nodes A_1, A_2 (see below). Thus, this recursive partition construction algorithm can be described as follows:

1. *Initialization:* initialize the list containing the cells associated with the root of the tree $\mathcal{A} = (\mathcal{X})$ and the tree $\mathcal{A}_{final}$ as an empty list.
2. *Expansion:* for each node $A \in \mathcal{A}$:

    IF A satisfies the stopping criterion (number of observations in the leaf less than n_0),
    - Remove A from the list $\mathcal{A}$
    - Concatenate $\mathcal{A}_{final} = \mathcal{A}_{final} + \{A\}$.

    ELSE randomly choose a coordinate from $\{1, \ldots, p\}$, **choose** the best split s in the *segmentation test*, and **create** the two child nodes by splitting $\mathcal{N}$. Then remove parent node A and add the child nodes to the list $\mathcal{A} = \mathcal{A} - \{A\} + \{\text{child nodes } A_1 \text{ and } A_2\}$.

This algorithm, similar to the original algorithm by Breiman (2001), is described on an example with $n_0 = 2$ in Figures 2.1 and 2.2. To compute the prediction in a single-sample decision tree, we simply take the average of the corresponding Y_i outcomes

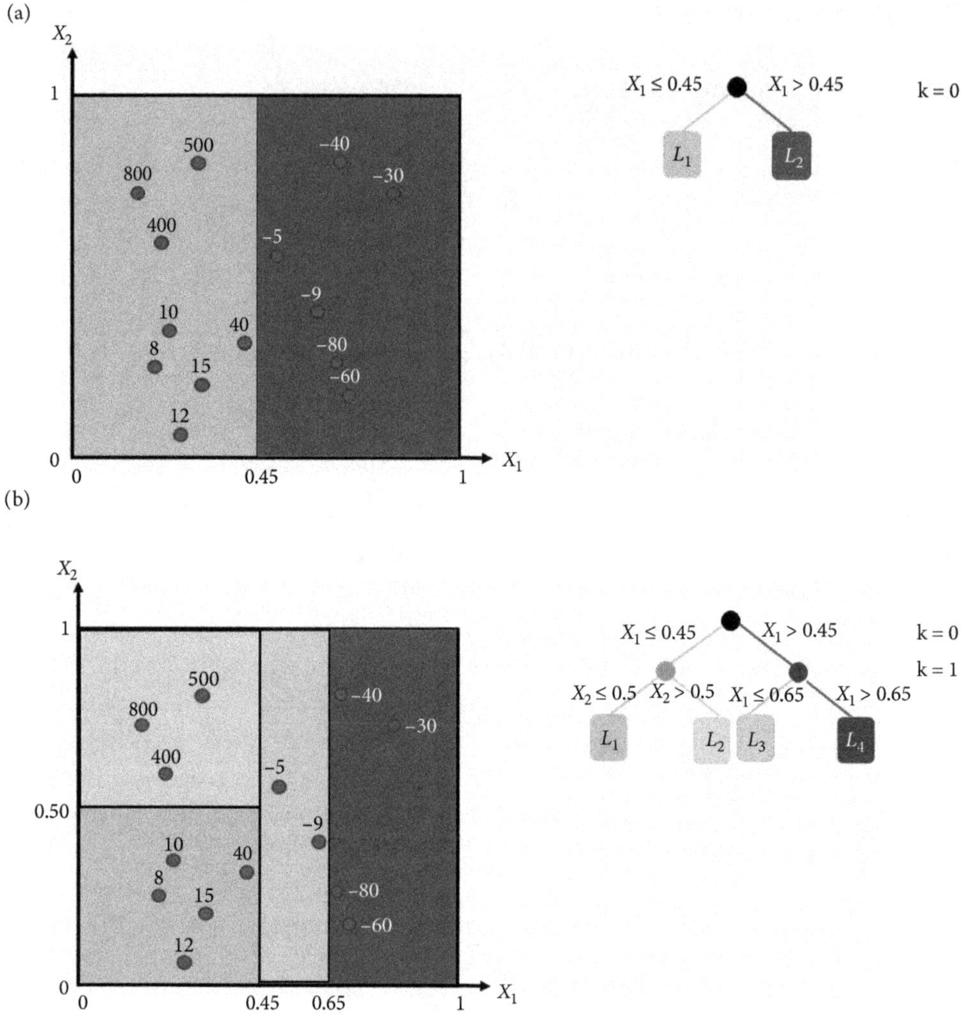

Figure 2.1 Decision tree algorithm: steps 1 and 2.

Note: Example of a randomized tree using a minimum number of observations $k = 2$ in each leaf as a stopping criterion.

of the observations that fall into the leaf $L(x)$. Note that an additional regularization step can be added to the above algorithm to cut the leaves according to a certain *pruning* criterion. This step is not necessary in our context and was not used in the original formulation by Breiman (2001).

2.7.2 Details on the segmentation test

For classification (when Y is binary), it is customary to use the initial CART (ClAssification and Regression Tree) criterion which consists in choosing s to maximize the homogeneity gain:

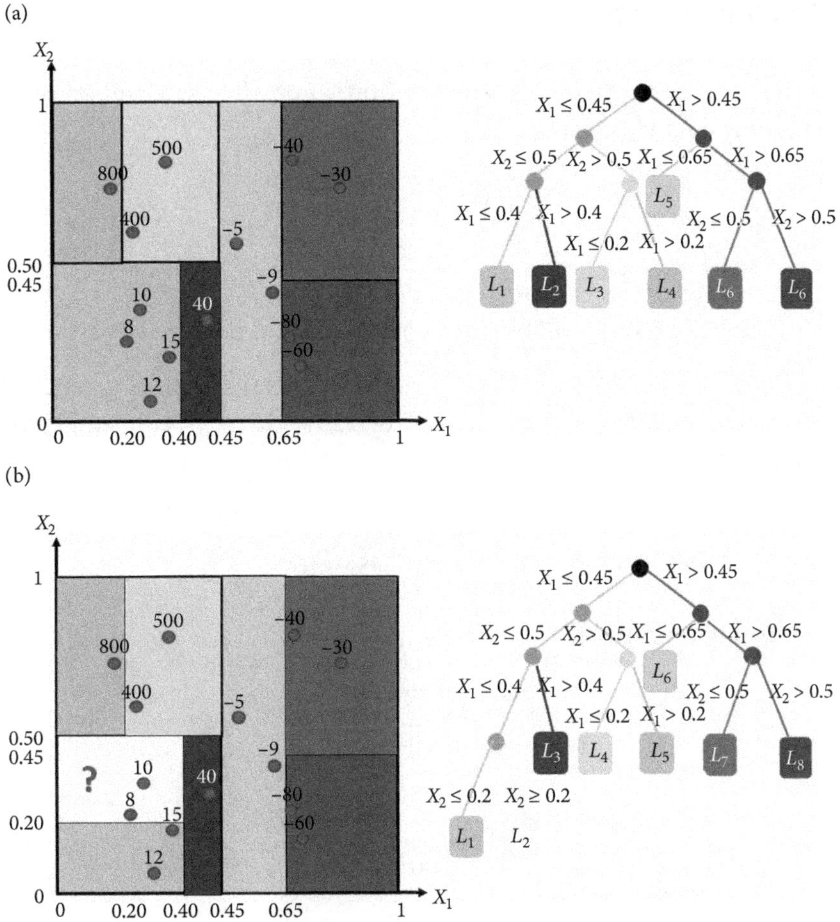

Figure 2.2 Decision tree algorithm: steps 3, 4, and evaluation.

Note: Example of a randomized tree using a minimum number of observations $k = 2$ in each leaf as a stopping criterion.

$$I(A_1, A_2) = G(A) - qG(A_1) - (1 - q)G(A_2),$$

where $q = N_{A_1}/N_A$, and $G(A) = 1 - \overline{Y}_A^2 - \left(1 - \overline{Y}_A\right)^2$ is the Gini index, i.e., a measure of homogeneity in the node. A good splitting generates two “heterogeneous” children containing “homogeneous” observations ($G(A) = 0$ if $\overline{Y}_A$ is equal to 0 or 1).

For regression, we consider a similar structure, where we maximize the decrease in variance, which can be rewritten as

$$I(A_1, A_2) = E(A) - (qE(A_1) + (1 - q)E(A_2)),$$

where $E(A) = \sum_{i, X_i \in A} \left(Y_i - \overline{Y}_A\right)^2 / N_A$. Thus, the segmentation criterion consists in finding the splits that decrease the variance the most, thus minimizing $qE(A_1) + (1 - q)E(A_2)$ for all splits.

2.7.3 Random forests

In a final step, we aggregate the trees formed on all possible subsamples of size s from the training data $U_1, \ldots, U_n$:

$$\hat{\mu}(x; U_1, \ldots, U_n) = \binom{n}{s}^{-1} \sum_{1 \le i_1 < \ldots < i_s \le n} T(x; U_{i_1}, \ldots, U_{i_s}), \tag{2.25}$$

where $\binom{n}{s}$ is the number of combinations of s elements among n. The estimator of Equation (2.25) is evaluated using Monte Carlo methods: we draw B samples without replacement denoted by $\mathcal{I}_b$, $b = 1, \ldots, B$ of size s, $(U^*_{i_1}, \ldots, U^*_{i_s})$, and consider the following approximation of (2.25):

$$\hat{\mu}(x; U_1, \ldots, U_n) \approx \frac{1}{B} \sum_{b=1}^{B} T(x; U^*_{b,1}, \ldots, U^*_{b,s}), \tag{2.26}$$

where the learning is based on

$$T(x; U^*_{b,1}, \ldots, U^*_{b,s}) = \sum_{i \in \mathcal{I}_b} \alpha^*_{b,i}(x) Y^*_{b,i},$$

$$\alpha^*_{b,i}(x) = \frac{1\left\{X^*_{b,i} \in L^*_b(x)\right\}}{\left|\{i : X^*_{b,i} \in L^*_b(x)\}\right|}. \tag{2.27}$$

This aggregation strategy, known as *bagging*, reduces the variance of the estimator of μ (see e.g., Bühlmann and Yu, 2002, for a more detailed analysis).

Additional references

Chapter 15 of Hastie et al. (2009) or Biau and Scornet (2016) provide a detailed explanation of how random forests work.

2.8 Neural networks

Neural networks are a difficult tool to introduce and comprehend without going into details and gaining practical experience. They can be perceived as a mere alternative algorithm for performing classification or regression tasks, i.e., to model the relationship between X and Y. In fact, to put it simply, a neural network is a composition of a multitude of non-linear functions in order to model the complex interaction between explanatory variables and the variable we are trying to predict. However, this is far too reductionist. On one hand, their flexibility, mainly due to automatic differentiation and the techniques developed to train them, make them suitable for a multitude of tasks that go well beyond simple classification or regression. On the other hand, the very philosophy of these tools makes them objects whose practical use requires making significant choices, both for the model and for the optimization algorithm – training neural networks is an art more than a scientific endeavor. Neural networks in general, and certain architectures in particular, are at the foundation of recent advances in artificial intelligence.

This section provides a brief introduction to neural networks, mainly to show their specificity compared to other methods and to build the prerequisites for the fifth part, which deals with text data. The use of neural networks in empirical economics is limited at present, partly because these techniques can be complex to implement, and partly because few theoretical results guarantee their performance, which also limits the ability to make inferences with this type of model. Nevertheless, this state of affairs could soon change. For example, Farrell et al. (2021) highlight non-asymptotic bounds and study the convergence rate of feed-forward neural networks.

2.8.1 Architecture

In a very basic way, a neural network can be seen as a function $\mu(.)$ that, given an input vector X, associates a representation or an *output*, $\mu(X)$. In general, and for most machine learning tasks, this output will take the form of a conditional expectation. For example, in a classification task, we would like the neural network to return the conditional probability of belonging to each category in the output space. However, we may simply want the neural network to return an abstract vector representation of the input in an arbitrarily high-dimensional space in order to both summarize the information contained in the input and create a space whose structure reflects logical relationships between the inputs. This latter use, aiming to create *embeddings*, constitutes one of the strengths of deep learning, which we will study in the fifth part, and more precisely in Chapter 13.

For now, let us focus on a classical prediction task using a simple neural network called a *feed-forward neural network.* The term *deep learning* that accompanies neural networks comes from the fact that the function $\mu(.)$ is constructed by composing multiple non-linear functions – the more functions there are, the deeper the network. Thus, a network with two layers can be written as follows:

$$\mu(x) = g_2(b_2 + \Theta_2 g_1(b_1 + \mathbf{\Theta}_1 x)), \tag{2.28}$$

where

$$h_1(.) = g_1(b_1 + \mathbf{\Theta}_1.)$$

is the first layer consisting of the parameter matrix $\mathbf{\Theta}_1$ of dimension $l_1 \times p$ (also called *weights* in the terminology of neural networks), the parameter vector b_1 of dimension l_1 (also called *bias*), and the activation function $g_1(.)$ that is applied element-wise. Similarly, $h_2(.) = g_2(b_2 + \mathbf{\Theta}_2.)$ is the second layer (final layer) consisting of the parameter matrix $\mathbf{\Theta}_2$ of dimension $1 \times l_1$, the scalar parameter b_2, and the activation function $g_2(.)$ that is also applied element-wise. In this sense, the *depth* of the network is defined by the number of layers it consists of, here two. In a very basic way, a linear regression is a shallow neural network, consisting of only one layer and an identity activation function since in this case $\mu(x) = X'\beta$. The *width* of a network is defined by the dimension of the intermediate space, or the *number of neurons*, here l_1. The larger and deeper a neural network is, the greater its capacity to approximate functions from a complex class – see the universal approximation theorems (e.g., Cybenko, 1989; Hornik, 1991; Rolnick and Tegmark, 2018). This generally implies that a performing neural network must consist of a large number of parameters, often exceeding the size of the training dataset. This is referred to as *over-parametrization.*

According to the traditional bias-variance trade-off to which standard machine learning models are subject – the model must be complex enough to capture the richness of the data, but not excessively so as to risk capturing noise – one might expect neural networks to suffer from chronic overfitting and be poorly generalizable. Belkin et al. (2019) show that neural networks surpass this trade-off by reducing the training loss to zero and entering a regime where the model interpolates the data without being less generalizable – on the contrary.

There are infinite possibilities for the choice of activation functions g_1, g_2. However, a number of them are commonly used for their ability to capture complex interactions between X and Y or for their impact on the network's learning speed, for example:

- Sigmoid: $g(x) = \exp(x)/(1 + \exp(x))$,
- Rectified Linear Unit (ReLU): $g(x) = \max(0, x)$,
- Soft-max: $g(x_1, \ldots, x_p) = (e^{x_j})_{j=1,\ldots,p} / \sum_{j=1,\ldots,p} e^{x_j}$.

Chapter 6 of Goodfellow et al. (2016) provides a comprehensive overview of commonly used activation functions. Generally, neural networks are often – but not exclusively – used for specific tasks involving unstructured data such as text or images. In a number of cases, it may be useful to base the architecture of a network on an existing network available on the internet: on one hand, these architectures have often proven themselves in well-known challenges such as the ImageNet Large Scale Visual Recognition Challenge (ILSVRC or simply ImageNet), and on the other hand, these pretrained networks with optimized parameter values for certain tasks can also be retrieved. This is referred to as *transfer learning* when initializing parameter values for a given task based on values obtained for another task. For example, in the field of computer-assisted vision, the VGG16 models (Simonyan and Zisserman, 2015) or GoogLeNet (Szegedy et al., 2015) are often interesting starting points.

2.8.2 Loss functions

Training a neural network means seeking to modify the values of the parameters $b_1, \mathbf{\Theta}_1, b_2, \mathbf{\Theta}_2$ in order to optimize the performance in terms of prediction. Therefore, a loss function that aligns with the training task is essential. Thus, the values of the parameters will be modified in order to minimize this loss function estimated on a sample:

$$\frac{1}{n}\sum_{i=1}^{n} \ell(Y_i, \mu(X_i)).$$

For a regression task, one could want to use loss functions such as:

- Mean Squared Error (MSE): $\ell(Y, \widehat{Y}) = (Y - \widehat{Y})^2$,
- Mean Absolute Error (MAE): $\ell(Y, \widehat{Y}) = |Y - \widehat{Y}|$.

For a classification task, the binary cross-entropy is typically the primary choice. It is defined as $\ell(Y, \widehat{Y}) = Y \log(\widehat{Y}) + (1 - Y)\log(1 - \widehat{Y})$. In general, one may seek to minimize the negative of a log-likelihood function (see Section 2.4).

2.8.3 Training through backpropagation

Once the structure of a neural network has been defined and a loss function has been chosen, a strategy must be defined to optimize the parameters. In general, this is not a problem when the objective function is convex, as a standard gradient descent can be implemented, possibly using the Hessian matrix to determine the step size at each iteration. However, in the case of neural networks, which are composed of functions that make the objective function non-convex and can contain thousands or millions of parameters, this is not the case, and alternative strategies must be established. In particular, stochastic gradient descent (SGD; Bottou, 2010) is the main optimization tool. The idea of this algorithm is that instead of computing the gradient over the entire training sample at each optimization step, it is only computed over a randomly selected subset of the sample. The true gradient is replaced with a noisy version in order to save computation time. At each optimization step, a random subset of the training sample, called a *batch* and denoted $\mathcal{B}$ with size $B \ll n$, is first randomly chosen. Then, for a given *learning rate* $\eta > 0$, the parameters are updated using the following rule:

$$\mathbf{\Theta}_{t+1} = \mathbf{\Theta}_t - \eta \frac{1}{B} \sum_{i \in \mathcal{B}} \partial_{\mathbf{\Theta}} \ell(Y_i, \mu(X_i)). \tag{2.29}$$

A full pass over the entire training set, partitioned into batches, is called an *epoch*. In practice, the gradient descent algorithms available in the software used to train neural networks are more complex and incorporate techniques aimed at speeding up convergence or move out of local minima (e.g., the famous Adam algorithm by Kingma and Ba, 2015). However, at the level of abstraction we are currently at, going into details is not necessary.

The first step is to compute the gradient recursively using the chain rule: $(g \circ f)' = f' \times (g' \circ f)$. Repeatedly applying this rule to optimize the parameters of each layer yields the backpropagation algorithm (Rumelhart et al., 1986). Here is what it would look like for our neural network (2.28) with an arbitrary loss function:

1. Since they will be involved in all subsequent calculations, we first compute the following two quantities:

$$\partial_{\mu(X_i)}\ell(Y_i, \mu(X_i)),$$
$$g_2'(b_2 + \boldsymbol{\Theta}_2 h_1(X_i)).$$

This gives us an initial value for the gradient:

$$\boldsymbol{g} \leftarrow \partial_{\mu(X_i)}\ell(Y_i, \mu(X_i)) \times g_2'(b_2 + \boldsymbol{\Theta}_2 h_1(X_i)).$$

2. Let us then compute the derivatives of the loss function with respect to the parameters of the second layer:

$$\partial_{b_2}\ell(Y_i, \mu(X_i)) = \partial_{\mu(X_i)}\ell(Y_i, \mu(X_i)) \times g_2'(b_2 + \boldsymbol{\Theta}_2 h_1(X_i)),$$
$$\partial_{\boldsymbol{\Theta}_2}\ell(Y_i, \mu(X_i)) = \partial_{\mu(X_i)}\ell(Y_i, \mu(X_i)) \times g_2'(b_2 + \boldsymbol{\Theta}_2 h_1(X_i)) \times h_1(X_i).$$

We can see that they depend on the value of our gradient, so we can directly compute them as follows:

$$\partial_{b_2}\ell(Y_i, \mu(X_i)) = \boldsymbol{g},$$
$$\partial_{\boldsymbol{\Theta}_2}\ell(Y_i, \mu(X_i)) = \boldsymbol{g} \times h_1(X_i).$$

We can then update these two parameters using the rule given by Equation (2.29).

3. Finally, we need to update the parameters of the first layer. For this, it is first necessary to backpropagate (update) the gradient:

$$\boldsymbol{g} \leftarrow \partial_{\mu(X_i)}\ell(Y_i, \mu(X_i)) \times g_2'(b_2 + \boldsymbol{\Theta}_2 h_1(X_i)) \times \boldsymbol{\Theta}_2' \odot \partial g_1(b_1 + \boldsymbol{\Theta}_1 X_i),$$

where $\boldsymbol{\Theta}_2'$ denotes the transpose of the matrix $\boldsymbol{\Theta}_2$, and $\odot$ represents element-wise vector multiplication. This amounts to using the recursive rule:

$$\boldsymbol{g} \leftarrow \boldsymbol{g} \times \boldsymbol{\Theta}_2' \odot \partial g_1(b_1 + \boldsymbol{\Theta}_1 X_i).$$

4. We can then compute the gradient for each parameter in the first layer. A calculation yields:

$$\begin{aligned}
&\partial_{b_1}\ell(Y_i,\mu(X_i))\\
&= \partial_{\mu(X_i)}\ell(Y_i,\mu(X_i)) \times g_2'(b_2 + \boldsymbol{\Theta}_2 h_1(X_i)) \times \boldsymbol{\Theta}_2{}' \odot \partial g_1(b_1 + \boldsymbol{\Theta}_1 X_i),\\
&\partial_{\boldsymbol{\Theta}_1}\ell(Y_i,\mu(X_i))\\
&= \partial_{\mu(X_i)}\ell(Y_i,\mu(X_i)) \times g_2'(b_2 + \boldsymbol{\Theta}_2 h_1(X_i)) \times \boldsymbol{\Theta}_2{}' \odot \partial g_1(b_1 + \boldsymbol{\Theta}_1 X_i) \times X_i'.
\end{aligned}$$

As previously, it is therefore sufficient to perform the calculation:

$$\partial_{b_1}\ell(Y_i,\mu(X_i)) = \boldsymbol{g},$$
$$\partial_{\boldsymbol{\Theta}_1}\ell(Y_i,\mu(X_i)) = \boldsymbol{g} \times X_i',$$

and then update according to Equation (2.29).

In a nutshell, the backpropagation method operates by recursively updating the gradient to compute, at each step, the gradient corresponding to each parameter. The calculation is done from the layer closest to the output to the layer closest to the input, hence the term "backpropagation." For more details or a more abstract explanation, the reader can refer to Goodfellow et al. (2016, p. 206). The most commonly used softwares such as `pytorch` (Paszke et al., 2019) or `tensorflow` (Abadi et al., 2016) define objects called tensors that store the sequence of operations that led to their value – the computational graph – in order to perform this gradient calculation automatically. This is called "automatic differentiation" or "auto-diff." The term "neural network" reflects the importance of the graph that connects each neuron to achieve the output layer prediction.

One of the dangers of this technique, which is inherent to neural networks in general, is the vanishing gradient problem, where the gradient becomes very close to zero so that the network stops learning. Indeed, if at any moment during the descent process the gradient becomes too close to zero – for example, due to an activation function whose derivative is very small, as is the case for the sigmoid function – information no longer passes through the network, and the parameters belonging to the first layers are no longer updated. In other words, the network no longer learns properly. In general, one could say of stochastic gradient descent what Winston Churchill said about democracy: it is the worst system, except for all the others. Given the structure of neural networks, it is not reasonable or even possible to use efficient optimization algorithms. Instead, we are forced to use stochastic gradient descent, knowing that there are very few theoretical guarantees on its convergence properties. In order to guide the training process of a neural network towards obtaining parameters that allow optimal performance (i.e., minimize generalization error), a number of regularization techniques can be implemented, such as choosing a certain smoothing of the gradient, adjusting the learning rate, penalizing high parameter values with an ℓ_2 norm, randomly setting some parameters to zero via dropout layers, augmenting the data through specific transformations, etc. But their description goes beyond the introductory scope of this section.

2.8.4 Training tips

Neural networks are notoriously difficult objects to train, due to the multitude of parameters to tune. However, we can provide a set of tricks that make it easier to successfully train them. Several of these tricks are inspired by an excellent blog post by Andrej Karpathy: karpathy.github.io/2019/04/25/recipe.

The first reflex to adopt applies more broadly to any machine learning project: it consists of thoroughly exploring the data. The goal of this step is to get a better idea of the variability in the data, evaluate the respective quantities of noise and signal in order to find a possible strategy for filtering the noise (e.g., removing ambiguous examples or mislabeled data), identify outliers, compare the frequency of certain classes or features to identify imbalances, etc.

Because their optimization is generally not a convex problem, neural networks require the use of stochastic gradient descent to learn, which poses a number of complications compared to more standard methods. In addition, debugging a model that does not perform as expected can quickly become frustrating. Therefore, a number of principles can guide practice:

- **Start with a simple model and gradually add complexity**. Large models (very deep or containing millions of parameters) can be difficult to train, especially due to the problem of *vanishing gradient,* i.e., the gradient of the layers close to the input becomes close to zero, which impairs the ability of these layers to learn during gradient descent. It is therefore preferable to start with a rudimentary model to which, for example, layers are gradually added. Similarly, it is not necessary to be creative: starting from a well-known architecture that has proven its worth should ensure a certain level of performance. At this stage of research, the goal is to have a model that: (i) learns, (ii) without its cost being exorbitant, in order to (iii) obtain a correct performance that can serve as a starting baseline.
- **Early stopping.** During training, it is important to regularly report the metrics of interest (e.g., at each epoch, possibly every ten batches if an epoch takes considerable time), both on the training sample and on a validation sample. In this regard, the closer the metric is to the application, and interpretable by

the practitioner, the better the training can be monitored. Thus, when training a classifier, it is important to report both the value of the loss function (usually binary cross-entropy) and accuracy, as well as precision or recall if relevant. It is important to monitor the learning curve of the model in order to check, on the one hand, that the loss function decreases with each epoch, and on the other hand, that the model does not start to overfit, which can be detected when the validation loss starts to increase while the training loss continues to decrease. In this regard, it may be interesting to implement what is called early stopping, by saving the model during training every time the validation loss decreases, to be able to go back to the best model even if training diverges.

- **Data augmentation**. Data augmentation is a practice that involves generating new observations through random transformations, in order to make the model robust to small deviations in the datasets. This is a very common practice when it comes to image processing, by randomly applying rotations, translations, truncations, adding noise to pixels, etc., to training data. Some practitioners even suggest adding unlabeled data with the model's prediction when it is above 90% in case of a shortage of observations when training a classifier. In natural language processing, this practice is rarer because non-meaningful strings of characters can be more easily identified and eliminated with regular expressions, but some strategies seem promising (Feng et al., 2021).
- **Regularizing the model**. Given that they often contain a number of parameters much larger than the number of observations, neural networks are highly prone to overfitting. Several strategies can be implemented to minimize this risk, including early stopping of training and data augmentation (refer to previous points for details). To regularize more directly, it is possible to consider models with lower dimension, introduce dropout layers that set certain weights to zero according to a Bernoulli distribution with an arbitrary parameter, or modify the loss function to incorporate an ℓ_2 penalty similar to Ridge regression in order to force the parameters to not deviate too much from zero (see Section 2.3.2 – a practice known as *weight decay* in deep learning).
- **Retraining the same model with different parameters**. Unlike other machine learning algorithms, neural networks can be retrained to improve performance. It may be interesting to let the model "simmer" for a bit longer than planned, or with a different learning rate, by modifying the batch size, changing the training data, etc. Similarly, when new observations are available, it is recommended to start from the previous parameter values rather than starting from scratch – in a logic akin to transfer learning. Section 14.3 explores these options in the context of language models.

As a word of conclusion, neural networks are powerful tools, and we will illustrate their performance in this book, notably for language-processing tasks. Nevertheless, note that some papers such as Grinsztajn et al. (2022) point out that when it comes to tabular data which are ubiquitous in empirical economics, tree-based methods still outperform neural networks.

Additional references

The book Goodfellow et al. (2016) is a reference on the subject. Fan et al. (2021) offers a statistical perspective on these somewhat peculiar objects called neural networks. Specifically, in non-parametric regression, when estimating functions that have some form of structured sparsity, Schmidt-Hieber (2020) shows that estimators based on sparsely connected deep neural networks with ReLU activation function achieve minimax optimal convergence rates.

Currently, training neural networks is primarily a matter of practice rather than theory. Tricks can be found in academic literature, as well as on dedicated forums or blogs. In this regard, we can mention Lilian Weng's blog (lilianweng.github.io/lil-log/), this excellent post by Andrej Karpathy (karpathy.github.io/2019/04/25/recipe/), as well as the digital book Godbole et al. (2023).

2.9 Summary

Key concepts

Linear regression (ordinary least squares, OLS), Ridge estimator, Lasso estimator, cross-validation, maximum likelihood, ℓ_1 or ℓ_2 penalization, generalized method of moments (GMM), factor model, singular value decomposition (SVD), principal component analysis (PCA), decision tree, random forest, bagging, neural network, feed-forward neural network, deep learning, stochastic gradient descent (SGD), backpropagation algorithm.

Additional references

Specific references have been provided at the end of each section, but readers coming from an economics background may find it beneficial to read Athey and Imbens (2019).

2.10 Proofs and additional results

Proof of Lemma 2.1 Following Section 2.2, we can see that from the SVD of $\boldsymbol{X} = \boldsymbol{U}\boldsymbol{S}\boldsymbol{V}'$ we get $\boldsymbol{X}'\boldsymbol{X} = \boldsymbol{V}\boldsymbol{S}'\boldsymbol{S}\boldsymbol{V}'$. So using matrix notations and the fact that $\boldsymbol{V}'\boldsymbol{V} = \mathbb{I}_p$, we can write:

$$\begin{aligned}\beta^R(\lambda) &= \left[\boldsymbol{X}'\boldsymbol{X} + \lambda\mathbb{I}_p\right]^{-1}\boldsymbol{X}'\boldsymbol{y} \\ &= \left[\boldsymbol{V}\boldsymbol{S}'\boldsymbol{S}\boldsymbol{V}' + \lambda\mathbb{I}_p\right]^{-1}\boldsymbol{V}\boldsymbol{S}'\boldsymbol{U}'\boldsymbol{y} \\ &= \boldsymbol{V}\left[\boldsymbol{S}'\boldsymbol{S} + \lambda\mathbb{I}_p\right]^{-1}\boldsymbol{S}'\boldsymbol{U}'\boldsymbol{y}.\end{aligned}$$

Then because all these matrices are diagonal, we have:

$$\text{diag}\left(\left[\boldsymbol{S}'\boldsymbol{S} + \lambda\mathbb{I}_p\right]^{-1}\boldsymbol{S}'\right) = \left(\frac{s_j}{s_j^2 + \lambda}\right)_{j=1,\dots,p}.$$

As $\lambda \to 0$, this last term is either equal to s_j^{-1} if $s_j > 0$ or to 0 if $s_j = 0$. Hence, $\left[\boldsymbol{S}'\boldsymbol{S} + \lambda\mathbb{I}_p\right]^{-1}\boldsymbol{S}' \to \boldsymbol{S}^+$ and

$$\beta^R(\lambda) \to \boldsymbol{V}\boldsymbol{S}^+\boldsymbol{U}'\boldsymbol{y} = \left[\boldsymbol{X}'\boldsymbol{X}\right]^+\boldsymbol{X}'\boldsymbol{y}.$$

□

Chapter 3
Causal inference

This chapter presents the intellectual framework underlying causal inference, which is the process by which one can establish a causal relationship between a phenomenon (often referred to as a *treatment* or *policy* in economics) and its effects. We first introduce the potential outcomes model, and then discuss the associated tools.

3.1 Definitions

We start by distinguishing between different types of parameters: probabilistic, statistical, and causal. Probabilistic parameters are defined based on the joint probabilities of the variables in the model, whether they are observed or not. Statistical parameters are defined based on the joint probabilities of the observed variables, for example, the conditional expectation of the outcome variable given observed characteristics or correlations between observed variables. Finally, causal parameters are defined based on a causal model and are not statistical parameters, for example, the causal effect of a treatment on a variable, all else being equal (see Section 1.5 in Pearl, 2000). The identification of these causal parameters requires assumptions that may not be testable. This difference in the status of the different parameters is important for understanding the interpretations made in this book.

We now formally define the causal effect of a treatment within the framework of the potential outcome model of Rubin (1974). $Y_i(0)$ is defined as the potential outcome for individual i if they are not treated, and $Y_i(1)$ as the potential outcome if they are treated. In reality, for a given individual, only the treatment status $D_i \in \{0, 1\}$ is observed, as well as the realized outcome Y_i defined by:

$$Y_i := Y_i(D_i) = \begin{cases} Y_i(0) & \text{if } D_i = 0, \\ Y_i(1) & \text{if } D_i = 1. \end{cases}$$

The treatment effect for an individual i is then:

$$\Delta_i = Y_i(1) - Y_i(0).$$

The fundamental problem of causal inference arises from the fact that, for an individual i, one can only ever observe $Y_i(0)$ or $Y_i(1)$, and thus never the effect Δ_i directly. This situation presents a missing variable problem, making the estimation

Machine Learning for Econometrics. Christophe Gaillac and Jérémy L'Hour, Oxford University Press.
 DOI: 10.1093/9780198918868.003.0003

of Δ_i unfeasible without additional assumptions. Therefore, we focus on making inferences about different features of the treatment effect at the population level.

A first quantity of interest is the average treatment effect (ATE)

$$\tau_0 := \mathbb{E}[Y_i(1) - Y_i(0)],$$

which represents the average impact of the intervention in the population. A second usual parameter of interest is the average treatment effect on the treated (ATT), which is defined as

$$\tau_0^{ATT} := \mathbb{E}[Y_i(1) - Y_i(0)|D_i = 1].$$

Finally, when we observe characteristics X_i, we may be interested in describing the potential heterogeneity of the treatment effect with respect to these variables. In fact, τ_0 represents an average effect that could mask significant disparities across the population. Subsequently, our attention shifts towards the conditional average treatment effect (CATE), defined as the function:

$$\tau : x \mapsto \mathbb{E}\,[Y_i(1) - Y_i(0)|X_i = x].$$

The estimation of this parameter will be further developed in Chapter 8.

3.2 Randomized controlled trials

Randomized controlled trials (RCTs) are the simplest conceptual framework for identifying causal effects, as well as the most reliable level of proof in terms of internal validity. In fact, Abadie and Cattaneo (2018) refer to them as the "gold standard." They consist of randomly assigning an individual to receive treatment ($D_i = 1$) or not receive treatment ($D_i = 0$). In this case, the group of untreated individuals constitutes what is called the *control group*, which serves as the baseline for comparison. The aim is to measure the effect of this treatment on an outcome variable. In doing so, it is crucial to consider the *counterfactual* situation, the value of the outcome variable that would have been observed if the treatment had not been administered. For example, to determine the causal effect of a training program on employment outcomes, we would want to compare the outcome of an individual after they have undergone training to the outcome they would have obtained *if they had not undergone training*. Therefore, we seek to obtain a control group that is as similar as possible to the treated individuals.

Random assignment to treatment thus helps to avoid the effects of *selection into treatment*, which is the idea that individuals who have the most to gain from treatment have incentives to enter the treatment group, biasing the comparison with the group of untreated individuals, who do not have such incentives. Even when random allocation is not feasible, the context of RCTs continues to serve as a foundational framework for the development of more sophisticated identification strategies.

We now develop simple methods and the statistical framework for estimating the parameters mentioned in the previous section. Suppose we observe an i.i.d. sample of pairs of random variables (Y_i, D_i), $i = 1, \dots, n$, and:

Assumption 3.1 (SUTVA).

$$Y_i := Y_i(D_i).$$

Hypothesis 3.1 is known as the *stable unit treatment value* (SUTVA) assumption, and assumes that the effect of the treatment on one individual does not affect the outcome of the other individuals. This assumption may be questionable if, for example, there are network or peer effects, more generally if there are externalities (e.g., the impact of a vaccine). An alternative model would be to assume that $Y_i = Y_i(D_1, \dots, D_n)$, i.e., an individual's outcome depends on the treatment status of other individuals. However, this model is generally too complex to be useful.

Assumption 3.2 (Random assignment).

$$(Y_i(0), Y_i(1)) \perp\!\!\!\perp D_i.$$

Assumption 3.2 expresses the independence of treatment with respect to potential outcomes, which is credible if and only if treatment is randomly assigned, without reference to the individual's potential outcome.

By comparing the average outcomes between the treated group and the control group, we have:

$$\begin{aligned}
&\mathbb{E}[Y|D=1] - \mathbb{E}[Y|D=0] \\
&= \mathbb{E}[Y(1)|D=1] - \mathbb{E}[Y(0)|D=0] \qquad \text{(under SUTVA)} \\
&= \mathbb{E}[Y(1)|D=1] - \mathbb{E}[Y(0)|D=0] + \mathbb{E}[Y(0)|D=1] - \mathbb{E}[Y(0)|D=1] \\
&= \mathbb{E}[Y(1)|D=1] - \mathbb{E}[Y(0)|D=1] + \underbrace{\mathbb{E}[Y(0)|D=1] - \mathbb{E}[Y(0)|D=0]}_{=0,\text{ using assumption 3.2}} \\
&= \tau_0,
\end{aligned} \tag{3.1}$$

where the last line is obtained using Assumption 3.2, which implies the equality of the average treatment on the treated (ATT) to the average treatment effect (ATE). In this sense, it means that the group of treated individuals in the absence of treatment would have been comparable to the group of untreated individuals. We can then deduce the *difference-in-means* (DM) estimator, denoting by n_d the number of individuals in group $d \in \{0, 1\}$:

$$\widehat{\tau}_{DM} = \frac{1}{n_1} \sum_{D_i=1} Y_i - \frac{1}{n_0} \sum_{D_i=0} Y_i. \tag{3.2}$$

Using the central limit theorem and (3.1), we obtain that the estimator (3.2) is asymptotically normal:

$$\sqrt{n}(\widehat{\tau}_{DM} - \tau_0) \overset{d}{\to} \mathcal{N}(0, \sigma_{DM}^2),$$

where $\sigma_{DM}^2 := \text{Var}(Y(1))/P(D = 1) + \text{Var}(Y(0))/P(D = 0)$, and we can derive confidence intervals on the ATE.

Remark 3.1 OLS estimation of the treatment effect

Assume that we observe (Y_i, D_i, X_i) satisfying the linear model

$$Y_i = \tau_0 D_i + X_i'\beta + \varepsilon_i, \quad \mathbb{E}[\varepsilon_i|D_i, X_i] = 0. \tag{3.3}$$

Then we can estimate the average treatment effect using OLS of Y_i on (D_i, X_i), and the estimator is asymptotically normal, under the standard OLS assumptions.

In fact, if agents are randomly assigned to two groups of equal size, even when the model is not linear in X_i, using OLS cannot lead to an estimator that is less precise than the estimator based on average differences, and is often even better (see Freedman, 2008; Lin, 2013). However, this gain relies on the linearity assumption of Model (3.3). As proven in (see Lin, 2013), this improvement in term of precision also holds when the groups have different sizes, but we regress Y_i on D_i, X_i, and the interactions between treatment D_i and covariates X_i. The other advantage of the latter *interactive* model is that it allows to describe heterogeneous effects of treatment.

3.3 Conditional independence and the propensity score

3.3.1 Baseline assumptions

The idealized framework of randomized experiments described above is often difficult to implement in practice. Moreover, it is often not desirable if the treatment is costly and one wishes to estimate its impact while limiting its cost, for example by excluding populations for which it is assumed a priori that the effect will be smaller. Nevertheless, this framework can be extended to cases where the treatment is not purely random but can be considered random once observable individual characteristics are controlled for. Assume that we observe an i.i.d. sample (Y_i, D_i, X_i), $i = 1, \ldots, n$, where X_i is a vector of observable characteristics. The key assumption is that once the observable individual characteristics X_i are controlled for, the assignment to treatment is as good as random.

Assumption 3.3 (Conditional independence or unconfoundedness).

$$(Y_i(0), Y_i(1)) \perp\!\!\!\perp D_i \,|X_i$$

Assumption 3.3 of conditional independence or selection on observables, often discussed in the economic literature, assumes that, conditional on these observable variables, the treatment is independent of potential outcomes. Rosenbaum and Rubin (1983) show that an important consequence of this assumption is that the propensity score defined as:

$$p : x \in \mathcal{X} \mapsto \mathbb{P}(D = 1|X = x)$$

allows to reduce the dimension of the problem, since it satisfies:

$$(Y_i(0), Y_i(1)) \perp\!\!\!\perp D_i \mid p(X_i). \tag{3.4}$$

3.3.2 Two characterizations of the ATE

There are multiple ways to characterize the ATE. We focus here on two of the most commonly used ones, i.e., using the inverse-propensity weighting (IPW)

Using the propensity score. A first characterization of the ATE uses inverse-propensity weighting for estimation. The idea is to estimate the score p in a first step using non-parametric regression $\widehat{p}$. Note that, when X is discrete and takes values x_k, $k = 1, \ldots, K$, a natural estimator of p is $\widehat{p}(x) = n_{x,1}/n_x$ when $x \in \{x_1, \ldots, x_K\}$, with n_x and $n_{x,1}$ being respectively the number of observations and the number of treated observations $D = 1$ such that $X = x$ in the sample of size n. Then, we use:

$$\widehat{\tau}_{IPW} = \frac{1}{n}\sum_{i=1}^{n}\left[\frac{D_i Y_i}{\widehat{p}(X_i)} - \frac{(1 - D_i)Y_i}{1 - \widehat{p}(X_i)}\right]. \tag{3.5}$$

Define τ^*_{IPW} the *oracle* estimator which is obtained assuming the propensity score is known:

$$\tau^*_{IPW} = \frac{1}{n}\sum_{i=1}^{n}\left[\frac{D_i Y_i}{p(X_i)} - \frac{(1 - D_i)Y_i}{1 - p(X_i)}\right]. \tag{3.6}$$

The analysis of the asymptotic properties of $\widehat{\tau}_{IPW}$ proceeds by decomposing

$$\widehat{\tau}_{IPW} - \tau_0 = \underbrace{\widehat{\tau}_{IPW} - \tau^*_{IPW}}_{(A)} + \underbrace{\tau^*_{IPW} - \tau_0}_{(B)}.$$

Notice that term (B) vanishes since τ^*_{IPW} is unbiased:

$$\begin{aligned}
\mathbb{E}(\tau^*_{IPW}) &= \mathbb{E}\left[\frac{D_i Y_i}{p(X_i)} - \frac{(1-D_i)Y_i}{1-p(X_i)}\right] \\
&= \mathbb{E}\left[\frac{D_i Y_i(1)}{p(X_i)} - \frac{(1-D_i)Y_i(0)}{1-p(X_i)}\right] \\
&= \mathbb{E}\left[\mathbb{E}\left[\frac{D_i Y_i(1)}{p(X_i)} - \frac{(1-D_i)Y_i(0)}{1-p(X_i)}\middle| p(X_i)\right]\right] \quad \text{(law of iterated expectations)} \\
&= \mathbb{E}\left[Y_i(1) - Y_i(0)\right] \quad \text{(with Assumption 3.3).}
\end{aligned}$$

Then, under the following overlap condition:

Assumption 3.4 (Overlap condition).

$$\exists \eta > 0, \textit{ such that, for all } x \in \mathcal{X},\ \eta \le p(x) \le 1 - \eta,$$

and assuming bounded outcome variables $|Y_i| \le M$, we obtain a control in probability for the distance to the oracle estimator (A):

$$|\widehat{\tau}_{IPW} - \tau^*_{IPW}| = \mathcal{O}_p\left(\frac{M \sup_{x\in\mathcal{X}} |\widehat{p}(x) - p(x)|}{\eta}\right).$$

Thus, under the sufficient condition of having a convergent estimator in sup-norm of the propensity score, $\sup_{x\in\mathcal{X}} |\widehat{p}(x) - p(x)| \underset{n\to\infty}{\to} 0$, the estimator $\widehat{\tau}_{IPW}$ is consistent.

Using difference between regression functions

A second characterization of the ATE is based on, for each $x \in \mathcal{X}$:

$$\begin{aligned}
&\mathbb{E}\left[Y_i(1) - Y_i(0)|X_i = x\right] \\
&= \mathbb{E}\left[Y_i(1)|X_i = x\right] - \mathbb{E}\left[Y_i(0)|X_i = x\right] \\
&= \mathbb{E}\left[Y_i(1)|X_i = x, D_i = 1\right] - \mathbb{E}\left[Y_i(0)|X_i = x, D_i = 0\right] \quad \text{(using assumption 3.3)} \\
&= \mathbb{E}\left[Y_i|X_i = x, D_i = 1\right] - \mathbb{E}\left[Y_i|X_i = x, D_i = 0\right] \quad \text{(using assumption 3.1)} \\
&= \mu_1(x) - \mu_0(x),
\end{aligned}$$

where $\mu_j(x) = \mathbb{E}\left[Y_i|X_i = x, D_i = j\right]$ for $j = 1, 2$, and thus

$$\tau_0 = \mathbb{E}\left[\mu_1(X_i) - \mu_0(X_i)\right]. \tag{3.7}$$

One way to obtain a consistent estimator of the ATE with this characterization would be to use a consistent non-parametric estimator $\widehat{\mu}_{(j)}$ of $\mu_{(j)}$ and then average over the observations:

$$\widehat{\tau}_{Diff} = \frac{1}{n}\sum_{i=1}^{n}(\mu_1(X_i) - \mu_0(X_i)). \tag{3.8}$$

In these two contexts, the functions μ and p appear as nuisance parameters that would need to be known in order to estimate the parameter of interest τ_0. Using separate machine learning estimators for $\mu_1(\cdot)$ and $\mu_0(\cdot)$, an estimator of $\tau(\cdot)$ does not necessitate the estimation of the propensity score. A challenge arises as biases in the separate estimations of $\mu_1(\cdot)$ and $\mu_0(\cdot)$ can accumulate and result in significant and unpredictable biases in the estimation of $\tau(\cdot)$.

An estimator following the first approach, $\widehat{\tau}_{IPW}$, often exhibits higher variance in contrast to a conditional mean regression estimator, $\widehat{\tau}_{Diff}$, attributed to the division by the propensity score in (3.5) (see the interesting example in Section 3 of Powers et al., 2017).

3.3.3 Efficient estimation of treatment effect

The augmented inverse propensity score (AIPW) estimator, defined by Robins et al. (1994) and Hahn (1998), is designed to correct the bias in (3.8) due to the estimation of $\mu_{(j)}$. It is given by

$$\widehat{\tau}_{AIPW} = \frac{1}{n}\sum_{i=1}^{n}\mu_1(X_i) - \mu_0(X_i) + \frac{D_i(Y_i - \mu_1(X_i))}{p(X_i)} - \frac{(1 - D_i)(Y_i - \mu_0(X_i))}{1 - p(X_i)}. \tag{3.9}$$

This AIPW estimator has two important properties:

1. It achieves the semi-parametric efficiency bound (Robins et al., 1994; Hahn, 1998), with

$$\sqrt{n}(\widehat{\tau}_{AIPW} - \tau_0) \overset{d}{\to} \mathcal{N}\left(0, \mathrm{Var}(\tau(X)) + \mathbb{E}\left[\frac{\sigma_0^2(X)}{1 - p(X)}\right] + \mathbb{E}\left[\frac{\sigma_1^2(X)}{p(X)}\right]\right),$$

   where $\sigma_j^2(x) = \mathrm{Var}(Y(j)|X = x)$ for $j = 0, 1$.
2. It is doubly robust, meaning that it is consistent either if the estimators $\widehat{\mu}_{(j)}$ for $j = 0, 1$ are consistent, or if $\widehat{p}$ is consistent.

3.4 Instrumental variables

3.4.1 Endogeneity and instrumental variables

We specialize here the presentation of the instrumental variables method to the context of the estimation of the treatment effect mentioned in the previous section. We aim to generalize the approach of randomized experiments to so-called natural experiments, where the treatment D is not random and therefore not independent from the potential outcomes. Consider a linear model allowing to estimate the effect of the treatment $D \in \mathbb{R}$ (discrete or continuous, and of dimension 1 here) while controlling for variables $X \in \mathbb{R}^{p_x}$ (also generally includes the intercept):

$$Y = D\tau_0 + X'\beta_0 + \varepsilon, \text{ with } \mathbb{E}[\varepsilon] = 0, \tag{3.10}$$

$$\mathbb{E}[\varepsilon|D,X] = 0. \tag{3.11}$$

In general, if we are outside the realm of RCTs or if the latter does not exactly adhere to the previous theoretical framework, the exogeneity assumption $\mathbb{E}[D\varepsilon] = 0$ may not hold. While it is always possible to define quantities $(\tilde{\tau}_0, \tilde{\beta}_0, \tilde{\varepsilon})$ such that

$$Y = D\tilde{\tau}_0 + X'\tilde{\beta}_0 + \tilde{\varepsilon},$$

with $\mathbb{E}[\tilde{\varepsilon}|D,X] = 0$. Under the usual rank conditions, the ordinary least squares estimator will estimate $(\tilde{\tau}_0, \tilde{\beta}_0)$, which generally differ from the true parameters (τ_0, β_0). Here, $D\tilde{\tau}_0 + X'\tilde{\beta}_0$ is the best linear predictor of Y on (D,X), but it is no longer the causal effect.

In this context where $\mathbb{E}[\varepsilon X] = 0$ but not $\mathbb{E}[\varepsilon D] = 0$, a possible strategy is to identify instrumental variables $W = (Z', X')' \in \mathbb{R}^{p+p_x}$, where p is larger than the number of endogenous variables D (here 1). An instrument is a variable that (i) is correlated with the endogenous variable and (ii) is uncorrelated with the residuals. We define D^* the best linear prediction of D using W, i.e. $D^* = W'\gamma$ where $\gamma = \arg\min_{g \in \mathbb{R}^p} \mathbb{E}\left[(D_i - W_i'g)^2\right]$, and denote by $W^* = (D^*, X')'$. More formally, assume:

Assumption 3.5 (Rank condition). $\mathbb{E}[W^*(W^*)']$ *is non-singular.*

Assumption 3.6 (Exogeneity). $\mathbb{E}[\varepsilon W] = 0$.

Under Assumptions (3.10), (3.5), and (3.6), the true parameters take the form:

$$(\tau_0, \beta_0')' = \mathbb{E}[W^*(W^*)']^{-1}\mathbb{E}[W^*Y]. \tag{3.12}$$

Lower levels conditions for Assumption (3.5), i.e., the relevance of the instruments Z for D are that $\mathbb{E}[WW']$ is non-singular and $\gamma \neq 0$. The estimator obtained by taking the empirical counterpart of (3.12) is the two-stage least squares (2SLS) estimator. The 2SLS estimator can thus be obtained by the following two steps: (i) regress D on the instrument Z and controls X, and then (ii) regress Y on the prediction of D obtained from step (i) and controls X. When there is only one instrument Z and without controls, we obtain in particular $\tau_0 = \text{Cov}(Y,Z)/\text{Cov}(Z,D)$.

In practice, the researcher may have access to multiple instruments or may want to consider transformations of the initial instrument $A(W)$, since they also satisfy

Assumption (3.6). Indeed, the moment condition $\mathbb{E}[\varepsilon|W] = 0$, where $W = (Z', X')'$, implies a sequence of unconditional moment conditions $\mathbb{E}[\varepsilon A(W)] = 0$, indexed by a vector of instruments $A(W)$ such that $\mathbb{E}[A(W)^2] < \infty$. This raises the legitimate question of choosing the function $A(\cdot)$ in order to minimize the asymptotic variance of the GMM estimator of $\theta_0 := (\tau_0, \beta_0')'$.

While this choice may not affect the identification of the causal effect, it does impact the precision of the 2SLS estimator. Therefore, we provide an overview of the classical results on the *problem of optimal instruments*. For simplicity here, we limit ourselves to the case of conditional homoscedasticity:

$$\mathbb{E}\left[\varepsilon^2|W\right] = \sigma^2. \tag{3.13}$$

3.4.2 The problem of optimal instruments

In this section, we assume that only D is endogenous and of dimension 1, and we recall the results concerning the optimal choice of $A(\cdot)$ in the moment equation $\mathbb{E}[\varepsilon A(W)] = 0$ such that $\mathbb{E}[A(W)^2] < \infty$ in order to obtain more precise estimates. We denote $S := (D, X')' \in \mathbb{R}^{p+1}$. We study the estimator of the generalized method of moments (GMM) (see the reminders in Section 2.5), based on the moment conditions:

$$M(\theta_0, A) := \mathbb{E}\left[A(W)\left(Y - S'\theta_0\right)\right] = 0.$$

Using the properties of GMM and the notations of Section 2.5: $\psi(U, \theta_0, A) := A(W)\left(Y - S'\theta_0\right)$, we obtain that the estimator $\widehat{\theta}_n$ satisfies:

$$\widehat{\theta}_n = \left[\frac{1}{n}\sum_{i=1}^{n} A(W_i)S_i'\right]^{-1} \frac{1}{n}\sum_{i=1}^{n} A(W_i)Y_i$$

and converges in probability $\widehat{\theta}_n \xrightarrow{p} \theta_0$ (see Theorem 5.7 in Van der Vaart, 1998). It is also asymptotically normal and we obtain:

$$\sqrt{n}\left(\widehat{\theta}_n - \theta_0\right) \xrightarrow{d} \mathcal{N}\left(0, \mathbf{G}(A)^{-1}\boldsymbol{\Sigma}(\theta_0, A)\left(\mathbf{G}(A)^{-1}\right)'\right), \tag{3.14}$$

where $\mathbf{G}(A) = \mathbb{E}\left[A(W)S'\right]$ and $\boldsymbol{\Sigma}(\theta_0, A) = \mathbb{E}\left[\psi(U, \theta_0, A)\psi(U, \theta_0, A)'\right]$. The optimal form of A minimizes the asymptotic variance in (3.14), as specified by Theorem 3.1 below.

Theorem 3.1. (Necessary condition for optimal instruments (Theorem 5.3 in Newey and McFadden, 1994, p. 2166)) *If an efficient choice $\overline{A}$ of A exists for the estimator (2.13), then it must satisfy*

$$\mathbf{G}(A) = \mathbb{E}\left[\psi(U, \theta_0, A)\psi\left(U, \theta_0, \overline{A}\right)'\right], \textit{ for all } A \textit{ such that } \mathbb{E}\left[A(W)^2\right] < \infty.$$

This condition can be reformulated as follows:

$$\mathbb{E}\left[A(W)S'\right] = \mathbb{E}\left[A(W)(Y - S'\theta_0)^2\overline{A}(W)'\right].$$

Thus, using the law of iterated expectations, we obtain

$$\mathbb{E}\left[A(W)\left(\mathbb{E}\left[S'|W\right] - \mathbb{E}\left[(Y - S'\theta_0)^2\middle|W\right]\overline{A}(W)'\right)\right] = 0.$$

Using the assumption of homoscedasticity (3.13), which can be written here as

$$\mathbb{E}[(Y - S'\theta_0)^2|W] = \sigma^2,$$

this last condition is satisfied when $\overline{A}(W) = \mathbb{E}\left[S|W\right]/\sigma^2$. Being invariant to multiplication by a constant matrix, the function $A(W) = \mathbb{E}\left[S|W\right]$ minimizes the asymptotic variance, which becomes:

$$\mathbf{\Lambda}^* = \sigma^2\mathbb{E}\left[\mathbb{E}\left[S|W\right]\mathbb{E}\left[S|W\right]'\right]^{-1}. \tag{3.15}$$

$\mathbf{\Lambda}^*$ is the semi-parametric efficiency bound (see Chapter 25 in Van der Vaart, 1998). Here, $A(W)$ is called the *optimal instrument*. The optimal instrument is therefore the regression function of S on W, $w \mapsto \mathbb{E}\left[S|W = w\right]$. Without further restrictions, it is naturally an object of high dimension (see, e.g., Tsybakov, 2009). With few instruments, Newey and McFadden (1994) propose nonparametric estimators in the form of series.

Remark 3.2 LATE

In the case of a binary treatment, some individuals *assigned* to the control group may still receive treatment. Conversely, some individuals *assigned* to the treatment group may refuse it. In these cases, we need to distinguish between the *treatment allocation* $Z \in \{0, 1\}$ and the *treatment actually received* $D \in \{0, 1\}$. While the allocation Z remains random, the treatment D generally no longer satisfies Assumption 3.2.

The approach, introduced by Imbens and Angrist (1994), consists of defining the potential treatment $D(Z)$, where for example $D(0) = 1$ if the individual was assigned to the control group but managed to receive treatment. Assuming that the allocation is indeed random:

$$Z \perp\!\!\!\perp (Y(0), Y(1), D(0), D(1)) \tag{3.16}$$

and under the assumption of *monotonicity*:

$$D(1) \geq D(0) \; p.s., \tag{3.17}$$

Continued

Remark 3.2 *Continued*

we can identify the coefficient:

$$\tau_0^C = \mathbb{E}[Y(1) - Y(0)|D(1) - D(0) = 1]$$
$$= \frac{\mathbb{E}[Y|Z = 1] - \mathbb{E}[Y|Z = 0]}{\mathbb{E}[D|Z = 1] - \mathbb{E}[D|Z = 0]}. \tag{3.18}$$

τ_0^C represents the causal effect of the treatment on the subpopulation of "compliers" $D(1)-D(0)=1$, meaning those who behave according to their allocation $D=Z$. The assumption in Equation 3.17 implies that there are no "defiers," i.e., individuals who would take the treatment if they were in the control group but would not take it if they were in the treatment group. Since τ_0^C measures a causal effect on the subpopulation of compliers, it is referred to as the "local average treatment effect" (LATE). It can also be identified as the coefficient of the regression of Y on D using Z as an instrumental variable, as described in Section 3.4.

Remark 3.3 Nonparametric regression and IV

A first way to generalize the linear model (3.10) (see, e.g., Newey and Powell, 2003; Darolles et al., 2011) is to consider

$$Y = \varphi(D, X) + \varepsilon, \text{ with } \mathbb{E}[\varepsilon|Z] = 0,$$

where the parameter of interest is the non-parametric function φ. The identification of this function is obtained by taking the conditional expectation with respect to Z:

$$\mathbb{E}[Y|Z] = \mathbb{E}[\varphi(X)|Z] \tag{3.19}$$

and assuming the *completeness* condition (see, e.g., D'Haultfoeuille, 2011), namely assuming that for any measurable and integrable function g,

$$\mathbb{E}[g(X)|Z] = 0 \; a.e \implies g(X) = 0 \; a.e$$

Equation (3.19) is a moment equation that reflects an *inverse problem*, where the associated operator is the conditional expectation operator with respect to Z (see, e.g., Carrasco et al., 2007; Darolles et al., 2011). Note that we can also relax the additivity assumption (see, e.g., Chernozhukov and Hansen, 2005).

The regularization methods classically used in this inverse problems literature, such as the Tikhonov method, are equivalent to some machine learning methods introduced in Chapter 2, such as ridge regularization. They provide "dense" alternatives to the use of the sparsity assumption and Lasso regularization, which are the focus of Chapters 4 and 6 (see also the discussion in Chapter 11). Also in this context, machine learning methods such as deep neural networks can be used (Hartford et al., 2017) to estimate the regression function $\mathbb{E}[Y|Z]$ and the conditional distribution $F_{X|Z}$ and then solve the inverse problem (3.19).

3.5 Summary

Key concepts

Causal inference, randomized controlled trial (RCT), counterfactual situation, treatment effect, average treatment effect (ATE), average treatment effect on the treated (ATT), heterogeneity of treatment effect, conditional average treatment effect (CATE), stable unit treatment value (SUTVA), average treatment effect in differences estimator, propensity score, inverse-propensity weighting (IPW), conditional independence or unconfoundedness, augmented propensity score, optimal instrumental variable problem, local average treatment effect (LATE).

Additional references

Angrist and Pischke (2009) and Imbens and Rubin (2015) are two reference books that provide a comprehensive treatment of classical tools for causal inference in the potential outcomes framework. Abadie and Cattaneo (2018) offer a review of the most commonly used methods.

PART II

HIGH-DIMENSION AND VARIABLE SELECTION

Chapter 4
Post-selection inference

Model selection and sparsity among explanatory variables are traditional scientific problems that hold particular importance in statistics and econometrics. These topics have received increasing attention over the past two decades, as statisticians from various fields more frequently have access to high-dimensional datasets, i.e., datasets that contain a large number of explanatory variables. Even with a moderately sized dataset, high-dimensional problems can arise, for example when estimating a non-parametric model using sieves. In practice, empirical economists often select variables through trial and error, guided by their intuition, and report results under the assumption that the selected model is the correct one. These results are supported by sensitivity analyses and additional robustness checks. However, empirical works rarely fully acknowledged the variable selection step, although it is far from innocuous. In particular, neglecting to account for it can lead to fallacious results. Leamer (1983) was one of the first to sound the alarm. For a modern presentation, see Leeb and Pötscher (2005) and, in the context of policy evaluation, Belloni et al. (2014).

This chapter specifically deals with the case of selecting control variables. Section 4.1 illustrates, in a simplified case, the post-selection inference problem. Sections 4.2 and 4.3 present and study the Lasso estimator as it is often used as an automatic variable selection tool. Section 4.4 builds on the intuition from Section 4.1 to illustrate the regularization bias in a case closer to practical applications. Section 4.5 proposes a particular solution in a fully linear framework, called the "double selection method."

This chapter is limited to the linear framework, but Chapter 5, and specifically Section 5.1, presents the key theoretical concepts for handling post-machine learning inference, of which post-selection inference can be seen as a particular case. Chapter 6 applies this theory to the instrumental variable model. And Chapter 7 covers further theoretical developments.

4.1 The post-selection inference problem

We begin by analyzing the two-step inference method described in the introduction: first selecting a model, followed by reporting the results of this model as if it were the "true" model. This section is based on the work of Leeb and Pötscher (2005). We consider here a very simple framework, where we assume that a maximum number

Machine Learning for Econometrics. Christophe Gaillac and Jérémy L'Hour, Oxford University Press.
 DOI: 10.1093/9780198918868.003.0004

of parameters are known, in order to illustrate, as clearly as possible, the intuition found throughout this chapter.

4.1.1 The model

Assumption 4.1 (Possibly sparse Gaussian linear model). *Consider the i.i.d. sequence of random variables $(Y_i, X_i)_{i=1,\dots,n}$ such that:*

$$Y_i = X_{i,1}\tau_0 + X_{i,2}\beta_0 + \varepsilon_i,$$

where $\varepsilon_i \sim \mathcal{N}(0,\sigma^2)$, σ^2 is known, $X_i = (X_{i,1}, X_{i,2})$ is of dimension two, $\varepsilon_i \perp\!\!\!\perp X_i$, and $\mathbb{E}[X_iX_i']$ is an non-singular matrix. We use the following notation for the elements of the OLS covariance matrix:

$$\begin{bmatrix} \sigma_\tau^2 & \sigma_{\tau,\beta} \\ \sigma_{\tau,\beta} & \sigma_\beta^2 \end{bmatrix} := \sigma^2 \left[\frac{1}{n} \sum_{i=1}^{n} X_iX_i' \right]^{-1}.$$

The most sparse true model is encoded by M_0, defined as a random variable taking the value R ("restricted") if $\beta_0 = 0$ and U ("unrestricted") otherwise.

Assumption 4.1 defines a simple regression model with two variables, where the effect of one variable is of interest, while the effect of the other is only a nuisance parameter, i.e., it is not directly of interest, but it may be necessary to take it into account to ensure the validity of the model, i.e., to validate the exogeneity condition. The reasoning in this section will be conditional on the covariates $(X_i)_{1\leq i\leq n}$, but we leave this dependence hidden. In particular, conditional on the covariates, the unrestricted estimator is normally distributed:

$$\sqrt{n}\begin{bmatrix} \widehat{\beta}(U) - \beta_0 \\ \widehat{\tau}(U) - \tau_0 \end{bmatrix} \sim \mathcal{N}\left(\begin{bmatrix} 0 \\ 0 \end{bmatrix}, \begin{bmatrix} \sigma_\beta^2 & \rho\sigma_\beta\sigma_\tau \\ \rho\sigma_\beta\sigma_\tau & \sigma_\tau^2 \end{bmatrix} \right),$$

where $\rho := \sigma_{\tau,\beta}/\sigma_\tau\sigma_\beta$ is the correlation between the estimators of the two parameters.

Remark 4.1 Inclusion of control variables

The term "control variables" refers to the variables that are included in the regression model in order to make the exogeneity assumption valid. In the terminology specific to causal inference and directed acyclic graphs, they are called "confounders." A good control variable is one that must both predict the variable of interest (relevance condition) and be correlated with the main explanatory variable (confounding condition). If a control variable is omitted, then the estimation is not valid since it suffers from an omitted variable bias.

The opposite case of adding a variable that is not a control variable has an ambiguous effect, depending on the condition it does not fulfill:

1. If a variable that does not satisfy the relevance condition is added, then the precision of the estimation deteriorates since it decreases the variance of the main explanatory variable, once purged of the effect of this superfluous variable.
2. If a variable is added that only satisfies the relevance condition, then the precision of the estimation increases since it decreases the variance of the residual term without decreasing the variance of the main explanatory variable.

4.1.2 Consistent model selection

The econometrician wants to perform inference on the parameter τ_0 associated with the effect of the variable $X_{i,1}$ and wonders whether to include $X_{i,2}$ in the regression or not – a more parsimonious model potentially leads to a more precise estimation, at the cost of an increased chance of being biased.

In the end, the econometrician reports the result of the model $\widehat{M}$ that was selected in a first step. Let $\widehat{\tau}(U)$ and $\widehat{\beta}(U)$ be the OLS estimators in the unrestricted model (U model), and let $\widehat{\tau}(R)$ and $\widehat{\beta}(R) = 0$ be the OLS estimators in the restricted model (R model). The economist includes $X_{i,2}$ in the model if and only if the t-statistic is sufficiently large:

Assumption 4.2 (Decision rule).

$$\widehat{M} = \begin{cases} U & \text{if } \left|\frac{\sqrt{n}\widehat{\beta}(U)}{\sigma_\beta}\right| > c_n \\ R & \text{otherwise,} \end{cases} \tag{4.1}$$

where c_n is such that $c_n \to \infty$ and $c_n/\sqrt{n} \to 0$ as $n \to \infty$.

Note that the BIC criterion corresponds to $c_n = \sqrt{\log n}$ and the AIC to $c_n = \sqrt{2}$. What are the asymptotic performances of this selection method?

Lemma 4.1 (Model selection consistency of rule 4.2). *For $M_0 \in \{U, R\}$,*

$$\mathbb{P}_{M_0}\left(\widehat{M} = M_0\right) \to 1,$$

as $n \to \infty$, where $\mathbb{P}_{M_0}$ indicates the probability distribution of $\widehat{M}$ under the true model M_0.

The proofs of lemmas and theorems are given at the end of the chapter.

Since the probability of selecting the true model tends to one as the sample size increases, Lemma 4.1 might suggest that a consistent model selection procedure allows for inference to be performed "as usual," i.e., that the model selection step can be neglected since for sufficiently large n, the correct model is selected with high probability. Indeed, in a "pointwise" sense, i.e., for a fixed and constant β_0 value with respect to the sample size, this is true. However, for any given sample size n, the probability of selecting the true model can be very low if β_0 is close to zero but not exactly zero. For example, suppose that $\beta_0 = \delta\sigma_\beta c_n/\sqrt{n}$ with $|\delta| < 1$ then: $\sqrt{n}\beta_0/\sigma_\beta = \delta c_n$ and the probability of selecting the unrestricted model in the proof of Lemma 4.1 is equal to $1 - \Phi(c_n(1+\delta)) + \Phi((\delta-1)c_n)$, which tends to zero even if the true model is U because $\beta_0 \neq 0$! This quick analysis indicates that the model selection procedure is not robust to deviations of the order of $c_n/\sqrt{n}$ from the restricted model ($\beta_0 = 0$). Statisticians say that, in this case, the model selection procedure is not *uniformly consistent* with respect to β_0. For the econometrician, this means that the standard inference procedure, i.e., the procedure that assumes that the selected model is true, or that is conditional on the selected model being true, and uses asymptotic normality to conduct tests and construct confidence intervals, may require very large samples to be accurate. Moreover, this required sample size depends on the unknown parameter β_0 (see the numerical simulations of Leeb and Pötscher, 2005).

4.1.3 Distribution of the post-selection estimator

Leeb and Pötscher (2005) analyze the distribution of the post-selection estimator $\tilde{\tau}$, defined by:

$$\tilde{\tau} := \hat{\tau}(\widehat{M}) = \hat{\tau}(R)\mathbf{1}_{\widehat{M}=R} + \hat{\tau}(U)\mathbf{1}_{\widehat{M}=U}. \tag{4.2}$$

Despite the warning issued in the previous paragraph, is a convergent model selection procedure sufficient to alleviate concerns about the post-selection approach? Indeed, using Lemma 4.1, it is tempting to think that $\tilde{\tau}$ will be asymptotically distributed according to a Gaussian distribution and that standard inference applies as well. However, we will show that the distribution of the finite sample of the post-selection estimator can be very different from a standard Gaussian distribution. The result presented here can be found in Leeb (2006) and is proven at the end of the chapter.

Lemma 4.2 (Density of the post-selection estimator Leeb, 2006). *The finite-distance density (conditionally on $(X_i)_{i=1,\dots,n}$) of $\sqrt{n}(\tilde{\tau}-\tau_0)$ is given by:*

$$f_{\sqrt{n}(\tilde{\tau}-\tau_0)}(x) = \Delta\left(\sqrt{n}\frac{\beta_0}{\sigma_\beta}, c_n\right)\frac{1}{\sigma_\tau\sqrt{1-\rho^2}}\varphi\left(\frac{x}{\sigma_\tau\sqrt{1-\rho^2}} + \frac{\rho}{\sqrt{1-\rho^2}}\frac{\sqrt{n}\beta_0}{\sigma_\beta}\right)$$
$$+\left[1 - \Delta\left(\frac{\sqrt{n}\beta_0/\sigma_\beta + \rho x/\sigma_\tau}{\sqrt{1-\rho^2}}, \frac{c_n}{\sqrt{1-\rho^2}}\right)\right]\frac{1}{\sigma_\tau}\varphi\left(\frac{x}{\sigma_\tau}\right),$$

where $\rho = \sigma_{\tau,\beta}/\sigma_\tau\sigma_\beta$ and $\Delta(a,b) := \Phi(a+b) - \Phi(a-b)$.

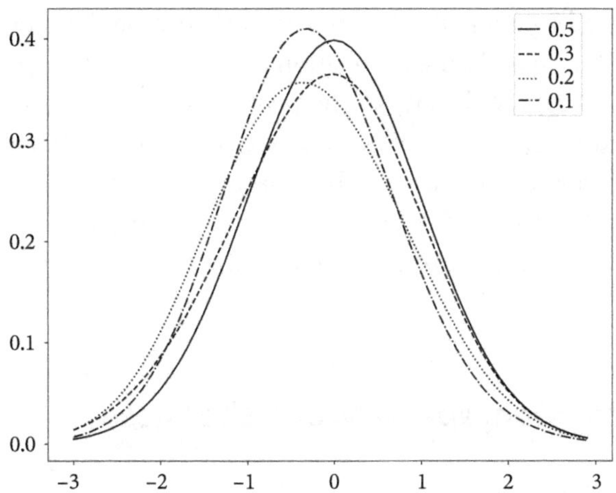

Figure 4.1 Finite-distance density of $\sqrt{n}(\tilde{\tau} - \tau_0), \rho = .4$

Note: Density of the post-selection estimator $\tilde{\tau}$ for different values of β_0/σ_β, see the legend. The other parameters are: $c_n = \sqrt{\log n}, n = 100, \sigma_\tau = 1$, and $\rho = .4$. See Lemma 4.2 for the mathematical formula.

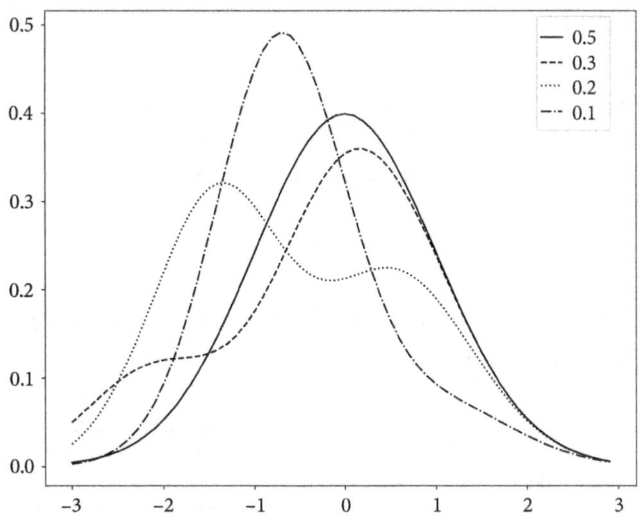

Figure 4.2 Finite-distance density of $\sqrt{n}(\tilde{\tau} - \tau_0), \rho = .7$

Note: See Figure 4.1. $\rho = .7$. This graph is the same as the one in Leeb and Pötscher (2005).

Lemma 4.2 gives the finite-distance density of the post-selection estimator. The least we can say is that it is not Gaussian. There is an omitted variable bias which the post-selection estimator can only overcome if the control variable has no effect on the outcome ($\beta_0 = 0$) or if there is no correlation between the explanatory variables ($\rho = 0$). Indeed, when $\rho = 0$, $\sqrt{n}(\tilde{\tau} - \tau_0) \sim \mathcal{N}(0, \sigma_\tau^2)$; whereas when $\beta_0 = 0$, $\sqrt{n}(\tilde{\tau} - \tau_0) \sim \mathcal{N}(0, \sigma_\tau^2/(1 - \rho^2))$ approximately, since $\Delta(0, c_n) \geq 1 - \exp(-c_n^2/2)$ – the probability of selecting the restricted model – is large. Figures 4.1 and 4.2 represent the finite-distance density of the post-selection estimator for several values of β_0/σ_β in the cases $\rho = .4$ and $\rho = .7$, respectively. Figure 4.1 shows a slight but significant distortion compared to a standard Gaussian distribution. The post-selection estimator clearly exhibits bias. As the correlation between the two explanatory variables intensifies (Figure 4.2), the density of the post-selection estimator becomes highly non-Gaussian and even exhibits two modes. See Leeb and Pötscher (2005) for a more in-depth discussion. Following this analysis, it is clear that inference procedures (i.e., tests and confidence intervals) based on standard Gaussian quantiles can generally give a distorted picture compared to the (true) distribution illustrated in Figure 4.2.

4.2 High dimension, sparsity, and the Lasso

A popular tool for automatically performing the variable selection step described in the previous section is the Lasso of Tibshirani (1994). In this section, we temporarily deviate from the post-selection inference problem to provide a proof of the Lasso in the linear model based on strong assumptions. These assumptions can and are relaxed in the Lasso literature, but they nevertheless allow us to simplify the proof. We start with a Gaussian linear model.

Assumption 4.3 (Sparse gaussian linear model). *Let* $(Y_i, X_i)_{i=1,...,n}$ *a sequence of i.i.d. random variables. The vector X is of dimension p. We assume that p is greater than 1 and can be much larger than n. We assume the following linear relationship:*

$$Y = X'\beta_0 + \varepsilon,$$

where $\varepsilon \sim \mathcal{N}(0, \sigma^2)$, $\varepsilon \perp\!\!\!\perp X_i$, $\|\beta_0\|_0 \leq s < p$. *Additionally, the explanatory variables are almost surely bounded,* $\max_{i=1,\dots,n} \|X_i\|_\infty \leq M$.

Remark 4.2 Sparsity

One element of assumption 4.3 requires special attention. The assumption of *sparsity*, $\|\beta_0\|_0 = \sum_{j=1}^{p} \mathbf{1}\{\beta_j \neq 0\} \leq s$, means that at most s components of β_0 are different from zero. This notion, i.e., the assumption that, although we consider many variables, only a small number of elements of the parameter vector are different from zero, is an inherent element in the literature on high dimensionality. This amounts to recasting the problem of high dimensionality as a variable selection problem, where a good estimator should be able to correctly select the relevant variables or estimate the quantities of interest consistently at a rate close to $\sqrt{n}$, paying only a price dependent on s and p. Before proceeding, we introduce the *sparsity set*, i.e., the set of indices corresponding to the non-zero elements of β_0: $S_0 := \{j \in \{1, \dots, p\}, \beta_{0j} \neq 0\}$. A less restrictive concept was introduced by Belloni et al. (2012). Called *approximate sparsity*, it assumes that the high-dimensional parameter can be decomposed into a sparse component, which has many zero entries and a few large entries, and a dense component for which all entries are small and decay to zero without ever being exactly zero, see Assumption 6.2 in Chapter 6. Although more general, this assumption complicates the proof without helping to understand the intuition.

Let

$$L(\beta) = \frac{1}{n}\sum_{i=1}^{n}\left(Y_i - X_i'\beta\right)^2$$

denote the mean squared error loss function. As in Section 2.3, the Lasso estimator is defined as:

$$\widehat{\beta} \in \arg\min_{\beta\in\mathbb{R}^p} L(\beta) + \lambda_n\|\beta\|_1. \tag{4.3}$$

The Lasso minimizes the sum of the empirical mean squared loss and a penalty or regularization term $\lambda_n\|\beta\|_1$. Note that the solution to (4.3) is not necessarily unique. As the ℓ_1 norm has a kink at zero, the resulting solution of the program, $\widehat{\beta}$, will be sparse. The parameter λ_n defines the trade-off between fitting the data on one side and sparsity on the other. Generally, the value of λ_n is chosen via the cross-validation procedure described in Section 2.3.5. It has been shown that Lasso-type estimators can provide a good approximation of parameters subject to a sparse structure, whether they are finite or infinite dimensional. However, in the presence of a large-dimensional β_0 for which the sparsity assumption is not supposed to hold, using the Lasso estimator is not a good idea. Thus, if for example, β_0 is assumed to be dense (i.e., many small entries but no real zeros), the use of ℓ_2 regularization (Ridge estimator) is more effective. For more information on the use of different types of regularization, see Section 2.3.4 as well as Abadie and Kasy (2019).

The Lasso and related techniques for dealing with high dimension have led to a vast literature since the seminal article of Tibshirani (1994). Bühlmann and Van de Geer (2011) and Giraud (2014) are reference textbooks. Other key articles include, for example, Candes and Tao (2007), Van de Geer (2008), Bickel et al. (2009).

To establish the convergence of the Lasso estimator, another ingredient is needed: a restricted eigenvalue condition. Let

$$\widehat{\Sigma} := \frac{1}{n}\sum_{i=1}^{n} X_i X_i'$$

the empirical Gram matrix. In a high-dimensional framework, we are particularly concerned with cases where the number of covariates is greater than the sample size ($p > n$), as then $\widehat{\Sigma}$ is degenerate in the sense that it is not full rank:

$$\min_{\substack{\delta\in\mathbb{R}^p \\ \delta\neq 0}} \frac{\delta'\widehat{\Sigma}\delta}{\|\delta\|_2^2} = 0.$$

In this case, least squares estimators cannot be computed. This is why a restricted eigenvalue assumption is necessary: all square sub-matrices contained in the empirical Gram matrix of dimension less than or equal to s must have a positive minimum eigenvalue. More precisely: for a non-empty subset $S \subset \{1, \ldots, p\}$ and $\alpha > 0$, we define the set:

$$C[S, \alpha] := \left\{ v \in \mathbb{R}^p : \|v_{S^C}\|_1 \leq \alpha \|v_S\|_1, v \neq 0 \right\} \tag{4.4}$$

Assumption 4.4 (Restricted eigenvalue). *The empirical Gram matrix $\widehat{\Sigma}$ satisfies:*

$$\kappa_\alpha^2(\widehat{\Sigma}) := \min_{\substack{S \subset \{1,\ldots,p\} \\ |S| \leq s}} \min_{\delta \in C[S,\alpha]} \frac{\delta' \widehat{\Sigma} \delta}{\|\delta_S\|_2^2} > 0.$$

This condition appears and is discussed in particular in Bickel et al. (2009) and Rudelson and Zhou (2013). We make this assumption directly on the empirical Gram matrix, instead of on the population Gram matrix $\mathbb{E}[XX']$, in order to simplify the proof. For a probabilistic link between population and empirical Gram matrices under fairly weak conditions, see, e.g., Oliveira (2013). Conditions that serve the same purpose as restricted eigenvalue conditions have been used before, notably the *compatibility condition*, the *coherence condition*, and the *restricted isometry condition*, see for example Bühlmann and Van de Geer (2011, p. 106).

4.3 Theoretical elements on the Lasso

This section provides a simple proof of the consistency of the Lasso and introduces the post-Lasso estimator.

Theorem 4.1 (Consistency in ℓ_1 norm of Lasso) *Under Assumption 4.3 and a restricted eigenvalue condition 4.4 with $C[S_0, 3]$, the Lasso estimator defined in 4.3 with a regularization parameter $\lambda_n = (4\sigma M/\alpha)\sqrt{2\log(2p)/n}$, where $\alpha \in]0, 1[$, satisfies, with a probability greater than $1 - \alpha$:*

$$\|\widehat{\beta} - \beta_0\|_1 \leq \frac{4^2 \sigma M}{\alpha \kappa_3^2(\widehat{\Sigma})} \sqrt{\frac{2s^2 \log(2p)}{n}}. \tag{4.5}$$

The main insight from Theorem 4.1 is that the Lasso is consistent in ℓ_1 norm to the true value β_0 at a rate of $s\sqrt{\log(p)/n}$. This rate should be compared to the rate of least squares estimator under full knowledge of the sparsity model, which is $s/\sqrt{n}$. The conclusion is that there is a price to pay for our ignorance, expressed by the term $\sqrt{\log(p)}$. This rate is called *fast* in comparison to a slower rate that exists without Assumption 4.4.

By adding a modified version of Assumption 4.4, an ℓ_2 rate can be obtained: $\|\beta_0 - \widehat{\beta}\|_2 \lesssim \sqrt{s\log(p)/n}$. The prediction error (i.e. $\|Y - X'\widehat{\beta}\|_2$) has also been widely discussed in the literature, see e.g., Bickel et al. (2009), but is of less interest in this book focused on inference.

Furthermore, note that the Lasso is *not* asymptotically Gaussian: the event $\widehat{\beta}_j = 0$ has a non-zero probability of occurring. Therefore, it is not possible to construct confidence intervals for β_0 using the usual method (i.e., Gaussian, asymptotic).

Remark 4.3: The post-Lasso estimator

Before proceeding, it is worth mentioning the post-Lasso estimator, an estimator related to the Lasso that has been notably studied by Belloni and Chernozhukov (2011) in the book by Alquier et al. (2011) and by Belloni and Chernozhukov (2013). It is a two-stage estimator in which a second stage is added to the Lasso procedure in order to eliminate the bias arising from the fact that ℓ_1 penalization pulls all coefficients towards zero, including those that are not zero (*shrinkage bias*). This second stage consists of computing the least squares estimator using only the covariates associated with a nonzero coefficient in the Lasso stage. More precisely, the procedure is as follows:

1. Compute the Lasso estimator as in Equation (4.3), and let $\widehat{S}$ be the set of non-zero Lasso coefficients.
2. Compute the least squares estimator in a model including only the covariates corresponding to the non-zero coefficients above:

$$\widehat{\beta}^{PL} = \underset{\beta \in \mathbb{R}^p, \beta_{\widehat{S}^C}=0}{\arg\min} \; L(\beta)$$

The performance is comparable to that of the Lasso in theory, although the bias appears to be smaller in empirical applications since the induced shrinkage of the nonzero coefficients is removed. We reiterate one of the lessons from this chapter: the post-Lasso estimator is still *not* asymptotically normal as it is subject to the post-selection inference problem highlighted by Leeb and Pötscher (2005) in Section 4.1.

4.4 Regularization bias

In this section, we discuss the regularization bias which is an omitted variable bias arising from the same mechanism as described more simply in Section 4.1.

4.4.1 Selection and estimation cannot be optimally done at the same time

The previous section focused on defining and understanding the Lasso estimator. Due to the sparsity property of the resulting solution (e.g., Belloni and

Chernozhukov, 2013, show that $\|\widehat{\beta}\|_0 \lesssim s$) and the natural appeal of the post-Lasso estimator, it is easy to place excessive confidence in the Lasso. Indeed, one might think that the Lasso can both serve as a device for recovering the support of β_0 and accurately or rapidly estimating this same quantity. That is, both selecting the right variables and estimating their associated coefficients accurately. However, Yang (2005) shows that for a model selection procedure to be convergent, it must behave sub-optimally in estimating the regression function and vice versa. In fact, the condition on the penalty parameter λ_n in Zhao and Yu (2006) is very different from our requirement of $\lambda_n = 4\sigma M\sqrt{2\log(2p)/n}/\alpha$ in Theorem 4.1. The moral of the story is that even when using the Lasso estimator, selecting relevant covariates and accurately estimating their effects are two objectives that cannot be pursued simultaneously. Furthermore, the warnings issued in Section 4.1 also apply to the Lasso: replacing Assumption 4.2 with Lasso selection does not overcome the problem of post-selection inference.

In the presence of a high-dimensional parameter to estimate, the econometric literature has chosen to pursue a high-quality estimation of β_0. Indeed, since most economic applications deal with a specific causal question like "what is the effect of A on B?" the identity of relevant regressors matters less than the accurate estimation of certain nuisance parameters: think, for example, of estimating a control function or the first stage of an instrumental variable regression.

But even when focusing solely on accurately estimating β_0, the Lasso is not sufficient. Indeed, high-dimensional statistics pose a specific challenge in that p, the number of variables, is not negligible compared to the sample size. In other words, if we were to assume that p remains constant with respect to n as $n \to \infty$, the problem could be reduced to a low-dimensional problem where $n >> p$. Thus, to adequately tackle the problem, we must adopt a framework that assumes $p \to \infty$ as $n \to \infty$. We will see that, within this high-dimensional framework, there exists an asymptotic bias that we will call a regularization bias.

4.4.2 The bias of the naive "plug-in" estimator

Assumption 4.5 (Linear model with controls). *Consider the i.i.d. sequence of random variables $(Y_i, D_i, X_i)_{i=1,\dots,n}$ such that, omitting the index i:*

$$Y = D\tau_0 + X'\beta_0 + \varepsilon,$$

with ε such that $\mathbb{E}[\varepsilon] = 0$, $\mathbb{E}[\varepsilon^2] = \sigma^2 < \infty$, and $\mathbb{E}[\varepsilon|D, X] = 0$. $D \in \{0, 1\}$. X is of dimension $p > 1$. We allow p to be much larger than n and to grow with n. We denote by $\mu_d := \mathbb{E}[X|D = d]$ for $d \in \{0, 1\}$ and $\pi_0 := \mathbb{E}[D_i] \neq 0$.

Suppose the econometrician wants to estimate the treatment effect τ_0 of D on Y in the model 4.5 above, while β_0 is simply a nuisance parameter. In this part as well as in the rest of the chapter, we assume that the random variable D is binary, but the stated results also apply in the case of a real-valued variable. In the presence of a high-dimensional set of controls X_i, a naive post-selection procedure (e.g., Belloni et al., 2014, [p. 36]) follows two steps:

1. (Selection) Compute the Lasso estimator of Y on D and X, forcing D to remain in the model by excluding τ from the penalty part in the Lasso, Equation (4.3). Obtain $\widehat{\beta}^L$. Exclude all elements of X that correspond to a null coefficient in $\widehat{\beta}^L$,
2. (Estimation) Compute the OLS estimator of Y on D and the set of selected elements of X to obtain the post-selection estimator $\widehat{\tau}$.

We denote $\widehat{\beta}$ the corresponding estimator of β_0 obtained in step 2. We note that for $j \in \{1, ..., p\}$, if $\widehat{\beta}_j^L = 0$ then $\widehat{\beta}_j = 0$. We also denote $\widehat{\pi} := n^{-1} \sum_{i=1}^n D_i$.

$$\widehat{\tau} := \frac{\frac{1}{n}\sum_{i=1}^n D_i(Y_i - X_i'\widehat{\beta})}{\widehat{\pi}} = \frac{1}{n_1} \sum_{D_i=1} (Y_i - X_i'\widehat{\beta}),$$

where $n_d := \sum_{i=1}^n \mathbf{1}\{D_i = d\}$, $d \in \{0, 1\}$ is a random quantity.

Lemma 4.3 (Regularization bias of $\widehat{\tau}$). *Under Assumption 4.5, if* $\mu_1 \neq 0$ *then:* $\sqrt{n}|\widehat{\tau} - \tau_0| \to \infty$.

Remark 4.4: Regularization bias

Lemma 4.3 is a disappointing result: in the high-dimensional case, the naive "plug-in" strategy does not work. This is due to two ingredients: $\mu_1 \neq 0$ and $p \to \infty$. If we were in a low-dimensional case and had, for example, an OLS estimator for β_0, $\sqrt{n}(\beta_0 - \widehat{\beta})$ would be asymptotically normal and the problem would not exist. It should be noted that in this low-dimensional case, there is no selection step. What are the limitations of the approach introduced in this section? It is a single-equation procedure. Recall that the selection step only uses the outcome equation, meaning that elements of X tend to be selected if they correspond to a large value in the coefficient β_0. Consequently, this procedure tends to overlook variables that have a moderate effect on Y but a significant effect on D, thus creating an omitted variable bias in the estimator of τ_0. As expressed by Belloni et al. (2014): "Intuitively, any such variable has a moderate direct effect on the outcome, which will be incorrectly misattributed to the effect of the treatment when this variable is strongly related to the treatment and the variable is not included in the regression." In this case, the regularization bias resulting from non-orthogonal procedures that use machine learning tools such as Lasso in a first step is referred to as "regularization bias."

Now, let's focus on a particular case that works. While this case is highly specific, it serves as a focal point for identifying underlying issues. For this, we will make two assumptions. The first one limits the growth rate of p. It is technical but trivial. The second assumption is probabilistic in nature and provides intuition for more general results in the following section.

Assumption 4.6 (Growth condition).

$$\frac{s \log p}{\sqrt{n}} \to 0.$$

Assumption 4.7 (Balanced design). *Let's assume that:*

1. $\mu_1 = \mathbb{E}[X|D=1] = 0$,
2. *Concentration bound:*

$$\left\| \frac{1}{\sqrt{n}} \sum_{i=1}^{n} D_i X_i \right\|_{\infty} \lesssim \sqrt{\log p}. \tag{4.6}$$

Assumption 4.6 aims to restrict the size of p in relation to the sample size. The second part of Assumption 4.7, which allows for control over the maximum elements of a random vector based on its dimension, is quite technical but can be proven under lower-level assumptions such as normality or sub-gaussianity of X and the application of Lemma 4.6, recalling that $\mathbb{E}[DX] = 0$ under the first part of Assumption 4.7.

Lemma 4.4 (A favorable case). *Under Assumptions 4.5, 4.6, and 4.7:*

$$\sqrt{n}\left(\widehat{\tau} - \tau_0\right) \xrightarrow{d} \mathcal{N}\left(0, \frac{\sigma^2}{\pi_0}\right).$$

We note that Assumption 4.7 (1) implies:

$$\mathbb{E}\left[\frac{\partial \sqrt{n}(\widehat{\tau} - \tau_0)}{\partial(\widehat{\beta} - \beta_0)}\right] = -\mathbb{E}\left[\frac{n^{-1/2}}{\widehat{\pi}} \sum_{i=1}^{n} D_i X_i\right] \approx 0.$$

Under this assumption, the estimator $\widehat{\tau}$ is first-order insensitive to small deviations around the true value β_0. This is what we will exploit in the following section.

4.5 The double selection method

Remember our estimation strategy for model 4.5: the idea was to select the elements of X related to Y in a first step, and then to regress Y on D and the selected elements of X in this first step. Generally, this strategy is subject to a bias. Let's see how we can eliminate it. Omitting the individual index, assume that the equation determining the treatment is given by:

$$D = X'\delta_0 + \xi,$$

where $\mathbb{E}[\xi|X] = 0$ and $\xi \perp\!\!\!\perp \varepsilon$. We denote $\eta := (\beta, \delta)'$, which we will now refer to as the *nuisance parameter*. We will show that the following moment condition:

$$\mathbb{E}\left[\psi(Z, \tau_0, \eta_0)\right] := \mathbb{E}[(Y - D\tau_0 - X'\beta_0)(D - X'\delta_0)] = 0, \tag{4.7}$$

is insensitive to small deviations around the true values of the nuisance parameters – we will say in Section 5.1 that this condition is orthogonal in the Neyman sense, or that it satisfies Equation 5.1 (Chapter 5) – and therefore allows us to obtain an estimator of τ_0 with desirable properties. ψ is a known function depending on the observables (the data) $Z := (Y, D, X)$, the parameter of interest τ_0, and the nuisance parameter $\eta_0 = (\beta_0, \delta_0)'$. For more details, the reader is referred to Example 2.1 in Chernozhukov et al. (2018) which deals with the broader framework underlying this choice. Let's first notice that:

$$\partial_\eta \psi(Z, \tau, \eta) = \begin{bmatrix} \partial_\beta \psi(Z, \tau, \eta) \\ \partial_\delta \psi(Z, \tau, \eta) \end{bmatrix} = \begin{bmatrix} -(D - X'\delta)X \\ -(Y - D\tau - X'\beta)X \end{bmatrix}.$$

In Assumption 4.5, β_0 was implicitly defined by the orthogonality condition, i.e., normal equations, or the theoretical first order conditions of the least squares program (see Section 2.1 for a refresher):

$$\mathbb{E}\left[(Y - D\tau_0 - X'\beta_0)X\right] = \mathbb{E}\left[\varepsilon X\right] = 0.$$

According to the orthogonality condition in the treatment equation above, δ_0 is such that:

$$\mathbb{E}\left[(D - X'\delta_0)X\right] = \mathbb{E}\left[\xi X\right] = 0. \tag{4.8}$$

It can be observed that we have $\mathbb{E}\partial_\eta \psi(Z, \tau_0, \eta_0) = 0$, which will be explained in Section 5.1. Equation (4.7) is reminiscent of the Frish–Waugh–Lovell theorem:

$$\mathbb{E}[(\underbrace{Y - D\tau_0 - X'\beta_0}_{\substack{\text{Residual from} \\ \text{the outcome regression}}})(\underbrace{D - X'\delta_0}_{\substack{\text{Residual from} \\ \text{the treatment regression}}})] = \mathbb{E}[\xi\varepsilon] = 0,$$

or more clearly, thanks to Equation (4.8):

$$\mathbb{E}[\underbrace{(Y - X'\beta_0 - (D - X'\delta_0)\tau_0)}_{\substack{\text{Residual from} \\ \text{the outcome regression}}} \underbrace{(D - X'\delta_0)}_{\substack{\text{Residual from} \\ \text{the treatment regression}}}] = 0,$$

which is the orthogonality condition in a problem where Y is regressed on the residual of the treatment regression and X. We can also see τ_0 as the following parameter:

$$\tau_0 = \frac{\text{Cov}[D - X'\delta_0, Y - X'\beta_0]}{\mathbb{E}[(D - X'\delta_0)^2]}. \tag{4.9}$$

τ_0 is the coefficient of the regression of the residual from the regression of Y on X on the residual from the regression of D on X.

Remark 4.5: Double selection method

This observation gives rise to the double selection method of Belloni et al. (2014) or the double machine learning estimator of Chernozhukov et al. (2017):

1. (Selection on the treatment) Regress D on X using Lasso to obtain $\widehat{\delta}^L$. We define $\widehat{S}_D := \left\{j = 1, \ldots, p, \widehat{\delta}_j^L \neq 0\right\}$ the set of selected variables,
2. (Selection on the outcome) Regress Y on X using Lasso to obtain $\widehat{\beta}^L$. We define $\widehat{S}_Y := \left\{j = 1, \ldots, p, \widehat{\beta}_j^L \neq 0\right\}$;
3. (Estimation) Finish by regressing Y on D and the $\widehat{s} = |\widehat{S}_D \cup \widehat{S}_Y|$ elements of X that correspond to the indices $j \in \widehat{S}_D \cup \widehat{S}_Y$, using the OLS.

Note that in the first two steps, we can use either a Lasso or a post-Lasso. We define the post-double selection estimators $\widehat{\beta}$ and $\widehat{\delta}$ as follows:

$$\widehat{\beta} = \underset{\beta:\beta_j = 0, \forall j \notin \widehat{S}_D \cup \widehat{S}_Y}{\arg\min} \sum_{i=1}^{n} (Y_i - D_i\widehat{\tau} - X_i'\beta)^2, \tag{4.10}$$

$$\widehat{\delta} = \underset{\delta:\delta_j = 0, \forall j \notin \widehat{S}_D \cup \widehat{S}_Y}{\arg\min} \sum_{i=1}^{n} (D_i - X_i'\delta)^2. \tag{4.11}$$

Based on Equation (4.7), the post-double selection estimator $\check{\tau}$ has the following explicit form:

$$\check{\tau} = \frac{n^{-1} \sum_{i=1}^{n} (Y_i - X_i'\widehat{\beta})(D_i - X_i'\widehat{\delta})}{n^{-1} \sum_{i=1}^{n} D_i(D_i - X_i'\widehat{\delta})}. \tag{4.12}$$

In relation to the previous paragraph, the third step may be surprising since we regress Y on D and the union of the selected X instead of regressing $Y - X'\widehat{\beta}^L$ on $D - X'\widehat{\delta}^L$. Using the Frisch-Waugh–Lovell theorem (Theorem 4.2 in the appendix), we can show that this third step is equivalent to regressing the residuals of the equation of Y including the selected X (during the first two steps) on the residuals of the equation of D on the selected X (during the first two steps). Conversely, estimating τ_0 directly through (4.9) is equivalent to regressing the residuals of the equation of Y on the selected X (only during the second step) on the residuals of the equation of D on the selected X (only during the first step). Therefore, they are not rigorously the same estimator. However, these two approaches often yield very close numerical results, given that the X that were not selected in one of the two steps are expected to have a quasi-undetectable effect in these regressions. The numerical difference may also come from the difference between the Lasso estimator and the post-Lasso estimator, if a Lasso rather than a post-Lasso is used in steps 1 and 2.

Belloni et al. (2014) show that the estimator $\check{\tau}$ is asymptotically Gaussian under relatively weak assumptions:

$$\sqrt{n}\,(\check{\tau} - \tau_0) \xrightarrow{d} \mathcal{N}(0, \sigma_\tau^2),$$

with $\sigma_\tau^2 = \mathbb{E}[\xi_i^2 \varepsilon_i^2]/\mathbb{E}[\xi_i^2]^2$, which can be consistently estimated by:

$$\widehat{\sigma}_\tau^2 = \left[\frac{1}{n}\sum_{i=1}^{n} \widehat{\xi}_i^2\right]^{-2} \frac{1}{n - \widehat{s} - 1} \sum_{i=1}^{n} \widehat{\xi}_i^2 \widehat{\varepsilon}_i^2,$$

with $\widehat{\varepsilon}_i = Y_i - \widehat{\tau} D_i - X_i'\widehat{\beta}$, $\widehat{\xi}_i = D_i - X_i'\widehat{\delta}$, and the post-double selection estimators defined in (4.10) and (4.11). Note that this result is a special case of the result given by Theorem 5.1 that we will see in the next chapter.

Remark 4.6: Post-selection inference

We note that the selection procedure advocated here is based on a two-equation approach. The intuition behind this result is explained in Section 4.4 on regularization bias: by selecting the elements of X in relation to both D and Y, it does not miss any confounding factor as was the case with the more naive approach, based on a single equation. This result is important because it allows for tests and confidence intervals on τ_0. Thus, for example, a two-sided confidence interval of asymptotic level $1 - \alpha$ is given by:

$$\left[\check{\tau} \pm \Phi^{-1}\left(1 - \frac{\alpha}{2}\right) \frac{\widehat{\sigma}_\tau}{\sqrt{n}}\right].$$

4.6 Empirical application: the effect of education on wage

In L'Hour (2020), we applied the concepts described earlier to quantify the impact of education on earnings using data from the French *Enquête Emploi* – we reproduce this application without modification. The four quarters of the years 2017, 2018, and 2019 from the employment survey are used, which represents a total of 162,254 observations.

Education level is measured by a categorical variable with sixteen modalities. We aim to estimate a linear model where the dependent variable is the logarithm of monthly salary, and the explanatory variables are composed of education level in binary variables (15 variables in total) and other control variables. We consider a total of 393 other control variables, among which are usual determinants of salary such as number of hours worked, individual's age, as well as a large number of socio-demographic and geographic variables (e.g., gender, social origin, marital status, nationality, number of children). When appropriate, we also consider relevant transformations of these variables (e.g., square, cross-product). Finally, we automatically remove variables that generate multicollinearity.

In the present case, we have 15 parameters of interest, i.e., one for each education level minus the baseline level (no education). We could directly apply the double selection method by replicating 15 times the step 1 described in Section 4.5, which consists in estimating a Lasso regression of the variable of interest on the control variables. However, we prefer to estimate a single stacked regression using a group-Lasso estimator, described in Section 2.3.4. Indeed, given that each binary variable represents a different education level, we can a priori think that the main determinants are shared and therefore the sparsity pattern is the same for each equation. The group-Lasso approach allows combining information across each equation to achieve a more accurate variable selection. This is especially important as an approach where each education level is separately analyzed is likely to fail since some education modalities are very rare in the population (less than 2%). The methodology followed to adapt the double selection method to a framework where the parameter of interest is multi-dimensional, including the use of group-Lasso, is described in the appendix of L'Hour (2020).

Figure 4.3 presents the estimates from two different models: (i) the complete model including the 393 control variables estimated by OLS (in black), (ii) the model estimated by double selection (in gray). The first step of double selection, which consists of selecting the control variables related to the logarithm of wages, selects 71 variables, while the second step, which consists of selecting the control variables related to the level of education via Group-Lasso, selects 68 variables. In total, 105 unique control variables are selected. The level of penalization was fixed theoretically, proportionally to $\sqrt{\log p/n}$ where p denotes the number of parameters in the model, which is $393 + 1$ in the first step and $15 \times (393 + 1)$ in the second. The confidence intervals have a level of 95% and are constructed using robust standard errors based on clustering at the household level. We can first observe that the double selection method leads to an estimator that is much more precise than in the complete model. Furthermore, the estimated effects are generally of smaller magnitude, so that some confidence intervals for the two models have no intersection, and we distinguish four groups of diplomas: (i) no diploma/up to middle school diploma which constitutes the baseline, (ii) high school diploma, which corresponds to a wage difference of +15% compared to the baseline, (iii) from a two-year college

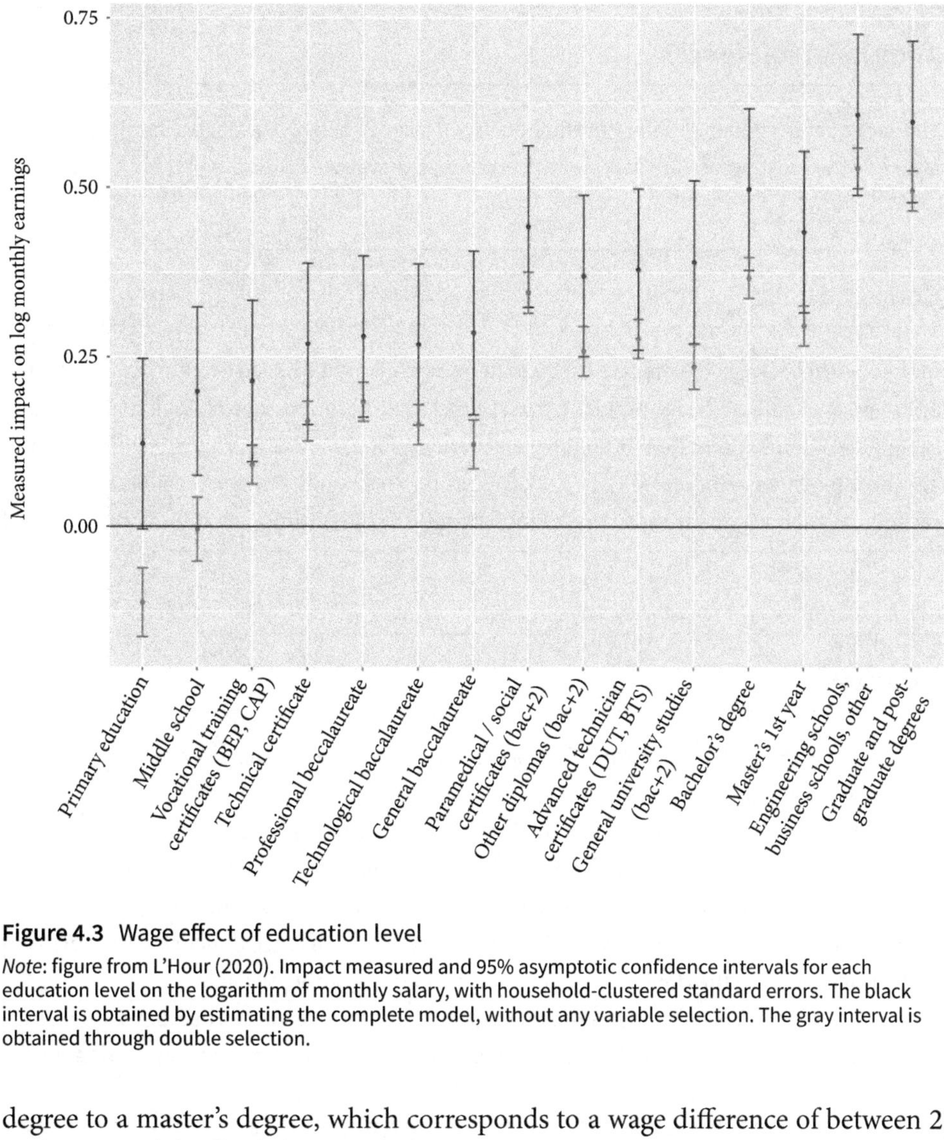

Figure 4.3 Wage effect of education level

Note: figure from L'Hour (2020). Impact measured and 95% asymptotic confidence intervals for each education level on the logarithm of monthly salary, with household-clustered standard errors. The black interval is obtained by estimating the complete model, without any variable selection. The gray interval is obtained through double selection.

degree to a master's degree, which corresponds to a wage difference of between 25 and 35%, and finally, (iv) master's degree, graduate school, and beyond, which are associated with a wage difference of +50%.

4.7 Summary

Key concepts

Nuisance parameter, parameter of interest, post-selection inference, sparsity, Lasso/post-Lasso estimator, regularization bias, plug-in estimator, double selection method.

Additional references

The Lasso regression is detailed in the book by Hastie et al. (2009). Belloni et al. (2014) is arguably the most accessible econometric reference that covers the core of this chapter.

Code and data

`hdm` is an R package developed by Victor Chernozhukov, Christian Hansen, and Martin Spindler, available at cran.r-project.org/web/packages/hdm/index.html, which allows for the practical implementation of double selection. github.com/demirermert/MLInference is also an interesting resource. A Stata package, `LASSOPACK`, has also been developed more recently, available at ideas.repec.org/c/boc/bocode/s458458.html.

Questions

1. What is the Lasso estimator? What is the key assumption for the Lasso to be consistent?
2. What is the convergence rate of the Lasso? When does this pose a problem?
3. Explain why estimating a nuisance parameter using a Lasso estimator can be problematic when we are interested in a specific parameter of interest.
4. What is the regularization bias? Can it exist in the case of small dimension ($p < n$)?
5. Briefly explain the double selection method and the problem it solves.
6. What problem is raised by Leeb and Potscher? Does the result of Theorem 5.1 (asymptotic normality of the immunized estimator) contradict the analysis of Leeb and Potscher? Why?

4.8 Proofs and additional results

4.8.1 Proof of the main results

Proof of Lemma 4.1 Considering the selection rule (4.2) and the assumption of Gaussian distribution in the model (4.1):

$$\begin{aligned}\mathbb{P}\left(\widehat{M} = R\right) &= \mathbb{P}\left(|\sqrt{n}\widehat{\beta}(U)/\sigma_\beta| \leq c_n\right)\\ &= \mathbb{P}\left(-c_n - \sqrt{n}\beta_0/\sigma_\beta \leq \sqrt{n}(\widehat{\beta}(U) - \beta_0)/\sigma_\beta \leq c_n - \sqrt{n}\beta_0/\sigma_\beta\right)\end{aligned}$$

$$= \Phi\left(c_n - \sqrt{n}\beta_0/\sigma_\beta\right) - \Phi\left(-c_n - \sqrt{n}\beta_0/\sigma_\beta\right)$$
$$= \Phi\left(\sqrt{n}\beta_0/\sigma_\beta + c_n\right) - \Phi\left(\sqrt{n}\beta_0/\sigma_\beta - c_n\right)$$
$$= \Delta\left(\sqrt{n}\beta_0/\sigma_\beta, c_n\right),$$

with $\Delta(a, b) := \Phi(a + b) - \Phi(a - b)$ and the fourth equality uses the symmetry of the Gaussian distribution, $\Phi(-x) = 1 - \Phi(x)$. According to this equation and the restrictions on c_n, the probability of the event $\widehat{M} = R$ tends to one if $\beta_0 = 0$ $(M_0 = R)$ and tends to zero otherwise $(M_0 = U)$. □

Proof of Lemma 4.2 Start from Equation (4.2):

$$\mathbb{P}\left(x \leq \sqrt{n}(\tilde{\tau} - \tau_0) \leq x + \mathrm{d}x\right)$$
$$= \mathbb{P}\left(x \leq \sqrt{n}(\widehat{\tau}(R) - \tau_0) \leq x + \mathrm{d}x \mid \widehat{M} = R\right)\mathbb{P}\left(\widehat{M} = R\right)$$
$$+ \mathbb{P}\left(x \leq \sqrt{n}(\widehat{\tau}(U) - \tau_0) \leq x + \mathrm{d}x \mid \widehat{M} = U\right)\mathbb{P}\left(\widehat{M} = U\right).$$

Let's consider the first term of the sum. According to Lemma 4.5, for any real number x, we have:

$$\mathbb{P}\left(x \leq \sqrt{n}(\widehat{\tau}(R) - \tau_0) \leq x + \mathrm{d}x \mid \widehat{M} = R\right) = \mathbb{P}\left(x \leq \sqrt{n}(\widehat{\tau}(R) - \tau_0) \leq x + \mathrm{d}x\right).$$

Thus, as $\mathrm{d}x \to 0$, the first part of the sum (multiplied by $1/\mathrm{d}x$) is the probability of selecting the model R multiplied by the density of $\sqrt{n}(\widehat{\tau}(R) - \tau_0)$. The probability of selecting the model R is $\mathbb{P}\left(\widehat{M} = R\right) = \Delta\left(\sqrt{n}\beta_0/\sigma_\beta, c_n\right)$. Before continuing, let's note the relationship between the moments of X_i and those of the OLS estimators in model U, according to Assumption 4.1:

$$\left[\frac{1}{n}\sum_{i=1}^{n} X_i X_i'\right] = \frac{\sigma^2}{\sigma_\beta^2\sigma_\tau^2(1-\rho^2)}\begin{bmatrix}\sigma_\beta^2 & -\rho\sigma_\beta\sigma_\tau \\ -\rho\sigma_\beta\sigma_\tau & \sigma_\tau^2\end{bmatrix}.$$

To compute the density of $\sqrt{n}(\widehat{\tau}(R) - \tau_0)$, we use the usual formula for OLS in which we substitute Y_i by the model in Assumption 4.1:

$$\sqrt{n}(\widehat{\tau}(R) - \tau_0) = -\sqrt{n}\beta_0\rho\frac{\sigma_\tau}{\sigma_\beta} + \sqrt{n}\frac{\sigma_\tau^2}{\sigma^2}(1-\rho^2)\left(\frac{1}{n}\sum_{i=1}^{n} X_{i,1}\varepsilon_i\right).$$

Since the ε_i are i.i.d. Gaussian and conditionally on X_i, we obtain:

$$\sqrt{n}(\widehat{\tau}(R) - \tau_0) \sim \mathcal{N}\left(-\sqrt{n}\beta_0\rho\frac{\sigma_\tau}{\sigma_\beta}, \sigma_\tau^2(1-\rho^2)\right).$$

The bias $-\sqrt{n}\beta_0\rho\sigma_\tau/\sigma_\beta$ corresponds to the usual omitted variable bias (OVB) Angrist and Pischke (2009, p. 59):

$$-\sqrt{n}\beta_0\frac{\rho\sigma_\tau\sigma_\beta}{\sigma_\beta^2} = \sqrt{n}\beta_0\frac{\mathrm{Cov}(X_{i,1}, X_{i,2})}{\mathrm{V}(X_{i,1})}.$$

Now let's focus on the second part of the sum and swap the order of the events:

$$\begin{aligned}&\mathbb{P}\left(x \leq \sqrt{n}(\widehat{\tau}(U) - \tau_0) \leq x + \mathrm{d}x \mid \widehat{M} = U\right)\mathbb{P}\left(\widehat{M} = U\right) = \\ &\mathbb{P}\left(\widehat{M} = U \mid x \leq \sqrt{n}(\widehat{\tau}(U) - \tau_0) \leq x + \mathrm{d}x\right)\mathbb{P}\left(x \leq \sqrt{n}(\widehat{\tau}(U) - \tau_0) \leq x + \mathrm{d}x\right).\end{aligned}$$

Let's recall that

$$\begin{bmatrix}\sqrt{n}(\widehat{\beta}(U) - \beta_0) \\ \sqrt{n}(\widehat{\tau}(U) - \tau_0)\end{bmatrix} \sim \mathcal{N}\left(\begin{bmatrix}0\\0\end{bmatrix}, \begin{bmatrix}\sigma_\beta^2 & \rho\sigma_\beta\sigma_\tau \\ \rho\sigma_\beta\sigma_\tau & \sigma_\tau^2\end{bmatrix}\right).$$

Therefore, we directly have

$$\frac{\mathbb{P}\left(x \leq \sqrt{n}(\widehat{\tau}(U) - \tau_0) \leq x + \mathrm{d}x\right)}{\mathrm{d}x} \to \frac{1}{\sigma_\tau}\varphi\left(\frac{x}{\sigma_\tau}\right),$$

as $\mathrm{d}x \to 0$. Due to the properties of Gaussian vectors, we obtain:

$$\sqrt{n}(\widehat{\beta}(U) - \beta_0) \mid \sqrt{n}(\widehat{\tau}(U) - \tau_0) \sim \mathcal{N}\left(\rho\frac{\sigma_\beta}{\sigma_\tau}\sqrt{n}(\widehat{\tau}(U) - \tau_0), \sigma_\beta^2(1 - \rho^2)\right).$$

Now let's calculate $\mathbb{P}(|\sqrt{n}\widehat{\beta}(U)/\sigma_\beta| > c_n|\sqrt{n}(\widehat{\tau}(U) - \tau_0) = x)$. On one hand:

$$\begin{aligned}&\mathbb{P}\left(\sqrt{n}\frac{\widehat{\beta}(U)}{\sigma_\beta} > c_n \middle| \sqrt{n}(\widehat{\tau}(U) - \tau_0) = x\right) \\ &= \Phi\left(\frac{1}{\sqrt{1-\rho^2}}\left(\sqrt{n}\frac{\beta_0}{\sigma_\beta} + \rho\frac{x}{\sigma_\tau} - c_n\right)\right).\end{aligned}$$

On the other hand:

$$\begin{aligned}&\mathbb{P}\left(\sqrt{n}\frac{\widehat{\beta}(U)}{\sigma_\beta} < -c_n \middle| \sqrt{n}(\widehat{\tau}(U) - \tau_0) = x\right) \\ &= 1 - \Phi\left(\frac{1}{\sqrt{1-\rho^2}}\left(\sqrt{n}\frac{\beta_0}{\sigma_\beta} + \rho\frac{x}{\sigma_\tau} + c_n\right)\right),\end{aligned}$$

which gives the intended result. □

Proof of Theorem 4.1 Since $\widehat{\beta}$ is a solution of the minimization program, we necessarily have:

$$L(\widehat{\beta}) + \lambda_n \|\widehat{\beta}\|_1 \leq L(\beta_0) + \lambda_n \|\beta_0\|_1. \tag{4.13}$$

Step 1: differences in loss functions. We decompose the difference between the two loss functions into two elements and replace Y_i:

$$\begin{aligned}
L(\widehat{\beta}) - L(\beta_0) &= \frac{1}{n}\sum_{i=1}^{n} \left(Y_i - X_i'\widehat{\beta}\right)^2 - \left(Y_i - X_i'\beta_0\right)^2 \\
&= \frac{1}{n}\sum_{i=1}^{n} \left(X_i'(\beta_0 - \widehat{\beta}) + \varepsilon_i\right)^2 - \varepsilon_i^2 \\
&= (\widehat{\beta} - \beta_0)' \underbrace{\left[\frac{1}{n}\sum_{i=1}^{n} X_i X_i'\right]}_{=\widehat{\Sigma}} (\widehat{\beta} - \beta_0) + 2(\widehat{\beta} - \beta_0)' \left[\frac{1}{n}\sum_{i=1}^{n} \varepsilon_i X_i\right].
\end{aligned}$$

Therefore, from Equation (4.13), we obtain:

$$\begin{aligned}
(\widehat{\beta} - \beta_0)'\widehat{\Sigma}(\widehat{\beta} - \beta_0) &\leq \lambda_n \left(\|\beta_0\|_1 - \|\widehat{\beta}\|_1\right) - 2(\widehat{\beta} - \beta_0)' \left[\frac{1}{n}\sum_{i=1}^{n} \varepsilon_i X_i\right] \\
&\leq \lambda_n \left(\|\beta_0\|_1 - \|\widehat{\beta}\|_1\right) + 2\|\widehat{\beta} - \beta_0\|_1 \|\frac{1}{n}\sum_{i=1}^{n} \varepsilon_i X_i\|_\infty,
\end{aligned}$$

Step 2: concentration inequality. It is time to apply the concentration inequality from Lemma 4.6 to $\|\frac{1}{n}\sum_{i=1}^{n} \varepsilon_i X_i\|_\infty$. Using Markov's inequality:

$$\begin{aligned}
&\mathbb{P}\left(\max_{j=1,\dots,p} \left|\frac{1}{n}\sum_{i=1}^{n} \varepsilon_i X_{ij}\right| \geq \frac{\lambda_n}{4} \middle| X_1, \dots, X_n\right) \\
&\leq \frac{4\mathbb{E}\left(\max_{j=1,\dots,p} |\frac{1}{n}\sum_{i=1}^{n} \varepsilon_i X_{ij}| \middle| X_1, \dots, X_n\right)}{\lambda_n} \\
&\lesssim \frac{4\sigma M}{\sqrt{n}} \frac{\sqrt{2\log(2p)}}{\lambda_n} \\
&\leq \alpha,
\end{aligned}$$

since $\lambda_n = \frac{4\sigma M}{\alpha}\sqrt{\frac{2\log(2p)}{n}}$. Since the right-hand side is non-probabilistic, we have:

$$\mathbb{P}\left(\max_{j=1,\dots,p} \left|\frac{1}{n}\sum_{i=1}^{n} \varepsilon_i X_{ij}\right| \geq \frac{\lambda_n}{4}\right) \leq \alpha.$$

During the event $\left\{\max_{j=1,\ldots,p} \left|\frac{2}{n}\sum_{i=1}^{n} \varepsilon_i X_{ij}\right| < \frac{\lambda_n}{2}\right\}$, which occurs with a probability greater than $1-\alpha$:

$$(\widehat{\beta}-\beta_0)'\widehat{\Sigma}(\widehat{\beta}-\beta_0) \leq \lambda_n\left(\|\beta_0\|_1 - \|\widehat{\beta}\|_1\right) + \frac{\lambda_n}{2}\|\widehat{\beta}-\beta_0\|_1. \tag{4.14}$$

Step 3: decomposition of ℓ_1 norms. From now on, we will use the notation β_{S_0} to denote the p-dimensional vector β in which the elements that are not in S_0 are replaced by 0. Note that $\beta = \beta_{S_0} + \beta_{S_0^C}$. Using the reverse triangle inequality, we have:

$$\|\beta_{0,S_0}\|_1 - \|\widehat{\beta}_{S_0}\|_1 \leq \|\beta_{0,S_0} - \widehat{\beta}_{S_0}\|_1.$$

We also note that $\beta_{0,S_0^C} = 0$, so $\|\beta_{0,S_0^C}\|_1 - \|\widehat{\beta}_{S_0^C}\|_1 = -\|\beta_{0,S_0^C} - \widehat{\beta}_{S_0^C}\|_1$. Thus, from (4.14), we obtain:

$$(\widehat{\beta}-\beta_0)'\widehat{\Sigma}(\widehat{\beta}-\beta_0) \leq \frac{3\lambda_n}{2}\|\beta_{0,S_0} - \widehat{\beta}_{S_0}\|_1 - \frac{\lambda_n}{2}\|\beta_{0,S_0^C} - \widehat{\beta}_{S_0^C}\|_1. \tag{4.15}$$

Step 4: cone condition and restricted eigenvalues. This means that we have the following cone condition:

$$\|\beta_{0,S_0^C} - \widehat{\beta}_{S_0^C}\|_1 \leq 3\|\beta_{0,S_0} - \widehat{\beta}_{S_0}\|_1,$$

so $\widehat{\beta}-\beta_0 \in \mathcal{C}[S_0, 3]$. Using Assumption 4.4 on the restricted eigenvalue of the empirical Gram matrix and the Cauchy–Schwarz inequality $\|\delta_{S_0}\|_1 \leq \sqrt{s}\|\delta_{S_0}\|_2$, we have:

$$(\widehat{\beta}-\beta_0)'\widehat{\Sigma}(\widehat{\beta}-\beta_0) \geq \kappa_3^2(\widehat{\Sigma})\|\beta_{0,S_0} - \widehat{\beta}_{S_0}\|_2^2 \geq \kappa_3^2(\widehat{\Sigma})\frac{\|\beta_{0,S_0} - \widehat{\beta}_{S_0}\|_1^2}{s}. \tag{4.16}$$

Step 5: conclusion. Using inequalities (4.15) and (4.16), notice that:

$$\begin{aligned}
2(\widehat{\beta}-\beta_0)'\widehat{\Sigma}(\widehat{\beta}-\beta_0) + \lambda_n\|\beta_0 - \widehat{\beta}\|_1 &\leq 4\lambda_n\|\beta_{0,S_0} - \widehat{\beta}_{S_0}\|_1 \\
&\leq 4\lambda_n\frac{\sqrt{s}}{\kappa_3(\widehat{\Sigma})}\sqrt{(\widehat{\beta}-\beta_0)'\widehat{\Sigma}(\widehat{\beta}-\beta_0)} \\
&\leq 4\lambda_n^2\frac{s}{\kappa_3^2(\widehat{\Sigma})} + (\widehat{\beta}-\beta_0)'\widehat{\Sigma}(\widehat{\beta}-\beta_0),
\end{aligned}$$

where the last inequality uses $4uv \leq u^2 + 4v^2$. We finally obtain:

$$(\widehat{\beta}-\beta_0)'\widehat{\Sigma}(\widehat{\beta}-\beta_0) + \lambda_n\|\beta_0 - \widehat{\beta}\|_1 \leq 4\lambda_n^2\frac{s}{\kappa_3^2(\widehat{\Sigma})}.$$

Finally, with probability greater than $1 - \alpha$:

$$\|\beta_0 - \widehat{\beta}\|_1 \leq \frac{4^2\sigma M}{\alpha\kappa_3^2(\widehat{\Sigma})}\sqrt{\frac{2s^2\log(2p)}{n}}.$$

□

Proof of Lemma 4.3. By substituting the model 4.5, we obtain:

$$\sqrt{n}\left(\widehat{\tau} - \tau_0\right) = \widehat{\pi}^{-1}\left[\frac{1}{n}\sum_{i=1}^{n} D_iX_i\right]'\sqrt{n}\left(\beta_0 - \widehat{\beta}\right) + \widehat{\pi}^{-1}\sqrt{n}\left[\frac{1}{n}\sum_{i=1}^{n} D_i\varepsilon_i\right]. \tag{4.17}$$

From the equation above, we could hope that since $\widehat{\beta}$ converges in ℓ_1 norm, the first term converges to zero in probability and we are left only with the second term. This is not the case. By the central limit theorem – using also the law of large numbers and the continuous mapping theorem to prove $\widehat{\pi} \xrightarrow{p} \pi_0$ – and Slutsky's theorem, we have:

$$\widehat{\pi}^{-1}\left[\frac{1}{\sqrt{n}}\sum_{i=1}^{n} D_i\varepsilon_i\right] \xrightarrow{d} \mathcal{N}\left(0, \frac{\sigma^2}{\pi_0}\right).$$

Moreover, in general, we can show that:

$$\left|\left[\frac{1}{n}\sum_{i=1}^{n} D_iX_i\right]'\sqrt{n}\left(\beta_0 - \widehat{\beta}\right)\right| \approx s\sqrt{\log p} \to \infty.$$

The underlying intuition is twofold. By the law of large numbers, we have:

$$\left[\frac{1}{n}\sum_{i=1}^{n} D_iX_i\right] \xrightarrow{p} \pi_0\mu_1.$$

Generally, $\mu_1 \neq 0$ and this term does not become zero. Moreover, since $p \to \infty$, we have $\|\sqrt{n}(\widehat{\beta} - \beta_0)\|_1 \approx s\sqrt{\log p}$ which does not become zero, proving the result. □

Proof of Lemma 4.4. We start from the proof of Lemma 4.3. Now, thanks to assumption 4.7, we obtain:

$$\left\|\frac{1}{\sqrt{n}}\sum_{i=1}^{n} D_iX_i\right\|_\infty \lesssim \sqrt{\log p}.$$

Using Theorem 4.1 and the inequality $|a'b| \leq \|a\|_\infty \|b\|_1$, we have:

$$\left|\left[\frac{1}{\sqrt{n}}\sum_{i=1}^{n} D_iX_i\right]'\left[\beta_0 - \widehat{\beta}\right]\right| \leq \left\|\frac{1}{\sqrt{n}}\sum_{i=1}^{n} D_iX_i\right\|_\infty \left\|\beta_0 - \widehat{\beta}\right\|_1$$

$$\lesssim \frac{s \log p}{\sqrt{n}} \to 0,$$

by the growth condition Assumption 4.6. Therefore, the quantity on the left-hand side of the above inequality converges to zero in probability (convergence in ℓ_1 norm implies convergence in probability). Using Slutsky's theorem and Equation (4.17), we obtain the result. □

4.8.2 Additional results

Lemma 4.5 was used in the calculation of the distribution of the post-selection estimator.

Lemma 4.5 (Independence, according to Leeb, 2006).

$$\widehat{\tau}(R) \perp\!\!\!\perp \widehat{\beta}(U).$$

Proof of Lemma 4.5 We use the following matrix notations: $\mathbf{X_j} = (X_{i,j})_{1 \leq i \leq n}$ for all $j = 1, 2$, $\mathbf{y} = (Y_i)_{1 \leq i \leq n}$, and $\mathbf{X} = (X_i')_{1 \leq i \leq n}$. We note that $\widehat{\tau}(R) = [\mathbf{X_1}'\mathbf{X_1}]^{-1}\mathbf{X_1}'\mathbf{y}$, and we define $\mathcal{M}_{\mathbf{X}_1} := \mathbf{I_n} - \mathbf{X_1}[\mathbf{X_1}'\mathbf{X_1}]^{-1}\mathbf{X_1}'$, the projector onto the orthogonal complement of the column space of $\mathbf{X_1}$. Let $\mathbf{X}^O := [\mathbf{X_1} : \mathcal{M}_{\mathbf{X}_1}\mathbf{X_2}]$ be the matrix, and $\widehat{\beta}^O$ be the coefficient obtained by regressing $\mathbf{y}$ on $\mathbf{X}^O$, i.e., $\widehat{\beta}^O = \left[\mathbf{X}^{O\prime}\mathbf{X}^O\right]^{-1}\left[\mathbf{X}^{O\prime}\mathbf{y}\right]$. We can show that:

$$\widehat{\beta}^O = \begin{bmatrix} \widehat{\tau}(R) \\ [\mathbf{X_2}'\mathcal{M}_{\mathbf{X}_1}\mathbf{X_2}]^{-1}\mathbf{X_2}'\mathcal{M}_{\mathbf{X}_1}\mathbf{y} \end{bmatrix},$$

and that $\widehat{\tau}(R)$ and $[\mathbf{X_2}'\mathcal{M}_{\mathbf{X}_1}\mathbf{X_2}]^{-1}\mathbf{X_2}'\mathcal{M}_{\mathbf{X}_1}\mathbf{y}$ are uncorrelated, according to Cochran's theorem. Using Frish–Waugh–Lovell theorem (Theorem 4.2 at the end of this chapter), $[\mathbf{X_2}'\mathcal{M}_{\mathbf{X}_1}\mathbf{X_2}]^{-1}\mathbf{X_2}'\mathcal{M}_{\mathbf{X}_1}\mathbf{y} = \widehat{\beta}(U)$, which completes the proof. □

Lemma 4.6, taken from Chatterjee (2013), provides a bound on the tail distribution of the maximum of Gaussian random variables. This lemma is actually more general and applies to sub-Gaussian random variables. The reader can refer to Vershynin (2018) for a definition of sub-Gaussian property as well as results on probabilities in high dimensions. We also recall the Frisch–Waugh–Lovell theorem (4.2). In this regard, the reader can also consult the *regression anatomy formula* in Angrist and Pischke (2009, p. 35–36).

Lemma 4.6 (Concentration inequality for Gaussian random variables). *Consider p Gaussian random variables, such that for $j = 1, \dots, p$, $\xi_j \sim \mathcal{N}(0, \sigma_j^2)$, and let $L = \max_{j=1,\dots,p} \sigma_j$. Then:*

$$\mathbb{E}\left[\max_{j=1,\ldots,p}|\xi_j|\right] \leq L\sqrt{2\log(2p)}.$$

Proof of Lemma 4.6 Since $\xi_j \sim \mathcal{N}(0, \sigma_j^2)$, a direct calculation shows that $\mathbb{E}\left[e^{c\xi_j}\right] = e^{\frac{c^2\sigma_j^2}{2}}$ for all $c \in \mathbb{R}$. It should be noted that the proof will only use that ξ_j is sub-Gaussian, i.e., $\mathbb{E}\left[e^{c\xi_j}\right] \leq e^{\frac{c^2\sigma_j^2}{2}}$.

$$\begin{aligned}
\mathbb{E}\left[\max_{j=1,\ldots,p}|\xi_j|\right] &= \frac{1}{c}\mathbb{E}\left[\log\left\{\exp\left(\max_{j=1,\ldots,p} c|\xi_j|\right)\right\}\right] \\
&\leq \frac{1}{c}\mathbb{E}\left[\log\left\{\sum_{j=1}^{p} e^{c|\xi_j|}\right\}\right] \\
&\leq \frac{1}{c}\mathbb{E}\left[\log\left\{\sum_{j=1}^{p} e^{c\xi_j} + e^{-c\xi_j}\right\}\right] \\
&\leq \frac{1}{c}\log\left\{\sum_{j=1}^{p} \mathbb{E}\left[e^{c\xi_j}\right] + \mathbb{E}\left[e^{-c\xi_j}\right]\right\} \\
&\leq \frac{1}{c}\log\left\{2pe^{\frac{c^2L^2}{2}}\right\} \\
&= \frac{\log(2p)}{c} + \frac{cL^2}{2},
\end{aligned}$$

where the third inequality uses Jensen's inequality and the fourth uses the remark at the beginning of the proof. The bound is minimized for the value $c^* = \sqrt{2\log(2p)}/L$ and equals $L\sqrt{2\log(2p)}$, which completes the proof. □

Theorem 4.2 (Frisch–Waugh–Lovell, Frisch and Waugh, 1933; Lovell, 1963) *Let's consider the regression of the n-dimensional vector* $\mathbf{y}$ *on the full rank* $n \times p$ *matrix* $\mathbf{X}$. *We consider the partition:* $\mathbf{X} = [\mathbf{X}_1 : \mathbf{X}_2]$, *and define* $\mathcal{P}_{\mathbf{X}_1} := \mathbf{X}_1[\mathbf{X}_1{}'\mathbf{X}_1]^{-1}\mathbf{X}_1{}'$, $\mathcal{M}_{\mathbf{X}_1} := \mathbf{I_n} - \mathcal{P}_{\mathbf{X}_1}$, *and* $\mathcal{P}_{\mathbf{X}}$ *and* $\mathcal{M}_{\mathbf{X}}$ *for* $\mathbf{X}$, *respectively. Let's consider these two quantities:*

1. $\widehat{\beta} = (\widehat{\beta}_1', \widehat{\beta}_2')' = (\mathbf{X}'\mathbf{X})^{-1}\mathbf{X}'\mathbf{y}$,
2. $\tilde{\beta}_2 = (\mathbf{X}_2{}'\mathcal{M}_{\mathbf{X}_1}\mathbf{X}_2)^{-1}\mathbf{X}_2{}'\mathcal{M}_{\mathbf{X}_1}\mathbf{y}$,

then $\tilde{\beta}_2 = \widehat{\beta}_2$.

Proof of Theorem 4.2. Let's consider the decomposition:

$$\mathbf{y} = \mathcal{P}_{\mathbf{X}}\mathbf{y} + \mathcal{M}_{\mathbf{y}}\mathbf{y} = \mathbf{X}\widehat{\beta} + \mathcal{M}_{\mathbf{y}}\mathbf{y} = \mathbf{X}_1\widehat{\beta}_1 + \mathbf{X}_2\widehat{\beta}_2 + \mathcal{M}_{\mathbf{X}}\mathbf{y}.$$

Pre-multiply by $\mathbf{X}_2'\mathcal{M}_{\mathbf{X}_1}$:

$$\begin{aligned}\mathbf{X}_2'\mathcal{M}_{\mathbf{X}_1}\mathbf{y} &= \mathbf{X}_2'\mathcal{M}_{\mathbf{X}_1}\mathbf{X}_1\widehat{\beta}_1 + \mathbf{X}_2'\mathcal{M}_{\mathbf{X}_1}\mathbf{X}_2\widehat{\beta}_2 + \mathbf{X}_2'\mathcal{M}_{\mathbf{X}_1}\mathcal{M}_{\mathbf{X}}\mathbf{y} \\ &= 0 + \mathbf{X}_2'\mathcal{M}_{\mathbf{X}_1}\mathbf{X}_2\widehat{\beta}_2 + 0.\end{aligned}$$

Therefore, $\widehat{\beta}_2 = (\mathbf{X}_2'\mathcal{M}_{\mathbf{X}_1}\mathbf{X}_2)^{-1}\mathbf{X}_2'\mathcal{M}_{\mathbf{X}_1}\mathbf{y} = \tilde{\beta}_2$. □

Chapter 5
Generalization and methodology

This chapter extends the intuition behind the double selection method, presented in the previous chapter, in two ways. First, it goes beyond the linear case to encompass a more general model summarized by an orthogonal score function $\psi(Z, \tau, \eta)$ that is used to make inference on the low-dimensional target parameter τ_0 in the presence of a high-dimensional nuisance parameter η_0. Second, it applies to a more general problem, of which variable selection is a part. In this context, we assume at a minimum that η_0 is a complex object that will be estimated using machine learning tools. This can reflect the idea of a parsimonious nuisance parameter requiring variable selection, but it can also reflect the presence of a nuisance parameter that is believed to be better estimated by nonlinear methods, such as random forests or neural networks. The ultimate goal is to obtain favorable properties for the estimator of τ_0, in order to guarantee theoretically reliable tests and confidence intervals.

Here, the intention is not to exhaustively list all possible machine learning methods to estimate η_0 – that would be pointless – we can mention Lasso, post-Lasso and Ridge regressions, elastic nets, regression trees and random forests, neural networks, aggregated methods, etc. The use of each of these methods is justified by the assumptions we are willing to make about the form of the parameter η_0. We simply give a general framework that can support the use of these methods.

Section 5.1 therefore generalizes the intuition given in the previous chapter. Section 5.2 applies this theory to orthogonal scores for estimating treatment effects, as already encountered in Chapter 3. Section 5.3 presents estimation by sample splitting, which is strongly recommended in this context because it allows for more robust estimation by relaxing overly strict assumptions (in theory) and avoiding overfitting (in practice). The following two sections present simulations and empirical examples.

5.1 Theory: immunization

5.1.1 Intuition

In the previous chapter (Section 4.5), we showed that the double selection method allows to ensure that the estimation of the high-dimensional nuisance parameter does not affect the asymptotic distribution of the estimator of the parameter of interest. This section will allow to move to an additional level of abstraction, beyond the

Machine Learning for Econometrics. Christophe Gaillac and Jérémy L'Hour, Oxford University Press.
 DOI: 10.1093/9780198918868.003.0005

case of linear regression. For this purpose, let's assume that the parameter of interest, τ_0, solves the equation $\mathbb{E}[m(Z_i, \tau_0, \beta_0)] = 0$ for a known score function $m(.)$, a vector of observables Z_i, and a nuisance parameter β_0. To make these objects less abstract, we can think of the fully parametric case where $m(.)$ is the derivative of the log-likelihood Wasserman (2010, Chapter 9). In the previous section, we had $Z_i = (Y_i, D_i, X_i)$, and $m(Z_i, \tau, \beta) := (Y_i - D_i\tau - X_i'\beta)D_i$. In Lemma 4.3, the source of the problem was that the derivative of the estimating equation with respect to the nuisance parameter was not zero:

$$\mathbb{E}\left[\partial_\beta m(Z_i, \tau_0, \beta_0)\right] = -\pi_0\mu_1 \neq 0.$$

We would like to replace m with another score function or estimating moment ψ and a potentially different nuisance parameter from β_0, η_0, so that:

$$\mathbb{E}\left[\partial_\eta \psi(Z_i, \tau_0, \eta_0)\right] = 0. \tag{5.1}$$

The condition (5.1) means that the moment condition to estimate τ_0 is not affected by small perturbations around the true value of the nuisance parameter η_0. This is the intuition behind the double selection or *immunized* or *Neyman-orthogonalized* procedure (Chernozhukov et al., 2017; Belloni et al., 2017; Chernozhukov et al., 2018). Modifying the estimating equation allows us to neutralize the effect of first-stage estimation and remove the regularization bias. We will say that any function ψ which satisfies condition (5.1) is a *Neyman-orthogonal* or simply *orthogonal score.*

5.1.2 Asymptotic normality

The ideas presented in this section have been developed by Chernozhukov et al. (2015a, 2015b, 2017); Belloni et al. (2017), and Chernozhukov et al. (2018).

Assumption 5.1 (Orthogonal moment condition). *The parameter of interest τ_0 is the root to the equation:*

$$\mathbb{E}\left[\psi(Z_i, \tau_0, \eta_0)\right] = 0,$$

with a known real-valued function $\psi(.)$ that satisfies the orthogonality condition (5.1), a vector of observable variables Z_i, and a high-dimensional parsimonious nuisance parameter η_0 such that $\|\eta_0\|_0 \leq s$. The design satisfies the growth condition Assumption 4.6.

Furthermore, suppose we have a first-stage estimator $\widehat{\eta}$ of η_0 that is of sufficient quality.

Assumption 5.2 (Nuisance parameter estimation). *Let $\widehat{\eta}$ be a first-stage estimator such that with high probability:*

$$\|\widehat{\eta}\|_0 \lesssim s,$$

$$\|\widehat{\eta} - \eta_0\|_1 \lesssim \sqrt{s^2 \log p/n},$$

$$\|\widehat{\eta} - \eta_0\|_2 \lesssim \sqrt{s \log p/n}.$$

We consider this estimator to be given. It does not need to be a Lasso, but the Lasso or post-Lasso clearly satisfy these assumptions in a *sparse* or *approximately sparse* scenario, i.e., in cases where only a few control variables matter. Chernozhukov et al. (2018) extend these conditions to any machine learning procedure of sufficient quality. They will be discussed in Section 5.3. Note that the recommended ML procedure depends on the assumptions made about η_0 since they will determine the performance of this tool. For example, if we assume that η_0 is sparse, a Lasso should work well. On the other hand, if we assume that η_0 should capture a piecewise-constant relationship between an explanatory variable and control variables, we would rather choose a random forest. The estimator of τ_0 that we will consider is $\check{\tau}$ such that:

$$\frac{1}{n}\sum_{i=1}^{n} \psi(Z_i, \check{\tau}, \widehat{\eta}) = 0. \tag{5.2}$$

For clearer exposition, we consider the simple case of Assumption 5.3 below.

Assumption 5.3 (Affine-quadratic Model). *The function $\psi(.)$ is such that:*

$$\psi(Z_i, \tau, \eta) = \Gamma_1(Z_i, \eta)\tau - \Gamma_2(Z_i, \eta),$$

where $\Gamma_j, j = 1, 2$, are functions whose second-order derivatives with respect to η are constant over the convex parameter space of η.

The class of models above may seem restrictive, but it includes many usual parameters of interest such as the average treatment effect (ATE), the average treatment effect on the treated (ATT), the local average treatment effect (LATE), as well as any coefficient in a linear regression.

Theorem 5.1 (Asymptotic normality of the immunized estimator) *The immunized estimator $\check{\tau}$, defined by (5.2) in the affine-quadratic model of Assumption 5.3 under Assumptions 4.6, 5.1, and using a first-stage nuisance estimator satisfying Assumption 5.2, has the property that:*

$$\sqrt{n}(\check{\tau} - \tau_0) \xrightarrow{d} \mathcal{N}(0, \sigma_\Gamma^2),$$

where $\sigma_\Gamma^2 := \mathbb{E}[\psi(Z_i, \tau_0, \eta_0)^2]/\mathbb{E}[\Gamma_1(Z_i, \eta_0)]^2$.

In practice, σ_Γ^2 is simply estimated from averages, replacing the unknown quantities with their estimators. The proofs can be found in the appendix of this chapter.

Remark 5.1 Importance of Theorem 5.1

Theorem 5.1 is relatively powerful: if one finds an estimator defined as the root of an orthogonal moment condition, i.e., one that satisfies condition (5.1), then this estimator will be asymptotically Gaussian with a variance that can be estimated. This theorem covers the case of double selection seen in Section 4.5. This thus offers the possibility of inference on the parameter of interest. It is worth highlighting the assumptions that matter the most. Assumption 5.1 is extremely important and constitutes the object of this entire section. The key element is that ψ must satisfy condition (5.1), without which we cannot control the term I_2' in the proof. Assumption 5.2 concerns the quality of the estimation of the nuisance parameter: although it can be made more general to accommodate for other methods from the literature on machine learning, the estimator of the nuisance parameter must have good performance. Assumption 4.6 about the growth condition is necessary but not very restrictive: p can grow as fast as e^{n^α} for $\alpha \in]0, 1/2[$! Assumption 5.3 is not important: it is a simplification in the context of this course to make the proof easier. Moreover, it is not very restrictive: many parameters of interest fall within this framework.

Remark 5.2 Overidentified case

Since we consider a scalar parameter of interest τ_0 identified by a single equation, Equation (5.2) was suitable as a definition. In general, when τ_0 is identified by a set of equations of higher dimension, the GMM estimator will take the form:

$$\hat{\tau} = \arg\min_{\tau \in \mathbb{R}^d} \left\| \frac{1}{n} \sum_{i=1}^{n} \psi(Z_i, \tau, \hat{\eta}) \right\|_2^2 .$$

The reason is that $n^{-1} \sum_{i=1}^{n} \psi(Z_i, \tau, \hat{\eta}) = 0$ will generally not have a solution.

For a given score function $m(.)$ that does not satisfy condition (5.1), how can we find a $\psi(.)$ that does satisfy it? We note that the nuisance parameter is denoted by β_0 in the first case and by η_0 in the second. This different notation means that most of the time, η_0 is different from β_0 and is generally of higher dimension. Section 4.5 covered the linear case. Chernozhukov et al. (2015a) address the cases of maximum likelihood and GMM, while Section 2.2 of Chernozhukov et al. (2018) covers an even wider range of models. Beyond the linear case, Farrell (2015) presents a more general method for estimating treatment effect parameters (ATE, ATT) using similar ideas, as we will see in the next section.

5.2 Orthogonal scores for treatment effect estimation

We consider the model from Section 5.1 of Chernozhukov et al. (2017). This is a more flexible model where we allow for heterogeneous treatment effects. Let (Y, D, X) be a vector such that $D \in \{0, 1\}$ and:

$$Y = g_0(D, X) + \varepsilon, \mathbb{E}[\varepsilon \mid D, X] = 0,$$
$$D = m_0(X) + \xi, \mathbb{E}[\xi \mid X] = 0.$$

Section 4.5 was a particular case where we had $g_0(D, X) = D\tau_0 + X'\beta_0$ and $m_0(X) = X'\delta_0$. In this type of configuration, there are usually two standard parameters of interest: the average treatment effect (ATE) and the average treatment effect on the treated (ATT),

$$\tau_0^{ATE} = \mathbb{E}[g_0(1, X) - g_0(0, X)],$$
$$\tau_0^{ATT} = \mathbb{E}[g_0(1, X) - g_0(0, X) \mid D = 1].$$

In Section 4.5, $\tau_0^{ATE} = \tau_0^{ATT} = \tau_0$ because the treatment effect was homogeneous. For ATE, the orthogonal score from Hahn (1998) is defined as:

$$\psi^{ATE}(Z_i, \tau, \eta)$$
$$= g(1, X) - g(0, X) + \frac{D(Y - g(1, X))}{m(X)} - \frac{(1 - D)(Y - g(0, X))}{1 - m(X)} - \tau.$$

The true value of the nuisance parameter is $\eta_0 = (g_0, m_0)$. For ATT, the orthogonal score is:

$$\psi^{ATT}(Z_i, \tau, \eta) = \frac{1}{\pi_0}\left(D - \frac{m(X)}{1 - m(X)}(1 - D)\right)(Y - g(0, X)) - \frac{D}{\pi_0}\tau.$$

The true value of the nuisance parameter is $\eta_0 = (g_0, m_0, \pi_0)$ with $\pi_0 = \mathbb{P}(D = 1)$. These orthogonal scores form the basis of Farrell (2015) and Bléhaut et al. (2023). Similar expressions exist for the local average treatment effect (LATE), and we refer to Chernozhukov et al. (2018).

Remark 5.3 Trick for computing the variance

These orthogonal scores fall into the affine-quadratic type of Assumption 5.3, so that the standard error computation will simply result from the expression of Theorem 5.1. Moreover, in both cases, $\mathbb{E}[\Gamma_1(Z_i, \eta_0)] = -1$ which implies that $\tau_0 = \mathbb{E}[\Gamma_2(Z_i, \eta_0)]$. As a result, according to Theorem 5.1, $\sigma_\Gamma^2 = \mathbb{V}[\Gamma_2(Z_i, \eta_0)]$. This observation makes the computation of the standard error quite simple: for each observation, it suffices to store $\widehat{\Gamma}_2(Z_i, \widehat{\eta})$ in a vector `gamma` and compute the standard error using `std(gamma)/sqrt(n)`.

5.3 Sample-splitting

In this section, we introduce an additional technique that further generalizes the immunization method discussed in the previous section. Indeed, *sample splitting* is the ingredient that relaxes some of the constraints on the estimation quality of the nuisance parameter (Assumption 5.2). This section presents the method without going into the theoretical details, which will be covered in Section 7.2.

As previously, we consider a low-dimensional parameter of interest τ_0, a high-dimensional nuisance parameter η_0, and, most importantly, an orthogonal score function $\psi(Z, \tau, \eta)$. It is necessary for ψ to satisfy (5.1), as emphasized in Section 5.1. We present the double-machine learning method with cross-fitting proposed by Chernozhukov et al. (2017).

Remark 5.4 Double machine learning with cross-fitting

We assume that we have a sample of n copies of the random vector Z_i, where n is divisible by an integer K for simplicity of notation.

1. Let $(I_k)_{k=1,...,K}$ be a random partition of indices $\{1, ..., n\}$ such that each set I_k has a size of n/k. For each $k \in \{1, ..., K\}$, we define $I_k^C := \{1, ..., n\} \backslash I_k$.
2. For each $k \in \{1, ..., K\}$, we construct an estimator based on a machine learning procedure for η_0 using only the auxiliary sample I_k^C:

$$\widehat{\eta}_k = \widehat{\eta}\left((Z_i)_{i \in I_k^C}\right).$$

3. For each $k \in \{1, ..., K\}$, using the main sample I_k, we construct the estimator $\check{\tau}_k$ as the solution of:

$$\frac{1}{n/K} \sum_{i \in I_k} \psi(Z_i, \check{\tau}_k, \widehat{\eta}_k) = 0.$$

4. We aggregate the estimators $\check{\tau}_k$ over each main sample:

$$\check{\tau} = \frac{1}{K} \sum_{k=1}^{K} \check{\tau}_k.$$

Theorem 3.1 in Chernozhukov et al. (2017) shows that the cross-fitted estimator $\check{\tau}$ is asymptotically Gaussian under reasonable conditions. There is no theory for choosing K, but traditionally recommended values are $K = 2, 4, 5$. The term *cross-fitting* comes from the particular technique of sample partitioning adopted here, where the auxiliary sample I_k^C used to estimate η_0 and the main sample I_k used to estimate τ_0 are permuted in order to maintain efficiency (the sample I_k is much smaller than n). Sample partitioning is necessary for technical reasons: it allows controlling the residual terms without relying on strong assumptions about the quality of nuisance parameter estimation. In particular cases, Assumption 5.2 can be replaced by the requirement that the nuisance parameter is estimated at a rate of $n^{-1/4}$ in the worst case scenario (Chernozhukov et al., 2018). Performance guarantees exist for certain versions of most classical machine learning methods, which makes it possible to satisfy this condition. This allows for the use of numerous methods to estimate the nuisance parameter. Intuitively, sample splitting eliminates bias arising from overfitting by using an auxiliary sample solely for estimating the nuisance parameter η_0 and then using the main sample solely for prediction.

Remark 5.5 Double machine learning, standard error estimation

The standard error of the previous estimator is easily estimated by computing:

$$\widehat{\sigma}^2 = \frac{1}{n}\sum_{i=1}^{n}\psi(Z_i, \check{\tau}, \widehat{\eta}_{k(i)})^2,$$

where $k(i) = \{k \in \{1, \ldots, K\} : i \in I_k\}$. Thus, an asymptotic $1 - \alpha$ confidence interval is given by:

$$\left[\check{\tau} \pm \Phi^{-1}\left(1 - \frac{\alpha}{2}\right)\frac{\widehat{\sigma}}{\sqrt{n}}\right].$$

Notice that the sample splitting technique advocated here introduces more uncertainty, which must be taken into account when presenting the results. Chernozhukov et al. (2017) propose to replicate this procedure S times by considering S different random partitions of the sample and recommend reporting the average estimator through cross-fitting, along with a corrected standard error.

Remark 5.6 In practice

Suppose that we observe the outcome, the treatment status, and a set of covariates $(Z_i)_{i=1,\ldots,n} = (Y_i, D_i, X_i)_{i=1,\ldots,n}$ from a population of interest and we want to estimate the treatment effect for the treated τ_0^{ATT}. Here is a possible strategy:

1. We partition the indices $\{1, \ldots, n\}$ into two, so that each set I_1, I_2 has a size $n/2$.
2. Using only the sample I_1, we construct a ML estimator of $g(0, X)$ and $m(X)$. For example, we can estimate $g(0, X)$ by training a feedforward neural network on Y_i and X_i for the untreated individuals in this sample. We denote this estimator by $\widehat{g}_{I_1}(x)$.

Continued

Remark 5.6 *Continued*

Similarly, $m(X)$ could be estimated by performing a Logit-Lasso on D_i and X_i in this sample. We denote this estimator by $\widehat{m}_{I_1}(x)$.

3. Now, let's use these estimators on sample I_2 to compute the treatment effect

$$\check{\tau}_{I_2} := \frac{1}{\sum_{i \in I_2} D_i} \sum_{i \in I_2} \left(D_i - \frac{\widehat{m}_{I_1}(X_i)}{1 - \widehat{m}_{I_1}(X_i)} (1 - D_i) \right) (Y_i - \widehat{g}_{I_1}(X_i))$$

4. We repeat steps 2–3, swapping the roles of I_1 and I_2 to obtain $\check{\tau}_{I_1}$.
5. We compute the average of the two estimators:

$$\check{\tau} = \frac{\check{\tau}_{I_1} + \check{\tau}_{I_2}}{2}.$$

5.4 Simulations: regularization bias

This simulation exercise illustrates two observations: (i) the naive post-selection estimator suffers from a significant regularization bias, (ii) the cross-fitting estimator trades off a higher bias for a lower mean squared error compared to the immunized estimator that uses the entire sample.

5.4.1 Data-generating process

Let's start by describing the DGP. The outcome equation is linear: $Y_i = D_i \tau_0 + X_i' \beta_0 + \varepsilon_i$, where $\tau_0 = 0.5$, $\varepsilon_i \perp\!\!\!\perp X_i$, and $\varepsilon_i \sim \mathcal{N}(0, 1)$. The treatment equation follows a Probit model, $D_i | X_i \sim \text{Probit}(X_i' \delta_0)$. The covariates are simulated as $X_i \sim \mathcal{N}(0, \Sigma)$, where each entry of the variance-covariance matrix is defined as follows: $\Sigma_{j,k} = .5^{|j-k|}$. Every other element of X_i is replaced by 1 if $X_{i,j} > 0$ and 0 otherwise. A crucial aspect of the DGP lies in the form of the coefficients δ_0 and β_0:

$$\beta_{0j} = \begin{cases} \rho_d(-1)^j / j^2, & \text{if } j < p/2 \\ 0, & \text{otherwise} \end{cases}, \quad \delta_{0j} = \begin{cases} \rho_y(-1)^j / j^2, & \text{if } j < p/2 \\ \rho_y(-1)^{j+1} / (p - j + 1)^2, & \text{otherwise} \end{cases}$$

Both equations are in an approximately sparse framework. The constants ρ_y and ρ_d are defined to set the signal-to-noise ratio, in the sense that a larger constant ρ_y implies a more important role for the covariates. For simplicity, we express them in terms of the R^2 of each equation in the DGP. The trick here is that some variables that are important for the treatment assignment are not relevant for the outcome equation. The fact that the selection procedure in one equation omits certain variables relevant for the outcome should create a bias and a non-Gaussian behavior.

5.4.2 Estimators

We estimate a model based on linear equations for both the outcome and the treatment as in Section 4.5, although it does not correspond to the DGP. We compare three estimators:

1. A post-selection estimator where a Lasso selection step is performed using the outcome equation described in Section 4.4;
2. A double selection estimator based on the Lasso, described in Section 4.5;
3. A double selection estimator based on the Lasso with cross-fitting ($K = 5$) as described in Section 5.3.

We report the bias, the RMSE and the coverage rate. The coverage rate is defined as the proportion of simulations for which the true τ_0 is contained in the 95% confidence interval. It is possible to play with these simulations using the script in the GitHub repository `DoubleML_Simulation.R`. This file defines each step and uses very few packages so that you can easily follow what is happening. The Lasso regression is coded from scratch in `functions/LassoFISTA.R`. Table 5.1 and Figure 5.1 show the result in a particular high-dimensional setting.

5.5 Empirical application: job training program

We revisit the dataset from LaLonde (1986) using the application in Bléhaut et al. (2023). This dataset was originally constructed to evaluate the impact of

Table 5.1 Estimation of τ_0

	Estimator:		
	Post-selection naive	Double selection simple	Double selection cross-fitting
	(1)	(2)	(3)
Bias	0.397	0.012	0.061
$\sqrt{MSE}$	0.457	0.186	0.235
Coverage rate	0.212	0.942	0.915

Note: Parameter values: $R = 10000$, $n = 200$, $p = 300$, $K = 5$, $\tau_0 = 0.5$, $R_y^2 = 0.1$, $R_d^2 = 0.8$. The curve represents the density of the best unbiased estimator.

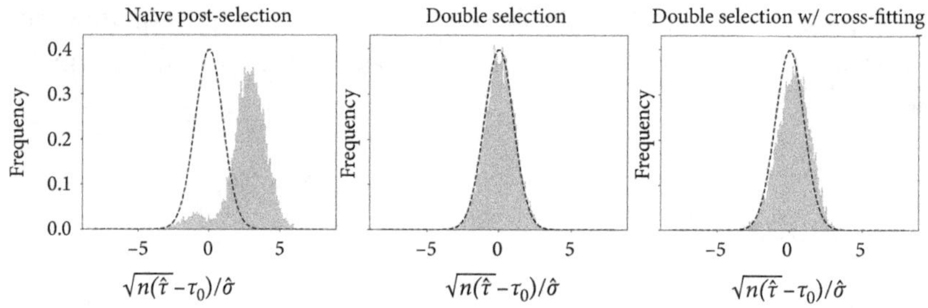

Figure 5.1 Simulated distributions of $\widehat{\tau} - \tau_0$

Note: $R = 10000, n = 200, p = 300, K = 5, \tau_0 = 0.5, R_y^2 = 0.1, R_d^2 = 0.8$. The curve represents the density of the best unbiased estimator.

the National Supported Work (NSW) program. The NSW is a temporary and subsidized vocational training program that targets individuals facing persistent employment access issues, such as former delinquents, recovering drug addicts, long-term social benefit recipients, and school dropouts. Here, the quantity of interest is the average treatment effect on the treated (ATT), defined as the impact of program participation on the annual earnings in 1978 in dollars. The treated group consists of individuals randomly assigned to this program from the at-risk population ($n_1 = 185$). Two control groups are available. The first is experimental: it is directly comparable to the treated group as it was generated by a randomized trial (sample size $n_0 = 260$). The second comes from the Panel Study of Income Dynamics (PSID) (sample size $n_0 = 2490$). The presence of the experimental sample allows to establish a benchmark to evaluate the ATT computed with observational data. We use these datasets to illustrate the tools discussed in the chapter.

To allow for a flexible specification, we consider the framework of Farrell (2015) and take the raw covariates in the dataset (age, education level, indicator of being African-American or Hispanic, marital status, absence of a diploma, income in 1974, income in 1975, absence of income in 1974, absence of income in 1975), two-way interactions between the four continuous variables and categorical variables, pairwise interactions between the dummy variables, and up to fifth-degree polynomial transformations of the continuous variables. The continuous variables are linearly rescaled to the interval [0, 1]. We end up with 172 variables among which we need to perform selection. The experimental benchmark for the estimation of the ATT is \$1,794 (633). We use the `hdm` package to implement Lasso and Logit-Lasso, and the `randomForest` package to grow a random forest of 500 trees. We divide the sample into five equally sized chunks.

The file `DoubleML_Lalonde.R` details each step and calculates an ATT estimate where the propensity score and the outcome functions are estimated using (i) a Lasso procedure and (ii) a random forest. We compute standard errors and confidence intervals. Table 5.2 presents the results. With or without taking into account

Table 5.2 Treatment effect in LaLonde (1986)

	Estimator		
	Experimental	Cross-fitting 1 Partition	Cross-fitting 20 Partitions
	(1)	(2)	(3)
OLS	1794 (633)		
Lasso		2305 (676)	2403 (685)
Random forest		7509 (6711)	1732 (1953)

multiple data partitions, the Lasso procedure ends up being quite close to the experimental estimate. The results are more mixed for the random forest: the simple cross-fitting procedure gives very imprecise results. This could be due to a particularly unfortunate split or a particularly poor performance of the standard random forest algorithm in this case. When considering multiple data partitions, the point estimate is reasonable but the standard error remains very high. Overall, the take-home message is to be cautious and test multiple machine learning algorithms when possible, and consider many data splits so that the results do not overly depend on the partitions. For a comparison of a wide range of machine learning tools, see Section 6.1 of Chernozhukov et al. (2018).

5.6 Summary

Key concepts

Neyman-orthogonal/immunization procedure, sample splitting, double-machine learning, orthogonal scores for treatment effect estimation.

Questions

1. Is the use of Lasso in the first step of Section 5.1 the key ingredient for solving the post-selection inference problem?
2. What is the *overfitting bias*? How can it be avoided?

Continued

Continued

3. In which case(s) do we prefer to use a random forest rather than a Lasso, and vice versa?
4. What is the objective of sample partitioning, and what is its cost?
5. Which part of the course could justify/motivate the use of the median?

$$\widehat{\tau} = \text{median}\left(\{\widehat{\tau}_k\}_{k=1}^K\right)$$
$$\widehat{\sigma}^{2,\text{ median}} = \text{median}\left(\left\{\widehat{\sigma}_k^2 + \left(\widehat{\tau}_k - \widehat{\tau}\right)^2\right\}_{k=1}^K\right).$$

6. In order to determine the true effect of gender on hourly wage (what is called the gender wage gap), an econometrician proposes to estimate a model with many control variables and present the estimates of a second model where the statistically insignificant control variables from the first model are removed. What do you think of this strategy?

Code and data

The git repository of this book allows the reproduction of the examples from this chapter: `DoubleML_Simulation.R` and `DoubleML_Lalonde.R`, respectively, for the simulations and the empirical application. The R program `functions/LassoFISTA.R` calculates the Lasso estimator.

Additional references

In addition to the prerequisites given in Chapter 2, Hastie et al. (2009) is the reference manual for standard machine learning methods. We also highly recommend reading Athey and Imbens (2019), which targets empirical economists. Regarding this chapter itself, the most complete and clear reference is Chernozhukov et al. (2017). Other similar references, although not necessarily as comprehensive, are Chernozhukov et al. (2015a,b). This presentation by Victor Chernozhukov is a good introduction: youtu.be/eHOjmyoPCFU.

5.7 Proofs and additional results

The proofs in this chapter are intentionally less rigorous than in the previous chapter, in order to provide intuition without getting lost in technical details. We refer the reader to Lemmas 2 and 3 in Chernozhukov et al. (2015a) and Belloni et al. (2017) for the technical details.

Proof of Theorem 5.1 $\check{\tau}$ defined by (5.2) is such that:

$$\check{\tau} = \left[\frac{1}{n}\sum_{i=1}^{n}\Gamma_1(Z_i,\widehat{\eta})\right]^{-1}\frac{1}{n}\sum_{i=1}^{n}\Gamma_2(Z_i,\widehat{\eta}).$$

According to Assumption 5.3, we can verify:

$$\sqrt{n}\,(\tau_0 - \check{\tau}) = \left[\frac{1}{n}\sum_{i=1}^{n}\Gamma_1(Z_i,\widehat{\eta})\right]^{-1}\frac{1}{\sqrt{n}}\sum_{i=1}^{n}\psi(Z_i,\tau_0,\widehat{\eta}). \tag{5.3}$$

First, we need to show that $n^{-1}\sum_{i=1}^{n}\Gamma_1(Z_i,\widehat{\eta}) \to \mathbb{E}\Gamma_1(Z_i,\eta_0)$. By the affine-quadratic Assumption 5.3:

$$\frac{1}{n}\sum_{i=1}^{n}\Gamma_1(Z_i,\widehat{\eta}) = \underbrace{\frac{1}{n}\sum_{i=1}^{n}\Gamma_1(Z_i,\eta_0)}_{:=I_1} + \underbrace{\left[\frac{1}{n}\sum_{i=1}^{n}\partial_\eta\Gamma_1(Z_i,\eta_0)\right]'(\widehat{\eta}-\eta_0)}_{:=I_2}$$
$$\underbrace{+\frac{1}{2}(\widehat{\eta}-\eta_0)'\left[\frac{1}{n}\sum_{i=1}^{n}\partial_\eta\partial_{\eta'}\Gamma_1(Z_i,\eta_0)\right](\widehat{\eta}-\eta_0).}_{:=I_3}$$

Under regularity assumptions, by the Law of Large Numbers, $I_1 \to \mathbb{E}[\Gamma_1(Z_i,\eta_0)]$. Then:

$$|I_2| \leq \left\|\frac{1}{n}\sum_{i=1}^{n}\partial_\eta\Gamma_1(Z_i,\eta_0)\right\|_\infty \|\widehat{\eta}-\eta_0\|_1 \lesssim \sqrt{\frac{s^2\log p}{n}} \to 0,$$

and finally:

$$|I_3| \leq \frac{1}{2}\|\widehat{\eta}-\eta_0\|_2^2\left\|\frac{1}{n}\sum_{i=1}^{n}\partial_\eta\partial_{\eta'}\Gamma_1(Z_i,\eta_0)\right\|_{sp(s\log n)} \lesssim \frac{s\log p}{n} \to 0,$$

if we assume that the sparse norm of the matrix of second-order derivatives (which does not depend on $\widehat{\eta}$) is bounded:

$$\left\|\frac{1}{n}\sum_{i=1}^{n}\partial_\eta\partial_{\eta'}\Gamma_1(Z_i,\eta_0)\right\|_{sp(s\log n)} \lesssim 1,$$

which occurs under reasonable conditions, see Rudelson and Zhou (2013). Secondly, we need to show that $\frac{1}{\sqrt{n}}\sum_{i=1}^{n}\psi(Z_i,\tau_0,\widehat{\eta}) \xrightarrow{d} \mathcal{N}(0,E[\psi^2(Z_i,\tau_0,\eta_0)])$. We consider a similar decomposition:

$$\frac{1}{\sqrt{n}}\sum_{i=1}^{n}\psi(Z_i,\tau_0,\widehat{\eta}) = \underbrace{\frac{1}{\sqrt{n}}\sum_{i=1}^{n}\psi(Z_i,\tau_0,\eta_0)}_{:=I_1'}$$
$$+\underbrace{\left[\frac{1}{\sqrt{n}}\sum_{i=1}^{n}\partial_\eta\psi(Z_i,\tau_0,\eta_0)\right]'(\widehat{\eta}-\eta_0)}_{:=I_2'} \tag{5.4}$$
$$+\underbrace{\frac{\sqrt{n}}{2}(\widehat{\eta}-\eta_0)'\left[\frac{1}{n}\sum_{i=1}^{n}\partial_\eta\partial_{\eta'}\psi(Z_i,\tau_0,\eta_0)\right](\widehat{\eta}-\eta_0).}_{:=I_3'}$$

A standard central limit theorem guarantees that $I_1' \overset{d}{\to} \mathcal{N}(0,\mathbb{E}[\psi^2(Z_i,\tau_0,\eta_0)])$ as long as $\mathbb{E}[\psi^2(Z_i,\tau_0,\eta_0)] < \infty$. We have:

$$|I_2'| \leq \left\|\frac{1}{\sqrt{n}}\sum_{i=1}^{n}\partial_\eta\psi(Z_i,\tau_0,\eta_0)\right\|_\infty \|\widehat{\eta}-\eta_0\|_1 \lesssim \frac{s\log p}{\sqrt{n}} \to 0,$$

provided we have a moderate deviation bound:

$$\left\|\frac{1}{\sqrt{n}}\sum_{i=1}^{n}\partial_\eta\psi(Z_i,\tau_0,\eta_0)\right\|_\infty \lesssim \sqrt{\log p},$$

which occurs under weak conditions using a more general version of lemma 4.6, thanks to condition (5.1) in Assumption 5.1. Finally:

$$|I_3'| \leq \frac{\sqrt{n}}{2}\|\widehat{\eta}-\eta_0\|_2^2\left\|\frac{1}{n}\sum_{i=1}^{n}\partial_\eta\partial_{\eta'}\psi(Z_i,\tau_0,\eta_0)\right\|_{sp(s\log n)} \lesssim \frac{s\log p}{\sqrt{n}} \to 0,$$

if we assume that the norm of the matrix is bounded:

$$\left\|\frac{1}{n}\sum_{i=1}^{n}\partial_\eta\partial_{\eta'}\psi(Z_i,\tau_0,\eta_0)\right\|_{sp(s\log n)} \lesssim 1.$$

These steps prove the desired result given Equation (5.3). □

Chapter 6
High dimension and endogeneity

This chapter reviews key findings related to variable selection in the instrumental variable (IV) linear model. In particular, we relax the exogeneity assumption, $\mathbb{E}[\varepsilon|D,X] = 0$, of the model (4.5) in Chapter 4. Instead, we assume that the econometrician is observing a set of IVs that satisfy an exogeneity assumption specified below, and ask how to select the best set of these instruments to obtain the most precise inference. The number of potential candidates can also be greater than the sample size. We distinguish two different cases of high dimension in the IV model:

- the case with *(truly) many instruments*, i.e., $p_n^z > n$, where the number of instruments p_n^z is allowed to grow with the sample size n,
- the case with *(truly) many endogenous variables*, i.e., $p_n^d > n$, where p_n^d is the number of endogenous variables. In this case, we always assume that we observe more instruments than endogenous variables, $p_n^z > p_n^d$.

These two frameworks are very natural in empirical applications, but inference in the second case is more complicated and will not be addressed here (see the remark at the end of the section). IV techniques for addressing endogeneity problems are widely used but can lead to imprecise inference. As introduced in Section 3.4.2, with few instruments and controls, and following Amemiya (1974), Chamberlain (1987), and Newey (1990), we can try to improve the precision of IV techniques by using *optimal instruments*. We consider the model below:

Assumption 6.1 (Linear IV model). *Consider n i.i.d. observations* (Y_i, D_i, X_i, Z_i) *such that:*

$$Y_i = D_i\tau_0 + X_i'\beta_0 + \varepsilon_i, \ \mathbb{E}[\varepsilon_i] = 0, \ \mathbb{E}[\varepsilon_i|Z_i, X_i] = 0, \tag{6.1}$$

where

1. *X_i is a vector of p_n^x exogenous control variables, including the constant;*
2. *D_i is an endogenous variable, $\mathbb{E}[\varepsilon_i|D_i] \neq 0$;*
3. *Z_i is a vector containing p_n^z instruments;*
4. ***There is a large number of controls** $p_n^x \gg n$ **and instruments** $p_n^z \gg n$.*

For simplicity, we define $p^x := p_n^x$ and $p^z := p_n^z$. Even when the researcher has only one valid instrument Z, they can still consider a large number of transformations of this initial instrument $(f_1(Z), \ldots, f_p(Z))'$ using series estimators based on B-Splines,

Machine Learning for Econometrics. Christophe Gaillac and Jérémy L'Hour, Oxford University Press.
 DOI: 10.1093/9780198918868.003.0006

polynomials, etc. This makes it a high-dimensional problem. This also highlights the generality of the context of the Assumption 6.1. In Section 6.1, we present the methodology of Belloni et al. (2012), using the Lasso and post-Lasso techniques to estimate the first stage regression of the endogenous variables on the instruments. As described in Chernozhukov et al. (2015b), this problem follows the structure of the double machine learning method described in Section 4.5. The estimation of the parameters of interest uses *orthogonal* or *immune* estimation equations that are robust to small perturbations in the nuisance parameter, similar to what we already introduced in Section 4.5. One can thus interpret this chapter as an other application of these tools. For simplicity, here we restrict our focus to the case of conditional homoscedasticity:

$$\mathbb{E}\left[\varepsilon^2|Z,X\right] = \sigma^2.$$

We refer to Belloni et al. (2012) for the general case. Building on the results of Section 3.4 on *optimal instruments*, in Section 6.1 we describe how to use the sparsity assumption to efficiently estimate the optimal instruments, which are conditional expectations $\mathbb{E}[S|Z,X]$ where $S := (D,X')$, in the present high-dimensional setting. Note that there are many ways to estimate $\mathbb{E}[S|Z,X]$ under different assumptions, but we limit ourselves to this context.

Remark 6.1 Large number of endogenous variables

In this book, we restrict ourselves to the case where the number p^d of endogenous regressors is fixed. However, several recent articles, in particular Gautier and Rose (2011), Gautier and Tsybakov (2013), and Belloni et al. (2017), consider the inference of a high-dimensional parameter τ_0 with a high-dimensional nuisance parameter.

This goes beyond the scope of this course but can be useful in the following situations:

- When economic theory is not explicit enough about the variables that belong to the true model. Here, the search for the "right" subset of potentially endogenous variables to select in the outcome equation may be impossible.
- We consider many non-linear functions of an endogenous regressor, especially when the outcome equation is of the form:

$$Y = \sum_{k=1}^{p^d} \tau_{0,k} f_k(D) + X'\beta_0 + \varepsilon,$$

where $\{f_k\}_{k=1}^{p^d}$ is a family of functions that capture non-linearities.

6.1 Specific model for instrumental variables

We now assume the linear first-stage model:

$$D = X'\gamma_0 + Z'\delta_0 + u, \quad u \perp\!\!\!\perp (Z, X), \tag{FS}$$

where, as described in Assumption 6.2 below, δ_0 only has a few important components (approximate sparsity). The instruments Z can be correlated with the controls X. To capture this correlation, we use the model:

$$Z = \mathbf{\Pi} X + \zeta, \quad X \perp\!\!\!\perp \zeta, \quad \mathbf{\Pi} \in \mathcal{M}_{p_n^x, p_n^x}(\mathbb{R}), \tag{6.2}$$

which gives the following two equations for D and Y:

$$\begin{aligned} D &= X'\gamma_0 + X'\mathbf{\Pi}'\delta_0 + u + \zeta'\delta_0 = X'\underbrace{(\gamma_0 + \mathbf{\Pi}'\delta_0)}_{:=\nu_0} + \underbrace{u + \zeta'\delta_0}_{:=\rho^d} \\ &= X'\nu_0 + \rho^d, \end{aligned} \tag{6.3}$$

where $\rho^d \perp\!\!\!\perp X$ and

$$\begin{aligned} Y &= X'(\nu_0\tau_0) + X'\beta_0 + \varepsilon + \tau_0\rho^d = X'\underbrace{(\nu_0\tau_0 + \beta_0)}_{:=\theta_0} + \underbrace{\varepsilon + \tau_0\rho^d}_{:=\rho^y} \\ &= X'\theta_0 + \rho^y, \end{aligned} \tag{6.4}$$

where $\rho^y \perp\!\!\!\perp X$. We make three preliminary remarks. First, the following two cases naturally arise in practice:

1. either the list of available and possible instruments is large, while the econometrician knows that only a few of them are relevant;
2. or, from a small list of regressors Z, optimal instruments can be approximated using a basis of functions (series estimators using B-Splines, polynomials, etc.). This case is treated by non-sparse methods in Newey (1990). In this decomposition, the potential number p^z of necessary functions $\{f_j\}_{j=1}^{p^z}$ can be higher than n. Note that instead of Z, one could also consider transformations of the initial instruments

$$f = (f_1, \ldots, f_p)' = (f_1(Z), \ldots, f_p(Z))'.$$

Second, as in Section 4.5, the key assumption that we make on *the nuisance component* is *approximate sparsity*. This means that $A(Z, X) = \mathbb{E}[S|Z, X]$ (recall that here $p^d = 1$) is assumed to be well approximated by a few ($s \ll n$) of these p^z instruments. We denote the nuisance component by $\eta_0 = (\theta_0, \nu_0, \delta_0, \gamma_0)$ and assume that it can be decomposed into a sparse component η_0^m and a non-sparse component but of relatively low amplitude η_0^r:

Assumption 6.2 (Approximate sparsity). *There exists $c > 0$ such that*

$$\eta_0 = \eta_0^m + \eta_0^r, \quad supp(\eta_0^m) \cap supp(\eta_0^r) = \emptyset$$
$$\|\eta_0^m\|_0 \leq s, \quad \|\eta_0^r\|_2 \leq c\sqrt{s/n}, \quad \|\eta_0^r\|_1 \leq c\sqrt{s^2/n}.$$

Third, similarly to Section 4.5, we must carefully choose the moment equations so that model selection errors in the estimation of the nuisance parameter component (here, the optimal instrument or its coefficients in its decomposition on a basis) have a limited impact on the estimation of the parameter of interest τ_0. We now show how the problem of optimal instruments can be transposed into the framework of the immunization procedure developed in Section 4.5, and in particular in the quadratic-affine model defined in (5.3).

6.2 Immunization for instrumental variables

Starting from Equation (6.1), Chernozhukov et al. (2015b) propose to estimate the parameter of interest using orthogonalized moments, following the idea described in Section 5.1 and the Frisch–Waugh–Lovell theorem.

Noting that the optimal instrument is $\mathbb{E}[D|X, Z] = X'\gamma_0 + Z'\delta_0$, the problem arises from the fact that the moment condition

$$\mathbb{E}[\varphi(W, \tau_0, \eta_0)] = 0 \text{ where } \varphi(W, \tau_0, \eta_0) := (Y - \tau_0 D - X'\beta_0)(X'\gamma_0 + Z'\delta_0),$$

does not satisfy the orthogonality conditions:

$$\mathbb{E}\left[\frac{\partial\varphi(W, \tau_0, \eta_0)}{\partial\beta}\right] = \mathbb{E}[X(X'\gamma_0 + Z'\delta_0)] \neq 0. \tag{6.5}$$

As in the proof of Theorem 5.1 in Section 5.7, a key tool for obtaining asymptotic behavior is the Taylor expansion of the empirical counterpart of this equation, $(\tau, \eta) \mapsto \sum_{i=1}^n \varphi(W_i, \tau, \eta)/n$ around (τ_0, η_0). Here, as in Equation (5.4), the first-order term related to the nuisance parameter will be problematic to obtain asymptotic normality. Indeed, under weak conditions on the convergence of the parameter estimation η_0, typically $\|\widehat{\eta} - \eta_0\| = O_p(n^{-1/4})$, this term does not vanish.

The idea is then to use an auxiliary moment equation $\mathbb{E}(g(W, \tau_0, \eta_0)) = 0$, such that the linear combination of the two $\psi := \varphi - \lambda' g$, with $\lambda \in \mathbb{R}^p$, satisfies the orthogonality conditions. In theory, we should take as many auxiliary moment equations as the dimensions of the nuisance parameter η_0. However, we simplify directly here since the equation related to φ is already orthogonal with respect to γ_0 and δ_0, and we will simply ensure that the one related to g is also orthogonal. The natural equation in our framework comes from the exogeneity condition of X, which gives:

$$\mathbb{E}[g(W,\tau_0,\eta_0)] = 0 \text{ with } g(W,\tau_0,\eta_0) := (Y - \tau_0 D - X'\beta_0)X.$$

Imposing the orthogonality condition thus amounts to choosing $\lambda \in \mathbb{R}^p$ such that $\mathbb{E}\left[\frac{\partial\psi(W,\tau_0,\eta_0)}{\partial\beta}\right] = 0$. This can be rewritten as $\lambda \in \mathbb{R}^p$ satisfying the system:

$$\mathbb{E}\left[\frac{\partial\varphi(W,\tau_0,\eta_0)}{\partial\beta}\right] = \mathbb{E}\left[\frac{\partial g(W,\tau_0,\eta_0)'}{\partial\beta}\right]\lambda.$$

We then obtain directly using (6.5) and (6.2) that taking $\lambda = \gamma_0 + \Pi'\delta_0 = \nu_0$ ensures this condition and therefore

$$\mathbb{E}\left[\psi(W,\tau_0,\eta_0)\right] = 0, \tag{6.6}$$

where:

$$\begin{aligned}
\psi(W,\tau_0,\eta_0) &= \left(Y - \tau_0 D - X'\beta_0\right)\left(Z'\delta_0 + X'\gamma_0 - X'\nu_0\right) &(6.7)\\
&= \left(Y - \tau_0 D - X'\left(\theta_0 - \nu_0\tau_0\right)\right)\left(Z'\delta_0 + X'\gamma_0 - X'\nu_0\right)\\
&= \left(Y - X'\theta_0 - (D - X'\nu_0)\tau_0\right)\left(Z'\delta_0 + X'\gamma_0 - X'\nu_0\right) &(6.8)\\
&= \left((Y - \mathbb{E}\left[Y|X\right]) - (D - \mathbb{E}\left[D|X\right])\tau_0\right)\left(\mathbb{E}\left[D|X,Z\right] - \mathbb{E}\left[D|X\right]\right).
\end{aligned}$$

We provide in Section 6.6 another way to derive this equation using projections. The instrument for D, controlling for the correlation between Z and X, is given by

$$\begin{aligned}
A(W) &= \mathbb{E}\left[D|Z,X\right] - \mathbb{E}\left[D|X\right] &(6.9)\\
&= Z'\delta_0 + X'\gamma_0 - X'(\gamma_0 + \mathbf{\Pi}'\delta_0)\\
&= (Z - \mathbf{\Pi}X)'\delta_0 &(6.10)\\
&= \zeta'\delta_0.
\end{aligned}$$

It is important to note that model (6.8) can be rewritten as the affine-quadratic model (5.3) using:

$$\begin{aligned}
M(\tau_0,\eta) &= \mathbb{E}\left[\Gamma_1(W,\eta)\tau_0 - \Gamma_2(W,\eta)\right] = \Gamma_1(\eta)\tau_0 - \Gamma_2(\eta), &(6.11)\\
\Gamma_1(\eta) &:= \mathbb{E}\left[\Gamma_1(W,\eta)\right] := \mathbb{E}\left[\left(D - X'\nu\right)\left(Z'\delta + X'\gamma - X'\nu\right)\right],\\
\Gamma_2(\eta) &:= \mathbb{E}\left[\Gamma_2(W,\eta)\right] := \mathbb{E}\left[\left(Y - X'\theta\right)\left(Z'\delta + X'\gamma - X'\nu\right)\right].
\end{aligned}$$

We summarize the estimation algorithm proposed by Chernozhukov et al. (2015b) before studying its theoretical properties, which follow from those established for the affine-quadratic model (5.3):

- **Step 1:** Perform a Lasso or post-Lasso regression of D on (X, Z) to obtain $\hat{\gamma}$ and $\hat{\delta}$ via (FS);
- **Step 2:** Perform a Lasso or post-Lasso regression of Y on X to obtain $\hat{\theta}$ via (6.4);
- **Step 3:** Perform a Lasso or post-Lasso regression of $\hat{D} = X'\hat{\gamma}+Z'\hat{\delta}$ on X to obtain $\hat{\nu}$ via (6.3);
- **Step 4:** The estimator of η_0 is $\hat{\eta} = (\hat{\theta}, \hat{\nu}, \hat{\gamma}, \hat{\delta})'$;
- **Step 5:** Finally, the estimator of τ is

$$\check{\tau} = \underset{\tau \in \mathbb{R}}{\operatorname{argmin}} \left\| \sqrt{n}\widehat{M}(\tau, \hat{\eta}) \right\|^2 = \left[\widehat{\Gamma}_1(\hat{\eta})'\widehat{\Gamma}_1(\hat{\eta})\right]^{-1} \widehat{\Gamma}_1(\hat{\eta})'\widehat{\Gamma}_2(\hat{\eta}).$$

Note that step 5 consists of performing two-stage least squares (2SLS) using the residuals $Y - X'\hat{\theta}$ from step 2 as the dependent variable, the residuals $D - \hat{D}$ from step 1 as the covariate, and the residuals $\hat{D} - \hat{\nu}'X$ from step 3 as the instruments.

Using the formulation (6.11) of the model as an affine-quadratic model (see Assumption 5.3) and if the assumptions of Theorem 5.1 are satisfied, namely if

1. the model is parsimonious, i.e., assumption 6.2 with $\eta_0 = \eta_0^m$;
2. the assumption (ORT) $\partial_\eta M(\tau_0, \eta_0) = 0$ is satisfied;
3. we assume high-quality estimation of the nuisance parameter;
4. the condition of growing number of relevant components s with the number of observations $s \log(p)/\sqrt{n} \to 0$, where $p := p^z + p^x$, is satisfied;

then we can apply Theorem 5.1 and obtain directly the asymptotic normality

$$\sqrt{n}\,(\check{\tau} - \tau_0) \to \mathcal{N}(0, \sigma_\Gamma^2), \tag{6.12}$$

where $\sigma_\Gamma^2 := \mathbb{E}[\psi(W, \tau_0, \eta_0)^2]/\mathbb{E}[\Gamma_1(W, \eta_0)]^2$.

Remark 6.2 "Small number" of controls

In the case of a "small number" of controls (see Belloni et al., 2012), θ_0 is no longer a "nuisance" parameter in the sense that no selection needs to be made on X. In this case, we can take $A(W) = \mathbb{E}[D|Z, X]$, as the (ORT) condition does not need to be satisfied with respect to θ, i.e., we can have $\partial_\theta M(\tau_0, \eta_0) \neq 0$.

Remark 6.3 Approximate sparsity

If we use the assumption of approximate sparsity 6.2, we must impose the following assumption, and the result (6.12) is still valid (see Chernozhukov et al., 2015b).

Assumption 6.3 (Estimation of nuisance parameters with high quality and approximate sparsity) *We make Assumption 6.2 and assume that $\hat{\eta}$ satisfies, with high probability,*

$$\|\hat{\eta}\|_0 \leq s,$$

$$\|\hat{\eta} - \eta_0^m\|_2 \leq \sqrt{\frac{s}{n}\log p},$$

$$\|\hat{\eta} - \eta_0^m\|_1 \leq \sqrt{\frac{s^2}{n}\log p}.$$

6.3 Simulations

Data generating process (DGP). We use a DGP similar to that of Chernozhukov et al. (2015a): $(Y_i, D_i, Z_i, X_i)_{i=1}^n$ i.i.d. and satisfying

$$\begin{aligned} Y_i &= \tau_0 D_i + X_i'\beta_0 + 2\varepsilon_i \\ D_i &= X_i'\gamma_0 + Z_i'\delta_0 + U_i \\ Z_i &= \mathbf{\Pi} X_i + \alpha\zeta_i, \end{aligned}$$

where $\alpha = 0.125$ and

$$\begin{pmatrix} \varepsilon_i \\ u_i \\ \zeta_i \\ x_i \end{pmatrix} \sim \mathcal{N}\left(0, \begin{pmatrix} 1 & 0.6 & 0 & 0 \\ 0.6 & 1 & 0 & 0 \\ 0 & 0 & I_{p^z} & 0 \\ 0 & 0 & 0 & \Sigma \end{pmatrix}\right),$$

where

- $\mathbf{\Sigma}$ is a $p^x \times p^x$ matrix with $\Sigma_{kj} = (0.5)^{|j-k|}$ and $\boldsymbol{I}_{p^z}$ is the identity matrix of size $p^z \times p^z$;
- The number of controls is set to 100, the number of instruments to 50, and the number of observations to 300;

Table 6.1 Simulation results for estimation of τ_0

	Estimator:		
	Naive post-selection (1)	Double selection (2)	Oracle (3)
Bias	0.07	0.01	0.00
Root MSE	0.28	0.30	0.05
MAD	0.19	0.20	0.03

Note: Based on 2000 simulations with the following parameters: $n = 300$, $p^x = 100$, $p^z = 50$, $K = 3$, $\tau_0 = 1.5$. Root MSE: root mean square error; MAD: mean absolute deviation.

- The most interesting part of the DGP is the form of the coefficients β_0, γ_0, and δ_0:

$$\beta_{0j} = \begin{cases} 1/4, j < 4 \\ 0, \text{otherwise} \end{cases},$$

$\gamma_0 = \beta_0$, and $\delta_{0j} = 3/j^2$. We are in a framework where approximate sparsity holds for these two equations.
- $\mathbf{\Pi} = \left[\boldsymbol{I}_{p^z}, \mathbf{0}_{p^z \times (p^x - p^z)}\right]$ and $\tau_0 = 1.5$.

We compare here three estimators:

1. An "oracle" estimator, where the nuisance parameter coefficients are known, and where we run a standard IV regression of $Y_i - \mathbb{E}[Y_i|X_i]$ on $D_i - \mathbb{E}[D_i|X_i]$ using the oracle $\zeta_i'\delta_0$ as an instrument;
2. A naive non-orthogonal estimator, where we use the Lasso regression of D on (X, Z) to select the set of controls and instruments that enter the instrumental equation: $I_X^D = \{j : \hat{\delta}_j \neq 0\}$, $I_Z^D = \{j : \hat{\delta}_j \neq 0\}$. We perform a Lasso regression of Y on X to select the set of controls that enter the outcome equation: $I_X^Y = \{j : \hat{\delta}_j \neq 0\}$. We then perform the 2SLS regression of Y on D and the selected controls and two selected sets $I_X^D \cup I_X^Y$ and I_Z^D;
3. A double selection estimator using Lasso as described in Section 5.

Table 6.1 and Figure 6.1 present the results of this simulation exercise. They show that the naive post-selection estimator has a larger regularization bias.

6.4 Applications

6.4.1 Logistic demand model

We present the logistic demand model in a context where only market share data is observed. We refer to the important articles by Berry et al. (1995), Berry (1994),

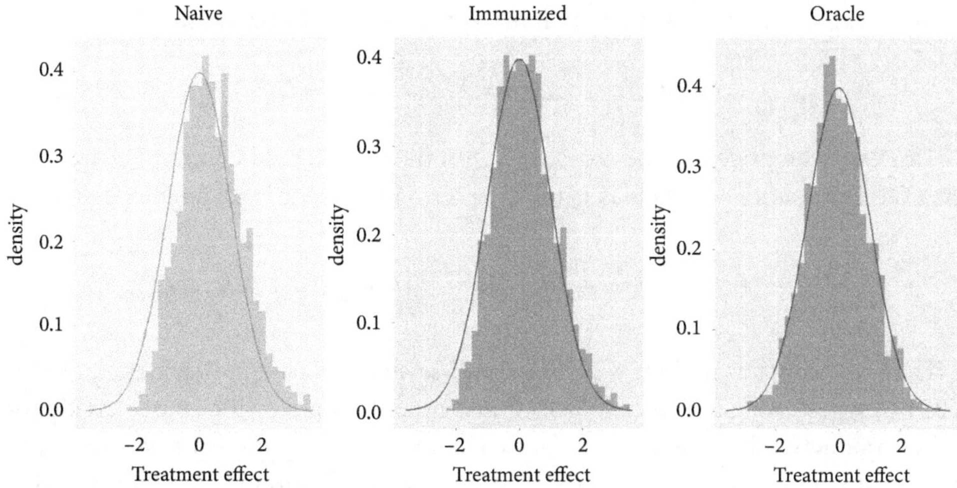

Figure 6.1 Distribution of $\hat{\tau} - \tau_0$
Note: See Table (6.1) .

and Nevo (2001) for more details on this classic context. The model describes the demand for a product in the space of characteristics. This description is based on the idea that a product can be described by a number of its characteristics and that consumers assign value to them. For example, for a car: efficiency, fuel type, engine power, etc. We assume to know the set of all possible choices for the consumer, who chooses among J products the one that maximizes their utility. The individual utility for choosing product $j \in \{0, \dots, J\}$ is random from the econometrician's point of view and is modeled by

$$u_{i,j} = X_j'\beta_0 - \tau_0 P_j + \zeta_j + \varepsilon_{i,j}, \quad (\varepsilon_{ij}, \zeta_j) \perp\!\!\!\perp X_j, \tag{6.13}$$

where $\varepsilon_{ij} \sim F(\cdot) = \exp(-\exp(-\cdot))$ is an idiosyncratic component that follows a type I extreme value distribution; and ζ_j is a component representing the average market's specific taste for product j, which is arbitrarily correlated with the price. This gives the expression for the choice probabilities as follows

$$P_{i,j} = \frac{\exp(\delta_j)}{1 + \sum_{k=1}^{J} \exp(\delta_k)}, \quad \delta_j = X_j^T\beta_0 - \tau_0 P_j + \zeta_j. \tag{6.14}$$

Moreover, the econometrician does not observe individual choices, but only the market shares of product j: $s_{j,t} = Q_{jt}/M_t$ in market t, where M_t and $Q_{j,t}$ are respectively the total number of households and number of people choosing product j in this market. This gives

$$s_{j,t} = \frac{\exp\left(X_{j,t}'\beta_0 - \tau_0 P_{j,t} + \zeta_{j,t}\right)}{1 + \sum_{k=1}^{J} \left(X_{k,t}'\beta_0 - \tau_0 P_{k,t} + \zeta_{k,t}\right)}.$$

Thus, using $s_{j,t}/s_{0,t}$ and assuming that market shares are non-zero, we obtain

$$\log(s_{j,t}) - \log(s_{0,t}) = X'_{j,t}\beta_0 - \tau_0 P_{j,t} + \zeta_{j,t}. \tag{6.15}$$

However, the price may be correlated with the unobserved component $\zeta_{j,t}$, such that OLS estimation would bias τ_0 towards zero. We use the instrumental equation:

$$P_{j,t} = Z'_{j,t}\delta_0 + X'_{j,t}\gamma_0 + u_{j,t}, \quad \mathbb{E}\left[u_{j,t}|Z_{j,t}, X_{j,t}\right] = 0. \tag{6.16}$$

Here, the controls include a constant and several covariates. Berry et al. (1995) (BLP) suggest using the so-called "BLP instruments," namely the characteristics of other products, which may satisfy an exclusion restriction, for any $j' \neq j$ and t', as well as any function of these characteristics. The justification is that if a product is close in the characteristic space to its competitors, this can have an impact on margins, and then on prices – however, cost-based instruments should be preferred, but they are rarely available. Thus, we are left with a set of potentially high-dimensional instruments to address the endogeneity of prices $P_{j,t}$.

Berry et al. (1995) solve this problem by considering sums of product characteristics excluding product j produced by firm f, namely, for the k-th characteristic of this product:

$$Z_{k,j,t} = \left(\sum_{j' \neq j, j' \in \mathcal{I}_f} X_{k,j',t}, \sum_{j' \neq j, j' \notin \mathcal{I}_f} X_{k,j',t} \right),$$

where $\mathcal{I}_f$ is the set of products manufactured by firm f. But the tools developed in the previous section allow for broader possibilities. Chernozhukov et al. (2015a) apply these techniques to revisit the results of Berry et al. (1995). We apply the same tools to a (semi-synthetic) dataset from Nevo (2001) on the demand for ready-to-eat cereals (see the dataset `cerealps3.csv`).

We augment the set of potential controls with all first-order interactions of the baseline variables, quadratics and cubics in all continuous baseline variables, and a time trend that yields a total of 24 "augmented" controls. Then sums of these characteristics define potential instruments following Berry et al. (1995), which yields 48 potential instruments. Table 6.2 presents the results using all constructed instruments (labeled "z1-z20"), and in the "augmented 2SLS selection," the squares and cubes of all these instruments. The identity of the controls and the instruments selected in the "augmented" set reveals important non-linearities missing from the base set of variables. Moreover, the selection method provides more plausible estimates for the important quantities of the model, such as price elasticities:

$$\frac{\partial s_j}{\partial P_k}\frac{P_k}{s_j} = \begin{cases} -\tau_0 P_j(1 - S_j) & \text{if } j = k \\ \tau_0 P_k s_k \text{ otherwise} \end{cases}.$$

Table 6.2 Estimation of τ_0

	Price coefficient	Standard error	Number of inelastic products
		Estimator without selection	
OLS Base	–9.63	0.84	586
2SLS Base	–9.48	0.87	990
		2SLS Estimator with "double selection"	
2SLS Base with Selection	−11.29	0.93	224
2SLS Augmented with selection	−11.44	0.91	212

Aside from the classical problems posed by these specific forms (price elasticities nearly proportional to prices, symmetry of cross-price elasticity for the products), facing inelastic demand is also inconsistent with a profit-maximizing price choice in this framework. Therefore, theory predicts that the demand should be elastic for all products, which is not the case with the estimations without selection in Table 6.2. The estimators with selection provide much more plausible estimates in this regard.

6.4.2 Instrument selection for estimating returns to education

We now revisit the analysis of returns to education conducted in Card (1993), where we show how the results are modified when we expand the set of possible instruments. David Card first considers the model with instrumental variables:

$$Y = \tau_0 D + X'\beta_0 + \varepsilon, \quad \varepsilon \perp\!\!\!\perp X$$
$$D = Z'\delta_0 + X'\delta_0 + u, \quad u \perp\!\!\!\perp (Z, X),$$

where Y denotes the logarithm of the individual's weekly wage, D denotes education (in years), X represents a vector of controls, potentially of high dimension, and Z a vector of instrumental variables for education.

In this example, the instruments are the two indicators that determine if a subject grew up near a two-year or a four-year high school. It also suggests using IQ as an instrument for the results of the Knowledge of World Work (KWW) test, when added as a control. The control variables X consist of: age and work experience at the time of the survey, the number of years of education of the subject's father and mother, an indicator of the family situation at the age of 14 (whether the subject lived with both parents or with a single mother), nine indicators related to the region of residence, an indicator coding whether the subject lives in a standard metropolitan statistical area (SMSA) and another indicating whether the subject lives in the south,

Table 6.3 Estimation of returns to education τ_0

	Nb. of instruments	Estimated	Std. error	Fuller estimate	Fuller std. error
OLS		0.065	0.0062		
2SLS	3	0.115	0.033	0.119	0.034
2SLS	66	0.075	0.019	0.083	0.025
DML, post-Lasso	66	0.102	0.031		

Note: Number of observations: 1,604 and number of controls: 19 including KWW. "Fuller" refers to Fuller (1977). OLS: ordinary least squares, 2SLS: two-stage least squares, DML: double machine learning.

an indicator to determine if the subject's race is Black, marital status at the time of the survey, an indicator to determine if the subject had a library card at the age of 14, the results of the KWW test, and interactions. Two options are possible without using selection: either use these four instruments, or interact these instruments with the controls, resulting in 66 instruments in the latter case. In this second case, we must correct the use of many instruments using the estimator of Fuller (1977), implemented in the R package `ivmodel`.

The results presented in Table 6.3, using the code provided on GitHub, show that the post-Lasso selects five instruments from the 66 potential ones, thus providing a relevant selection without prior knowledge. Comparing the standard errors in the case of Lasso with the Fuller estimates with 66 instruments only shows a slight increase.

6.5 Summary

Key concepts

Endogeneity, instrumental variables, optimal instruments, double machine learning, Neyman-orthogonal, sparse model.

Additional references

The framework presented here follows the formalization of Chernozhukov et al. (2015a) and Chernozhukov et al. (2017), but reading Belloni et al. (2012) will provide a slightly different perspective on these methods. From a practical standpoint, the R package **hdm** is complemented by vignettes available at cran.r-project.org/web/packages/hdm/vignettes/hdm.pdf, which summarize the essential results and provide empirical illustrations. Finally, Angrist and Frandsen (2022) propose several applications and demonstrate some limits of using estimators based on the sparsity assumption for causal effect estimation with a large number of instruments, where the first-stage equation may not satisfy this assumption. In this chapter, we studied the Lasso as a regularization technique in this context, but there are other regularizations that are more suitable in these situations where the sparsity assumption seems strong, such as Ridge penalization, spectral cut-off, or principal component approaches (see, e.g., Carrasco, 2012).

Questions

1. Justify why, in the context of treatment effect estimation with endogeneity, the problem of numerous instruments frequently arises. What is the solution that we have described in this chapter?
2. Show that the orthogonality condition (ORT) is not satisfied if the term $\mathbb{E}[D|X]$ is not present in Equation (6.9).
3. Show that when there are no controls X (taking $Z = \zeta$), we have $\Lambda^* = \sigma_\Gamma^2$, where with Equation (3.15), $\Lambda^* = \sigma^2\mathbb{E}\left[\mathbb{E}\left[D|Z\right]^2\right]^{-1}$. Conclude that this optimal IV estimator of τ_0 estimated by Lasso or post-Lasso achieves the efficiency bound. This extends to the "small number" of controls.
4. In the context of Equation (6.11), verify that the orthogonality assumption (ORT) is satisfied: $\partial_\eta M(\tau_0, \eta_0) = 0$.
5. Show that for the model (6.13), we obtain (6.14).

Code and data

The course's GitHub repository contains the different datasets and codes used in this section. The code **SimulationsIV.R** provides the simulations from Section 6.3. The code **NevoIV.R** and the data **cerealps3.csv** detail the application to demand estimation in Section 6.4.1. Chernozhukov et al. (2015a) apply these techniques to revisit the results of Berry et al. (1995), and the data is available in the R package **hdm**. The code **CardIV.R** is associated with the application in Section 6.4.2. The course's GitHub repository also contains a code **BonusAngristKrueger.R** that reproduces the application of the instrument selection techniques developed in the previous sections to the dataset **NEW7080.dta** from Angrist and Krueger (1991), performed in Belloni et al. (2010), which can be found at the following address: economics.mit.edu/faculty/angrist/data1/data/angkru1991.

6.6 Additional remark

Another derivation of the moment equation (6.6) using projections. Consider the space of random variables that are square integrable on the canonical probability space $(\Omega, \mathcal{A}, P)$, which we denote by $L^2(P)$. This is a Hilbert space associated with the inner product $< X, W >= \mathbb{E}[XW]$ and the norm $\|X\| = \mathbb{E}[X^2]^{1/2}$. Define $p_X(W) = \mathbb{E}[W|X]$, the orthogonal projection of W onto the subspace of $L^2(P)$, $\{\xi = h(X), \mathbb{E}[h(X)^2] < \infty\}$ of square integrable random variables that are measurable with respect to X. Applying $m_X(W) = W - p_X(W) = W - \mathbb{E}[W|X]$ to (6.1), we obtain the equations:

$$m_X Y = m_X D\tau_0 + m_X\varepsilon, \quad \mathbb{E}\left[\varepsilon|X, Z\right] = 0, \tag{6.17}$$

where

$$\begin{aligned} m_X D &= D - \mathbb{E}\left[D|X\right] = D - X'\nu_0, \\ m_X Y &= Y - \mathbb{E}\left[Y|X\right] = Y - X'(\nu_0\tau_0 + \beta_0). \end{aligned}$$

For estimation, we use the following implication of (6.1):

$$\mathbb{E}\left[m_X\varepsilon\left(m_X p_{X,Z} D\right)\right] = 0, \tag{6.18}$$

where

$$\begin{aligned} m_X p_{X,Z} D &= m_X \mathbb{E}[D|X, Z] \\ &= \mathbb{E}[D|X, Z] - \mathbb{E}[\mathbb{E}[D|X, Z]|X] \\ &= X'\gamma_0 + Z'\delta_0 - X'\nu_0. \end{aligned}$$

Note that if D were exogenous, (6.18) would simply be $\mathbb{E}\left[m_X\varepsilon m_X D\right] = 0$. In the current context, following the same idea as the optimal instrument, we should use $\mathbb{E}\left[\varepsilon\mathbb{E}\left[D|X, Z\right]\right] = 0$. However, to be able to handle errors arising from selection in the estimation of the covariates X, we need to subtract the term $\mathbb{E}\left[D|X\right]$ to obtain a robust estimator, which gives

$$\mathbb{E}\left[\left(\varepsilon - \mathbb{E}\left[\varepsilon|X\right]\right)\left(\mathbb{E}\left[D|X, Z\right] - \mathbb{E}\left[D|X\right]\right)\right] = 0$$

hence Equation (6.18). The moment condition (6.17) can be rewritten as (6.6) and we also have

$$\begin{aligned} \psi(W, \tau_0, \eta_0) &= \left(\rho^y - \rho^d\tau_0\right)\left(Z'\delta_0 + X'\gamma_0 - X'\nu_0\right) \\ &= \varepsilon\left(Z'\delta_0 + X'\gamma_0 - X'\nu_0\right). \end{aligned} \tag{6.19}$$

Chapter 7
Going further

The objective of this chapter is to present specific developments of the tools introduced in the previous sections, particularly focusing on the properties of the Lasso. The Lasso and the choice of its penalty have been presented so far in the case of non-Gaussian errors or using cross-validation in a more general framework, but with less strong theoretical foundations. Section 7.1 shows that it is also possible to theoretically justify a choice of penalty in the case of non-Gaussian errors and provides the intuition behind this choice, based on the theory of self-normalized sums. Section 7.2 then analyzes the contribution of sample-splitting, especially for relaxing certain assumptions on the growth of the number of variables that can be included as a function of the sample size. We have presented the double selection procedure, which allows for inference on a coefficient in this high-dimensional context. This procedure can be adapted to perform joint inference on a small number of coefficients (see Section 4.2 in Chernozhukov et al., 2021). Another procedure called "desparsification," equivalent at the first order, uses a bias correction in order to obtain simultaneous confidence regions for a small number of coefficients. In order to present the different possible approaches, this procedure is introduced in Section 7.3. It is then used, for example, in Section 11.3.1 to test Granger causality. Finally, the Lasso has so far been introduced in an i.i.d. framework. However, this regularization and way to select instruments can also be extended to panel data, which we present in Section 7.4. Finally, we study an application of these tools to estimate the effect of the number of police officers per capita on crime rates.

7.1 Estimation with non-Gaussian errors

We have already described the properties of the Lasso assuming that the error term is Gaussian. Belloni et al. (2012) relaxed this assumption while also describing how to choose the parameter λ in a more general case. We describe their strategy. Consider the selection linear model, with a high number of covariates Z_i:

$$D_i = Z_i'\delta_0 + \varepsilon_i, \quad \mathbb{E}\left[\varepsilon_i | Z_i\right] = 0 \tag{7.1}$$

and the Lasso estimator of δ_0,

$$\widehat{\delta} \in \underset{\delta \in \mathbb{R}^p}{\operatorname{argmin}} \quad \frac{1}{n}\sum_{i=1}^{n}\left(D_i - Z_i'\delta\right)^2 + \frac{\lambda}{n}\left\|\widehat{\Gamma}\delta\right\|_1, \tag{7.2}$$

Machine Learning for Econometrics. Christophe Gaillac and Jérémy L'Hour, Oxford University Press.
 DOI: 10.1093/9780198918868.003.0007

where $\left\|\hat{\Gamma}\delta\right\|_1 = \sum_{j=1}^{p} \left|\hat{\Gamma}_j\delta_j\right|$. The penalty $\hat{\Gamma} \in \mathcal{M}_{p,p}(\mathbb{R})$ is an estimator of the weights of the "ideal" penalty:

$$\hat{\Gamma}^0 = \text{diag}(\hat{\gamma}_1^0, \ldots, \hat{\gamma}_p^0), \text{ where } \hat{\gamma}_j^0 = \sqrt{\frac{1}{n}\sum_{i=1}^{n} Z_{i,j}^2\varepsilon_i^2}. \tag{7.3}$$

$\hat{\Gamma}^0$ are the weights for the "ideal" penalty in the sense that they depend on the error ε_i, which is not actually observed. Thus, **in practice:**

1. We set $\lambda = 2c\sqrt{n}\Phi^{-1}(1 - 0.1/(2p\log(p \vee n)))$, where $c = 1.1$ and $\Phi^{-1}(\cdot)$ is the inverse of the standard normal cumulative distribution function.
2. We estimate the ideal penalty in two steps, 1) using weights in the "conservative" penalty and 2) by inserting the resulting estimated residuals in place of ε_i to obtain more suitable weights.

Assumption 7.1 (Moment conditions). *Assume that*

(i) $\max_{j=1,\ldots,p} \mathbb{E}\left[D_i^2\right] + \mathbb{E}\left[D_i^2 Z_{j,i}^2\right] + 1/\mathbb{E}\left[Z_{j,i}^2\varepsilon_i^2\right] \le K_1$;
(ii) $\max_{j=1,\ldots,p} \mathbb{E}\left[Z_{j,i}^3\varepsilon_i^3\right] \le K_2$, *where* $K_1, K_2 < \infty$.

Under these moment conditions, Theorem 7.1 below provides convergence rates for the Lasso with non-Gaussian and heteroscedastic errors, relaxing the assumptions made in Theorem 4.1. Of course, these assumptions are more realistic in most applications.

Theorem 7.1 (Convergence rates for the Lasso with non-Gaussian and heteroscedastic errors, Theorem 1 in Belloni et al., 2012) *Consider the model (7.1), the sparsity assumption* $|\delta_0|_0 \le s$, *and Assumptions 4.4 and 7.1. Let* $\varepsilon > 0$, *there exist* C_1 *and* C_2, *such that the Lasso estimator defined in (7.2) with tuning parameter* $\lambda = 2c\sqrt{n}\Phi^{-1}(1 - \alpha/(2p))$, *where* $\alpha \to 0$, $\log(1/\alpha) \le c_1 \log(\max(p, n))$, $c_1 > 0$, *and with asymptotic weights for the penalties* $l\hat{\gamma}^0 \le \hat{\gamma} \le u\hat{\gamma}^0$ *where* $l \xrightarrow{P} 1$, $u \xrightarrow{P} 1$ *satisfies, with probability* $1 - \varepsilon$

$$\left\|\hat{\delta} - \delta_0\right\|_1 \le \frac{C_1}{\kappa_{\overline{C}}^2}\sqrt{\frac{s^2\log(\max(p, n))}{n}}, \tag{7.4}$$

where $\kappa_{\overline{C}} := \kappa_{\overline{C}}\left(\frac{1}{n}\sum_{i=1}^{n} Z_i Z_i'\right)$ *and*

$$\overline{C} = \frac{\left\|\hat{\gamma}^0\right\|_\infty}{\left\|1/\hat{\gamma}^0\right\|_\infty}\frac{uc + 1}{lc - 1}.$$

Important intuitions for understanding Theorem 7.1: the regularization event and concentration inequality. The proof of the Lasso with Gaussian errors, in step 2 of the proof of Theorem 4.1, is based on the fact that with a probability of at least $1 - \alpha$, we have the following *regularization event*:

$$\left\{ \max_{j=1,\dots,p} \left| \frac{1}{n} \sum_{i=1}^{n} \varepsilon_i X_{ij} \right| \leq \frac{\lambda_n}{4} \right\}.$$

To ensure this, we used Markov's inequality, conditioned on $X_1, \dots, X_n$, and the concentration inequality (see Lemma 4.6), which, for p Gaussian random variables $\xi_j \sim \mathcal{N}(0, \sigma_j^2)$, ensures that

$$\mathbb{E}\left[\max_{j=1,\dots,p} |\xi_j| \right] \leq \max_{j=1,\dots,p} \sigma_j \sqrt{2 \log(2p)}.$$

In the general case of Lasso with non-Gaussian and heteroskedastic errors, to choose λ and the weights γ^0, we generalize these ideas. We ensure that we have the regularization event with high probability

$$\left\{ \max_{j=1,\dots,p} \left| \frac{\sum_{i=1}^{n} Z_{i,j}\varepsilon_i / \sqrt{n}}{\widehat{\gamma}_j^0} \right| \leq \frac{\lambda}{2c\sqrt{n}} \right\}, \tag{7.5}$$

using the following concentration inequality applied to $U_{i,j} := Z_{i,j}\varepsilon_i$. This guarantees that there exists a finite constant $A > 0$ such that

$$\mathbb{P}\left(\max_{j=1,\dots,p} \left| \frac{\sum_{i=1}^{n} U_{i,j}/\sqrt{n}}{\sqrt{\sum_{i=1}^{n} U_{i,j}^2 / n}} \right| \leq \Phi^{-1}\left(1 - \frac{\alpha}{2p}\right) \right) \geq 1 - \alpha\left(1 + \frac{A}{l_n}\right), \tag{7.6}$$

where $l_n \to \infty$. This result is obtained from the moderate deviation theorems for self-normalized sums (see Lemma 5 in Belloni et al., 2012 and Belloni et al., 2018). The idea is to choose the weights $\widehat{\Gamma}^0$ in the penalty in such a way that the term:

$$\frac{\sum_{i=1}^{n} Z_{i,j}\varepsilon_i / \sqrt{n}}{\widehat{\gamma}_j^0}$$

behaves like a standard normal random variable. In this case, we can obtain the desired condition (7.5) by letting $\lambda/(2c\sqrt{n})$ be sufficiently large to dominate the maximum of p standard normal random variables with high probability. Belloni et al. (2012) show that choosing $(\gamma_j^0)^2 = \mathrm{Var}\left(Z_{i,j}\varepsilon_i\right)$ achieves this idea, even if the ε_i's are not i.i.d. Gaussian. This gives (7.6). Then, Lemma 7.1 below ensures that, on this regularization event, the desired inequalities hold.

Lemma 7.1 (Lemma 6 in Belloni et al., 2012). *Consider the model (7.1), the sparsity assumption $|\delta_0|_0 \leq s$, Assumptions 4.4 and 7.1. If the penalty dominates the score in* *the sense that*

$$\frac{\widehat{\gamma}_j^0 \lambda}{n} \geq \max_{1 \leq j \leq p} 2c \left| \frac{1}{n} \sum_{i=1}^{n} Z_{i,j} \varepsilon_i \right|,$$

or equivalently (7.5), then we obtain

$$\left\| \widehat{\Gamma}^0 \left(\widehat{\delta} - \delta_0 \right) \right\|_1 \leq \frac{(1 + c_0)}{\kappa_{c_0}} \left(u + \frac{1}{c} \right) \frac{\lambda s}{n \kappa_{c_0}}, \tag{7.7}$$

with $c_0 = (uc + 1)/(lc - 1)$.

Bootstrap-after-cross-validation in generalized linear models. The selection method (7.2) firstly might remain conservative, as can be seen from (7.6), and secondly can be extended to generalized linear models, where one is interested in the true value δ_0, which is given by the solution to

$$\delta_0 = \operatorname*{argmin}_{\delta \in \delta} \mathbb{E}[m(Z'\delta, Y)],$$

where $m : \mathbb{R} \times \mathcal{Y} \to \mathbb{R}$ is a known function that is convex in its first argument, $Z \in \mathbb{R}^p$ is a (high-dimensional) vector of regressors, Y is the outcome variable or vector, and Δ is a convex parameter space. This more general context includes in particular the binary response model (see example in Exercise 15.2), or the logistic calibration of balancing. Denote by $\partial_1 m$ the derivative of the loss function m with respect to its first argument. Under some sparsity assumption, Chetverikov and Sørensen (2022) show that for the following adapted ℓ_1 penalized M-estimator:

$$\widehat{\delta} \in \operatorname*{argmin}_{\delta \in \delta} \quad \frac{1}{n} \sum_{i=1}^{n} m(Z_i'\delta, Y_i) + \frac{\lambda}{n} \|\delta\|_1,$$

if we can choose λ so that

$$\frac{\lambda}{n} \geq \max_{1 \leq j \leq p} c \left| \frac{1}{n} \sum_{i=1}^{n} Z_{i,j} \partial_1 m(Z_i'\delta_0, Y_i) \right|,$$

we get a bound similar to (7.7). If the residuals $\partial_1 m(Z_i'\delta_0, Y_i)$ were known, this would suggest setting $\lambda = cnq_{1-\alpha}$, where $q_{1-\alpha}$ is the $1 - \alpha$ quantile of the absolute value of the maximum of the scores

$$\max_{1 \leq j \leq p} \left| \frac{1}{n} \sum_{i=1}^{n} Z_{i,j} \partial_1 m(Z_i'\delta_0, Y_i) \right|.$$

While this choice is not feasible, Chetverikov and Sørensen (2022) show that a *bootstrap-after-cross-validation* procedure works theoretically and in practice, where 1) we obtain a preliminary estimator $\widehat{\theta}^{cv}$ based on $\widehat{\lambda}^{cv}$ selected by cross-validation, 2) then use this to estimate the $1 - \alpha$ quantile of the score using Gaussian multiplier bootstrap, i.e., using the $1 - \alpha$ quantile of

$$\max_{1 \leq j \leq p} \left| \frac{1}{n} \sum_{i=1}^{n} e_i Z_{i,j} \partial_1 m(Z_i' \widehat{\theta}^{cv}, Y_i) \right|,$$

where $\{e_i\}_{i=1,\ldots,n}$ are independent standard normal random variables that are independent of the data. The key is to prove that cross-validation provides a sufficiently good estimator of the residuals $\partial_1 m(Z_i' \delta_0, Y_i)$. Under appropriate regularity conditions, this leads to convergence rates similar to those in Theorem 7.1.

7.2 Sample splitting

We analyze how to use sample splitting to relax the assumption (4) of a growing number of non-zero components. We replace it with the weaker condition:

$$\frac{s \log(\max(p, n))}{n} \to 0. \tag{7.8}$$

As in Belloni et al. (2012), we consider the case of two samples, but this can easily be extended to the case of K samples.

Let a and b be the two samples of sizes $n_a = \lfloor n/2 \rfloor$ and $n_b = n - n_a$, $j^c = \{a, b\} \backslash j$ for $j \in \{a, b\}$, and define the estimator based on sample splitting as follows:

$$\begin{aligned} \check{\tau} = & \left[\sum_{i=1}^{n_a} \Gamma_1 \left(W_i^a, \widehat{\eta}^b \right) + \sum_{i=1}^{n_b} \Gamma_1 \left(W_i^b, \widehat{\eta}^a \right) \right]^{-1} \\ & \times \left(\left(\sum_{i=1}^{n_a} \Gamma_1 \left(W_i^a, \widehat{\eta}^b \right) \right) \check{\tau}_a + \left(\sum_{i=1}^{n_b} \Gamma_1 \left(W_i^b, \widehat{\eta}^a \right) \right) \check{\tau}_b \right), \end{aligned} \tag{7.9}$$

which uses

$$\check{\tau}_j = \left[\frac{1}{n_j} \sum_{i=1}^{n_j} \Gamma_1 \left(W_i^j, \widehat{\eta}^{j^c} \right) \right]^{-1} \frac{1}{n_j} \sum_{i=1}^{n_j} \Gamma_2 \left(W_i^j, \widehat{\eta}^{j^c} \right) \quad \text{for } j \in \{a, b\}.$$

This estimator combines the two treatment effect estimators based on each sample, each using a preliminary estimator of the nuisance parameter based on the other sample only.

Theorem 7.2 (Asymptotic normality of the split-sample immune estimator, Theorem 7 in Belloni et al., 2012) *The immune estimator $\check{\tau}$ defined by (7.9) in the affine-quadratic model (5.3), under Assumption 5.1 and* ***the growth condition (7.8)****, using a first-stage nuisance estimator satisfying Assumption 5.2, is asymptotically normal:*

$$\sqrt{n}(\check{\tau} - \tau_0) \to \mathcal{N}(0, \sigma_\Gamma^2),$$

with $\sigma_\Gamma^2 := \mathbb{E}[\psi(W_i, \tau_0, \eta_0)^2] / \mathbb{E}[\Gamma_1(W_i, \eta_0)]^2$.

7.3 Joint inference on a group of coefficients

We start by describing the link between the double selection procedure, introduced in Part 3, and the bias correction procedure of Lasso (or *desparsification*) introduced by Zhang and Zhang (2014) and Van de Geer et al. (2014). This correction then allows us to establish in Section 7.3.2 the joint asymptotic normality of the lasso estimator for a small number of coefficients once the bias has been corrected. This in turn allows one to derive *simultaneous* confidence bands for these coefficients rather than *marginal* ones when the double Lasso procedure introduced in Chapter 4 is applied coefficient by coefficient. The latter is potentially misleading as the number of coefficients increases. Chernozhuokov et al. (2013); Belloni et al. (2015) also propose a method for making inference on a group of coefficients based on the double selection estimation procedure described in Part 3 (see respectively Bach et al., 2018; Chernozhukov et al., 2021, for a survey and extension to time and space). In order to present multiple possible approaches, we will instead describe here the approach of explicit bias correction, after establishing the link between the *double selection* and *desparsification* procedures.

7.3.1 Double selection and Lasso desparsification

Consider in an i.i.d. sample $(Y_i, X_i)_{i=1,\ldots,n}$ and the following model:

$$Y = X'\beta_0 + \varepsilon, \tag{7.10}$$

where ε is such that $\mathbb{E}[\varepsilon] = 0$, $\mathbb{E}[\varepsilon^2] = \sigma^2 < \infty$, $\mathbb{E}[\varepsilon|D, X] = 0$, and p is the dimension of X, which is allowed to be much larger than n. The parameter of interest is the coefficient $\beta_{0,k}$ for $k \in \{1, \ldots, p\}$. This model has been studied in Section 4.5; where we presented the double selection method introduced by Chernozhukov et al. (2018). Remark 3.4 details this method in three steps, which leads to the following expression (7.11) for the estimator of $\beta_{0,k}$:

$$\check{\beta}_k = \frac{n^{-1}\sum_{i=1}^n (Y_i - X'_{i,-k}\widehat{\beta}_{-k})(X_{i,k} - X'_{i,-k}\widehat{\gamma})}{n^{-1}\sum_{i=1}^n X_{i,k}(X_{i,k} - X'_{i,-k}\widehat{\gamma})}, \tag{7.11}$$

where $\widehat{\beta}_{-k}$ is an estimator of β_{-k}, the coefficient vector of the post-Lasso regression of Y on X, from which the k-th component has been removed, and $\widehat{\gamma}$ is an estimator of γ, the coefficient of the post-Lasso regression of X_k on X_{-k}. This procedure is equivalent at first order to the following procedure:

1. We regress Y on (X_k, X_{-k}) using a (post-)Lasso. We denote by $\widehat{\beta}^{[1]}$ the associated estimator.
2. We regress X_k on X_{-k} using a (post-)Lasso. We denote by $\widehat{\gamma}^{[1]}$ the associated estimator and $\widehat{\nu} := X_k - X'_{-k}\widehat{\gamma}^{[1]}$ the residual.

3. We use an IV regression of $Y - X'_{-k}\widehat{\beta}^{[1]}_{-k}$ on X_k using $\widehat{\nu}$ as an instrument, leading to the final estimator of $\beta_{0,k}$:

$$\check{\beta}^{[1]}_k = \frac{n^{-1}\sum_{i=1}^n (Y_i - X'_{i,-k}\widehat{\beta}^{[1]}_{-k})(X_{i,k} - X'_{i,-k}\widehat{\gamma}^{[1]})}{n^{-1}\sum_{i=1}^n X_{i,k}(X_{i,k} - X'_{i,-k}\widehat{\gamma}^{[1]})}, \tag{7.12}$$

which has the same form as (7.11).

This procedure is described in Belloni et al. (2014). Developing (7.12) and using the definition of $\widehat{\nu}_i$, we can rewrite $\check{\beta}^{[1]}_k$ as a correction of the bias of the initial estimator $\widehat{\beta}^{[1]}$ (Zhang and Zhang, 2014; Van de Geer et al., 2014):

$$\check{\beta}^{[1]}_k = \left(\frac{1}{n}\sum_{i=1}^n X_{i,k}\widehat{\nu}_i\right)^{-1} \frac{1}{n}\sum_{i=1}^n \widehat{\nu}_i Y_i - \underbrace{\sum_{m\neq k} \widehat{\beta}^{[1]}_m \frac{n^{-1}\sum_{i=1}^n X_{i,m}\widehat{\nu}_i}{n^{-1}\sum_{i=1}^n X_{i,k}\widehat{\nu}_i}}_{\text{Bias correction}}. \tag{7.13}$$

Let us describe the intuition behind (7.12). Using the notations from Theorem 4.2, let $\mathbf{X} = [\mathbf{X}_1, \ldots, \mathbf{X}_p]$ be the $n \times p$ matrix of column vectors $\mathbf{X}_k$ of size $n \times 1$ and $\mathbf{y}$ be the $n \times 1$ vector of Y_i. Using the Frisch–Waugh–Lovell theorem (see Theorem 4.2) and denoting by $\boldsymbol{\nu}_k = \mathcal{M}_{\mathbf{X}_{-k}}\mathbf{X}_k$ the projection of $\mathbf{X}_k$ onto the orthogonal complement of the space generated by the columns of $\mathbf{X}_{-k}$, it is traditionally known that $\beta_{0,k}$ can be estimated via

$$\widehat{\beta}_k = (\mathbf{X}_k{}'\boldsymbol{\nu}_k)^{-1}\boldsymbol{\nu}_k{}'\mathbf{y}.$$

The problem when considering $p > n$ comes from the fact that the projection $\boldsymbol{\nu}_k$ is no longer defined. The "desparsification" proposed by Zhang and Zhang (2014) therefore consists in correcting $\boldsymbol{\nu}_k$ for the bias that is generated.

7.3.2 Asymptotic normality of the bias-corrected estimator

We now describe how to use this correction to perform inference on a group $G \subseteq \{1, \ldots, p\}$ of coefficients $\beta_{0,G} = \{\beta_{0,j}, j \in G\}$. The definition of the Lasso estimator

$$\widehat{\beta} = \arg\min_{\beta\in\mathbb{R}^p} \frac{1}{n}\sum_{i=1}^n (Y_i - X_i'\beta)^2 + \lambda \|\beta\|_1,$$

implies that $\widehat{\beta}$ satisfies the Karush–Kuhn–Tucker (KKT) conditions:

$$-\frac{1}{n}\sum_{i=1}^n X_i(Y_i - X_i'\widehat{\beta}) + \frac{\lambda\widehat{\kappa}}{2} = 0, \tag{7.14}$$

$$\|\widehat{\kappa}\|_\infty \leq 1, \quad \widehat{\kappa}_k = \text{sign}(\widehat{\beta}_k) \text{ if } \widehat{\beta}_k \neq 0.$$

The model (7.10) yields

$$-\frac{1}{n}\sum_{i=1}^{n} X_i(Y_i - X_i'\widehat{\beta}) = \frac{1}{n}\sum_{i=1}^{n} X_iX_i'(\widehat{\beta} - \beta_0) - \frac{1}{n}\sum_{i=1}^{n} X_i\varepsilon_i.$$

Using $\widehat{\boldsymbol{\Sigma}} = \sum_{i=1}^{n} X_iX_i'/n$, we can rewrite the optimality condition (7.14) as:

$$\widehat{\boldsymbol{\Sigma}}(\widehat{\beta} - \beta_0) + \frac{\lambda\widehat{\kappa}}{2} = \frac{1}{n}\sum_{i=1}^{n} X_i\varepsilon_i.$$

If we have a good approximation $\widehat{\boldsymbol{\Theta}}$ of the inverse of $\widehat{\boldsymbol{\Sigma}}$, then we have the following decomposition:

$$\underbrace{\widehat{\beta} + \widehat{\boldsymbol{\Theta}}\frac{\lambda\widehat{\kappa}}{2}}_{\substack{\text{Estimator with} \\ \text{bias correction } \check{\beta}}} - \beta_0 = \underbrace{\widehat{\boldsymbol{\Theta}}\left(\frac{1}{n}\sum_{i=1}^{n} X_i\varepsilon_i\right)}_{\text{Asymptotically normal term}} - \underbrace{\frac{\Delta}{\sqrt{n}}}_{\text{Negligible term}},$$

where

$$\Delta = \sqrt{n}\left(\widehat{\boldsymbol{\Theta}}\widehat{\boldsymbol{\Sigma}} - \boldsymbol{I}\right)(\widehat{\beta} - \beta_0)$$

is an error term related to the approximation of the inverse $\widehat{\boldsymbol{\Theta}}\widehat{\boldsymbol{\Sigma}} \neq I$. It can be shown, under certain assumptions, that Δ is asymptotically negligible. Under these conditions, using the optimality condition (7.14), the bias of the estimator $\widehat{\beta}_G$ for the components β_G of group G is

$$B_G = \widehat{\boldsymbol{\Theta}}_G\left(\frac{1}{n}\sum_{i=1}^{n} X_i(Y_i - X_i'\widehat{\beta})\right), \tag{7.15}$$

where $\boldsymbol{\Theta}_G$ is the sub-matrix of $\boldsymbol{\Theta}$ corresponding to the coefficients of group G. Thus, the bias-corrected estimator $\check{\beta}_G = \widehat{\beta}_G + B_G$ has a similar form as (7.12).

With Gaussian errors $\varepsilon \sim \mathcal{N}(0, \sigma_\varepsilon^2 \boldsymbol{I})$ and using some assumptions about the growth rate of the number of regressors ($s^2 \log(p)^2/n \to 0$), Van de Geer et al. (2014) (Theorem 2.2) show that in this context the Lasso estimator is asymptotically Gaussian, for any group $G \subseteq \{1, \ldots, p\}$,

$$\sqrt{n}\left(\check{\beta}_G - \beta_{0,G}\right) \xrightarrow{d} \mathcal{N}(0, \Xi_G), \tag{7.16}$$

where Ξ_G is the asymptotic variance

$$\Xi_G = \lim_{n\to\infty} \text{Var}\left(\frac{1}{\sqrt{n}}\sum_{i=1}^{n} \varepsilon_i\boldsymbol{\Theta}_G X_i\right).$$

Note that Breunig et al. (2020) relax the assumption of Gaussian errors and use this bias correction of the Lasso to propose an alternative method to the immunization procedure developed in the instrumental variable models of Section 6. They obtain an IV estimator based on the Lasso that is asymptotically normal, which also allows for constructing simultaneous confidence regions in this context. We use this correction in a time series framework in Section 11.3.1 in order to test Granger causality (see Babii et al., 2019).

We now discuss the method for estimating the inverse of Σ, denoted $\widehat{\boldsymbol{\Theta}}$, initially proposed by Meinshausen and Bühlmann (2006). This method uses the fact that for every $k \in \{1, \ldots, p\}$, the matrix $\boldsymbol{\Sigma} = \mathbb{E}[XX']$ can be partitioned

$$\begin{pmatrix} \boldsymbol{\Sigma}_{k,k} & \boldsymbol{\Sigma}_{-k,k} \\ \boldsymbol{\Sigma}_{-k,k} & \boldsymbol{\Sigma}_{-k,-k} \end{pmatrix},$$

after rearranging the rows. The proposed estimator consists of two steps. First, we regress for $k \in \{1, \ldots, p\}$, the component X_k on the others using a Lasso:

$$\widehat{\gamma}_k = \arg\min_{\gamma \in \mathbb{R}^{p-1}} \left(\frac{1}{n} \sum_{i=1}^{n} (X_{i,k} - X'_{i,-k}\gamma)^2 + \lambda_k \|\gamma\|_1 \right).$$

Second, we consider the estimator $\widehat{\boldsymbol{\Theta}} := \widehat{\boldsymbol{B}}^{-2} \widehat{\mathbf{C}}$ of the inverse of $\boldsymbol{\Sigma}$, where

$$\widehat{\mathbf{C}} = \begin{pmatrix} 1 & -\widehat{\gamma}_{1,2} & \cdots & -\widehat{\gamma}_{1,p} \\ -\widehat{\gamma}_{1,2} & 1 & & -\widehat{\gamma}_{2,p} \\ \vdots & \vdots & & \vdots \\ -\widehat{\gamma}_{p,1} & -\widehat{\gamma}_{1,p} & \cdots & 1 \end{pmatrix},$$

where we denote the $(p-1)$ components of the vector $\widehat{\gamma}_k = \{\widehat{\gamma}_{k,j} : j = 1, \ldots, p, j \neq k\}$, $\widehat{\boldsymbol{B}}^2 = \mathrm{Diag}(\widehat{b}_1^2, \ldots, \widehat{b}_p^2)$, and $\widehat{b}_k^2 = \sum_{i=1}^{n} (X_{i,k} - X'_{i,-k}\widehat{\gamma}_k)^2/n + \lambda_k \|\widehat{\gamma}_k\|_1/2$. The useful property of this approximation of the inverse is that we control explicitly over the deviation between $\widehat{\boldsymbol{\Sigma}}\widehat{\boldsymbol{\Theta}}$ and the identity matrix in infinite norm, as a function of $\widehat{b}$ and the penalties λ_k (see (10) in Van de Geer et al., 2014).

7.4 Regularization and instrument selection for panel data

In this section, we briefly show how to use the lasso and the regularization procedures from Section 6.2 when the observations are identically distributed across individuals but correlated over time. If there is dependence, this should be taken into account in the selection procedure (7.2), as it will lead to a larger choice of penalty parameters, and thus fewer selected variables, than if this dependence is neglected. One way to take into account this dependence is to use the a variant of the lasso, the cluster-Lasso estimator developed by Belloni et al. (2016), which adapts to the clustered covariance structure. In the following, the results hold for $n \to \infty$ and fixed T, where n is the number of individuals and T is the number of observed periods, and with a joint asymptotic $n \to \infty$ and $T \to \infty$.

Consider the following panel data model:

$$Y_{it} = \tau_0 D_{it} + e_i + \varepsilon_{it} \tag{7.17}$$

$$D_{it} = Z'_{it}\delta_0 + f_i + u_{it}, \tag{7.18}$$

where $\mathbb{E}[\varepsilon_{it}u_{it}] \neq 0$ but $\mathbb{E}[\varepsilon_{it}|Z_{i1},\ldots,Z_{iT}] = \mathbb{E}[u_{it}|Z_{i1},\ldots,Z_{iT}] = 0$, and where we have a large number p_z of instruments Z_{it} satisfying $p_z \gg nT$. For simplicity, we do not consider cases where the number of controls is fixed or high-dimensional, but the ideas of double selection from Section 6.1 can be directly extended here. We use the classical *within* transformation:

$$\ddot{Y}_{it} = Y_{it} - \frac{1}{T}\sum_{t=1}^{T} Y_{it},$$

and respectively $\ddot{Z}_{it}$ and $\ddot{\varepsilon}_{it}$ are the within transformations of Z_{it} and ε_{it}, to partially remove the fixed effects in both equations. This reduces the model to

$$\ddot{Y}_{it} = \tau_0 \ddot{D}_{it} + \ddot{\varepsilon}_{it} \tag{7.19}$$

$$\ddot{D}_{it} = \ddot{Z}'_{it}\delta_0 + \ddot{u}_{it}. \tag{7.20}$$

We then use the sparsity assumption $\|\delta_0\|_0 \leq s$ and the cluster-Lasso regression of $\ddot{D}_{it}$ on $\ddot{Z}_{it}$ to estimate δ_0. Finally, to estimate τ_0, we use the orthogonal moment condition:

$$\mathbb{E}\left[\frac{1}{T}\sum_{t=1}^{T}\left(\ddot{Y}_{it} - \tau_0\ddot{D}_{it}\right)\ddot{Z}'_{it}\delta_0\right] = 0,$$

which satisfies (5.1) because there are no controls here. Using the notations of Assumption 5.3, this gives us the following estimator for τ:

$$\check{\tau} = \left[\frac{1}{nT}\sum_{i=1}^{n}\sum_{t=1}^{T}\Gamma_1\left(\ddot{D}_{it}, \ddot{Z}_{it}, \widehat{\delta}\right)\right]^{-1}\frac{1}{nT}\sum_{i=1}^{n}\sum_{t=1}^{T}\Gamma_2\left(\ddot{Y}_{it}, \ddot{Z}_{it}, \widehat{\delta}\right),$$

where $\Gamma_1(\ddot{D}_{it}, \ddot{Z}_{it}, \delta) = \ddot{D}_{it}\ddot{Z}'_{it}\delta$ and $\Gamma_2(\ddot{Y}_{it}, \ddot{Z}_{it}, \delta) = \ddot{Y}_{it}\ddot{Z}'_{it}\delta$.

7.4.1 The cluster-Lasso: intuition

We consider the regression (7.20). The estimation of the cluster-Lasso coefficient is based on

$$\widehat{\delta} \in \underset{\delta\in\mathbb{R}^{p_z}}{\operatorname{argmin}} \frac{1}{nT}\sum_{i=1}^{n}\sum_{i=1}^{T}\left(\ddot{D}_{it} - \ddot{Z}'_{it}\delta\right)^2 + \frac{\lambda}{nT}\sum_{k=1}^{p_Z}\widehat{\gamma}_k\left|\delta_k\right|. \tag{7.21}$$

Similar to Section 6.2, the penalty weights $\widehat{\gamma}_k$ are chosen such that the "regularizing event"

$$\frac{\lambda\widehat{\phi}_j}{nT} \geq 2c\left|\frac{1}{nT}\sum_{i=1}^{n}\sum_{t=1}^{T}\ddot{Z}_{itj}\ddot{\varepsilon}_{it}\right|$$

occurs with a high probability. To do this, as in (7.6), we use moderate deviations theorems from the theory of self-normalization (see Lemma 5 in Belloni et al., 2012). The variables $U_{ij} := \sum_{t=1}^{T}\ddot{Z}_{itj}\ddot{\varepsilon}_{it}/T$ are independent random variables with zero mean with respect to i, and they satisfy (if the third order moments are finite) when $n \to \infty$ and for α sufficiently small a concentration inequality of the type (7.6). This leads to a clustered ideal choice of penalty weights:

$$\begin{aligned}\left(\widehat{\gamma}_k^0\right)^2 &= \frac{1}{nT}\sum_{i=1}^{n}\left(\sum_{t=1}^{T}\ddot{Z}_{itj}\ddot{\varepsilon}_{it}\right)^2\\ &= \frac{1}{nT}\sum_{i=1}^{n}\sum_{t=1}^{T}\sum_{t'=1}^{T}\ddot{Z}_{itj}\ddot{Z}_{it'j}\ddot{\varepsilon}_{it}\ddot{\varepsilon}_{it'}.\end{aligned}$$

As in the previous section, $\ddot{\varepsilon}_{it}$ is unknown and thus we start with a conservative penalty, i.e., an estimator of $\mathrm{Var}\left(\sum_{i=1}^{T}\ddot{Z}_{itj}\ddot{D}_{it}/T\right)$, and then we iterate by re-inserting the estimated $\ddot{\varepsilon}_{it}$. As in Section 6.2, we take

$$\lambda = 2c\sqrt{nT}\Phi^{-1}\left(1-\frac{\alpha}{2p_z}\right).$$

We define the statistic Belloni et al. (2016) call this quantity i_T^Z the "information index." Indeed, it quantifies the impact of the dependence on the choice of the tuning parameter in the sense that it is inversely related to the strength of intra-individual dependence and can vary between $i_T^Z = 1$ (perfect dependence within cluster i) and $i_T^z = T$ (perfect independence within i). Theorem 7.3 shows that, through this quantity, this dependence has an impact on convergence rates.

$$i_T^Z = T\min_{1\leq k\leq p}\frac{\mathbb{E}\left[\sum_{t=1}^{T}\ddot{Z}_{itk}^2\ddot{\varepsilon}_{it}^2/T\right]}{\mathbb{E}\left[\left(\sum_{t=1}^{T}\ddot{Z}_{itk}\ddot{\varepsilon}_{it}\right)^2/T\right]}.$$

We define the empirical Gram matrix $\ddot{\Sigma} = \{\ddot{\Sigma}_{jk}\}_{j,k=1}^{p}$, where

$$\ddot{\Sigma}_{jk} - \frac{1}{nT}\sum_{i=1}^{n}\sum_{t=1}^{T}\ddot{Z}_{itj}\ddot{Z}_{itk}.$$

Theorem 7.3 (Convergence rates of panel cluster-Lasso, Theorem 1 in Belloni et al., 2016) *Let* $\varepsilon > 0$. *Let* $\{(D_{it}, Z_{it})\}_{i=1,\ldots,n,t=1,\ldots,T}$ *be an i.i.d. sample in i for which* $n, T \to \infty$

jointly. Assume $s = o(ni_T^Z)$, $s\log(\max(p, nT)) = o(ni_T^Z)$, *and the other regularity conditions (RE) and sparse eigenvalue condition SE (page 12 in Belloni et al., 2016) based on* $\ddot{\Sigma}$. *Consider an admissible cluster-Lasso estimator* $\widehat{\delta}$ *with a penalty* $\lambda = 2c\sqrt{nT}\Phi^{-1}(1-\alpha/(2p_Z))$ *and weights* $\{\widehat{\gamma}_j\}_{j=1}^{p_z}$, $l\widehat{\gamma}_j^0 \leq \widehat{\gamma}_j \leq u\widehat{\gamma}_j^0$ *where* $l \xrightarrow{p} 1, u \xrightarrow{p} 1$. *Then, there exist* C_1 *and* C_2 *such that with probability* $1 - \varepsilon$,

$$\left\|\delta_0 - \widehat{\delta}\right\|_1 \leq C_2\sqrt{\frac{s^2\log(\max(p, nT))}{ni_T^Z}}.$$

Note that in the theorem above, the effective sample size ni_T^Z is intuitively related to the structure of temporal dependence: when observations are completely independent over time ($i_T^Z = T$), the effective size is nT while if the observations are perfectly dependent ($i_T^Z = 1$), it is n.

Finally, note that under similar growth conditions to Theorem 7.1, namely

$$\frac{s^2\log(\max(p, nT))^2}{ni_T^D} = o(1),$$

then Belloni et al. (2016) also obtain the asymptotic normality of the IV estimator $\check{\tau}$ in this context:

$$\sqrt{ni_T^D}V^{-1/2}(\check{\tau} - \tau_0) \xrightarrow{d} \mathcal{N}(0, 1),$$

where

$$V := i_T^D\frac{\mathbb{E}\left[\left(\sum_{t=1}^T \psi\left(\ddot{Y}_{it}, \ddot{D}_{it}, \ddot{Z}_{it}, \delta_0\right)\right)^2/T\right]}{T\mathbb{E}\left[\sum_{t=1}^T \Gamma_1\left(\ddot{D}_{it}, \ddot{Z}_{it}, \delta_0\right)/T\right]^2},$$

where $\psi\left(\ddot{Y}_{it}, \ddot{D}_{it}, \ddot{Z}_{it}, \delta_0\right) := \left(\ddot{Y}_{it} - \tau_0\ddot{D}_{it}\right)\ddot{Z}'_{it}\delta_0$.

7.4.2 Application to the economics of crime

We consider an application to the economics of crime using the data from Baltagi (2008) which replicates Cornwell and Trumbull (1994). Note that Belloni et al. (2016) also develop an interesting application to gun control. The data consist of a panel of 90 counties in North Carolina over the period 1981–1987. All variables are in logarithm except for nominal regional and time variables. The main explanatory variables are the probability of an arrest (measured by the ratio of arrests to crimes), the probability of a conviction following an arrest (measured by the ratio of convictions to arrests), the probability of a prison sentence following a conviction (measured by the proportion of total convictions that result in prison sentences),

Table 7.1 Application to the economics of crime of estimation with double selection in cluster

	Estimator of the effect of the number of police officers per individual		
	Within (1)	Within "large set" (2)	Cluster-Lasso (3)
Estimator	0.477^{***}	0.306^{***}	0.714^{***}
Standard error	0.168	0.054	0.184

the average jail sentence in days as an indicator of the severity of the sanction, the number of police officers per capita as a measure of the county's ability to detect crime, and population density (i.e., the county's population divided by its area). To deal with the potential endogeneity of the number of police officers per capita, we use the same instruments as Cornwell and Trumbull (1994), namely the composition of crimes (ratio of direct contact crimes to non-contact crimes) and tax revenues per capita.

The variable selection method presented in this chapter allows us to resolve some of the trade-offs that researchers face in other circumstances: including a large number of covariates to account for all potential confounders without compromising the precision of the estimates. To illustrate this point, we consider Equations (7.17)–(7.18) with: the same set of controls (16) and instruments (2) as in Cornwell and Trumbull (1994) and Baltagi (2008) or a "large set" of controls (i.e., including interactions and polynomial transformations up to second order, resulting in 544 control variables) and IV (98). The idea is that one may not be sure of the exact identity of the controls entering the equation. Table 7.1 focuses on the effect of the number of policemen per inhabitant on crime rates. The cluster-Lasso estimator is different from the within estimator with few controls and IV (first column). The important point is that the cluster-Lasso estimator does not require a priori selection, and it selects controls and IVs different from those included in the reference set. The within estimation for the "large set" seems to be biased as the number of controls is close to the number of observations in all cases.

7.5 Summary

Key concepts

Non-Gaussian errors, Lasso parameter selection, concentration inequality, sample-splitting, regularization and instrument selection in panel data, within transformation, cluster-Lasso.

Additional references

There are many methods of selection of tuning parameters in non-parametric and ℓ_1 penalized estimation, which are surveyed and described in detail in Chetverikov (2024). Kock et al. (2024) extend the methods of Section 7.1 to high-dimensional vector autoregressions (VAR). These extensions are mainly based on Belloni et al. (2012) and Belloni et al. (2016), which we recommend reading. However, these concepts are also used in other contexts such as the generic machine learning by Chernozhukov et al. (2017) presented in Chapter 8, and nowcasting in Chernozhukov et al. (2021) presented in Chapter 11. Baltagi (2008) provides a more detailed exposition of the application, including motivations for the choice of instruments.

Code and data

The data for the application in Section 7.4.2 are directly accessible in the form of the dataset "Crime" in the package **R** *plm*. Baltagi (2008) provides a complete description of the data. The code "CrimeIV.R" is available on the course's GitHub and utilizes the **rlassoIV** function from the **hdm** R package.

Questions

1. How would you modify the standard Lasso estimation procedure when the errors are non-Gaussian and heteroscedastic, if you want to achieve the same convergence rates (up to a constant)?
2. Explain the principle and advantages of sample splitting. What disadvantages do you see?

7.6 Proofs and additional results

Proof of Lemma 7.1 Let $L(\delta) = \sum_{i=1}^{n} (D_i' - Z_i'\delta)^2 / n$. Since $\widehat{\delta}$ is the solution of the minimization problem:

$$L\left(\widehat{\delta}\right) - L(\delta_0) \leq \frac{\lambda}{n}\left(\left\|\widehat{\Gamma}\delta_0\right\|_1 - \left\|\widehat{\Gamma}\widehat{\delta}\right\|_1\right). \tag{7.22}$$

Then, using (7.1) and expanding the quadratic function $L(\cdot)$, we obtain

$$\begin{aligned}\left(D_i - Z_i'\widehat{\delta}\right)^2 &= \left(D_i - Z_i'\delta - Z_i'(\widehat{\delta} - \delta)\right)^2 \\ &= \varepsilon_i^2 - 2\varepsilon_i Z_i'(\widehat{\delta} - \delta) + \left(Z_i'(\widehat{\delta} - \delta)\right)^2.\end{aligned}$$

Using the Hölder inequality and $S := 2(\widehat{\mathbf{\Gamma}}^0)^{-1} \sum_{i=1}^n Z_i \varepsilon_i / n$,

$$\left| L\left(\widehat{\delta}\right) - L\left(\delta_0\right) - \frac{1}{n}\sum_{i=1}^{n}\left(Z_i'\left(\widehat{\delta} - \delta_0\right)\right)^2 \right| = \left| \frac{2}{n}\sum_{i=1}^{n} \varepsilon_i Z_i'\left(\widehat{\delta} - \delta_0\right) \right|$$

$$\leq \|S\|_\infty \left\| \widehat{\mathbf{\Gamma}}^0\left(\widehat{\delta} - \delta_0\right)\right\|_1.$$

Combined with (7.22) and $\lambda/n \geq c\,\|S\|_\infty$, and denoting by

$$V := \frac{1}{n}\sum_{i=1}^{n}\left(Z_i'\left(\widehat{\delta} - \delta_0\right)\right)^2,$$

this leads to

$$\begin{aligned} V &\leq \frac{\lambda}{n}\left(\left\|\widehat{\mathbf{\Gamma}}\delta_0\right\|_1 - \left\|\widehat{\mathbf{\Gamma}}\widehat{\delta}\right\|_1\right) + \|S\|_\infty \left\|\widehat{\mathbf{\Gamma}}^0\left(\widehat{\delta} - \delta_0\right)\right\|_1 \\ &\leq \frac{\lambda}{n}\left(\left\|\widehat{\mathbf{\Gamma}}\left(\widehat{\delta} - \delta_0\right)_{S_0}\right\|_1 - \left\|\widehat{\mathbf{\Gamma}}\left(\widehat{\delta} - \delta_0\right)_{S_0^c}\right\|_1\right) + \|S\|_\infty \left\|\widehat{\mathbf{\Gamma}}^0\left(\widehat{\delta} - \delta_0\right)\right\|_1 \\ &\leq \left(u + \frac{1}{c}\right)\frac{\lambda}{n}\left\|\widehat{\mathbf{\Gamma}}^0\left(\widehat{\delta} - \delta_0\right)_{S_0}\right\|_1 - \left(l - \frac{1}{c}\right)\frac{\lambda}{n}\left\|\widehat{\mathbf{\Gamma}}^0\left(\widehat{\delta} - \delta_0\right)_{S_0^c}\right\|_1. \end{aligned} \tag{7.23}$$

Then, assumption 4.4 implies $\|\widehat{\mathbf{\Gamma}}^0(\widehat{\delta} - \delta_0)_{S_0^c}\|_1 \leq c_0 \|\widehat{\mathbf{\Gamma}}^0(\widehat{\delta} - \delta_0)_{S_0}\|_1$. By definition of κ_{c_0} we obtain

$$\kappa_{c_0}\left\|\widehat{\mathbf{\Gamma}}^0(\widehat{\delta} - \delta_0)_{S_0}\right\|_2 \leq V^{1/2}$$

and using the Cauchy–Schwarz inequality $\|\widehat{\mathbf{\Gamma}}^0(\widehat{\delta} - \delta_0)_{S_0}\|_2 \geq \|\widehat{\mathbf{\Gamma}}^0(\widehat{\delta} - \delta_0)_{S_0}\|_1/\sqrt{s}$,

$$\left\|\widehat{\mathbf{\Gamma}}^0\left(\widehat{\delta} - \delta_0\right)_{S_0}\right\|_1 \leq \frac{\sqrt{s}}{\kappa_{c_0}}V^{1/2} \tag{7.24}$$

which, in (7.23), leads to

$$V^{1/2} \leq \left(u + \frac{1}{c}\right)\frac{\lambda\sqrt{s}}{n\kappa_{c_0}}. \tag{7.25}$$

The result of the lemma is obtained by using (7.25),

$$\left\|\widehat{\mathbf{\Gamma}}^0\left(\widehat{\delta} - \delta_0\right)\right\|_1 \leq (1 + c_0)\left\|\widehat{\mathbf{\Gamma}}^0\left(\widehat{\delta} - \delta_0\right)_{S_0}\right\|_1$$

and (7.24). □

Proof elements for Theorem 7.1 The proof is based on three steps. First, for this choice of λ, using Lemma 5 in Belloni et al. (2012), we have as $\alpha \to 0$ and $n \to \infty$

$$\mathbb{P}\left(2c\sqrt{n}\left|\frac{\frac{1}{\sqrt{n}}\sum_{i=1}^{n} Z_{i,j}\varepsilon_i}{\gamma_j^0}\right| > \lambda\right) = o(1).$$

Thus, for sufficiently large n and sufficiently small α, we can consider the regularization event,

$$\mathcal{E} := \left\{ \left| \frac{\frac{1}{\sqrt{n}} \sum_{i=1}^{n} Z_{i,j}\varepsilon_i}{\gamma_j^0} \right| \leq \frac{\lambda}{2c\sqrt{n}} \right\},$$

which occurs with a probability greater than $1 - \alpha$. Second, using

$$\kappa_{c_0} \geq \frac{1}{\|\widehat{\gamma}^0\|_\infty} \kappa_{(\|\widehat{\gamma}^0\|_\infty / \|1/\widehat{\gamma}^0\|_\infty) c_0} \left(\frac{1}{n} \sum_{i=1}^{n} Z_i Z_i' \right) > 0.$$

Third, applying Lemma 7.1 to $\mathcal{E}$ with $\lambda = 2c\sqrt{n}\Phi^{-1}(1 - \alpha/(2p))$, and using that there exists C_3 such that $\Phi^{-1}(1 - \alpha/(2p)) \leq C_3\sqrt{\log(p/\alpha)}$, we obtain

$$\begin{aligned}
\left\| \widehat{\Gamma}^0 \left(\widehat{\delta} - \delta_0 \right) \right\|_1 &\leq \frac{(1 + c_0)}{\kappa_{c_0}} \left(u + \frac{1}{c} \right) \frac{\lambda s}{n\kappa_{c_0}} \\
&\leq \frac{(1 + c_0)}{\kappa_{c_0}} \left(u + \frac{1}{c} \right) \Phi^{-1} \left(1 - \frac{\alpha}{2p} \right) \frac{2cs}{\sqrt{n}\kappa_{c_0}} \\
&\leq \frac{(1 + c_0)}{\kappa_{c_0}} \left(u + \frac{1}{c} \right) \frac{2cC_3}{\kappa_{c_0}} \frac{s\sqrt{\log(p/\alpha)}}{\sqrt{n}},
\end{aligned}$$

which leads to the result. □

Proof of Theorem 7.2 The proof mainly consists of modifying the proof of Theorem 5.1 to use the independence between $(\varepsilon_i)_{i=1}^{n_j}$ and $\widehat{\eta}^{j^c}$ for $j \in \{a, b\}$.

Step 1: analysis of $\check{\tau}_j$. Let's take $j \in \{a, b\}$.
As in Theorem 5.1, the growth condition (7.8) suffices to obtain

$$n_j^{-1} \sum_{i=1}^{n_j} \Gamma_1 \left(W_i^j, \widehat{\eta}^{j^c} \right) \to \mathbb{E}\Gamma_1(W_i, \eta_0).$$

Then, we need to show that under the weaker condition (7.8), we still have

$$\frac{1}{\sqrt{n_j}} \sum_{i=1}^{n_j} \psi \left(W_i^j, \tau_0, \widehat{\eta}^{j^c} \right) \to \mathcal{N}(0, \text{Var}[\psi(W_i, \tau_0, \eta_0)]).$$

We use the fact that $\mathbb{E}[\varepsilon^j | X_i^j, \zeta_i^j] = 0$ and that $\{\varepsilon_i^j, \ 1 \le i \le n_j\}$ are independent from the j^c sample, to obtain

$$
\begin{aligned}
&\mathbb{E}\left[\psi\left(W_i^j, \tau_0, \widehat{\eta}^{j^c}\right) - \psi\left(W_i^j, \tau_0, \eta_0\right)\right] \\
&= \mathbb{E}\left[\mathbb{E}\left[\psi\left(W_i^j, \tau_0, \widehat{\eta}^{j^c}\right) - \psi(W_i^j, \tau_0, \eta_0) | X_i^j, \zeta_i^j, j^c\right]\right] \\
&= \mathbb{E}\left[\mathbb{E}\left[\varepsilon^j | X_i^j, \zeta_i^j\right]\left(\left(Z_i^j\right)' (\widehat{\delta}^{j^c} - \delta_0) + \left(X_i^j\right)' (\widehat{\gamma}^{j^c} - \gamma_0) - \left(X_i^j\right)' (\widehat{\nu}^{j^c} - \nu_0)\right)\right] \\
&= 0.
\end{aligned}
$$

Then, by letting $\mathcal{W}_j := (X_i^j, \zeta_i^j, j^c)$, and using Chebyshev's inequality, the fact that $\widehat{\eta}^{j^c} - \eta^{j^c}$ are independent of $\{\varepsilon_i^j, \ 1 \le i \le n_j\}$ due to the independence of the two sub-samples j and j^c, and that $\{\varepsilon_i^j, \ 1 \le i \le n_j\}$ have a conditional variance on $\left(X_i^j, \zeta_i^j\right)$ bounded above by K, we obtain

$$
\begin{aligned}
&\mathbb{P}\left(\left|\frac{\sqrt{n}}{n_j}\sum_{i=1}^{n_j}\left(\psi\left(W_i^j, \tau_0, \widehat{\eta}^{j^c}\right) - \psi\left(W_i^j, \tau_0, \eta_0\right)\right)\right| > \varepsilon\right) \\
&\le \frac{1}{\varepsilon^2}\mathbb{E}\left[\left|\frac{\sqrt{n}}{n_j}\sum_{i=1}^{n_j}\left(\psi\left(W_i^j, \tau_0, \widehat{\eta}^{j^c}\right) - \psi\left(W_i^j, \tau_0, \eta_0\right)\right)\right|^2\right] \\
&\le \mathbb{E}\left[\sum_{i=1}^{n_j}\left(\left(Z_i^j\right)'\left(\widehat{\delta}^{j^c} - \delta_0\right) + (X_i^j)'\left(\widehat{\gamma}^{j^c} - \gamma_0\right) - \left(X_i^j\right)'\left(\widehat{\nu}^{j^c} - \nu_0\right)\right)^2 \sum_{i=1}^{n_j}\frac{n(\varepsilon_i^j)^2}{\varepsilon^2 n_j^2}\right] \\
&\le \mathbb{E}\left[\mathbb{E}\left[\sum_{i=1}^{n_j}\left(\left(Z_i^j\right)'\left(\widehat{\delta}^{j^c} - \delta_0\right) + (X_i^j)'\left(\widehat{\gamma}^{j^c} - \gamma_0 - \widehat{\nu}^{j^c} + \nu_0\right)\right)^2 \sum_{i=1}^{n_j}\frac{n(\varepsilon_i^j)^2}{\varepsilon^2 n_j^2}\middle| \mathcal{W}_j\right]\right] \\
&\le \mathbb{E}\left[\sum_{i=1}^{n_j}\left((Z_i^j)'\left(\widehat{\delta}^{j^c} - \delta_0\right) + (X_i^j)'\left(\widehat{\gamma}^{j^c} - \gamma_0 - \widehat{\nu}^{j^c} + \nu_0\right)\right)^2\right]\mathbb{E}\left[\sum_{i=1}^{n_j}\frac{n(\varepsilon_i^j)^2}{\varepsilon^2 n_j^2}\middle| \mathcal{W}_j\right] \\
&\le \frac{K}{\varepsilon^2}\mathbb{E}\left[\frac{n}{n_j^2}\sum_{i=1}^{n_j}\left((Z_i^j)'\left(\widehat{\delta}^{j^c} - \delta_0\right) + (X_i^j)'\left(\widehat{\gamma}^{j^c} - \gamma_0\right) - (X_i^j)'\left(\widehat{\nu}^{j^c} - \nu_0\right)\right)^2\right] \\
&\le \frac{K}{\varepsilon^2}\frac{n}{n_j}\frac{C_2}{\kappa_{\overline{C}}}\frac{s\log(\max(p, n_j))}{n_j}.
\end{aligned}
$$

By using Theorem 7.1, we obtain

$$
\sqrt{n_j}\left(\check{\tau}_j - \tau_0\right) = \left[\frac{1}{n_j}\sum_{i=1}^{n_j}\Gamma_1\left(W_i^j, \eta_0\right)\right]^{-1}\frac{1}{\sqrt{n_j}}\sum_{i=1}^{n_j}\psi\left(W_i^j, \tau_0, \eta_0\right) + o_P(1). \qquad (7.26)
$$

Step 2: On the aggregate estimation $\check{\tau}$. By combining the two results, we obtain the asymptotic representation of $\sqrt{n}\left(\check{\tau} - \tau_0\right)$

$$
\begin{aligned}
&\sqrt{n}(\check{\tau} - \tau_0) \\
&= \left[\frac{1}{n} \sum_{i=1}^{n_a} \Gamma_1(W_i^a, \eta_0) + \frac{1}{n} \sum_{i=1}^{n_b} \Gamma_1(W_i^b, \eta_0) \right]^{-1} \\
&\times \left(\left(\sum_{i=1}^{n_a} \frac{\Gamma_1(W_i^a, \eta_0)}{\sqrt{n}} \right) (\check{\tau}_a - \tau_0) + \left(\sum_{i=1}^{n_b} \frac{\Gamma_1(W_i^b, \eta_0)}{\sqrt{n}} \right) (\check{\tau}_b - \tau_0) \right) + o_P(1) \\
&= \left[\frac{1}{n} \sum_{i=1}^{n} \Gamma_1(W_i, \eta_0) \right]^{-1} \left(\sum_{i=1}^{n_a} \frac{\psi(W_i^a, \tau_0, \eta_0)}{\sqrt{n}} + \sum_{i=1}^{n_b} \frac{\psi(W_i^b, \tau_0, \eta_0)}{\sqrt{n}} \right) + o_P(1),
\end{aligned}
$$

which concludes the proof. □

PART III
TREATMENT EFFECT HETEROGENEITY

Chapter 8
Inference on heterogeneous effects

In Chapter 3, we introduced the tools for estimating a specific statistic of the individual treatment effect $Y(1) - Y(0)$: the average treatment effect (ATE), $\tau_0 := \mathbb{E}[Y(1) - Y(0)]$. Chapter 5 detailed how these methods could be extended to the case of a large number of control variables. However, this average may hide important differences in treatment effect related to the observed individual characteristics X. For a treatment that produces a positive effect on average, we would be particularly interested in the possibility of detecting whether it does not harm certain subpopulations, which could then be characterized. This heterogeneity will be used in Chapter 9, where we will consider the question of how to best adjust the treatment allocation based on the individual characteristics X.

One of the tools for identifying this heterogeneity is the function

$$\tau : \quad x \in \mathcal{X} \mapsto \mathbb{E}[Y(1) - Y(0)|X = x],$$

that is, the average treatment effect conditional on the characteristics (conditional average treatment effect, or CATE). Because it is a function, this object is more complicated than the ATE, which is a scalar. This is especially the case when the support of X is continuous, where the CATE is inherently high-dimensional. This chapter introduces the recently developed tools for characterizing the heterogeneity of treatment effects and statistically testing whether there are subgroups of the population that are differentially affected by them.

Section 8.1 of this chapter begins by describing more formally the problem and the limitations of certain simple approaches. Sections 8.2 and 8.3 respectively describe the two main directions taken in the literature. The first proposes a direct estimation of the CATE under fairly general conditions on the machine learning methods used. The second, in particular, adapts certain methods presented in Chapter 2 to perform inference. In Section 8.3.6, we detail how the latter approach can be used to perform inference in the presence of endogeneity with causal random forests. The complexity of the CATE has also led to interest in simpler statistics that allow the heterogeneity of treatment effects to be described and tested. Section 8.4 therefore details inference on the properties of heterogeneous effects with selection on observables. Finally, Section 8.6 summarizes all the proofs and additional results of this chapter, and each section includes some applications of the tools developed.

Machine Learning for Econometrics. Christophe Gaillac and Jérémy L'Hour, Oxford University Press. © Christophe Gaillac and Jérémy L'Hour (2025). DOI: 10.1093/9780198918868.003.0008

8.1 Heterogeneous treatment effects

For an agent indexed by i, let $Y_i(0)$ denote the potential outcome if the agent is not treated, and $Y_i(1)$ denote the potential outcome if the agent is treated. We observe the treatment exposure D_i and the realized outcome $Y_i = D_iY_i(1) + (1 - D_i)Y_i(0)$. In this section, we consider an i.i.d. sample (Y_i, D_i, X_i) for $i = 1, \dots, n$, where $X_i \in \mathcal{X}$ contains observable characteristics of the agent i. We also maintain the assumption of treatment independence conditional on observables or unconfoundedness (see Chapter 3, Section 3.3):

Assumption 8.1 (Unconfoundedness assumption).

$$D \perp\!\!\!\perp (Y(0), Y(1)) \mid X. \tag{8.1}$$

A first idea to describe the heterogeneity of treatment effects would be to cluster the population into subgroups based on the observed characteristics X, in order to perform the following test:

$$H_0 : \forall x \in \mathcal{X}, \ \tau(x) = \tau_0, \text{ vs } H_1 : \exists x \in \mathcal{X}, \ \tau(x) \neq \tau_0,$$

where $\tau_0 = \mathbb{E}[Y(1) - Y(0)]$. The problem with this approach is that the researcher 1) often does not know all the subgroups of interest (i.e., sets of interactions between covariates) and 2) would like to perform multiple tests of this type to identify the sub-population of interest. However, if we assume that each test is performed at the α level, then the probability that some of the true null hypotheses are rejected by chance alone may be large. Indeed, if all tests are mutually independent, then the probability that at least one true null hypothesis will be rejected is $1 - (1 - \alpha)^K$, where K is the number of tests performed. This is greater than α for $K > 1$, and actually tends to 1 as $K \to \infty$. In other words, the test level is no longer controlled. This is the problem known as *multiple testing*.

There are corrections for this problem, such as the Bonferroni correction, which does not take into account the correlation between events and is therefore conservative (see also Romano and Wolf, 2005; List et al., 2016; Hsu, 2017, for other more advanced strategies). However, it is still necessary to specify the assumptions of the test. In general, the researcher has an intuition about the characteristics that are driving the heterogeneity of the treatment effect and can therefore test the hypothesis of equality of effects between these subgroups. However, it may be realized that this a priori is not the most relevant. Furthermore, we would also like to implement an automatic way to partition the population and test for the heterogeneity of effects in these groups. Ideally, we would like to form these partitions in a way that maximizes the heterogeneity between groups. This would allow for significant differences despite samples that are often of limited sizes due to the cost of experimentation.

Denoting by $\mu_j(\cdot) = \mathbb{E}[Y|X = \cdot, D = j]$ for $j = 0, 1$ and using the assumption of selection on observables (8.1), it can then be observed that the CATE can be written as follows:

$$\tau(x) = \mathbb{E}[Y(1)|X = x] - \mathbb{E}[Y(0)|X = x]$$
$$= \mu_1(x) - \mu_0(x).$$

These two functions μ_j, for $j = 0, 1$, are regression functions of the observed outcome variable Y on the variables X, which can be estimated separately on the treatment group $\{i : D_i = 1\}$ and the control group $\{i : D_i = 0\}$. However, in a finite sample, a major pitfall of this approach is that $\widehat{\mu}_1$ and $\widehat{\mu}_0$ will then have different regularization biases, which can lead, when we take the difference to form an estimator of the CATE, to estimating heterogeneity where there is none. The problem is partly exacerbated by the fact that the treatment and control groups may be of very different sizes, leading to very different precisions of the estimators of μ_1 and μ_0, which affects what can be inferred about their differences.

The literature has mainly followed two types of approaches. The first one historically (see e.g., Imai and Ratkovic, 2014; Athey et al., 2019; Farrell et al., 2021) aims to adapt different machine learning methods to the context of CATE estimation. These methods, studied in Section 8.3, allow for inference under sometimes quite restrictive conditions. In the context of the above remark and model (8.2), Imai and Ratkovic (2014) proposed to use the joint estimator:

$$(\widehat{\gamma}, \widehat{\delta}) = \arg\min_{\gamma,\delta} \sum_{i=1}^{n} (Y_i - X_i'\gamma + (D_i - 0.5)X_i'\delta)^2 + \lambda_1 \|\gamma\|_1 + \lambda_2 \|\delta\|_2,$$

with $\widehat{\tau}(x) = x'\widehat{\delta}$, which produces a parsimonious estimator of the treatment effect. Exercise 15.3 provides more details on this estimator. However, adapting each method requires the development of an associated theory, which limits the choice of the learning method to best estimate the functions $\mu_j(\cdot)$.

A second approach (see e.g., Robinson, 1988; Nie and Wager, 2020; Kennedy, 2023) considers the functions $m(\cdot) := \mathbb{E}[Y|X = \cdot]$ and $p(\cdot) := \mathbb{E}[D|X = \cdot]$ as *nuisance parameters*, i.e., parameters that are necessary for the estimation of the parameter of interest but not the focus of the study, involved in the estimation of the CATE. These two parameters can be estimated by a wide range of machine learning methods. The developed estimator possesses a *quasi-oracle* property, meaning that it is almost as performant as the CATE estimator obtained when the true functions m and p are known. We start by developing this approach in Section 8.2.

Remark 8.1 High-dimensional linear model

Here, we illustrate the problem when estimating the heterogeneity of treatment effects by performing separate regressions on the treatment and control groups without using a common objective. Consider an example using a high-dimensional linear model as developed in

Continued

Remark 8.1 *Continued*

the previous section:

$$Y(j) = X'\beta_j + \varepsilon_j,\ \mathbb{E}[\varepsilon_j|X] = 0,\ \text{for } j \in \{0,1\}, \tag{8.2}$$

where $\beta_0, \beta_1 \in \mathbb{R}^p$ and $p \gg n$. Under the assumption of sparsity of the two vectors β_0, β_1, $\|\beta_0\|_0, \|\beta_1\|_0 \leq s < p$, they can be separately estimated via Lasso on the treatment and control groups:

$$\widehat{\beta}_j \in \arg\min_{\beta_j \in \mathbb{R}^p} \frac{1}{|i : D_i = j|} \sum_{i:\, D_i = j} (Y_i - X_i'\beta_j)^2 + \lambda_{j,n}\|\beta_j\|_1.$$

We can derive an intuitive estimator of the CATE under this model as $\widehat{\tau}(x) = x'(\widehat{\beta}_1 - \widehat{\beta}_0)$.

However, in general the different regularizations of β_0, β_1 can then lead to inaccurate estimation of τ. As an example, consider the model (8.2) with 150 explanatory variables X with $\beta_{j,k} = 0$ for any k different from 1, $\beta_{1,1} = \beta_{0,1} = 1$, 400 observations, and D following a Bernoulli distribution with parameter 0.8. In Figure 8.1, we can observe heterogeneity when estimating β_0, β_1 separately, even though there is none in this DGP. The reader can refer to Künzel et al. (2019) for other examples.

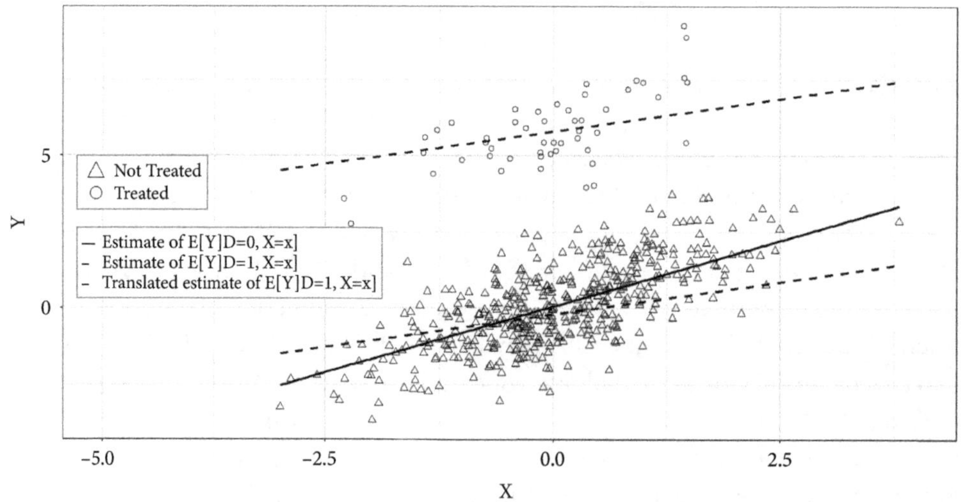

Figure 8.1 Example of estimation of the heterogeneity of treatment effects leading to artifacts: we detect heterogeneity where there is none.

Note: The points represent the 400 observations, treated (dots) or not (triangles). The top dotted line is the estimate of the regression function $E(Y|D = 1, X = \cdot)$ using the treated individuals, and the bottom line is simply its translation. Similarly, the solid line is the regression function $E(Y|D = 0, X = \cdot)$ using the untreated individuals.

8.2 Direct estimation

The two nuisance parameters, which can be directly estimated from the data, are denoted by:

$$p(x) := \mathbb{E}\left[D|X=x\right], \qquad \text{(PROPENSITY SCORE)}$$

$$m(x) := \mathbb{E}\left[Y|X=x\right] = \mu_0(x) + p(x)\tau(x). \qquad \text{(REGRESSION FUNCTION)}$$

Nie and Wager (2020) base their estimator of the treatment effects τ, called the *R-learner*, on the following representation proposed by Robinson (1988) in the context of the semi-parametric model discussed in the remark below:

$$Y_i - m(X_i) = (D_i - p(X_i))\tau(X_i) + \varepsilon_i, \quad \mathbb{E}\left[\varepsilon_i|X_i, D_i\right] = 0. \tag{8.3}$$

The parameter τ therefore satisfies

$$\tau(\cdot) = \arg\min_{\tau}\left\{\mathbb{E}\left[(Y_i - m(X_i) - (D_i - p(X_i))\tau(X_i))^2\right]\right\}. \tag{8.4}$$

To reflect an a priori potential for the form of the treatment effect (i.e., linear, discontinuous, regular, etc.) and limit the complexity of the problem, one can choose to restrict τ to belong to a class of functions Θ, thereby limiting its complexity. With preliminary knowledge of the estimators $\widehat{m}$ and $\widehat{p}$ of the functions m and p, we estimate τ by minimizing the empirical loss penalized by Λ_n, which takes into account the complexity of the function τ:

$$\widehat{\tau}(\cdot) = \arg\max_{\tau\in\Theta}\left\{\frac{1}{n}\sum_{i=1}^{n}\left((Y_i - \widehat{m}(X_i) - (D_i - \widehat{p}(X_i))\tau(X_i)\right)^2 + \Lambda_n(\tau(X_i))\right\}. \tag{8.5}$$

Nie and Wager (2020) propose a two-step estimator:

1. (Estimation of nuisance parameters) Adjustment of $\widehat{m}$ and $\widehat{p}$ by any method aiming to achieve good prediction performance (random forests, deep neural networks, Lasso, etc.).
2. (Estimation of treatment effects) Estimate the treatment effects via a plug-in version of (8.5), using cross-fitted estimators (for example, leave-one-out, where the partition described in Section 5.3 consists of a single observation per group):

$$\widetilde{Y}_{(i)}(X_i) := Y_i - \widehat{m}_{(i)}(X_i) \text{ and } \widetilde{D}_{(i)}(X_i) := D_i - \widehat{p}_{(i)}(X_i).$$

Allowing for a two-step estimation, as opposed to the formulation of the causal forest in Section 8.3, enables the selection of methods that are more suitable for the profiles of m and p in the initial stages. By generalizing the insights and methods of the semi-parametric model in (8.7), the details of which are presented in the remark below,

Nie and Wager (2020) show that it is thereby possible to replicate the performance of the oracle estimator based on (8.5), which assumes knowledge of m and p, given that:

$$\max\left(\mathbb{E}\left((\widehat{m}(X) - m(X))^2\right), \mathbb{E}\left((\widehat{p}(X) - p(X))^2\right)\right) = o_P(n^{-1/2}), \tag{8.6}$$

and where there is a uniformly consistent estimator of the propensity score $\sup_{x\in\mathcal{X}} |\widehat{p}(x) - p(x)| \to_P 0$. The method uses cross-fitting, introduced in Section 5.3, and the expectations in (8.6) are implicitly conditioned on the sample that was used to select the parameters of the estimators $\widehat{m}$ and $\widehat{p}$, which are considered deterministic in this equation. The condition (8.6) imposes a convergence rate in quadratic norm on the estimators of the regression function and propensity score. In practice, this condition is satisfied by a large number of classical non-parametric methods presented, for example, in Chapter 2, provided that the true functions p and m are sufficiently smooth.

Once estimated, however, it remains to test whether the potentially detected heterogeneity of treatment is statistically significant. The method proposed by Nie and Wager (2020) does not currently allow for inference without additional assumptions about the form of τ. An indirect approach consists of using the estimated CATE to guide the statistical analysis in subgroups. However, this is potentially subject to the risk of multiple testing (see Section 8.3.5 and the papers by Davis and Heller, 2020, and Davis and Heller, 2017). This involves separately estimating the average treatment effect for these subgroups, as in the second part of this book, and then testing whether the differences are statistically significant. Another approach is to use the estimated CATE to calculate the best linear prediction of the CATE based on $\widehat{\tau}(x)$, introduced in Chernozhukov et al. (2017) and discussed in detail in Section 8.4.1. The latter is a simpler object on which inference is possible. Finally, Section 8.3 proposes a less flexible method regarding the form of τ, but which allows for direct inference.

Remark 8.2 Semi-parametric model

To give the intuition for Equation (8.3), we consider the following semi-parametric model for $\tau(x) = \varphi(x)\beta$ and

$$Y(d) = f(X) + d\tau(X) + \varepsilon(d), \quad d \in \{0, 1\}, \tag{8.7}$$

where $\varphi : \mathcal{X} \to \mathbb{R}^p$ is a known function. In the spirit of Robinson (1988) and under Assumption 8.1, we obtain:

$$Y - m(X) = (D - p(X))\varphi(X)\beta + \varepsilon.$$

We can thus construct an asymptotically normal "oracle" estimator of β, that is, assuming m and p are known and regressing $Y - m(X)$ on $(D - p(X))\varphi(X)$.

To put this estimator into practice, a general technique is to use cross-fitting, introduced in Section 5.3:

1. Determine a partition $(I_k)_{k=1,...,K}$ of $\{1, \ldots, n\}$ and estimate m and p, respectively, by regressing, using the method of our choice, Y on X and D on X for $i \in \{1, \ldots, n\} \setminus I_k$;
2. Define the transformed variables $\widetilde{Y}_i := Y_i - \widehat{m}_{k(i)}(X_i)$ and $\widetilde{D}_i := (D - \widehat{p}_{k(i)}(X))\varphi(X)$ where $\widehat{m}_{k(i)}$ and $\widehat{p}_{k(i)}$ are the estimators obtained using the sample that does not contain i;
3. Finally, estimate β by ordinary least squares of $\widetilde{Y}_i$ on $\widetilde{D}_i$.

The important point is that when

$$\max(\mathbb{E}\left((\widehat{m}(X) - m(X))^2\right), \mathbb{E}\left((\widehat{p}(X) - p(X))^2\right)) = o_P(n^{-1/2}),$$

then the cross-fitting estimator converges in probability at a rate of $\sqrt{n}$ to the oracle estimator, and asymptotic normality is preserved.

8.3 Inference with causal random forests

One cannot directly use statistical learning methods such as random forests to estimate the treatment effect, as we never observe both Y_0 and Y_1 for the same individual. Therefore, it is not possible to calculate an error on a test sample for the treatment effect. As a result, part of the literature has adapted these tools to the causal inference framework. The main properties of *random forests* are recalled in Section 2.7, and we show here how to adapt these methods to estimate the CATE. Note that we restrict ourselves to random forests, but other methods have also been adapted to the causal inference framework: Lasso (Imai and Ratkovic, 2014), neural networks (Farrell et al., 2021), etc.

8.3.1 Double sample trees

One way to perform causal inference is to rely on the "honesty" property of the tree (Athey and Imbens, 2016; Athey and Wager, 2021), which we now detail. Compared to the standard tree explained in Chapter 2, an "honest" tree or "double sample tree" does not use the same sample to determine the splits that partition the variable space $\mathcal{X}$ and to evaluate the value of the estimator in the leaves. When observations are independent and identically distributed, this makes the construction of the partition independent of the given value on each leaf of the tree. In particular, this limits overfitting by avoiding overly fine partitions in a specific area of the space related to certain values of Y in the subsample used.

We also use "random split trees," where the direction of the split is randomly chosen. We will explain later why this choice is useful for proving the consistency of the estimator. We now study the properties of double sample trees, constructed according to the following algorithm:

1. For each possible subsample of size s in $\{1,\dots,n\}$, divide it into two disjoint sets $\mathcal{I}$ and $\mathcal{J}$ of sizes $|\mathcal{I}| = \lfloor s/2 \rfloor$ and $|\mathcal{J}| = \lceil s/2 \rceil$.
2. Build a decision tree through recursive partitioning, with splits chosen using the sample $\mathcal{J}$ (i.e., without using the observations of Y contained in the sample $\mathcal{I}$).
3. Estimate the responses only in the leaves using the sample $\mathcal{I}$.

8.3.2 Two-sample random forests

In a second step, we aggregate the trees formed on all possible subsamples of size s from the training data. This leads to the creation of two-sample random forests (*double sample random forests* or *bagging*), by aggregating decision trees formed on different subsamples of size s, where these subsamples are formed by randomly selecting the variables X, with this randomness represented by ξ distributed as Ξ:

$$\widehat{\mu}(x; Z_1,\dots,Z_n) = \begin{pmatrix} n \\ s \end{pmatrix}^{-1} \sum_{1\leq i_1<\dots<i_s\leq n} \mathbb{E}_{\xi\sim\Xi}\left[T_\xi(x; Z_{i_1},\dots,Z_{i_s})\right], \tag{8.8}$$

where:

- $T_\xi(x; Z_{i_1},\dots,Z_{i_s})$ is the decision tree based on $(Z_{i_1},\dots,Z_{i_s})$, $Z_i := (D_i, X_i, Y_i)$;
- $\begin{pmatrix} n \\ s \end{pmatrix}$ is the number of combinations of s elements among n;
- ξ summarizes the random aspect of the variable selection during the tree growth.

Given that the number of terms in the sum in (8.8) is very large $\begin{pmatrix} n \\ s \end{pmatrix}$, we use an approximation of the estimator from Equation (8.8) using a Monte Carlo method. Specifically, we draw B samples $\mathcal{I}_b$ of size s without replacement, where the b-th sample is $(Z^*_{b,1},\dots,Z^*_{b,s})$, and we consider the following approximation of (8.8):

$$\widehat{\mu}(x; Z_1,\dots,Z_n) \approx \frac{1}{B}\sum_{b=1}^{B} T_{\xi^*_b}(x; Z^*_{b,1},\dots,Z^*_{b,s}), \tag{8.9}$$

where the learning is based on:

$$T_{\xi_b^*}(x; Z_{b,1}^*, \ldots, Z_{b,s}^*) = \sum_{i \in \mathcal{I}_b} \alpha_{b,i}^*(x) Y_{b,i}^*, \tag{8.10}$$

$$\alpha_{b,i}^*(x) = \frac{1\{X_{b,i}^* \in L_b^*(x)\}}{|\{i : X_{b,i}^* \in L_b^*(x)\}|}.$$

This aggregation strategy, called bagging, reduces the variance of the estimator of μ (see, e.g., Bühlmann and Yu, 2002). It should be noted that the honesty property requires the partitions L_b^* in (8.10) to be independent of the values in the leaves $Y_{i,b}^*$.

8.3.3 Bias and honesty of the random forest regression

We consider hereafter i.i.d. observations $(Y_i, X_i)_{i=1}^n$ and show the consistency of an estimator $\widehat{\mu}(\cdot)$ of $\mu(\cdot) = \mathbb{E}[Y_i|X_i = \cdot]$. This helps to form an intuition about the necessary adaptations of usual statistical learning tools to obtain their consistency or asymptotic normality at the expense of predictive performance.

Definition 8.1 (Leaf diameter). *The diameter of the leaf $L(x)$ is the length of the longest segment contained in $L(x)$, which we denote by $Diam(L(x))$.*
The diameter of the leaf $L(x)$ parallel to the j-th axis is the length of the longest segment contained in $L(x)$ parallel to the j-th axis, which we denote by $Diam_j(L(x))$.

One way to ensure the consistency of the estimator is to impose that the leaves become small in **all directions of the feature space $\mathcal{X}$** when n (and therefore s) becomes large: $\text{Diam}(L(x)) \to 0$ as $s \to \infty$ (see Lemma 8.1). To do this, we impose randomness in the variable selection at each step (random-split tree). We need the following assumptions.

Assumption 8.2

- ***Random-split tree***: *the probability that the next split occurs along the j-th feature is bounded from below by δ/p, where $0 < \delta \leq 1$.*
- ***α-regular***: *from the sample $\mathcal{I}$, each split leaves at least a fraction α of observations of the training set on each side of the split.*
- ***Minimum leaf size** k: there are between k and $2k - 1$ observations in each terminal leaf of the tree.*
- ***Honest tree:*** *the samples used to construct the nodes and to evaluate the estimator on the leaves are different.*

The minimum leaf size k is a *regularization parameter* that must be set by the researcher. In practice, cross-validation can be used to choose k. The following lemma is essential, but it relies on a very strong assumption regarding the distribution of the covariates.

Lemma 8.1 (Control of leaf diameter in uniform random forests, Lemma 2 in Wager and Athey, 2017). *Let T be an α-regular tree satisfying Assumption 8.2 and $X_1, \ldots, X_s \sim \mathcal{U}([0,1]^p)$ independently. Let $0 < \eta < 1$, then for sufficiently large s,*

$$\mathbb{P}\left(Diam_j(L(x)) \geq \left(\frac{s}{2k-1}\right)^{-\alpha_1 \delta/p}\right) \leq \left(\frac{s}{2k-1}\right)^{-\alpha_2 \delta/p},$$

where $\alpha_1 = 0.99(1-\eta)\log(1-\alpha)/\log(\alpha)$ and $\alpha_2 = \eta^2/(-2\log(\alpha))$.

Finally, a key assumption to obtain a consistent estimator is that $x \mapsto \mu(x)$ is Lipschitz. This limits the use of these random forests to regression functions μ_j that are sufficiently regular. This is a classic assumption in non-parametric estimation, where many methods such as kernel estimation, smoothing splines, neural networks, etc. are used. All of these methods require some form of regularity in the object being estimated.

Lemma 8.2 (Control of the bias in double sample random forests, Theorem 3 in Wager and Athey, 2017). *Let T satisfy Assumption 8.2, $x \mapsto \mu(x)$ be Lipschitz, $\alpha \leq 0.2$, then the bias of the random forest for $x \in \mathcal{X}$ is bounded by*

$$\left|\mathbb{E}\left[\widehat{\mu}(x)\right] - \mu(x)\right| = \mathcal{O}\left(s^{-\alpha_3 \delta/p}\right),$$

where $\alpha_3 = \log(1-\alpha)/(2\log(\alpha))$.

Lemma 8.2 states that the bias of our double-sample random forest estimator $\widehat{\mu}(x)$ of $\mu(x)$ goes to zero at a rate that decreases with the dimension of the covariates (p), but increases with the regularity of the tree (α_3) and the parameter indexing the random split (δ).

8.3.4 Double sample causal trees

The asymptotic normality of random forest regression is proved in Theorem 8 of Wager and Athey (2017). Here, for simplicity, we state directly the asymptotic normality of causal forests (Theorem 11 in Wager and Athey, 2017). Causal forests are random forests for treatment effect estimation, and are particularly useful for causal inference where the difficulty is that the outcome of the regression is not directly observed.

The algorithm for double sample causal trees is similar to the algorithm for double sample trees, but the splits are chosen (splitting criterion) to maximize the variance of

$$\hat{\tau}(x) = \hat{\mu}_1(x) - \hat{\mu}_0(x) = \frac{1}{|\{i,\ D_i = 1,\ X_i \in L(x)\}|} \sum_{i:\ D_i=1,\ X_i \in L(x)} Y_i - \frac{1}{|\{i:\ D_i = 0,\ X_i \in L(x)\}|} \sum_{i,\ D_i=0,\ X_i \in L(x)} Y_i, \quad (8.11)$$

while Assumption 8.2 is replaced by:

Assumption 8.3

- ***α*-regularity**: *each leaf* $L(\cdot)$ *leaves at least a fraction* α *of the available training examples on each side of the split;*
- ***Minimum leaf size*** k: *there are between* k *and* $2k - 1$ *observations of each treatment group in each terminal leaf of the tree (with* $D_i = 1$ *or with* $D_i = 0$*);*
- ***Honest trees***: *the sample* $\mathcal{J}$ *used to place the splits is different from the sample* $\mathcal{I}$ *used to evaluate the estimator through (8.11).*

Without the honesty property, the treatment effect estimator would be based on leaves that lead to a high treatment effect, but this likely means that the treatment effect in these leaves is biased.

Remark 8.3 Causal forests: summary of the algorithm

We summarize the algorithm for causal forests. Starting from an i.i.d. sample (Y_i, X_i, D_i), $i = 1, \ldots, n$, where Y_i is the outcome variable, X_i are the features, and D_i is the treatment indicator, and after fixing a minimum leaf size k for each treatment group $D = 0, 1$:

1. Randomly draw a sample of size s from $\{1, \ldots, n\}$ without replacement, and split it into two subsamples $\mathcal{I}$ and $\mathcal{J}$ of respective sizes $\lfloor s/2 \rfloor$ and $\lceil s/2 \rceil$;
2. Build a decision tree through recursive partitioning, with splits chosen using the sample $\mathcal{J}$ (i.e., without using the Y observations contained in the sample $\mathcal{I}$) and minimizing on sample $\mathcal{J}$ an error criterion $MSE(\hat{\tau})$ adapted to the treatment effect, where $\hat{\tau}$ is defined in (8.11) and $MSE(\hat{\tau})$ is discussed in the remark below.
3. Estimate the responses $\hat{\tau}$ defined in (8.11) in the leaves using only the sample $\mathcal{I}$.

The following set of assumptions about the distribution of the covariates, the regularity of μ_j, and the existence of the conditional variance, allows us to obtain the asymptotic normality of causal random forests.

Assumption 8.4 (Regularity conditions for asymptotic normality). *The potential outcomes samples $(X_i, Y_i(1))$ and $(X_i, Y_i(0))$ satisfy, for $j \in \{0, 1\}$,*

- $X_i \sim \mathcal{U}([0, 1]^p)$ *independently;*
- $\mu_j : x \mapsto \mathbb{E}[Y(j)|X = x]$ *and* $\mu_{j,2} : x \mapsto \mathbb{E}[Y(j)^2|X = x]$ *are Lipschitz;*
- $Var(Y(j)|X = x) > 0$ *and* $\mathbb{E}[|Y(j) - \mathbb{E}[Y(j)|X = x]|^{2+\delta_1}] \leq M$ *for constants* $\delta_1, M > 0$ *uniformly over* $x \in [0, 1]^p$.

The infinitesimal jackknife estimator (Efron, 2014; Wager et al., 2014) is denoted by

$$\widehat{V}_{IJ}(x) = \frac{n-1}{n}\left(\frac{n}{n-s}\right)^2 \sum_{i=1}^{n} \left(\frac{1}{B-1} \sum_{b=1}^{B} \left(\widehat{\tau}_b^*(x) - \overline{\widehat{\tau}_b^*}(x)\right)\left(N_{i,b}^* - \overline{N_b^*}\right) \right),$$

where $N_{i,b}^*$ indicates whether the i-th observation has been used or not for the b-th bootstrap tree and $\overline{N_b^*}$, $\overline{\widehat{\tau}_b^*}$ are averages over the B bootstrap trees.

Theorem 8.1 (Asymptotic normality, double sample causal random forests, Theorem 1 in Wager and Athey, 2017) *Assume that we have i.i.d. samples $Z_i = (X_i, Y_i, D_i)_{i=1}^n \in [0, 1]^p \times \mathbb{R} \times \{0, 1\}$, Assumption 8.1, and that there exists $\varepsilon > 0$ such that $\varepsilon \leq \mathbb{P}(D = 1|X) \leq 1 - \varepsilon$. Let's assume that Assumption 8.4 is satisfied and consider a double-sample causal random forest satisfying Assumption 8.3 with $\alpha \leq 0.2$. Assume that*

$$s = \lfloor n^{\beta} \rfloor, \text{ for a certain } \beta_{\min} := 1 - \left(1 + \frac{p}{\delta} \frac{\log(\alpha^{-1})}{\log\left((1-\alpha)^{-1}\right)}\right)^{-1} < \beta < 1. \qquad (8.12)$$

Then, there exist a function $C(\cdot)$ and a constant $\gamma > 0$ both independent of n, such that the estimator $\widehat{\tau}(x)$ of the CATE at a point x is asymptotically normal:

$$\frac{\widehat{\tau}(x) - \tau(x)}{\sigma_n(x)} \to_d \mathcal{N}(0, 1),$$

where $\sigma_n(x) := \dfrac{s}{n} \dfrac{C(x)}{\log(n/s)^{\gamma}}$. The asymptotic variance $\sigma_n(x)$ can be consistently estimated using the infinitesimal jackknife*:*

$$\widehat{V}_{IJ}(x)/\sigma_n^2(x) \xrightarrow{p} 1.$$

Several comments are in order. First, because of the restrictions on β, we can specify the convergence rate $n^{-1/(1+p\alpha_3/\delta)}$, which does not allow a case of "high dimension" in the sense of the second part ($p \gg \log(n)$). Theorem 8.1 allows inference, i.e. testing the significance of the treatment effect for a population with covariates x, without imposing a priori on the groups formed from the characteristics X learned from the data. Third, the Theorem 8.1 relies on a very strong assumption about the distribution of the covariates.

Remark 8.4 On the segmentation criterion

If the result of the regression τ_i **was observed** and without dividing the training sample $\mathcal{S}^{\text{tr}}$ (as for the CART regression algorithm, see reminders in Section 2.7.2), then the cutoffs should minimize the empirical counterpart of the quadratic error loss

$$\mathbb{E}\left[(\tau_i - \widehat{\tau}(X_i))^2\right] = \mathbb{E}\left[\tau_i^2\right] - 2\mathbb{E}\left[\widehat{\tau}(X_i)\tau_i\right] + \mathbb{E}\left[\widehat{\tau}(X_i)^2\right]$$

on the test sample $\mathcal{S}^{\text{te}}$. This amounts to minimizing

$$\begin{aligned}\text{MSE}_{\widehat{\tau}}\left(\mathcal{S}^{\text{te}}, \mathcal{S}^{\text{tr}}, T\right) &:= \frac{1}{|\mathcal{S}^{\text{te}}|}\sum_{i\in\mathcal{S}^{\text{te}}}\left((\tau_i - \widehat{\tau}(X_i; \mathcal{S}^{\text{tr}}, T))^2 - \tau_i^2\right) \\ &= -\frac{2}{|\mathcal{S}^{\text{te}}|}\sum_{i\in\mathcal{S}^{\text{te}}}\tau_i\widehat{\tau}(X_i; \mathcal{S}^{\text{tr}}, T) + \frac{1}{|\mathcal{S}^{\text{te}}|}\widehat{\tau}(X_i; \mathcal{S}^{\text{tr}}, T)^2. \end{aligned} \quad (8.13)$$

However, since τ_i is not directly observed, Athey and Imbens (2016) use a criterion that mimics what is done in the CART algorithm. Here, using the fact that the estimators $\widehat{\mu}(X_i)$ are constant on each leaf L_m by definition, we have, for $x \in L_m$,

$$\begin{aligned}\sum_{i\in\mathcal{S},\, i \text{ s.t. } X_i\in L_m}\widehat{\mu}(X_i)^2 &= \sum_{i\in\mathcal{S},\, i \text{ s.t. } X_i\in L_m}\frac{\widehat{\mu}(X_i)}{|L_m|}\sum_{k\in\mathcal{S},\, k \text{ s.t. } X_k\in L_m} Y_k \\ &= \sum_{k\in\mathcal{S},\, k \text{ s.t. } X_k\in L_m}\frac{Y_k}{|L_m|}\sum_{i\in\mathcal{S},\, i \text{ s.t. } X_i\in L_m}\widehat{\mu}(X_i) \\ &= \sum_{k\in\mathcal{S},\, k \text{ s.t. } X_k\in L_m}\widehat{\mu}(X_k)Y_k.\end{aligned}$$

Thus, (8.13) shows that, in the context of regression, we want to minimize the unbiased estimator of $\text{MSE}_{\widehat{\mu}}\left(\mathcal{S}^{\text{te}}, \mathcal{S}^{\text{tr}}, T\right)$ which is

$$\text{MSE}_{\widehat{\mu}}\left(\mathcal{S}^{\text{tr}}, \mathcal{S}^{\text{tr}}, T\right) = -\frac{1}{|\mathcal{S}^{\text{tr}}|}\sum_{i\subset\mathcal{S}^{\text{tr}}}\widehat{\tau}(X_i; \mathcal{S}^{\text{tr}}, T)^2.$$

Continued

Remark 8.4 *Continued*

In the context of the treatment effect, this leads Athey and Imbens (2016) to consider, by analogy, the maximization of the achievable criterion

$$-\text{MSE}_{\widehat{\tau}}\left(\mathcal{S}^{\text{tr}}, \mathcal{S}^{\text{eval}}, T\right) = \frac{1}{|\mathcal{S}^{\text{eval}}|} \sum_{i \in \mathcal{S}^{\text{eval}}} \widehat{\tau}(X_i; \mathcal{S}^{\text{tr}}, T)^2,$$

where the training sample is divided into an evaluation sample $\mathcal{S}^{\text{eval}}$ and a true training sample $\mathcal{S}^{\text{tr}}$.

Another interesting criterion analyzed by Athey and Imbens (2016) is based on

$$T = \frac{|\widehat{\tau}_1 - \widehat{\tau}_2|}{\sqrt{\text{Var}(\widehat{\tau}_1) + \text{Var}(\widehat{\tau}_2)}},$$

where $\widehat{\tau}_1$ and $\widehat{\tau}_2$ are the estimated treatment effects in each child node, with the estimated variances $\text{Var}(\widehat{\tau}_1)$ and $\text{Var}(\widehat{\tau}_2)$, respectively. This criterion is a t-statistic type criterion, which tests the equality of treatment effects between the two potential child nodes, and aims to select the most different ones.

Remark 8.5 Local centering

The ideas derived from the literature considered in the first two sections (i.e., Chernozhukov et al., 2017) led Athey and Wager (2021) to consider a local centering pre-processing before estimating causal random forests. More specifically, they show, using simulations, that estimating the aforementioned double sample causal forests with orthogonalized results

$$\widetilde{Y}_i = Y_i - \mathbb{E}[Y_i|X_i = x],$$
$$\widetilde{D}_i = D_i - \mathbb{E}[D_i|X_i = x],$$

improves the algorithm's performance. In practice, they propose using estimators based on random forests for the regression function in the above equations. This translates into the use of recentered variables $\widetilde{Y}_i = Y_i - \widehat{Y}^{(-i)}(X_i)$ and $\widetilde{D}_i = D_i - \widehat{D}^{(-i)}(X_i)$, where $\widehat{Y}^{(-i)}(X_i)$ and $\widehat{D}^{(-i)}(X_i)$ are leave-one-out estimators (random forests evaluated without the i-th observation, which is computationally inexpensive).

8.3.5 Applications

Davis and Heller (2017) and Davis and Heller (2020) estimate the impact of two youth employment programs in Chicago. These two randomized controlled trials focus on the same summer employment program in 2012 and 2013. They have relatively large sample sizes (1,634 and 5,216 observations, respectively) and control for a wide range of covariates. The program provides disadvantaged youth between the ages of 14 and 22 with a 25-hours-per-week job and an adult mentor. Participants are paid Chicago's minimum wage. The researchers focus on two outcomes: arrests for violent crime in the two years following randomization and an indicator of employment status in the six quarters following the program.

They ask: if we divide the sample into a group that is predicted to respond positively to the program and a group that is not, will we be able to identify youth with larger treatment effects? To do this, they train the causal forest on half of the sample and then use the treatment effect predictions on the other half. Then they regress the outcomes on the two indicators $1\{\widehat{\tau}(X_i) > 0\}$, $D_i 1\{\widehat{\tau}(X_i) > 0\}$, and $D_i(1 - 1\{\widehat{\tau}(X_i) > 0\})$. They test the null hypothesis that the treatment effect is the same in both groups. Their results show that the test is rejected in the training sample for both outcome variables of interest, while it detects significant heterogeneity only for the employment outcome in the test sample. This could be an indication of overfitting. It is worth noting that changing the partitioning rule does not seem to change their results significantly. They conclude from this analysis that sampling error may prevent detection of the treatment effect with these sample sizes.

Hussam et al. (2022) use a causal random forest to assess the impact of providing a $100 subsidy to randomly selected entrepreneurs in India, particularly on their returns. In addition, they compare the predicted treatment when using causal forests based on entrepreneur characteristics with the treatment effect when the subsidy is allocated based on community members' rankings of the entrepreneurs. They find that peer rankings predict returns over and above observable characteristics, but that making the rankings public encourages lying, limiting their naive use for subsidy allocation.

8.3.6 The problem of estimating treatment heterogeneity with endogeneity

Athey et al. (2019) extend the estimation of treatment heterogeneity mentioned above to the case where there is potential endogeneity. The objective is to measure the causal effect of a policy while recognizing that the intervention and the outcome are linked by unobserved factors. The assumption of selection on observables (8.1) no longer holds, but instrumental variables are assumed to be available. For example, one may be interested in the causal effect of motherhood on female labor market participation. In this context, the instrumental variable traditionally used in the literature is the binary variable "mixed children," which means having children of different genders. The idea is that the desire to have children of different genders will impact the number of children but will not have a direct impact on labor market participation. Athey et al. (2019) consider the following model:

$$\begin{aligned} Y_i &= \mu(X_i) + \tau(X_i)D_i + \varepsilon_i, \\ \mathbb{E}[Z_i\varepsilon_i|X_i = x] &= 0, \quad \mathbb{E}[\varepsilon_i|X_i = x] = 0 \quad \forall x \in \mathcal{X}. \end{aligned} \tag{8.14}$$

In this context, τ is our parameter of interest, the causal effect of D on Y, μ is the nuisance parameter, and ε is a noise term correlated with D_i.

Remark 8.6 Link with NPIV

Note that model (8.14) is a very particular case of the so-called nonparametric instrumental variable (NPIV) model (see e.g., Chapter 3; Newey and Powell, 2003; Darolles et al., 2011), which takes the form:

$$Y_i = \varphi(D_i, X_i) + \varepsilon, \quad \mathbb{E}[Z_i\varepsilon_i|X_i = x] = 0, \mathbb{E}[\varepsilon_i|X_i = x] = 0,$$

where $\varphi(D_i, X_i) = \tau(X_i)D_i + \mu_0(X_i)$. $\tau(\cdot)$ is the heterogeneous causal impact of D_i on Y_i using Z_i as an instrument.

Using the following notations

$$m(W_i; \tau, \mu) := (Y_i - \tau(X_i)D_i - \mu(X_i)) \begin{pmatrix} Z_i \\ 1 \end{pmatrix},$$

where $W_i = (X_i, Y_i, D_i, Z_i)$, then estimation is based on the following moment conditions, for all $x \in \mathcal{X}$,

$$M(x; \tau, \mu) := \mathbb{E}[m(W_i; \tau, \mu)|X_i = x] = 0. \tag{8.15}$$

Specifically, when we have only one instrument Z with non-zero $\text{Cov}(D, Z|X = x)$ for all $x \in \mathcal{X}$, then note that $\tau(x)$ is identified from the moment conditions (8.15) as $\tau(x) = \text{Cov}(Y, Z|X = x)/\text{Cov}(D, Z|X = x)$.

At a specific point x, the idea is to use random forests to compute the weights $\alpha_i(x)$ that measure the importance of the i-th observation in the estimation of $\tau(x)$ by the moment equation,

$$(\widehat{\tau}(x), \widehat{\mu}(x)) \in \arg\min_{\tau,\mu} \left\{ \left\| \sum_{i=1}^{n} \alpha_i(x) m(W_i; \tau, \mu) \right\|_2 \right\},$$

where $\alpha_i(x) := 1\{X_i \in L(x)\}/|\{i : X_i \in L(x)\}|$ and $\|\cdot\|_2$ is the Euclidean norm. If there exists a unique solution $(\widehat{\tau}(x), \widehat{\mu}(x))$, then it solves

$$\sum_{i=1}^{n} \alpha_i(x) m\left(W_i; \widehat{\tau}(x), \widehat{\mu}(x)\right) = 0.$$

The idea is then to extend the previous random forests to learn the weights α_i using the data and obtain an asymptotically normal estimator $\widehat{\tau}$ of τ. The main difference compared to the case where Assumption (8.1) is satisfied is that both τ and μ are implicitly defined.

8.3.7 The gradient tree algorithm

The algorithm computes the splits (and thus the weights and the estimator) recursively. We start with a parent node P that we want to split into two children C_1, C_2 using a cut aligned with the axis, generating the best improvement in the accuracy of our estimator $\widehat{\tau}$, meaning minimizing:

$$\mathrm{err}(C_1, C_2) = \sum_{j=1}^{2} \mathbb{P}\left(X_i \in C_j | X_i \in P\right) \mathbb{E}\left[\left(\widehat{\tau}_{C_j}(\mathcal{J}) - \tau(X_i)\right)^2 | X_i \in C_j\right],$$

where $\widehat{\tau}_{C_j}(\mathcal{J})$ are adapted on the children C_j in the first part of the training sample $\mathcal{J}$. However, we do not have access to an unbiased direct estimate of $\mathrm{err}(C_1, C_2)$. This leads Athey et al. (2019) to propose a new procedure:

1. In a labeling step, we compute $(\widehat{\tau}_P(\mathcal{J}), \widehat{\mu}_P(\mathcal{J}))$ in the parent node using

$$(\widehat{\tau}_P(\mathcal{J}), \widehat{\mu}_P(\mathcal{J})) \in \arg\min \left\{ \left\| \sum_{\{i \in \mathcal{J},\, X_i \in P\}} m\left(W_i; \tau, \mu\right) \right\|_2 \right\}, \tag{8.16}$$

then we compute the gradients with respect to τ, μ:

$$\begin{aligned} \boldsymbol{A_P} &:= \frac{1}{|\{i : X_i \in P\}|} \sum_{\{i:\, X_i \in P\}} \nabla m\left(W_i; \widehat{\tau}_P, \widehat{\mu}_P\right) \\ &= \frac{1}{|\{i : X_i \in P\}|} \sum_{\{i:\, X_i \in P\}} \begin{pmatrix} -D_i Z_i & -Z_i \\ -D_i & -1 \end{pmatrix}. \end{aligned}$$

Note that in the instrumental variables model (8.14), the minimization problem in (8.16) has an explicit solution

$$\begin{pmatrix} \widehat{\tau}_P(\mathcal{J}) \\ \widehat{\mu}_P(\mathcal{J}) \end{pmatrix} = \begin{pmatrix} \dfrac{\sum_{\{i:\, X_i \in P\}} Z_i (Y_i - \overline{Y}_P)}{\sum_{\{i: X_i \in P\}} Z_i (D_i - \overline{D}_P)} \\ \dfrac{1}{|\{i : X_i \in P\}|} \sum_{\{i: X_i \in P\}} \left(Y_i - D_i \widehat{\tau}_P(\mathcal{J})\right) \end{pmatrix},$$

where $\overline{Y}_P = \sum_{\{i:\, X_i \in P\}} Y_i / |\{i : X_i \in P\}|$ and $\overline{D}_P = \sum_{\{i:\, X_i \in P\}} D_i / |\{i : X_i \in P\}|$. Then we compute the *pseudo-results*:

$$\rho_i := -(1, 0) \boldsymbol{A_P}^{-1} m\left(W_i; \widehat{\tau}_P, \widehat{\mu}_P\right) \in \mathbb{R}, \tag{8.17}$$

where $(1, 0)$ is the vector in $\mathbb{R}^2$ that takes the coordinate of τ.

2. In a regression step, we perform a CART regression on the pseudo-results, meaning we find the partition that maximizes the criterion:

$$\tilde{\Delta}(C_1, C_2) = \sum_{j=1}^{2} \frac{1}{|\{i : X_i \in C_j\}|} \left(\sum_{\{i: X_i \in C_j\}} \rho_i \right)^2 . \tag{8.18}$$

Then, we relabel the observations in each child by solving the estimation equation.

The motivation for this strategy comes from the fact that using $\tilde{\Delta}(C_1, C_2)$ as a criterion is a way to approximate the true error $\text{err}(C_1, C_2)$. Indeed, Proposition 1 in Athey et al. (2019) states that if: 1) A_P is a consistent estimator of $\nabla \mathbb{E}\left[m\left(W_i; \hat{\tau}_P, \hat{\mu}_P\right) | X_i \in P\right]$; 2) the parent node has a radius smaller than $r > 0$; 3) the regularity assumptions of Theorem 8.2 are satisfied; 4) the number of observations in the children nodes is considered fixed and large compared to $1/r^2$, then:

$$\text{err}(C_1, C_2) = K(P) - \mathbb{E}\left[\tilde{\Delta}(C_1, C_2)\right] + o(r^2), \tag{8.19}$$

where $K(P)$ is a deterministic term related to the uniformity (purity) of P.

Remark 8.7 Influence function

The intuition for using the *pseudo-results* ρ_i comes from the proof of the asymptotic normality for Z-estimators, which are estimators of θ_0 based on the moment condition

$$\mathbb{E}\left[m_{\theta_0}(X_i)\right] = 0.$$

Using the asymptotic representation of the Z-estimator $\hat{\theta}_n$, for example in Theorem 5.21 page 52 of Van der Vaart (1998),

$$\hat{\theta}_n = \theta_0 + \frac{1}{n} \nabla m_{\theta_0}^{-1} \sum_{i=1}^{n} m_{\theta_0}(X_i) + o_P\left(\frac{1}{\sqrt{n}}\right), \tag{8.20}$$

we obtain that the influence of the n-th observation on the estimator is given by

$$\begin{aligned}
&\hat{\theta}(X_1, \ldots, X_n) - \hat{\theta}(X_1, \ldots, X_{n-1}) \\
&= \frac{1}{n} \nabla m_{\theta_0}^{-1} m_{\theta_0}(X_n) + \frac{1}{n} \nabla m_{\theta_0}^{-1} \sum_{i=1}^{n-1} m_{\theta_0}(X_i) - \frac{1}{n-1} \nabla m_{\theta_0}^{-1} \sum_{i=1}^{n-1} m_{\theta_0}(X_i) \\
&= \frac{1}{n} \nabla m_{\theta_0}^{-1} m_{\theta_0}(X_n) - \frac{1}{n(n-1)} \nabla m_{\theta_0}^{-1} \sum_{i=1}^{n-1} m_{\theta_0}(X_i) \\
&= \frac{1}{n} \nabla m_{\theta_0}^{-1} m_{\theta_0}(X_n) + o_P(1),
\end{aligned}$$

which has the same shape as ρ_i. The update of the estimator error when dividing the parent P into two children (C_1, C_2) is approximated via the result (8.19) using the average of the influence functions on C_1 and C_2. This strategy is similar to the analysis of the asymptotic behavior of a Z-estimator using (8.20).

8.3.8 Central limit theorem for generalized random forests

We only study the case of the triangular model (8.14) and we refer to Athey et al. (2019) for the more general case of asymptotic normality for generalized random forests (GRF hereafter). We denote by

$$V(x) = \nabla\mathbb{E}\left[m(W_i; \tau, \mu)|X_i = x\right] = -\begin{pmatrix} \mathbb{E}\left[D_iZ_i|X_i = x\right] & \mathbb{E}\left[Z_i|X_i = x\right] \\ \mathbb{E}\left[D_i|X_i = x\right] & 1 \end{pmatrix},$$

the dependent pseudo-variables ρ_i^* which are oracles (that is to say not accessible) given by

$$\rho_i^*(x) = -(1,0)V(x)^{-1}m(W_i; \tau(x), \mu(x)) \in \mathbb{R}$$

and let the resulting pseudo-forest be

$$\tilde{\tau}^*(x) := \tau(x) + \sum_{i=1}^{n} \alpha_i(x)\rho_i^*(x) = \sum_{i=1}^{n} \alpha_i(x)\left(\tau(x) + \rho_i^*(x)\right).$$

$\tilde{\tau}^*(x)$ is useful as it has the same form as the basic element for learning in the U-statistic studied in Wager and Athey (2017). Thus, the tools developed in Wager and Athey (2017) and in Section 8.3 can be applied, which establishes the asymptotic normality of $\hat{\tau}(x)$ under the condition that $\hat{\tau}(x)$ and $\tilde{\tau}^*(x)$ are asymptotically close, which is guaranteed by Assumption 8.5. $\tilde{\tau}^*(x)$ is the result of the ideal regression forest trained with the dependent variables $\tau(x) + \rho_i^*(x)$.

Assumption 8.5 (Smoothness conditions for asymptotic normality of GRF).
Assume that:

- *for fixed values of* (τ, μ),

$$M_{\tau,\mu}(x) := \mathbb{E}\left[m(W_i; \tau, \mu)|X_i = x\right];$$

  is Lipschitz in the variable x*;*
- ***Regular identification**:* $V(x)$ *is invertible for all* $x \in \mathcal{X}$*. This comes from the fact that the instrument is valid.*

Theorem 8.2 (Asymptotic normality of GRF for instrumental variable model 8.14, Theorem 5 in Athey et al., 2019) *Assume that we have i.i.d. samples*

$W_i = (X_i, Z_i, Y_i, D_i)_{i=1}^n \in [0,1]^p \times \mathbb{R} \times \mathbb{R} \times \{0,1\}$, and there exists $\varepsilon > 0$ such that $\varepsilon \leq \mathbb{P}(D = 1|X) \leq 1 - \varepsilon$. Suppose Assumptions 8.4 and 8.5 hold, and consider a causal double sample random forest satisfying Assumption 8.3 with $\alpha \leq 0.2$. Suppose β satisfies (8.12). Then, there exist $C(\cdot)$ and $\gamma > 0$, such that the estimator $\widehat{\tau}(x)$ of the CATE at point x is asymptotically normal:

$$\frac{\widehat{\tau}(x) - \tau(x)}{\sigma_n(x)} \to_d \mathcal{N}(0,1),$$

with $\sigma_n(x) := sC(x)/(n \log(n/s)^\gamma)$.

Athey et al. (2019), just like Nie and Wager (2020), recommend orthogonalizing the variables Y_i, D_i, and Z_i, with the leave-one-out preliminary estimators $\widehat{m}^{(-i)}$, $\widehat{p}^{(-i)}$, and $\widehat{z}^{(-i)}$ of $\mathbb{E}[Y_i|X_i = x]$, $\mathbb{E}[D_i|X_i = x]$, and $\mathbb{E}[Z_i|X_i = x]$, which gives

$$\widehat{\tau}(\cdot) = \frac{\sum_{i=1}^n \alpha_i(x)\left(Y_i - \widehat{m}^{(-i)}(X_i)\right)\left(Z_i - \widehat{z}^{(-i)}(X_i)\right)}{\sum_{i=1}^n \alpha_i(x)\left(D_i - \widehat{p}^{(-i)}(X_i)\right)\left(Z_i - \widehat{z}^{(-i)}(X_i)\right)}. \tag{8.21}$$

This option is implemented in the R package `grf`. Confidence intervals can be constructed for the value of the treatment effect at a point $\tau(x)$, such as

$$\lim_{n\to\infty} \mathbb{E}\left[\tau(x) \in \left(\widehat{\tau}(x) \pm \Phi^{-1}(1 - \alpha/2)\widehat{\sigma}_n^2(x)\right)\right] = 1 - \alpha,$$

from the fact that $\mathrm{Var}[\tilde{\tau}^*(x)]/\sigma_n^2 \to 1$ and using the definition of $\rho_i^*(x)$ to construct $\widehat{\sigma}_n^2(x)$.

8.3.9 Application to the heterogeneity of the effect of subsidized training on trainees' income

Firstly, we strongly recommend consulting the simulations used in Athey and Wager (2019) using the `grf` package, which illustrate the performance of GRF.

Here we consider an application of GRF to estimate the heterogeneity of the effect of subsidized training on participants' future income. We use the data from Abadie et al. (2002). We reanalyze data from the Job Training Partnership Act (JTPA), a large-scale, government-funded training program. Individuals are randomly assigned to the JTPA treatment group or the control group, where the treatment consists of offering training. Only 60% of individuals in the treatment group actually accepted training, but the random assignment of treatment provides an instrument for treatment status. In addition, since only 2% of individuals receiving JTPA services are in the control group, the effect for the latter is interpreted as the effect for those who are treated. See Abadie et al. (2002) for more details and an alternative method of estimating the effects of this training on the earnings distribution based on quantile regression that deals with the endogeneity of the treatment. We focus on the heterogeneity of the training effect based on interactions of baseline

Table 8.1 The estimated treatment effect on 30-month earnings

	ATE, OLS	ATE, 2SLS	ATE, RF	ATE, GRF	Quartile 1	Med.	Quartile 3
Men	3,754 (536)	1,593 (895)	3,185	2,365	962	2,247	4,276
Women	2,215 (334)	1,780 (532)	1,843	1,634	706	1,408	2,053

characteristics: age, an indicator for high school completion, marital status, indicators for Black and Hispanic race, perceptions of Aid to Families with Dependent Children (AFDC), and a binary variable indicating whether one worked less than 13 weeks in the previous year. We denote by Y earnings at a 30-month horizon, D enrollment in JTPA services, and Z service provision.

We train a generalized random forest on 80% of the sample, separating men and women, and using instrumental variables (referred to as "GRF") or not (referred to as "CRF"). We establish several comparisons.

We compare the distributions of the predicted treatment effects for 20% of the sample, which is our test sample, using GRF or CRF. Of course, a more in-depth analysis of the results is necessary and could be done by reporting the precise estimate of the treatment effect for subgroups of the sample (here, all covariates are binary variables, so we cannot plot the estimated treatment as in the simulations of the `grf` package). Similar to Abadie et al. (2002), the Table 8.1 shows that there is a significant difference between the two. This highlights the importance of using an instrumental variable in this context. The results from Table 8.1 can also be compared to the quantile treatment effect (QTE) estimates on the test sample from Abadie et al. (2002) using a quantile regression that accounts for endogeneity. The two are very close, which is consistent, but the lack of a uniform confidence region for the GRF prevents us from making further comparisons, such as testing whether the effects are the same for two populations $H_0 : \tau(x_1) = \tau(x_2)$, for given $x_1, x_2 \in \mathcal{X}$ vs $H_1 : \tau(x_1) \neq \tau(x_2)$.

8.4 Inference on characteristics of heterogeneous effects

The previous sections have shown that inference on the CATE often requires strong assumptions that may not always hold (e.g., uniformly distributed covariates in causal forests) or are not testable. Furthermore, the practical implementation of these methods often differs from their theoretical counterparts (e.g., tuning parameters are chosen by cross-validation). There may be a trade-off between the assumptions we are willing to make and the information we want to learn about the target object. Thus, following a branch of the statistical literature (see, e.g., Lei et al., 2017), Chernozhukov et al. (2017) propose to change the perspective on the CATE and make inference on selected **key characteristics** of the CATE rather than the true object itself. This change of objective still allows to describe the heterogeneity of the effects while providing proper tests of some of its characteristics.

For simplicity of exposition, we present this approach in the case of experiments where the propensity score is known, but note that the results can also be extended to the case where we have a consistent estimator of the propensity score. Changing our parameters of interest allows to use many machine learning methods that can be considered as proxies for the CATE, and to limit the number of assumptions we have to make (in particular, the resulting estimators from these methods no longer necessarily need to be consistent). The idea is to post-process these machine learning estimators to obtain consistent estimators *of concise summaries* of the CATE, rather than of the CATE itself. The requirement that the propensity score be known is an important constraint, but it is also a fairly common framework, for example in randomized controlled experiments, possibly stratified by certain observed variables.

The model is similar to that of Section 8.1: we observe the outcome variable $Y = DY(1) + (1 - D)Y(0)$, the binary treatment variable D, the covariates $X \in \mathbb{R}^p$, and assume selection on observables 8.1 and the overlap assumption ($\exists\ \varepsilon > 0,\ s.t.\ \varepsilon \leq p(X) \leq 1 - \varepsilon$). For simplicity, we first consider that the propensity score $p(x) := \mathbb{P}(D = 1|X = x)$ known. We have the following model:

$$Y = \mu_0(X) + D\tau(X) + U, \quad \mathbb{E}\left[U|X, D\right] = 0, \tag{8.22}$$

$$\tau(X) = \mu_1(X) - \mu_0(X) = \mathbb{E}[Y(1)|X] - \mathbb{E}[Y(0)|X]. \tag{8.23}$$

8.4.1 Estimation of key characteristics of CATE

Chernozhukov et al. (2017) propose to separate the i.i.d. data (Y_i, D_i, X_i) for $i = 1, \ldots, n$ into an auxiliary sample (denoted $Data_A$) and a main sample (denoted $Data_M$). The first step is to estimate $x \to \mu_0(x)$ and $x \to \tau(x)$ on the auxiliary sample. The following estimators are the estimators of μ_0 and τ respectively, resulting from a machine learning algorithm (any algorithm can be considered):

$$m_0 : x \to m_0(x|\text{Data}_A), \tag{8.24}$$

$$T : x \to T(x|\text{Data}_A). \tag{8.25}$$

m_0 and T are called *ML proxy predictors* because no assumption about their performance is imposed. They can simply be proxies for the true functions. Then, they propose to reprocess these estimators to make inference on the following key characteristics of the CATE on the main sample:

1. the **best linear predictor** (BLP) of the CATE $\tau(\cdot)$ based on the approximate predictor $T(\cdot)$;
2. **sorted group average treatment effects** (GATES), which is the average of $\tau(\cdot)$ over different groups induced by the heterogeneity of the estimator $T(\cdot)$;

3. **classification analysis** (CLAN), which is the average of the features X over the groups induced by the quantiles of $T(\cdot)$.

Best linear predictor (BLP) of the CATE. The first key characteristic (1), the BLP of the CATE using the proxy T, is defined as the linear projection of the CATE onto the plane spanned by 1 and this proxy in the $L^2(P)$ space:

$$\begin{aligned} BLP[\tau(X)|T(X)] &= \underset{f(X)\in \mathrm{Span}(1,T(X))}{\arg\min} \ \mathbb{E}\left[(\tau(X) - f(X))^2\right] \\ &= \mathbb{E}\left[\tau(X)\right] + \frac{\mathrm{Cov}(\tau(X), T(X))}{\mathrm{Var}(T(X))}\left(T(X) - \mathbb{E}[T(X)]\right) \\ &= b_1 + b_2\left(T(X) - \mathbb{E}[T(X)]\right), \end{aligned} \tag{8.26}$$

where

$$(b_1, b_2) \in \underset{(B_1,B_2)\in\mathbb{R}^2}{\arg\min} \ \mathbb{E}\left[(\tau(X) - B_1 - B_2 T(X))^2\right]. \tag{8.27}$$

We do not observe $\tau(\cdot)$, but we actually observe an unbiased signal of $\tau(\cdot)$, which is:

$$\mathbb{E}\left[\frac{D - p(X)}{p(X)(1 - p(X))} Y \middle| X\right] = \tau(X) \tag{8.28}$$

and from the auxiliary sample A, we can estimate a proxy $T(\cdot)$ for $\tau(\cdot)$. Thus, we can estimate $\mathrm{Cov}(\tau(X), T(X))/\mathrm{Var}(T(X))$ using (8.28) and the regression:

$$w(X)(D - p(X))Y = \beta_1 + \beta_2\left(T(X) - \mathbb{E}[T(X)]\right) + \varepsilon, \tag{8.29}$$

$$\mathbb{E}\left[\varepsilon\begin{pmatrix} 1 \\ T(X) - \mathbb{E}[T(X)] \end{pmatrix}\right] = \begin{pmatrix} 0 \\ 0 \end{pmatrix}, \tag{8.30}$$

where $w(X) = ((1 - p(X))p(X))^{-1}$.

Theorem 8.3. (Convergence of the estimator of the best linear predictor, Theorem 2.2 in Chernozhukov et al., 2017) *Consider the functions $x \mapsto T(x)$ and $x \mapsto m_0(x)$ as fixed and the propensity score p known. Suppose that Y and X have finite second moments and that $\mathbb{E}[XX']$ is full rank. Then, take (β_1, β_2) defined as in (8.29), which also solves the problem (8.27), so that*

$$\beta_1 = \mathbb{E}\left[\tau(X)\right] \quad \textit{and} \quad \beta_2 = \frac{Cov(\tau(X), T(X))}{Var(T(X))}.$$

Several remarks are in order. First, identification is constructive and simple: the estimation procedure of weighted MCO is described in 8.4.3. Second, this strategy does not assume that the estimator $T(X)$ is a consistent estimator of $\tau(X)$, which allows the use of the high-dimensional parameter $p \gg n$. However, we only estimate the best linear projection of τ onto $(T(X), 1)$, which means that if $T(X)$ is a poor predictor, this feature tells us very little about the true τ. Furthermore, unlike in Section 8.1, we assume that the propensity score p is known here. Finally, note two interesting extreme cases:

- if $T(X)$ is a perfect approximation of $\tau(X)$ and $\tau(X)$ is not a constant, then $\beta_2 = 1$;
- if $T(X)$ is completely noisy, uncorrelated with $\tau(X)$, then $\beta_2 = 0$.

Testing whether $\beta_2 = 0$ is equivalent to conducting a simple test of the joint hypothesis that there is heterogeneity and that $T(X)$ is relevant (which is a problem if it is not rejected, as the two hypotheses cannot be separated).

Remark 8.8 Alternative estimator

To reduce the noise generated by the Horvitz–Thompson type weight $H := (D - p(X))/(p(X)(1 - p(X)))$ in (8.30), Chernozhukov et al. (2017) recommend using the following regression instead of (8.29):

$$w(X)(D - p(X))Y = \mu' Z_1 H + \beta_0 + \beta_1 (T(X) - \mathbb{E}[T(X)]) + \varepsilon,$$

where $Z_1 = (1, m_0(X), T(X))$.

Sorted group average treatment effects. We can also divide the support of the machine learning predictor $T(X)$ into distinct regions to define groups of similar treatment response and make inferences about the expected effect of their treatment:

$$GATES: \quad \mathbb{E}[\tau(X)|G_1] \leq \cdots \leq \mathbb{E}[\tau(X)|G_K],$$

for $G_k = 1\{l_{k-1} \leq T(X) \leq l_k\}$ with $-\infty = l_0 \leq l_1 \cdots \leq l_K = \infty$. To do this, Chernozhukov et al. (2017) consider the regression of the unbiased signal $w(X)(D-p(X)Y$ on the indicators $1\{i \in G_1\}, \ldots, 1\{i \in G_K\}$. The resulting projection parameters are the GATES.

8.4.2 Inference for key features of the CATE

For the following key features of the CATE:

- $\theta = \beta_2$, the parameter weighting the predictor of CATE heterogeneity (based on the BLP);
- $\theta = \beta_1 + \beta_2(T(x) - \mathbb{E}[T])$, the individual prediction of τ.

Chernozhukov et al. (2017) also propose methods for making inference by addressing the *two sources of uncertainty* that arise when using sample-splitting methods (see, for example, Section 5.3). Specifically, the use of different partitions into two parts $\{A, M\}$ of the initial sample and the aggregation of different estimations $\widehat{\theta}_A$ provide:

- *conditional uncertainty*, which is the uncertainty of the estimation concerning the parameter θ, *conditionally on the data division*;
- *variational uncertainty*, which is induced by the sample-splitting.

To perform inference with methods using sample-splitting, it is necessary to adjust the normal confidence level in a specific way. Denote:

- the *lower median* (which is the usual median) by

$$\underline{\text{Med}}(X) := \inf\{x \in \mathbb{R} : \mathbb{P}_X(X \leq x) \geq 1/2\};$$

- the *upper median* by $\overline{\text{Med}}(X) := \sup\{x \in \mathbb{R} : \mathbb{P}_X(X \geq x) \geq 1/2\}$ (the next distinct quantile of a random variable);
- $\text{Med}(X) := (\overline{\text{Med}}(X) + \underline{\text{Med}}(X))/2$,

where for a continuous variable these notions coincide. We precise the two sources of uncertainty, which arise from the repeated use of the partitions $\{A, M\}$ of the initial sample $\{Y_i, D_i, X_i\}_{i=1}^n$:

- *Conditional uncertainty*: conditionally on the data of the sample A (hereafter denoted $Data_A$), the ML estimators from the previous sections imply that, as the cardinality of the set M (denoted $|M|$) goes to infinity, with high probability and under the assumptions of Theorem 8.3:

$$\mathbb{P}\left(\frac{\widehat{\theta}_A - \theta_A}{\widehat{\sigma}_A} \leq z \,\middle|\, \text{Data}_A\right) \to \Phi(z),$$

  where Φ is the c.d.f. of the standard normal distribution. The following **conditional** confidence intervals are obtained:

$$\mathbb{P}(\theta_A \in [L_A, U_A] \,|\, \text{Data}_A) = 1 - \alpha + o_P(1),$$

  where $[L_A, U_A] := \left[\widehat{\theta}_A \pm \Phi^{-1}(1 - \alpha/2)\widehat{\sigma}_A\right]$.
- *Variational uncertainty*: To perform unconditional inference on the sample-splitting performed, Chernozhukov et al. (2017) propose:
  - either adjusting the standard p-values $p_A^+ = 1 - \Phi\left(\frac{\widehat{\theta}_A - \theta_A}{\widehat{\sigma}_A}\right)$ and

$p_A^- = \Phi\left(\frac{\widehat{\theta}_A - \theta_A}{\widehat{\sigma}_A}\right)$ for the testing the null $H_0 : \theta_A = \theta_0$ respectively

the one-sided hypotheses: $H_1 : \theta_A > \theta_0$ or $H_1 : \theta_A < \theta_0$, to account for the sample-splitting;
- or aggregating the estimators and adjusting the confidence intervals (see, for example, Section 5.3).

Note that conditionally on $Data_A, \widehat{\theta}_A$ is a random variable.

Adjusting p-values to account for sample-splitting. We describe the first option to handle the variational uncertainty. First, note that under H_0, asymptotically $p_A^{\pm} \sim \mathcal{U}(0,1)$ **conditionally on the data** A, but randomness still remains conditionally on the whole dataset. Thus, Meinshausen et al. (2009) and Chernozhukov et al. (2017) suggest using $p^{\pm}$ as the respective p-values for the one-sided tests, and $2\min(p^+, p^-)$ for the two-sided one, where

$$p^{\pm} = \underline{\text{Med}}(p_A^{\pm}|\text{Data}) \leq \alpha/2. \tag{8.31}$$

Thus, in the former case we would reject the null hypothesis if $p^{\pm} < \alpha$ (where α is the test level). This rule is based on the fact that the median M of J uniformly distributed random variables (not necessarily independent) satisfies $P(M \leq \alpha/2) \leq \alpha$, thus controlling the type I error. Theorem 8.4 shows the uniform validity (over distributions P in $\mathcal{P}$, all possible data distributions satisfying H_0) of the sample-splitting adjusted p-values.

Assumption 8.6 (Asymptotic uniform level for conditional testing). *Suppose that all partitions $Data_A$ of the data in set $\mathcal{A}$ are "regular," in the sense that under H_0, for all $x \in [0,1]$,*

$$\sup_{P \in \mathcal{P}} |\mathbb{P}_P(p_A^{\pm} \leq x | Data_A \in \mathcal{A}) - x| \leq \delta = o(1),$$

and $\inf_{P \in \mathcal{P}} P(Data_A \in \mathcal{A})$ *converges to 1.*

Assumption 8.6 guarantees that the unconditional distribution of the p-value $p_A^{\pm}$ asymptotically converges to the distribution of a uniform random variable, uniformly over the class $\mathcal{P}$.

Theorem 8.4 (Asymptotic uniform level, Theorem 3.1 in Chernozhukov et al., 2017) *If Assumption 8.6 holds, then under H_0, we have*

$$\sup_{P \in \mathbb{P}} \mathbb{P}_P(p^{\pm} \leq \alpha/2) \leq \alpha + 2\delta = \alpha + o(1).$$

Adapted estimator and confidence intervals. Chernozhukov et al. (2017) propose to aggregate estimators obtained from multiple partitions of the initial sample through:

$$\widehat{\theta} := \text{Med}\left(\widehat{\theta}_A \middle| \text{Data}\right)$$

and to report the following confidence intervals with nominal level $1 - 2\alpha$:

$$[l; u] := \left[\overline{\text{Med}}(L_A|\text{Data}); \underline{\text{Med}}(U_A|\text{Data})\right],$$

where $[L_A, U_A] := \left[\widehat{\theta}_A \pm \Phi^{-1}(1 - \alpha/2)\widehat{\sigma}_A\right]$. Theorem 3.2 in Chernozhukov et al. (2017) shows the uniform validity of this type of confidence interval, using the validity of the confidence interval *CI* introduced earlier, which is narrower but more difficult to compute.

8.4.3 Algorithm: inference on the main features of CATE

We describe the algorithm to perform inference on the main features of CATE, before considering simulation and applications in the following two sections. Consider the i.i.d. sample $(Y_i, X_i, D_i)_{i=1}^n$. These algorithms based on alternative estimators for BLP and GATES are more stable (see Chernozhukov et al., 2017, for a formal proof of theoretical equivalence).

Step 0 We fix the number of partitions (*sample-splitting*) S and the significance level α.

Step 1 We compute the propensity scores $p(X_i)$.

Step 2 We consider S partitions into two sets of indices $i \in \{1, \ldots, n\}$ in the main sample M, and the auxiliary sample A. For each partition $s \in \{1, \ldots, S\}$:

Step 2.1 Fit and train each ML method separately to learn m_0 and T using A. For each observation i in M, we compute the predicted base effect $m_0(X_i)$ and the predicted treatment effect $T(X_i)$.

Step 2.2 We estimate the BLP parameters using weighted OLS in M:

$$Y_i = \widehat{\alpha}' Z_{1,i} + \widehat{\beta}_1 (D_i - p(X_i)) + \widehat{\beta}_2 (D_i - p(X_i)) \left(T(X_i) - \overline{T}^M\right) + \widehat{\varepsilon}_i,$$

for $i \in M$, where $\overline{T}^M$ is the average of $T(X_i)$ in M, which is such that

$$\frac{1}{|M|} \sum_{i \in M} w(X_i) \widehat{\varepsilon}_i Z_i = 0,$$

where

$$Z_i = \left[Z_{1,i}', D_i - p(X_i), (D_i - p(X_i)) \left(T(X_i) - \overline{T}^M\right)\right]',$$
$$w(X_i) = (p(X_i)(1 - p(X_i)))^{-1},$$
$$Z_{1,i} = (1, m_0(X_i), T(X_i))'.$$

Step 2.3 We estimate the GATES parameters using weighted OLS in M *via*

$$Y_i = \widehat{\alpha}' Z_{1,i} + \sum_{k=1}^{K} \widehat{\gamma}_k (D_i - p(X_i))\, 1\{T(X_i) \in I_k\} + \widehat{\varepsilon}_i, \quad i \in M$$

such that

$$\frac{1}{|M|} \sum_{i \in M} w(X_i) \widehat{\varepsilon}_i W_i = 0,$$

$$W_i = \left[Z_{1,i}', \{(D_i - p(X_i)) 1\{T(X_i) \in I_k\}\}_{k=1}^{K}\right]',$$
$$I_k = [l_{k-1}, l_k], \; l_k = q_{k/K}(T(X_i)).$$

Step 2.4 We compute performance measures for each ML method

$$\widehat{\Lambda} = \left|\widehat{\beta}_2\right|^2 \widehat{\operatorname{Var}}(T(X)) \quad \text{and} \quad \widehat{\bar{\Lambda}} = \sum_{k=1}^{K} \widehat{\gamma}_k^2 \mathbb{P}(T(X) \in I_k).$$

Step 3 We select the ML methods that maximize $\widehat{\Lambda}$ and $\widehat{\bar{\Lambda}}$.

Step 4 We compute estimates, confidence level $(1 - \alpha)$, and conditional values of p for all parameters of interest.

Step 5 We compute adjusted confidence intervals $(1 - 2\alpha)$ and adjusted p-values using the variational method described in Section 8.4.2.

Several remarks are in order. First, note that maximizing $\widehat{\Lambda}$ in step 2.4 is equivalent to maximizing the correlation between the ML predictor proxy and the true τ. Maximizing $\widehat{\bar{\Lambda}}$ in step 2.4 is equivalent to maximizing the part of the variation of τ that is explained by

$$\sum_{k=1}^{K} \widehat{\gamma}_k (D_i - p(X_i))\, 1\{T(X_i) \in I_k\}.$$

8.4.4 Simulations

We illustrate the behavior of the introduced tools on simulations in this section and refer to Exercise 15.4 for an application to the heterogeneity of the gender wage gap. We implement this strategy in a framework where

$$\tau(x) = \zeta(x_1)\zeta(x_2), \quad \text{where } \zeta(u) = 1 + \frac{1}{1 + e^{-20(u-1/3)}},$$

based on an adaptation of the code github.com/demirermert/MLInference.

Table 8.2 Performance measures table for GATES and BLP using four ML methods

	Elastic net	Boosting	Neural networks	Random forests
$\widehat{\bar{\Lambda}}$	8,359	8,444	8,507	8,379
$\widehat{\Lambda}$	0,882	0,941	0,968	0,892

Note: Estimation based on 100 splits.

Table 8.3 Estimated ATE and parameter β_2 table for BLP.

	Neural networks	Neural networks	Boosting	Boosting	True
	ATE	HET	ATE	HET	ATE
	2,758	1,003	2,759	0,910	2,753
90% CI	(2,679 ; 2,836)	(0,921 ; 1,085)	(2,680 ; 2,838)	(0,832 ; 0,986)	

Note: Estimation using 100 partitions for the two best methods according to the selection procedure based on Λ: neural networks and boosting trees. β_2 is denoted HET.

Table 8.4 Average estimated characteristics for the most and least affected groups $\mathbb{E}[X_k|G_5]$ and $\mathbb{E}[X_k|G_1]$.

	Neural networks			Boosting		
	Most affected	Least affected	Difference	Most affected	Least affected	Difference
X_1	0.777	0.235	0.539	0.720	0.248	0.475
	(0.762 ; 0.793)	(0.219 ; 0.252)	(0.517 ; 0.561)	(0.703 ; 0.737)	(0.231 ; 0.264)	(0.451 ; 0.498)
X_2	0.768	0.238	0.529	0.715	0.268	0.453
	(0.752 ; 0.785)	(0.221 ; 0.256)	(0.504 ; 0.553)	(0.698 ; 0.734)	(0.250 ; 0.285)	(0.427 ; 0.478)

Note: Realized based on 100 divisions (see CLAN in Chernozhukov et al., 2017) for the two variables X_1 and X_2 with robust confidence intervals for the four used ML methods. "Least affected" corresponds to group G_1 and "most affected" corresponds to group G_5.

The neural network model is able to adapt well to heterogeneity, as β_2 is close to 1. This is reassuring because the shape of ζ is a sigmoid, which is the base function of the neural network here (i.e., the *activation function*, see Section 2.8). Now let's look at what we call the "CLAN" in Table 8.4, which are the average characteristics for the most and least affected groups $\mathbb{E}[X_k|G_5]$ and $\mathbb{E}[X_k|G_1]$ for the two variables X_1 and X_2. We show that ML methods are able to correctly identify that those in the upper right corner (resp. lower left corner) in the (X_1, X_2) space are those who benefit the most (resp. the least) from the treatment.

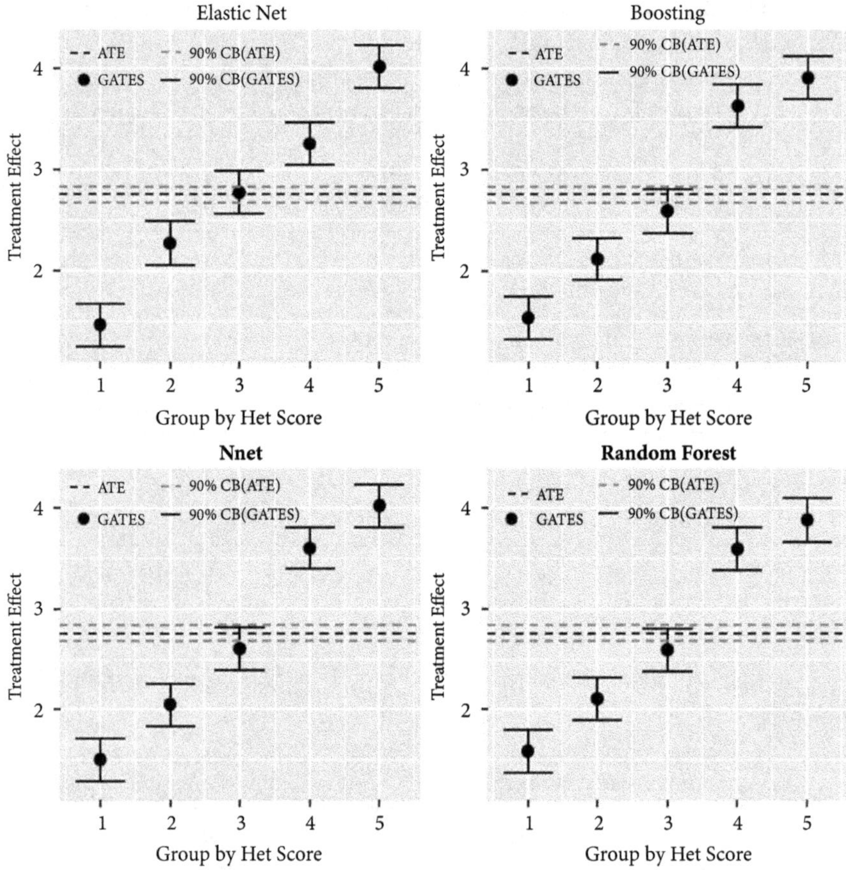

Figure 8.2 GATES estimate with robust confidence intervals.

Note: Estimation based on 100 partitions for the four used machine learning methods. The quantiles of the true treatment effect are min: 1.00, 25%: 2.00, 50%: 2.54, 75%: 3.92, max: 3.99.

8.5 Summary

Key concepts

Heterogeneous treatment effects, conditional average treatment effect (CATE), nuisance parameters, R-learner, "honest trees" property, bagging, causal forests, segmentation criterion, endogeneity, gradient tree, generic machine learning, key features of CATE, best linear predictor (BLP) of CATE, variational uncertainty.

Additional references

Athey and Wager (2019) develop an application of causal random forests using the `grf` package to estimate, based on data from the national study of learning attitudes, the effect of a "nudge" intervention (indirect suggestions) to instill in students the belief that intelligence can be developed through academic success. Baiardi and Naghi (2024) revisit influential empirical studies with the tools presented in this chapter, providing very interesting examples of the value added of such tools.

Code and data

The two-step estimation of (8.5) proposed by Nie and Wager (2020) is implemented in the R package `rlearner`, available at github.com/xnie/rlearner. The code and data associated with Athey and Wager (2019) are provided on github.com/grf-labs. Simulations for Section 8.3.9 are also available at this address.

The data from Abadie et al. (2002) for the application in Section 8.3.9 can be downloaded from economics.mit.edu/faculty/angrist/data1/data/abangim02.

The simulations in Section 8.4.4 use an adaptation of the code available at github.com/demirermert/MLInference. This github code also contains the dataset and code to reproduce the application in Chernozhukov et al. (2017).

Questions

1. What fundamental problem arises when using standard machine learning methods to estimate causal effects?
2. Explain briefly the problem highlighted by this citation from Athey (2017) and propose a method seen in this chapter to overcome it. "[In the context of evaluating the allocation of a treatment whose aim was to retain customers]. *The overlap between the group with highest risk of [not buying again] and the group who would respond most to interventions was only 50 %. Thus, treating the problem of retaining customers as if it were a prediction problem yielded lower payoffs to the firm.*"
3. Explain intuitively what random splits in the construction of causal random forests bring in theory. What do we lose compared to causal random forests with optimally selected splits?
4. Can we estimate the conditional average treatment effect

$$\tau : x \mapsto \mathbb{E}\left[Y(1) - Y(0) | X = x\right]$$

using the generic machine learning approach? Discuss.

5. We want to make inference on a parameter θ using only one sample, which is divided into two parts data $= \{A, M\}$. We use the subsample M to train an ML estimator $\widehat{\theta}$. We then use the subsample A to evaluate it, which leads to the estimator $\widehat{\theta}_A$. What type of inference can we make? What problem does it raise?

Continued

Continued

6. Explain intuitively why partitioning the sample is useful in the estimation of causal random forests to obtain the convergence of the estimator for heterogeneous treatment effects. What is this property called?
7. What are the main differences between random forests and causal random forests? How are they implemented in practice?
8. Describe the best linear predictor (BLP) of CATE using two machine learning proxies m_0 and T for, respectively, $\mathbb{E}[Y|X, D = 0]$ and the CATE.

8.6 Proofs and additional results

Proof of Lemma 8.1. Let $0 < \eta < 1$ and denote by

- $c(x)$ the number of splits leading to the leaf $L(x)$,
- $c_j(x)$ the number of splits creating the leaf $L(x)$ along the axis j.

Using the fact that T is α-regular, the minimum number of observations in $L(x)$ is $s\alpha^{c(x)}$, $\alpha > 1$, which is thus less than or equal to $2k - 1$. We obtain

$$c(x) \geq c_0 := \frac{\log(s/(2k-1))}{\log(\alpha^{-1})}.$$

Using the fact that T is a randomly divided tree, with high probability,

$$c_j(x) \geq Z, \quad Z \sim \text{Binomial}\left(c_0, \frac{\delta}{p}\right),$$

meaning that the minimum total number of splits leading to $L(x)$ is c_0 and at each of these nodes, the probability of choosing the j-th coordinate is bounded below by δ/p. Then, we use the Chernoff multiplicative bound

$$\mathbb{P}\left(c_j(x) \leq (1-\eta)\mu_0\right) \leq e^{-\eta^2\mu_0/2}, \tag{8.32}$$

where $\mu_0 = \mathbb{E}[Z] = \delta c_0/p$. Finally, Wager and Walther (2015) show that the diameter of the leaf along the axis j is related to the number of observations in the leaf, **when the covariates are uniformly distributed**, $L(x)$ *via*

$$\text{Diam}(L(x)) \leq (1-\alpha)^{0.99c_j(x)}.$$

Combining this inequality with (8.32) leads to the result. □

Proof of Lemma 8.2. We start with Definition (8.8) which implies $\mathbb{E}\left[\widehat{\mu}(x)\right] = \mathbb{E}\left[T(x; Z_i)\right]$. Then, we define $\tilde{\mu}(x)$ as $\widehat{\mu}(x)$ by replacing $\alpha_i(x)$ with

$$\tilde{\alpha}_i(x) = \frac{1\{X_i \in L(x)\}}{s|L(x)|},$$

where $|L(x)|$ is the Lebesgue measure of the leaf $L(x)$. Using the honesty assumption (i.e., Y is independent of $L(x)$) for the third equality and

$$\mathbb{P}(X_i \in L(x)|L(x)) = |L(x)|$$

for the fourth equality,

$$\begin{aligned}
&\mathbb{E}[\tilde{\mu}(x)] - \mu(x) \\
&= \mathbb{E}[T(x; Z)] - \mathbb{E}[Y|X = x] \\
&= \mathbb{E}\left[\mathbb{E}\left[\sum_{i\in\{i_1,\ldots,i_s\}} \frac{1\{X_i \in L(x)\}}{s|L(x)|} Y_i \middle| L(x), X_i \in L(x)\right]\right] - \mathbb{E}[Y|X = x] \\
&= \frac{1}{s} \sum_{i\in\{i_1,\ldots,i_s\}} \mathbb{E}\left[\frac{1\{X_i \in L(x)\}}{|L(x)|} |L(x)\right] \mathbb{E}[\mathbb{E}[Y_i|X_i \in L(x)]] - \mathbb{E}[Y|X = x] \\
&= \mathbb{E}[\mathbb{E}[Y|X \in L(x)] - \mathbb{E}[Y|X = x]].
\end{aligned}$$

Then, using the fact that $x \mapsto \mathbb{E}[Y|X = x]$ is Lipschitz, there exists a constant $C > 0$,

$$|\mathbb{E}[Y|X \in L(x)] - \mathbb{E}[Y|X = x]| \leq C\text{Diam}(L(x)). \tag{8.33}$$

Moreover, using the fact that the diagonal length of a unit hypercube in dimension p is $\sqrt{p}$,

$$\left\{\text{Diam}(L(x)) \geq \sqrt{p}\left(\frac{s}{2k-1}\right)^{-\alpha_1\delta/p}\right\}$$

is a subset of

$$\bigcup_{j=1}^{p}\left\{\text{Diam}_j(L(x)) \geq \left(\frac{s}{2k-1}\right)^{-\alpha_1\delta/p}\right\},$$

and using Lemma 8.1,

$$\begin{aligned}
&\mathbb{P}\left(\text{Diam}(L(x)) \geq \sqrt{p}\left(\frac{s}{2k-1}\right)^{-\alpha_1\delta/p}\right) \\
&\leq \sum_{j=1}^{p} \mathbb{P}\left(\text{Diam}_j(L(x)) \geq \left(\frac{s}{2k-1}\right)^{-\alpha_1\delta/p}\right) \\
&\leq p\left(\frac{s}{2k-1}\right)^{-\alpha_2\delta/p}.
\end{aligned}$$

We conclude by taking $\eta = \sqrt{\log((1-\alpha)^{-1})} \leq 0.49$ (thus $0.99(1-\eta) \geq 0.51$, hence the factor 1/2 in α_3) and with $\mathbb{E}\left[\tilde{\mu}(x) - \widehat{\mu}(x)\right] = \mathcal{O}\left(n^{-1/2}\right)$. □

Key ideas for the proof of Theorem 8.1. A random forest is a U-statistic, which means that it can be written as

$$\mu = \binom{n}{s}^{-1} \sum_{i \in \{1,\ldots,n\}^s,\text{ with } i_1 < \ldots < i_s} T(Z_{i_1}, \ldots, Z_{i_s})$$

for a bounded function T (see Chapter 12 p.162 in Van der Vaart, 1998). Note that under the assumptions of Ttheorem 8.1, the regression function being Lipschitz on a closed bounded interval, it is bounded. The usual way to show the asymptotic normality for U-statistics is to use the projection $\mathring{\widehat{\mu}}(x)$ of $\widehat{\mu}(x)$ onto the class $\mathcal{S}$ of all statistics of the form

$$\sum_{i=1}^{n} g_i^x(Z_i),$$

where $\mathbb{E}\left[\left(g_i^x(Z_i)\right)^2\right] < \infty$, which is called the Hájek projection. The Hájek projection can thus be understood as a linearization of our initial statistic.

Then, starting with $\widehat{\mu}(x) = (\widehat{\mu}(x) - \mathring{\widehat{\mu}}(x)) + \mathring{\widehat{\mu}}(x)$, the proof consists in showing that $\widehat{\mu}(x) - \mathring{\widehat{\mu}}(x) \xrightarrow{p} 0$ and applying the central limit theorem to the projection $\mathring{\widehat{\mu}}(x)$. More precisely, we useProposition 8.1 (which is Lemma 11.10 in Chapter 11 of Van der Vaart, 1998).

Proposition 8.1 *Let $Z_1, \ldots, Z_n$ be independent random vectors, then the projection of a random variable W with a finite second moment onto the class $\mathcal{S}$ is given by*

$$\mathring{W} = \mathbb{E}[W] + \sum_{i=1}^{n} \left(\mathbb{E}[W|Z_i] - \mathbb{E}[W]\right).$$

Proof of proposition 8.1. The proof follows from the fact that $\mathring{W}$ belongs to $\mathcal{S}$ and because we can verify that for all $S \in \mathcal{S}$,

$$\mathbb{E}\left[(W - \mathring{W})S\right] = 0.$$

Indeed, for all $i \in \{1, \ldots, n\}$,

$$\mathbb{E}\left[(W - \mathring{W})g_i(Z_i)\right] = \mathbb{E}\left[\underbrace{\left(\mathbb{E}[W|Z_i] - \mathbb{E}[\mathring{W}|Z_i]\right)}_{=0} g_i(Z_i)\right]$$

because for all $j \neq i$, by independence, $\mathbb{E}\left[\mathbb{E}[W|Z_i]\,|Z_j\right] = \mathbb{E}[W]$. □

Next, an important result (see Theorem 11.2 in Van der Vaart, 1998), which allows to reduce the asymptotic analysis of $(W - E(W))/\mathrm{Sd}(W)$ to that based on the projection $(\mathring{W} - \mathbb{E}[\mathring{W}])/\mathrm{Sd}(\mathring{W})$, states that if the projection $\mathring{W}$ satisfies

$$\lim_{n\to\infty} \frac{\mathrm{Var}(W)}{\mathrm{Var}(\mathring{W})} \to 1, \tag{8.34}$$

then

$$\frac{W - \mathbb{E}[W]}{\mathrm{Sd}(W)} - \frac{\mathring{W} - \mathbb{E}[\mathring{W}]}{\mathrm{Sd}(\mathring{W})} \xrightarrow{p} 0.$$

Thus, to prove the asymptotic normality of the random forest, one could try to show (8.34). However, this is not true for regression trees. Therefore, Wager and Athey (2017) show an adaptation close to this property (8.34) (i.e., regression trees are ν-incremental), which states that under the conditions of Theorem 8.1, there exists $C_1(\cdot)$ such that

$$\liminf_{s\to\infty} \frac{\mathrm{Var}(\mathring{T}(x))}{\mathrm{Var}(T(x))} \log(s)^p \geq C_1(x), \tag{8.35}$$

where for simplicity we denote $T(x) := \mathbb{E}_{\xi\sim\Xi}\left[T_\xi(x; Z_1, Z_2, \ldots, Z_s)\right]$ (where the expectation is only with respect to the randomness of ξ, so $T(x)$ depends on $Z_1, Z_2, \ldots, Z_s$). Then, they use the independence of the observations and the symmetry permutation of the trees T, for a subsample $\mathcal{I}_b$ of $\{1, \ldots, n\}$,

$$\mathbb{E}\left[T(x; Z_{b,1}, \ldots, Z_{b,s}) | Z_j = z\right] = \begin{cases} \mathbb{E}\left[T(x; z, Z_{b,2}, \ldots, Z_{b,s})\right] & \text{if } j \in \mathcal{I}_b \\ \mathbb{E}\left[T(x; Z_{b,1}, Z_{b,2}, \ldots, Z_{b,s})\right] & \text{if } j \notin \mathcal{I}_b \end{cases}$$

which in (8.8) yields that, for $i \in \{1, \ldots, n\}$, with $C_n^s = \binom{n}{s}$,

$$\begin{aligned} &\mathbb{E}[\widehat{\mu}(x)|Z_i = z] - \mathbb{E}[\widehat{\mu}(x)] \\ &= \sum_{\mathcal{I}_b : i \in \mathcal{I}_b} \frac{\mathbb{E}[\mathbb{E}_{\xi\sim\Xi}[T_\xi(x; Z_{b,1}, .., Z_{b,s})]|Z_i = z] - \mathbb{E}\left[\mathbb{E}_{\xi\sim\Xi}\left[T_\xi(x; Z_{b,1}, .., Z_{b,s})\right]\right]}{C_n^s}, \\ &= (C_n^s)^{-1} C_{n-1}^{s-1} (\mathbb{E}\left[\mathbb{E}_{\xi\sim\Xi}\left[T_\xi(x; z, Z_2, .., Z_s)\right]\right] - \mathbb{E}\left[\mathbb{E}_{\xi\sim\Xi}\left[T_\xi(x; Z_1, Z_2, .., Z_s)\right]\right]) \\ &= \frac{s}{n} (\mathbb{E}\left[\mathbb{E}_{\xi\sim\Xi}\left[T_\xi(x; z, Z_2, \ldots, Z_s)\right]\right] - \mathbb{E}\left[\mathbb{E}_{\xi\sim\Xi}\left[T_\xi(x; Z_1, Z_2, \ldots, Z_s)\right]\right]), \end{aligned}$$

and we have

$$\begin{aligned} \mathring{\widehat{\mu}}(x) &= \mathbb{E}\left[\widehat{\mu}(x)\right] + \sum_{i=1}^{n} (\mathbb{E}[\widehat{\mu}(x)|Z_i] - \mathbb{E}\left[\widehat{\mu}(x)\right]) \\ &= \mathbb{E}\left[T(x)\right] + \frac{s}{n} \sum_{i=1}^{n} (\mathbb{E}\left[T(x)|Z_i\right] - \mathbb{E}\left[T(x)\right]). \end{aligned} \tag{8.36}$$

In addition,

$$\mathring{T}(x) = \mathbb{E}\left[T(x)\right] + \sum_{i=1}^{s}(\mathbb{E}[T(x)|Z_i] - \mathbb{E}\left[T(x)\right]). \tag{8.37}$$

Using (8.36)–(8.37), we obtain $\sigma_n^2(x) = s\text{Var}(\mathring{T}(x))/n$. $\sigma_n^2(x)$ is the variance of $\mathring{\widehat{\mu}}(x)$. Lemma 7 in Wager and Athey (2017) shows that

$$\begin{aligned}\frac{\mathbb{E}\left[\left(\widehat{\mu}(x) - \mathring{\widehat{\mu}}(x)\right)^2\right]}{\sigma_n^2(x)} &\leq \left(\frac{s}{n}\right)^2 \frac{\text{Var}(T(x))}{\sigma_n^2(x)} \\ &= \frac{s}{n}\frac{\text{Var}(T(x))}{\text{Var}(\mathring{T}(x))} \quad (\text{avec } \sigma_n^2(x) = \frac{s}{n}\text{Var}(\mathring{T}(x))),\end{aligned}$$

which, with (8.35), results in

$$\frac{\mathbb{E}\left[\left(\widehat{\mu}(x) - \mathring{\widehat{\mu}}(x)\right)^2\right]}{\sigma_n^2(x)} \to 0.$$

It remains to be shown that the right hand side of Equation (8.36) satisfies the conditions of the Lyapunov central limit theorem.

Proof of Theorem 8.3. We show only that

$$\beta_2 = \frac{\text{Cov}(\tau(X), T(X))}{\text{Var}(T(X))},$$

since the proof for β_1 follows a similar reasoning. The normal equations (8.30) identifying (β_1, β_2) give, for β_2, the following values:

$$\beta_2 = \frac{\text{Cov}(w(X)(D - p(X))Y, T(X) - \mathbb{E}\left[T(X)\right])}{\text{Var}(T(X) - \mathbb{E}\left[T(X)\right])}. \tag{8.38}$$

The denominator is equal to $\text{Var}(T(X))$. Now, since $T(X) - \mathbb{E}\left[T(X)\right]$ has a zero mean, the numerator of (8.38) is given by

$$\begin{aligned}&\text{Cov}(w(X)(D - p(X))Y, T(X) - \mathbb{E}\left[T(X)\right]) \\ &= \mathbb{E}\left[w(X)(D - p(X))Y(T(X) - \mathbb{E}\left[T(X)\right])\right].\end{aligned} \tag{8.39}$$

Recall that $Y = \mu_0(X) + D\tau(X) + U$, so the result comes from (8.39) and the following three points. First, using the law of iterated expectations,

$$\begin{aligned}
&\mathbb{E}\left[w(X)(D - p(X))\mu_0(X)(T(X) - \mathbb{E}\left[T(X)\right])\right] \\
&= \mathbb{E}\left[w(X)\mu_0(X)(T(X) - \mathbb{E}\left[T(X)\right])\underbrace{\mathbb{E}\left[D - p(X)|X\right]}_{=0}\right] \\
&= 0.
\end{aligned}$$

Then, we have $D|X \sim \mathcal{B}(p(X))$ so that

$$\mathbb{E}\left[w(X)(D - p(X))D|X\right] = \mathbb{E}\left[w(X)(D - p(X))^2|X\right] = 1,$$

and therefore

$$\begin{aligned}
\mathbb{E}\left[w(X)(D - p(X))D\tau(X)(T(X) - \mathbb{E}\left[T(X)\right])\right] &= \mathbb{E}\left[\tau(X)(T(X) - \mathbb{E}\left[T(X)\right])\right] \\
&= \mathrm{Cov}\left(\tau(X), T(X)\right).
\end{aligned}$$

Finally, we have

$$\begin{aligned}
&\mathbb{E}\left[w(X)(D - p(X))U(T(X) - \mathbb{E}\left[T(X)\right])\right] \\
&= \mathbb{E}\left[w(X)(D - p(X))\underbrace{\mathbb{E}\left[U|D, X\right]}_{=0}(T(X) - \mathbb{E}\left[T(X)\right])\right] \\
&= 0,
\end{aligned}$$

which leads to the result. □

Intuitions for the proof of Theorem 8.2 The proof follows from the fact that $\tilde{\tau}^*(x)$ is formally equivalent to the result of a regression forest, so using Theorem 8.1,

$$\frac{\tilde{\tau}^*(x) - \tau(x)}{\sigma_n(x)} \to_d \mathcal{N}(0, 1).$$

Then, according to Theorem 3 (consistency of $(\widehat{\tau}, \widehat{\mu})$) and Lemma 4 of Athey et al. (2019) we have

$$\frac{n}{s}\left(\tilde{\tau}^*(x) - \widehat{\tau}(x)\right)^2 = \mathcal{O}_p\left(\left(\frac{s}{n}\right)^{2/3}\right), \tag{8.40}$$

so $(\tilde{\tau}^*(x) - \widehat{\tau}(x))/\sigma_n \xrightarrow{p} 0$ which gives the result. The technical part of the theorem is the proof of Lemma 4 which gives (8.40). □

Proof of Theorem 8.4. $p^{\pm} \leq \alpha/2$ is equivalent to $\mathbb{E}[1\{p_A^{\pm} \leq \alpha/2\}|\text{Data}] \geq 1/2$. This implies

$$\begin{aligned}\mathbb{P}_P\left(p^{\pm} \leq \alpha/2\right) &= \mathbb{E}_P[1\{\mathbb{E}_P[1\{p_A^{\pm} \leq \alpha/2\}|\text{Data}] \geq 1/2\}]\\ &\leq \mathbb{P}_P\left(p_A^{\pm} \leq \alpha/2\right)/(1/2) \quad \text{(using Markov's inequality)}\\ &\leq 2\left(\alpha/2 + \delta + P_P(Data \notin \mathcal{A})\right) \quad \text{(using assumption 8.6).}\end{aligned}$$

□

Chapter 9
Optimal policy learning

Consider the problem of a planner who has limited budget resources to subsidize a program. It is legitimate to wonder whether it is possible to inform their decision by learning the optimal allocation policy for this program (optimal policy learning) from the results of a randomized experiment. The problem therefore consists of determining a fixed allocation of resources, which constitutes the treatment, to a target population. Several objectives can be pursued, but for simplicity, we assume that the planner wants to maximize the expected average utility for this population, given the budget constraints. In practice, and for simplicity, utility will be associated here with a directly measurable outcome variable, such as return to employment or short/long-term income for a training program, or specified through a functional form, assumed to be known.

Section 9.1 begins by formally introducing the problem and providing the form of the optimal policy in a simplified framework. After introducing the minimax regret criterion as a performance measure, Section 9.2.1 details the tools for estimating the optimal policy by maximizing empirical welfare when the propensity score is known. However, in many cases, the propensity score must be estimated. Section 9.2.2 describes how to adapt the developed tools to this context. Finally, Section 9.3 presents an application to the optimization of a training program.

9.1 Problem: optimal policy learning

9.1.1 Optimal policy in a simplified framework

We formally present the simplified framework used in Bhattacharya and Dupas (2012). Let Y be the observed outcome at the individual level and D be a binary treatment, which must be determined by a specific decision rule. The researcher also has information X about the individuals. The latter is used to make the assignment decision $\pi : \mathcal{X} \to \{0, 1\}$, where $\mathcal{X}$ is the support of X. The function π represents the policy of assigning individuals with characteristics X to the treatment or control group. Note that π is a binary classifier. Here, we denote $Y = DY(1) + (1 - D)Y(0)$, where $Y(0)$ and $Y(1)$ are the potential outcomes of Y without and with treatment, respectively. We further assume that the treatment can be considered as good as random conditional on the observed variables (*unconfoundedness*).

Machine Learning for Econometrics. Christophe Gaillac and Jérémy L'Hour, Oxford University Press.
 DOI: 10.1093/9780198918868.003.0009

Assumption 9.1 (Conditional independence).

$$D \perp\!\!\!\perp (Y(0), Y(1)) \mid X. \tag{9.1}$$

In particular, this excludes the case where individuals with the most anticipated effects based on certain unobservable variables are also the most likely to be treated. One way to model this planner's problem is to determine an allocation $\pi : \mathcal{X} \to \{0, 1\}$ such that the expected utility:

$$W(\pi) := \mathbb{E}\,(Y(\pi(X))) = \int_{x \in \mathcal{X}} \mathbb{E}\,[Y(\pi(X)) | X = x]\, dF_X(x) \tag{9.2}$$

is maximized – here we assume, for simplicity, that utility and the outcome variable Y are equivalent – subject to the constraint $c \geq \mathbb{E}(\pi(X))$, where c is an upper bound on the fraction of individuals that can be treated, assumed to be proportional to the budget constraint. By using Assumption 9.1 to decompose (9.2), the problem can be rewritten as:

$$\begin{aligned} \max_{\pi(\cdot)} & \int_{x \in \mathcal{X}} \mu_1(x)\pi(x) + \mu_0(x)(1 - \pi(x)) dF_X(x) \\ s.t. & \int_{x \in \mathcal{X}} \pi(x) dF_X(x) \leq c, \end{aligned} \tag{9.3}$$

where $\mu_j(x) := \mathbb{E}\,[Y |\, X = x,\ D = j],\ j \in \{0, 1\}$. Under the same assumption 9.1, $\tau(x) := \mathbb{E}\,[Y(1) - Y(0) |\, X = x]$, the conditional average treatment effect (CATE), can be decomposed as:

$$\tau(x) = \mu_1(x) - \mu_0(x).$$

We then note that the objective function of problem (9.3) can be rewritten as:

$$\int_{x \in \mathcal{X}} \mu_0(x) + \tau(x)\pi(x) dF_X(x).$$

Assumption 9.2 *Assume that:*

(i) for a $\delta \geq 0$, $\mathbb{P}(\tau(X) > \delta) > c$ (the constraint is relevant),
(ii) $F_{\tau(X)}$ is strictly increasing and $\tau(X)$ has a bounded support.

Assumption 9.2 (ii) implies that $\gamma \in \mathcal{X} \mapsto \mathbb{P}\,(\tau(X) \geq \gamma)$ is decreasing.

Proposition 9.1 *Under assumptions 9.1–9.2, the optimal policy solution to (9.3) takes the form:*

$$\pi(x) = 1\,\{\tau(x) \geq \gamma\},\ \gamma\ s.t.\ c = \int_{x \in \mathcal{X}} \pi(x) dF_X(x). \tag{9.4}$$

The optimal policy (9.4) (or *Bayes classifier*) therefore consists of assigning treatment to agents for whom the benefit exceeds the cost. The empirical problem is twofold: the benefit must first be estimated, and this policy is potentially very complex to implement if the groups that benefit most from the treatment are highly heterogeneous. In (9.4), γ is the $(1 - c)$ quantile of the random variable $\tau(X)$, which is unique when $F_{\tau(X)}$ is increasing. This problem therefore illustrates in a simple way that knowledge of the heterogeneous treatment effect $\tau(\cdot)$ would ideally allow for efficient treatment allocation.

Remark 9.1 Dual formulation and extension

Note that the dual formulation of the problem is also interesting: we seek to estimate the minimum cost to obtain a given average value of the outcome in the population:

$$\min_{\pi(\cdot)} \int_{x\in\mathcal{X}} \pi(x)dF_X(x) \tag{9.5}$$

$$\text{s.t.} \quad \int_{x\in\mathcal{X}} \mu_1(x)\pi(x) + \mu_0(x)(1 - \pi(x))dF_X(x) = b.$$

Note also that a direct extension of (9.3) allows us to handle heterogeneity in the cost of treatment in the population $h(\cdot)$, which leads to the following modified budget constraint:

$$c = \int_{x\in\mathcal{X}} h(x)\pi(x)dF_X(x),$$

and the solution to the modified problem (9.3):

$$\pi(x) = 1\left\{\tau(x) - h(x) \geq \gamma\right\}, \ \gamma \ s.t. \ c = \int_{x\in\mathcal{X}} h(x)\pi(x)dF_X(x).$$

More generally, it is interesting to identify the populations that benefit more or less from the treatment. One limit that is not addressed in the above framework is the fact that there can be negative externalities: treated agents will benefit at the expense of non-treated agents. For example, Crépon et al. (2013) estimate these effects in the labor market. Another limit is that the above approach via (9.4) suggests for estimation an approach based on a *plug-in* estimate of the CATE to find the optimal policy. However, the problem of learning the optimal policy appears to be simpler, since we only want to determine a rule for treatment allocation (potentially under constraints) and not precisely estimate the heterogeneity of the treatment effect.

9.1.2 The minimax regret criterion

A trade-off emerges from this presentation: on one hand, the abundance of available variables X would allow for a more precise, targeted treatment allocation. On the other hand, the complexity of the allocation policy increases with the dimension of the available variables. This compromise becomes even more critical as the policies obtained, in order to be implemented, must often comply with certain constraints that limit the variables that can be used to make the treatment decision, for example, for legal or fairness concerns. This also limits the complexity of the policy: it must often be clear, explainable, and easy to implement. This justifies the search for the optimal policy within a class of policies Π that incorporate these constraints. We do not assume that the optimal policy given by (9.4) belongs to the class Π and we do not attempt to estimate it either. The objective, introduced and motivated in Manski (2004) then Stoye (2009, 2012), is rather to learn, from the data of a randomized experiment and a given specification, the expected utility W and its empirical counterpart, a policy $\widehat{\pi}$ that minimizes the regret

$$R(\pi) = W(\pi^*) - W(\pi), \tag{9.6}$$

with respect to *the best policy in the class* Π,

$$\pi^* = \arg\max\{W(\pi) : \pi \in \Pi\}$$

with a control on the worst-case regret (*minimax regret criterion*):

$$\sup_{P_n} \mathbb{E}(R(\widehat{\pi})),$$

where $\mathbb{E}$ is the expectation with respect to the distribution of the data $(Y_i, D_i, X_i)_{i=1}^n$.

9.2 Empirical welfare maximization

We present the learning of the optimal policy through empirical welfare maximization, (see Kitagawa and Tetenov, 2018), which consists of estimating $W(\pi)$ and considering a maximizer of this estimator. We start with the simple framework where the propensity score is known in Section 9.2.1, and then explain how to handle this additional complexity where we need to estimate this nuisance parameter in Section 9.2.2. There are, of course, now many variations of this initial case, for example with fairness constraints (Viviano and Bradic, 2020), in natural experiments (Athey and Wager, 2021), or in the presence of interactions (Viviano, 2019).

9.2.1 Empirical welfare maximization with known propensity score

Consider the framework of a randomized experiment described above, under the assumption of conditional independence (9.1). Similar to what is presented in the introductory example, and with the propensity score $p(x) = \mathbb{E}[D = 1|X = x]$, the welfare criterion $W(\pi)$ can be rewritten as:

$$\begin{aligned} W(\pi) &= \mathbb{E}\left[\frac{YD}{p(X)}\pi(X) + \frac{Y(1-D)}{1-p(X)}(1-\pi(X))\right] \\ &= \mathbb{E}(Y(0)) + \mathbb{E}\left[\left(\frac{YD}{p(X)} - \frac{Y(1-D)}{1-p(X)}\right)\pi(X)\right]. \end{aligned} \tag{9.7}$$

We recognize in (9.7) a structure similar to the inverse propensity score estimator described in (3.6). The idea proposed by Kitagawa and Tetenov (2018) is to maximize the empirical welfare:

$$\widetilde{\pi} = \arg\max_{\pi\in\Pi} \widehat{W}(\pi), \tag{9.8}$$

where

$$\widehat{W}(\pi) = \frac{1}{n}\sum_{i=1}^{n}\left[\frac{Y_iD_i}{p(X_i)} - \frac{Y_i(1-D_i)}{1-p(X_i)}\right]\pi(X_i).$$

Remark 9.2 Complexity of a class of binary decisions

The Vapnik-Chervonenkis dimension (or VC-dimension, see Vapnik, 1998; Van der vaart and Wellner, 1996) is often used to measure the complexity of a class of sets.

In our context, it is the largest value $l \in \mathbb{N}$ such that there exists a set of l points $x^l = \{x_1, \dots, x_l\}$ in $\mathcal{X}$ that is *shattered* by Π: that is, for every vector $v \in \{0,1\}^l$ there exists a policy π_v constrained to belong to the class Π such that $\pi_v(x_i) = v_i, i = 1, \dots, l$.

Consider examples with finite or infinite VC-dimension:

- *Linear eligibility rules*: the class of policies of the form $\pi(x) = 1\{\beta_0 + x'\beta_1 \geq 0\}$, with $(\beta_0, \beta_1) \in \mathbb{R}^{p+1}$ has a VC-dimension $VC(\Pi) = p + 1$;
- *Decision trees*: the class of decision trees of depth L has a VC-dimension of the order of $2^L \log(p)$;
- *Monotonic eligibility rules*: for example, for $x \in [0,1]^2$, and if we decide to treat agents such that $x_2 \geq f(x_1)$, where f is strictly increasing. Since any set of points $x^l = \{x_1, \dots, x_l\}$ with $x_i = (a_i, a_i^2)$, $a_1 < \cdots < a_l$ can be shattered by Π, the VC-dimension is infinite.

Assumption 9.3

- *Overlap assumption: there exists* $\eta > 0$ *such that*

$$0 < \eta \leq p(x) \leq 1 - \eta < 1, \quad x \in \mathcal{X}. \tag{9.9}$$

- *Bounded variables: there exists $M < \infty$ such that $|Y| < M$ almost surely.*
- *Complexity of Π: The class Π has a finite Vapnik–Chervonenkis dimension $VC(\Pi)$ and is countable.*

For simplicity, we will limit ourselves to the framework of finite VC-dimension in this chapter, but note that Mbakop and Tabord-Meehan (2021) consider maximization constrained to a collection of classes that approximate a more complex class, potentially of infinite VC-dimension, including the monotonic policies mentioned in the remark above. Let $\mathcal{P}(M, \eta)$ denote the set of data distributions that satisfy Assumptions (9.3).

Theorem 9. (Upper bound on the regret, Theorem 2.1 in Kitagawa and Tetenov, 2018) *Suppose (9.3), then the following uniform control holds*

$$\sup_{P \in \mathcal{P}(M,\eta)} \mathbb{E}_P (W(\pi^*) - W(\widetilde{\pi})) \leq \frac{CM}{\eta} \sqrt{\frac{VC(\Pi)}{n}}, \tag{9.10}$$

where C is a constant, $\pi^* = \arg\max\{W(\pi) : \pi \in \Pi\}$, and $\widetilde{\pi}$ defined in (9.8).

Theorem 9.1 therefore shows that the expected regret in the worst case scenario of data distribution $P \in \mathcal{P}(M, \eta)$ decreases as $\sqrt{VC(\Pi)/n}$. This allows for classes Π for which the complexity $VC(\Pi)$ increases with the sample size, but at a slower rate than n. Moreover, Kitagawa and Tetenov (2018) also provide a lower bound on the risk, which is the left term in (9.10). Indeed, the best risk is bounded by below by a term of the same order $\sqrt{VC(\Pi)/n}$ as the upper bound (9.10). This shows that the rate $\sqrt{VC(\Pi)/n}$ is optimal within the class $P \in \mathcal{P}(M, \eta)$.

We give some insights into the proof of Theorem 9.1. For any policy $\pi \in \Pi$:

$$\begin{aligned} W(\pi) - W(\widetilde{\pi}) &= W(\pi) - \widehat{W}(\widetilde{\pi}) + \widehat{W}(\widetilde{\pi}) - W(\widetilde{\pi}) \\ &\leq W(\pi) - \widehat{W}(\widetilde{\pi}) + \sup_{\pi' \in \Pi} |\widehat{W}(\pi') - W(\pi')| \\ &\leq 2 \sup_{\pi' \in \Pi} |\widehat{W}(\pi') - W(\pi')|, \end{aligned}$$

and therefore, for $\pi = \pi^*$,

$$R(\widetilde{\pi}) \leq 2 \sup_{\pi' \in \Pi} |\widehat{W}(\pi') - W(\pi')|.$$

The term $\widehat{W}(\pi') - W(\pi')$ can be seen as a centered empirical process, under the form:

$$\frac{1}{\sqrt{n}} \sum_{i=1}^{n} (f_{\pi'}(Y_i, X_i, D_i) - \mathbb{E}[f_{\pi'}(Y_i, X_i, D_i)]),$$

for functions indexed by $\pi' \in \Pi$:

$$f_{\pi'}(Y_i, X_i, D_i) := \left(\frac{Y_i D_i}{p(X_i)} - \frac{Y_i(1 - D_i)}{1 - p(X_i)}\right)\pi'(X_i).$$

The result then follows from inequalities on the expectation of the supremum of empirical processes indexed by classes Π whose complexity, through VC-dimension, is bounded (Van der vaart and Wellner, 1996).

Computational aspects. As we learn the optimal policy through an argmax in problem (9.8), it is important to also describe its computational aspects. Indeed, since problem (9.8) is not a convex optimization problem in general, these aspects are important. To do so, it is useful to re-parameterize the problem, noting that the objective function (9.7) can be centered and that it is equivalent to maximize the *advantage* of the policy π:

$$\begin{aligned} A(\pi) &= 2W(\pi) - \mathbb{E}[Y(0) + Y(1)] \\ &= \mathbb{E}[(2\pi(X) - 1)\tau(X)] \quad (\text{where } W(\pi) = \mathbb{E}[Y(\pi(X))]). \end{aligned} \tag{9.11}$$

We then maximize the empirical advantage:

$$\begin{aligned} \widetilde{A}(\pi) &= \frac{1}{n}\sum_{i=1}^{n}(2\pi(X_i) - 1)\left(\frac{Y_i D_i}{p(X_i)} - \frac{Y_i(1 - D_i)}{1 - p(X_i)}\right) \\ &= \frac{1}{n}\sum_{i=1}^{n}(2\pi(X_i) - 1)\Gamma_i, \quad \Gamma_i = \frac{Y_i D_i}{p(X_i)} - \frac{Y_i(1 - D_i)}{1 - p(X_i)} \qquad (9.12) \\ &= \frac{1}{n}\sum_{i=1}^{n}(2\pi(X_i) - 1)\text{sign}(\Gamma_i)\,|\Gamma_i|. \qquad (9.13) \end{aligned}$$

The formulation (9.13) shows that learning policies through empirical maximization can be seen as a *weighted optimization problem in the context of classification.* We can use tools developed in weighted classification (see e.g., Athey and Wager, 2021; Zhou et al., 2018; Kitagawa et al., 2021) to solve this problem. In some special cases of policy classes, the problem can be exactly solved using a reformulation as a *mixed integer programming* problem. This is the case for linear classes Π (see Appendix C in Kitagawa and Tetenov, 2018) or finite depth decision trees (see Zhou et al., 2018). However, the computational complexity increases with the sample size, which limits the use of this exact approach. There are also algorithms that provide approximate solutions (for classes Π of finite depth decision trees, see Zhou et al., 2018), but are much less computationally expensive. Kitagawa and Tetenov (2018) suggest *convexifying* the risk by minimizing instead:

$$\mathbb{E}[\phi(Yf(X))], \quad \text{where } \pi(x) = 1\{f(x) \geq 0\}, \tag{9.14}$$

for well-chosen convex functions ϕ and certain classes of functions f. When the true minimizer π^* belongs to the considered class Π, then the minimization of the substitution risk (9.14), which is a (convex) problem much simpler to solve than the original classification problem consisting in maximizing (9.11), also allows for the minimization of the initial risk (see, e.g., Zhang, 2004; Bartlett et al., 2006). However, this assumption is not desirable in the context of optimal policy estimation. Kitagawa and Tetenov (2018) provide conditions under which the minimization of the substitution risk (9.14) amounts to minimizing the initial risk, *without assuming that* the optimal policy belongs to class Π.

9.2.2 Maximization of empirical welfare with estimated propensity score

In the estimator from Section 9.2.1, we have so far assumed that the propensity score p is known. Following the same logic as in Section 8.1, we now construct a doubly robust estimator that is robust to the estimation of the propensity score p, which is a nuisance parameter in this case. In a similar spirit to the estimator proposed by Hahn (1998) – see the augmented inverse propensity score estimator (3.9) – Athey and Wager (2021) introduce a modification to the weights Γ_i in (9.12):

$$\widetilde{A}(\pi) = \frac{1}{n}\sum_{i=1}^{n}(2\pi(X_i) - 1)\Gamma_i^*,$$

$$\Gamma_i^* = \mu_1(X_i) - \mu_0(X_i) + \frac{(Y_i - \mu_1(X_i))D_i}{p(X_i)} - \frac{(Y_i - \mu_0(X_i))(1 - D_i)}{1 - p(X_i)}.$$

These modified weights only have an impact in a finite sample, and do not change in population of $\tilde{A}$, which remains A. They are introduced to make the moments defining A locally robust (or Neyman orthogonal) to the estimation of the nuisance parameters, which are μ_0, μ_1, and the propensity score p. The weights Γ_i^* are still *oracle* weights since the functions μ_j and p are assumed to be known. As in Section 8.1, Athey and Wager (2021) then use cross-fitting, introduced in Section 5.3, to propose an estimable estimator:

$$\widehat{A}(\pi) = \frac{1}{n}\sum_{i=1}^{n}(2\pi(X_i) - 1)\widehat{\Gamma}_i$$

$$\widehat{\Gamma}_i = \widehat{\mu}_1^{k(i)}(X_i) - \widehat{\mu}_0^{k(i)}(X_i) + \frac{(Y_i - \widehat{\mu}_1^{k(i)}(X_i))D_i}{\widehat{p}^{k(i)}(X_i)} - \frac{(Y_i - \widehat{\mu}_0^{k(i)}(X_i))(1 - D_i)}{1 - \widehat{p}^{k(i)}(X_i)}, \qquad (9.15)$$

where $k(i)$ indicates the index of the subgroup of the partition $(I_k)_{k=1,\ldots,K}$ of the indices of the sample $\{1, \ldots, n\}$ in which the individual i is located, and

$$\widehat{\pi} = \arg\max_{\pi \in \Pi} \widehat{A}(\pi). \tag{9.16}$$

We assume, as in Section 8.1, that the functions μ_j, $j = 1, 2$ and p are sufficiently well estimated according to the following criteria:

1. uniform consistency of the estimators

$$\sup_{x \in \mathcal{X}} |\widehat{\mu}_j(x) - \mu_j(x)|, \ \sup_{x \in \mathcal{X}} |\widehat{p}(x) - p(x)| \xrightarrow{p} 0;$$

2. convergence rate in L_2 norm

$$\max\left(\mathbb{E}\left[(\widehat{\mu}_j(X) - \mu_j(X))^2\right], \mathbb{E}\left[(\widehat{p}(X) - p(X))^2\right]\right) = o_P(n^{-1/2}).$$

This allows for a large number of machine learning methods under various assumptions of classical regularities in nonparametric estimation (see Zhou et al., 2018, for more references and different examples of rates for classes of functions, such as parametric functions, Holder or Sobolev classes, and Reproducing Kernel Hilbert Space – RKHS). To adapt the methods from Section 8.1, the goal is to ensure that the estimator with estimated nuisance parameters $\widehat{A}$ is close to the one where these parameters are known $\widetilde{A}$, for a fixed policy $\pi \in \Pi$:

$$\sqrt{n}(\widehat{A}(\pi) - \widetilde{A}(\pi)) \xrightarrow{p} 0.$$

However, to be able to reduce it to the case where the propensity score is known, and since the estimator maximizes the empirical risk over $\pi \in \Pi$, a stronger result is needed, valid uniformly over the set of policies $\pi \in \Pi$. Athey and Wager (2021) obtain the following key result (Lemma 4), which guarantees that if $VC(\Pi) \leq n^{1/2}$, then

$$\sqrt{n} \sup_{\pi \in \Pi} |\widehat{A}(\pi) - A^*(\pi)| \xrightarrow{p} 0.$$

Theorem 1 from Athey and Wager (2021) then provides an upper bound of the form (9.10) in Theorem 9.1, with the functions μ_0, μ_1, and p being estimated.

9.3 Application: optimization of a training program

We continue the study of the randomized experiment developed in Section 8.3.9 and in Kitagawa and Tetenov (2018) and Mbakop and Tabord-Meehan (2021). We reanalyze here the data from the Job Training Partnership Act (JTPA), which is a large training program funded by the US federal government, with the aim of determining an optimal training policy based, for simplicity, solely on past wages and education.

Two-thirds of individuals are randomly assigned to the JTPA treatment group and the control group, with the treatment consisting of offering training. We focus here on the intention-to-treat, and on the effect on individual earnings at 30 months. Despite the fact that the propensity score is known, we use the approach (9.15)–(9.16) of Athey and Wager (2021), where the treatment effect τ and the propensity score are estimated using random forests (causal ones for τ). The optimal policy is then estimated via (9.16) using decision trees of fixed depth (1, 2, and 3 presented in Figure 9.1). The advantage is estimated using sample splitting with $K = 10$, *via*

$$\widehat{A}_{CV} = \frac{1}{n}\sum_{k=1}^{K}\sum_{i\in S_k}(2\widehat{\pi}^{(-k)}(X_i) - 1)\widehat{\Gamma}_i,$$

on the different sample splits S_k, and the gain reported in Table 9.1 in the same manner.

Figure 9.2 shows the treatment policies obtained by minimizing the empirical risk, while restricting to the class of decision trees of fixed depth and without restriction. In the case of the class of decision trees of depth 1, we obtain the same policy as the class of quadrant policies presented in Figure 1 of Kitagawa and Tetenov (2018). It can be observed from Table 9.1 that this relatively simple policy already brings a gain compared to the uniform policy where the entire population is treated. The gain increases gradually with the complexity of the class of trees considered. The "optimal" gain without restrictions is large compared to the uniform policy, but it can be noted from Figure 9.2 that the latter gives a relatively complex allocation plan with respect to the two relevant variables here, which are education and previous wage. This analysis quantifies what would be lost by using the very simple allocation rule based on decision trees of depth 1 rather than an optimal but complex rule to implement. The decrease in gains with tree depth for these relatively low depths that are fixed in advance suggests that these classes are not particularly well suited to the problem, and that linear or polynomial classes in education as in Kitagawa and Tetenov (2018) would be better choices. It should be noted that Kitagawa and Tetenov (2018) also illustrates how the obtained policies are modified when treatment costs are taken into account.

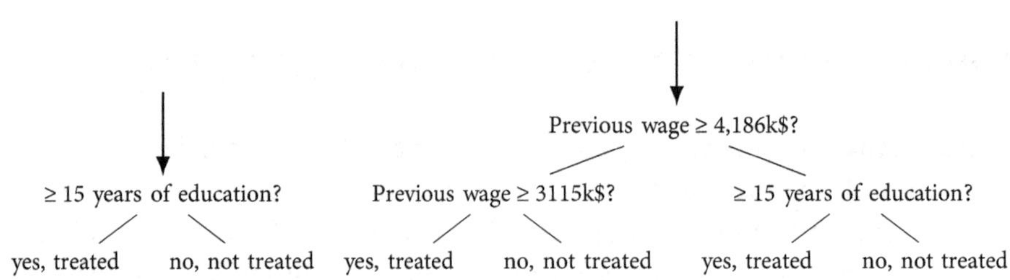

Figure 9.1 Example of decision trees of fixed depths 1 (left) and 2 (right) obtained by maximizing the empirical welfare.

Table 9.1 Estimated gains according to the chosen policy using years of education and annual wage before entering the program.

	Known propensity score		Estimated propensity score	
	Estimated average gain ($)	Treated population (%)	Estimated average gain ($)	Treated population (%)
All treated	1,179.99 (333.16)	100	1,254.22 (327.50)	100
Depth 1 tree	1,260.71 (322.30)	96	1,343.78 (316.63)	96
Depth 2 tree	1,352.88 (304.53)	87	1,436.73 (298.20)	86
Depth 3 tree	1,584.59 (304.24)	88	1,620.49 (299.65)	88
Optimal	2,131.32 (278.10)	77	2,166.80 (273.92)	77

Note: We adopt the same convention as Kitagawa and Tetenov (2018), and the reported gains are the differences from the average income in the 30 months following the training. Unlike Kitagawa and Tetenov (2018), we use AIPW for estimation but like them IPW for gain calculation.

9.4 Summary

Key concepts

Optimal policy learning, minimax regret criterion, maximization of empirical welfare, complexity of a class of sets, VC-dimension.

Code and data

The code `policy_learning_jtpa.R` associated with the application in Section 9.3 is available on the GitHub. The data and code to replicate the application by Mbakop and Tabord-Meehan (2021) can be downloaded from onlinelibrary.wiley.com/doi/abs/10.3982/ECTA16437.

Questions

1. Show Proposition 9.1.
2. What is the objective introduced for learning the optimal policy? Give the advantages and disadvantages of considering worst-case as a measure.

Continued

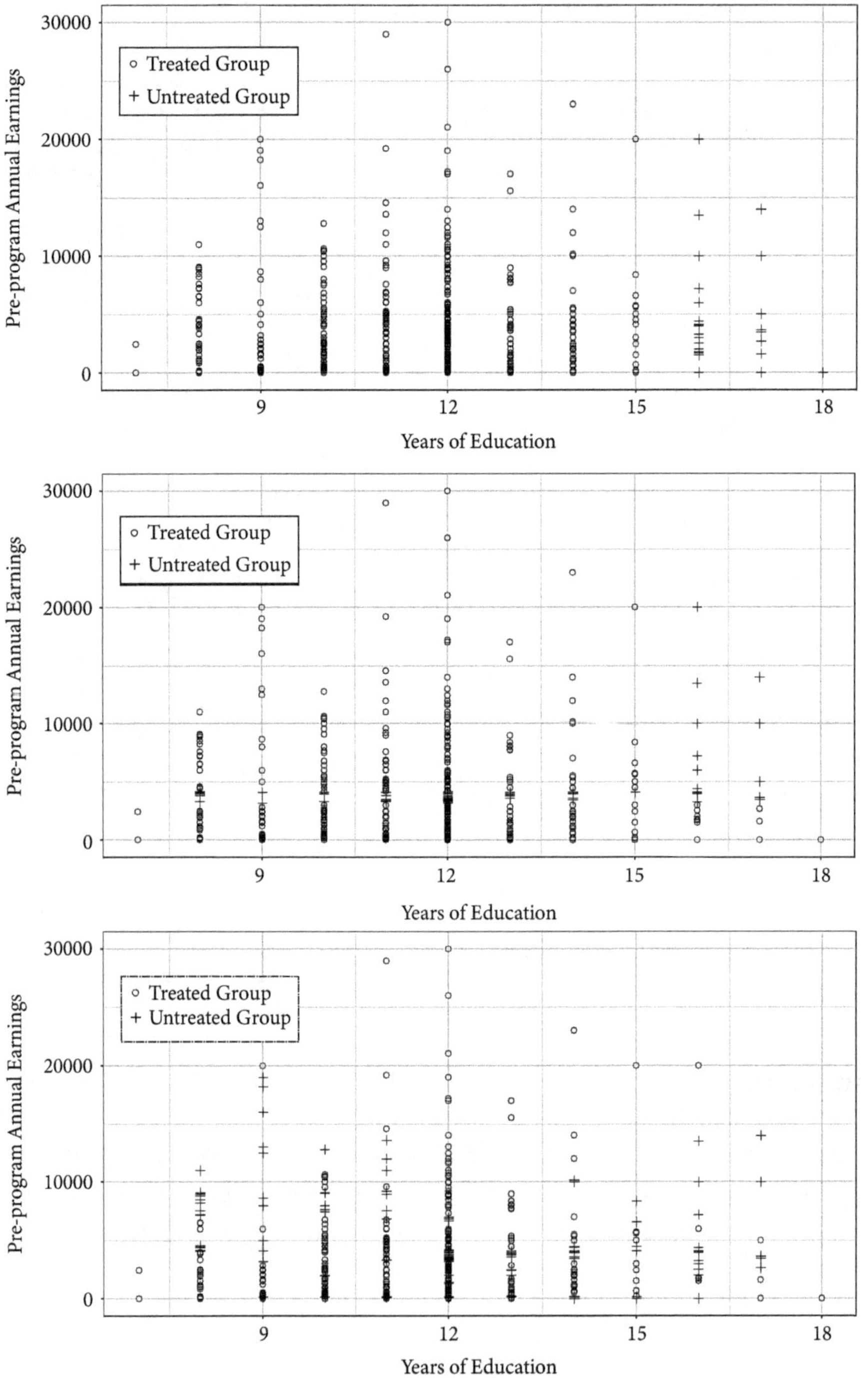

Figure 9.2 Treatment decisions obtained by maximizing empirical risk and non-parametric plug-in of the estimated treatment effect.

Note: Each point represents a sample of 1,000 randomly drawn observations from the 11,008 observations.

3. For what statistical and operational reasons is it desirable to limit the complexity of the class of policies considered?
4. What measure is used for the complexity of the class of policies considered? Can it grow with the number of observations, and if so, how?
5. Give three examples of classes of policies that can be considered and discuss the ranking of their complexities.
6. What is the computational gain in rewriting the maximization of empirical risk in the form of the maximization of the advantage:

$$\widetilde{A}(\pi) = \frac{1}{n}\sum_{i=1}^{n}(2\pi(X_i) - 1)\,\mathrm{sign}(\Gamma_i)\|\Gamma_i\|?$$

Additional references

We recommend reading the foundational articles by Manski (2004), Stoye (2009), and Kitagawa and Tetenov (2018). In particular, we suggest reading the treatment of the application in Section 9.3 by Kitagawa and Tetenov (2018): they consider different classes than those considered here and also illustrate how the obtained policies are modified when taking into account the cost of treatment. Finally, the literature on the subject is flourishing and now addresses more realistic and complex contexts than the one developed here, see Viviano and Bradic (2020); Athey and Wager (2021); Viviano, (2019).

PART IV

AGGREGATED DATA AND MACROECONOMIC FORECASTING

Chapter 10
The synthetic control method

The synthetic control method has been considered by Athey and Imbens (2017) as "arguably the most important innovation in the policy evaluation literature in the last fifteen years." Introduced in particular by Abadie and Gardeazabal (2003) and Abadie et al. (2010), its popularity in empirical studies is constantly growing, as evidenced by applications in various fields such as taxation and football player migration (Kleven et al., 2013), immigration (Bohn et al., 2014), health policies (Hackmann et al., 2015), minimum wage (Allegretto et al., 2017), regional policies (Gobillon and Magnac, 2016), sex work laws (Cunningham and Shah, 2017), financial value of connections to policymakers (Acemoglu et al., 2016), the effect of COVID-19 certification on health outcomes (Oliu-Barton et al., 2022), and many more.

Often considered as an alternative to difference-in-differences methods especially in situations where only aggregated data is available (Angrist and Pischke, 2009, Section 5.2), the synthetic control method offers a data-driven procedure for selecting a comparison unit, called the "synthetic unit" in comparative case studies. The synthetic unit is constructed as a weighted combination of control units, also known as the "donor pool." It aims to best replicate the behavior of the treated unit during the pre-treatment period. This approach enhances the likelihood of satisfying a crucial assumption for the credibility of such comparison: the *common trend assumption* (CTA). The CTA posits that, in the absence of the policy change, the treated and control groups would have followed the same trajectory. Moreover, due to the characteristics of the synthetic control solution, certain units in the control group may receive a weight of zero. In contrast, the difference-in-differences estimator assigns a weight of $1/n_0$ to every control unit, where n_0 represents the size of the control group. These nuances will be discussed in detail in the core of the chapter. However, these insights provide a preliminary understanding of the flexibility offered by the synthetic control method. It allows for the individual weighing of control units to obtain the best possible *counterfactual* – an estimate of the outcome variable in the absence of treatment – in the sense that it replicates the treated unit during the pre-treatment period.

Although the link with the difference-in-differences approach is direct, the synthetic control method is also related to matching estimators (Abadie and Cattaneo, 2018, Section 4, for a brief introduction) because solving the synthetic control program is equivalent to performing matching by minimizing a certain distance. To

Machine Learning for Econometrics. Christophe Gaillac and Jérémy L'Hour, Oxford University Press.
 DOI: 10.1093/9780198918868.003.0010

learn more about this topic, the reader can refer to Section 10.6 as well as Abadie and L'Hour (2021). Apart from these technical considerations, the effectiveness of this method can be attributed to its simplicity and visual nature, as demonstrated later on. It also offers a quantitative tool for comparative case studies, a type of task traditionally more qualitative in nature.

Section 10.1 introduces the method, while Section 10.2 presents a result on the bias of the estimator that colors the intuition behind the method. Section 10.3 is more methodological in nature and explores the use cases of the synthetic control method as well as the potential pitfalls. Section 10.4 presents how to perform tests and construct confidence intervals. The seminal article by Abadie et al. (2010) is reproduced in Section 10.5. Finally, Section 10.6 discusses the extension to cases where multiple units are treated.

10.1 Framework and estimation

To present the synthetic control method, consider a panel data framework. We observe $n_0 + 1$ units at each date $t = 1, \dots, T$. Unit 1 is treated starting from date $T_0 + 1$, while units 2 to $n_0 + 1$ are never treated. Units 2 to $n_0 + 1$ form what is called the "donor pool" because these units can be selected or not to be a part of the synthetic unit. $Y_{i,t}(0)$ represent the potential outcome of unit i at date t if it is not treated, and $Y_{i,t}(1)$ the potential outcome if it is treated. We observe the treatment exposure of each unit at each date ($D_{i,t}$) and the realized outcome $Y_{i,t}{}^{obs}$ defined by:

$$Y_{i,t}^{obs} = Y_{i,t}(D_{i,t}) = \begin{cases} Y_{i,t}(0) & \text{if } D_{i,t} = 0 \\ Y_{i,t}(1) & \text{if } D_{i,t} = 1 \end{cases}$$

The parameter of interest is the effect of the intervention on unit 1 during the post-treatment period, i.e., between dates $T_0 + 1$ and T:

$$\tau_t := Y_{1,t}(1) - Y_{1,t}(0), \quad t = T_0 + 1, \dots, T$$

Remark 10.1 About the dimensions

Most empirical articles that use the synthetic control method deal with long panel data where T is relatively large or proportional to n_0, and where there are at most a dozen treated units. For example, in Abadie et al. (2010), $T = 40$, $n_0 = 38$ for a single treated unit; in Acemoglu et al. (2016), $T \approx 300$, $n_0 = 513$ for about 10 treated units. This contrasts strongly with traditional applications that make use of standard panel data or repeated cross-sectional data where n_0 is very large while T varies from two to 10 dates. In most applications where the method is used, a "unit" is a city, a region, or even a country, hence the limited sample size.

T_0 is necessarily greater than 1 but is generally located after the middle of the period, i.e., $T_0 > (T-1)/2$, in order to have a long pre-treatment period that allows the synthetic unit to be "learned" in machine learning parlance (see Theorem 10.1 for a justification). As a consequence, the standard asymptotic framework where the number of units tends to infinity is less relevant for this type of applications.

Matrix notations give a better illustration of the nature of the problem, by recasting it as a missing variable problem. We observe the following matrix:

$$\mathbf{Y}^{obs} := \left(Y_{i,t}^{obs}\right)_{\substack{t=T,\dots,1\\ i=1,\dots,n_0+1}} = \begin{pmatrix} Y_{1,T}(1) & Y_{2,T}(0) & \cdots & Y_{n_0+1,T}(0) \\ \vdots & \vdots & & \vdots \\ Y_{1,T_0+1}(1) & Y_{2,T_0+1}(0) & \cdots & Y_{n_0+1,T_0+1}(0) \\ Y_{1,T_0}(0) & Y_{2,T_0}(0) & \cdots & Y_{n_0+1,T_0}(0) \\ \vdots & \vdots & & \vdots \\ Y_{1,1}(0) & Y_{2,1}(0) & \cdots & Y_{n_0+1,1}(0) \end{pmatrix}.$$

However, the matrix of outcomes in the absence of treatment has the following form:

$$\mathbf{Y}(0) := \begin{pmatrix} ? & Y_{2,T}(0) & \cdots & Y_{N+1,T}(0) \\ \vdots & \vdots & & \vdots \\ ? & Y_{2,T_0+1}(0) & \cdots & Y_{n_0+1,T_0+1}(0) \\ Y_{1,T_0}(0) & Y_{2,T_0}(0) & \cdots & Y_{n_0+1,T_0}(0) \\ \vdots & \vdots & & \vdots \\ Y_{1,1}(0) & Y_{2,1}(0) & \cdots & Y_{n_0+1,1}(0) \end{pmatrix}.$$

Thus, we encounter a missing variable problem, also called the "fundamental problem of causal inference" (Holland, 1986). The synthetic control method aims to estimate the $T - T_0 - 1$ missing elements on the first column by reweighting the n_0 observed elements at the end of each row to produce a counterfactual:

$$\mathbf{Y}(0) = \begin{pmatrix} \boxed{?} & \boxed{Y_{2,T}(0)} & \boxed{\cdots} & \boxed{Y_{n_0+1,T}(0)} \\ \vdots & \vdots & & \vdots \\ ? & Y_{2,T_0+1}(0) & \cdots & Y_{n_0+1,T_0+1}(0) \\ Y_{1,T_0}(0) & Y_{2,T_0}(0) & \cdots & Y_{n_0+1,T_0}(0) \\ \vdots & \vdots & & \vdots \\ Y_{1,1}(0) & Y_{2,1}(0) & \cdots & Y_{n_0+1,1}(0) \end{pmatrix}.$$

Once this basic intuition is established, weights need to be calculated to apply to each unit $i = 2, \dots, n_0 + 1$. For $i = 1, \dots, n_0 + 1$, we define X_i as the p-dimensional vector measuring the pre-intervention characteristics of unit i. In many applications, the p pre-intervention characteristics will only include pre-treatment outcomes (in this case $p = T_0$), but we may want to add other predictors of the observed outcome during the pre-treatment period, which may or may not be time-varying. We gather them in a vector Z_i such that for the treated unit:

$$\underset{(p\times 1)}{X_i} := \begin{pmatrix} Y_{i,1}^{obs} \\ Y_{i,2}^{obs} \\ \vdots \\ Y_{i,T_0}^{obs} \\ Z_i \end{pmatrix}.$$

We define X_c to be a $p \times n_0$ matrix obtained by concatenating $[X_2, \ldots, X_{n_0+1}]$. For a diagonal $p \times p$ matrix V, we define the norm $\|X\|_V = \sqrt{X'VX}$. Let $\omega = (\omega_2, \ldots, \omega_{n_0+1})$ be vector of parameters of size n_0 subject to the following constraints:

$$\omega_i \geq 0, \;\text{ for } i = 2, \ldots, n_0 + 1\,, \tag{10.1}$$

$$\sum_{i \geq 2} \omega_i = 1. \tag{10.2}$$

These constraints prevent extrapolation beyond the support of the data, i.e., the counterfactual cannot take a value greater than the maximum or lower than the minimum observed value for a control unit. The solution to the synthetic control problem ω^* is obtained by solving the following program:

$$\min_{\omega} \|X_1 - X_c\omega\|_V^2, \tag{10.3}$$

subject to the constraints (10.1) and (10.2). In other words, the synthetic unit is the projection of the treated unit onto the convex hull defined by the control units.

The synthetic control estimator is defined as the difference between the observed outcome for the treated unit and the synthetic outcome:

$$\hat{\tau}_t := Y_{1,t}^{obs} - \sum_{i=2}^{n_0+1} \omega_i^* Y_{i,t}^{obs}.$$

We note that the difference-in-differences estimator would be:

$$\hat{\tau}_t^{DID} := Y_{1,t}^{obs} - \left(Y_{1,T_0}^{obs} + \frac{1}{n_0} \sum_{i=2}^{n_0+1} Y_{i,t}^{obs} - Y_{i,T_0}^{obs} \right),$$

by equally weighting each member of the donor pool and taking as counterfactual the observed outcome measure during the last period for the treated unit, adjusted for the average variation of the observed outcome variable in the control group.

Remark 10.2 About the choice of X_i

X_1 and X_c must contain pre-treatment variables that are good predictors of the variable of interest. In the example of the Mariel boatlift (Card, 1990), where the variables of interest are wages and unemployment, these include aggregated demographic indicators (gender, ethnicity, age), education levels, median income, and GDP per capita. Due to the chronological nature of the problem, including pre-treatment outcomes is strongly advised by Theorem 10.1. e.g., including unemployment rates from 1975–1979 provides a way to create a control unit that verifies the CTA. It is noted that the validity of the synthetic control method relies implicitly on an assumption of conditional independence with observable factors of the form $\mathbb{E}[Y_{i,t}(0)|X_i, D_i] = \mathbb{E}[Y_{i,t}(0)|X_i]$. As long as the synthetic unit is sufficiently similar to the treated unit in terms of the selected variables, it is believed to form a credible counterfactual.

Remark 10.3 About the choice of V

The matrix V in the objective function is a diagonal matrix whose each element (positive) on the diagonal reflects the researcher's prior beliefs on the importance of each variable for the studied intervention. Let v_j be the j-th element of the diagonal. In this case, the synthetic control program (10.3) can be written as:

$$\arg\min_{\omega} \sum_{j=1}^{p} v_j \left[X_{1,j} - \sum_{i=2}^{n_0+1} \omega_i X_{c,ij} \right]^2.$$

Since ω^* depends on V, we use the notation $\omega^*(V)$. However, the applied econometrician does not always have a preconceived idea about the weighting matrix V to adopt. Abadie et al. (2010) then propose to choose $v_1, \ldots, v_p$ by using nested minimization of the mean-squared prediction error (MSPE) on the period preceding the treatment:

$$MSPE(V) := \sum_{t=1}^{T_0} \left[Y_{1,t}^{obs} - \sum_{i=2}^{n_0+1} \omega_i^*(V) Y_{i,t}^{obs} \right]^2.$$

A form of cross-validation can also be used (Abadie and L'Hour, 2021). For simplicity of exposition and because it is the most natural choice, we assume that the validation period is within the second half of the pre-intervention period, although other choices are possible. The procedure is as follows:

1. We partition the pre-intervention period containing T_0 dates into $T_0 - k$ initial learning dates and k subsequent validation dates.

Continued

Remark 10.3 *Continued*

2. For each validation period, $t \in \{T_0 - k, \dots, T_0\}$, we calculate

$$\widehat{\tau}_t(V) = Y_{1,t}^{obs} - \sum_{i=2}^{n_0+1} \omega_i^*(V) Y_{i,t}^{obs},$$

where $\omega_i^*(V)$ solves (10.3) with X measured in the learning period $\{1, \dots, T_0 - k - 1\}$.

3. We choose V to minimize the mean squared prediction error in the validation period,

$$\text{MSPE}(V) = \frac{1}{k} \sum_{t=T_0-k}^{T_0} \widehat{\tau}_t(V)^2.$$

The intuition behind this strategy is based on the nullity of the estimated treatment effect during the validation period.

10.2 A result on the bias

Why does synthetic control work? This section details the result given by Abadie et al. (2010) on the bias of the estimator. We assume the data generating process for the outcome variable in the absence of treatment is given by a factor model similar to the model (2.21) studied in Chapter 11:

$$Y_{i,t}(0) = \delta_t + Z_i'\theta_t + \lambda_t'\mu_i + \varepsilon_{i,t}, \tag{10.4}$$

where δ_t is a time-fixed effect, θ_t is a time-varying parameter vector, Z_i are observed covariates, λ_t are unobserved common factors of dimension F, μ_i are unobserved loading factors (dimension F), and $\varepsilon_{i,t}$ are unobserved transitory shocks. For readers unfamiliar with factor models, the vector λ_t can be considered as the underlying macroeconomic dynamics that affect each unit differently through μ_i. Instead of taking this into account using multiple observed macroeconomic variables, one may want to capture them with a small number of factors, similar to what is done in principal component analysis. In essence, synthetic control works because it offers a simple method to approximate the factor dynamics $\lambda_t'\mu_i$.

Assumption 10.1 (i.i.d. transitory shocks). $(\varepsilon_{i,t})_{i=1,\dots,n_0+1,t=1,\dots,T}$ *are i.i.d. random variables in both i and t, with mean zero and variance* σ^2. *Moreover, for an integer* $m > 2$, $\mathbb{E}|\varepsilon_{i,t}|^m < \infty$.

Assumption 10.2 (Perfect synthetic matching). *The matching distance is zero:*

$$\|X_1 - X_c\omega^*\|_V^2 = 0.$$

In other words, the synthetic unit perfectly replicates the treated unit during the pre-treatment period.

This is a crucial point in proving the following theorem. Note that this is a frequent situation in many applications due to some overfitting when $n_0 > p$ since there are more parameters than variables to fit. However, as p increases, this assumption is less likely to be verified because the probability for the treated unit to be included in the convex hull formed by the untreated units tends to zero exponentially (a problem known as the "curse of dimensionality"). A detailed discussion is given in Ferman and Pinto (2016). Let $\xi(M)$ be the smallest eigenvalue of:

$$\frac{1}{M}\sum_{t=T_0-M+1}^{T_0}\lambda_t\lambda_t'.$$

Let $\lambda^{\mathbf{P}}$ be the $T_0 \times F$ matrix whose t-th row is equal to λ_t'. We make the following assumption:

Assumption 10.3 (Invertibility of the factor matrix). *$\xi(M) \geq c_\xi > 0$ for every positive integer $M \geq F$. Consequently, $\lambda^{\mathbf{P}\prime}\lambda^{\mathbf{P}}$ is invertible. Also, suppose that $|\lambda_t|_\infty \leq \bar{\lambda}$, for $1 \leq t \leq T$.*

Theorem 10.1 (Bias of the synthetic control) *Under Assumptions 10.1, 10.2, and 10.3, for $t \in \{T_0 + 1, \ldots, T\}$:*

$$\mathbb{E}\hat{\tau}_t - \tau_t \underset{T_0 \to +\infty}{\to} 0.$$

The proof of this result, which is interesting in itself, is provided in the appendix of this chapter. Embedded in the proof, you can notice that using pre-treatment outcomes as variables to compute the synthetic control weights is important because they allow to approximate the factor part of the counterfactual outcome equation, $\lambda_t'\mu_i$.

Remark 10.4

This result, due to Abadie et al. (2010), shows that the bias of the synthetic control estimator tends to zero as the number of pre-treatment dates increases. For example, it does not address ℓ_1 or ℓ_2 convergence, mainly because in the appendix proof $\mathbb{E}(|R_{3,t}|) = \mathbb{E}(|\varepsilon_{1,t} - \varepsilon_{2,t}|)$ does not decrease as T_0 increases. Indeed, we only observe a single treated unit, hence the existence of a variance term that does not disappear.

10.3 When and why should synthetic controls be used

When is it a good idea to use synthetic control? Abadie (2021) provides some guidelines to frame the use of this method. We start with three general conditions, which are not strictly specific to synthetic control. Then, we discuss conditions that apply more specifically to comparative studies of a macroeconomic nature and to synthetic control.

First, there should be no anticipation of the policy by the agents. In practice, the effect of the policy may occur before its formal implementation if forward-looking agents react in anticipation, as soon as it is announced. To remedy this problem, it is possible to backdate the intervention to the date of its announcement, rather than to the date of its application. Second, it is necessary to ensure the absence of spillover effects. Indeed, if the spillover effects of a policy are significant and affect geographically neighboring units, selecting these neighbors to be part of the donor pool can also lead to biasing the results by underestimating the actual effect of the policy. It may therefore be preferable to eliminate units that may have been affected by the policy, or to consider them as treated themselves. Third, there must be enough post-intervention dates to detect an effect that may take time to surface.

Fourth, the treatment effect must be sufficiently large to be distinguished from the volatility present in the variable of interest. In other words, configurations in which synthetic control has a good chance of detecting an effect are those for which the signal-to-noise ratio is relatively high a priori. Unlike more conventional microeconometric configurations where uncertainty can be reduced through averaging over a large number of individuals, the framework of synthetic control, where we only have a small number of treated units, limits this possibility. It can therefore only be used to evaluate effects that are suspected to have a significant economic impact. Note also that too much volatility in the variable of interest increases the risk of overfitting. Indeed, in the factor model (10.4), if the variance of the transitory shocks is relatively large compared to the unobserved term that we are trying to approximate ($\lambda_t'\mu_i$), and given that the number of pre-treatment dates T_0 is not always sufficiently large, the synthetic unit may result from fitting the noise ($\varepsilon_{i,t}$) rather than the factor component. In cases where this volatility is too high, it may be wise to pre-filter the time series via a moving average.

Fifth, the donor pool must be composed only of units that are homogeneous in terms of treatment or non-treatment. In other words, we want to ensure that no unit that can be included in the construction of the synthetic unit has undergone a treatment or policy aimed at acting on the same outcome variable, as this could bias the results. Thus, in the example of the tobacco control program that we will study later, we do not want to take into account certain US states that have also changed their anti-tobacco legislation during the period under consideration. Furthermore, these units must also be sufficiently similar to the treated units in terms of characteristics to justify a comparison. Thus, it is not always possible to apply the synthetic control method, especially when a valid donor pool is unavailable. This condition can be verified via a *convex hull condition*: the synthetic unit is a convex combination of units from the donor pool. Therefore, the counterfactual is within the convex envelope defined by the donor pool. Once constructed, the researcher must verify that the characteristics of the synthetic unit are sufficiently close to those of the treated unit. In some cases, the treated unit is so particular that it is impossible to construct a credible counterfactual, as indicated by the significant distance between it and the synthetic unit during the pre-treatment period.

When these conditions are met, the synthetic control method offers certain advantages. The first one is the absence of extrapolation: the counterfactual cannot take a value higher than the maximum or lower than the minimum observed in the donor pool at each date. The synthetic control estimator prevents extrapolation because the weights are positive and their sum is equal to one. The second one is the transparency of the adjustment. Echoing the convex hull condition from the previous paragraph, when $\|X_1 - X_c\omega^*\|_V^2 > 0$, it means that X_1 is not in the convex hull defined from the untreated units, and thus X_1 cannot be perfectly replicated. On the contrary, the use of linear regression always allows for a perfect reproduction of the treated unit, but this can lead to spurious results (Abadie et al., 2015). Thirdly, it provides protection against specification searching. Indeed, only the characteristics measured during the period preceding the treatment are necessary to calculate the weights. They can therefore be calculated before the treatment takes place in order to avoid engaging in *p-hacking*. Finally, the sparsity of the solution facilitates the qualitative interpretation of the counterfactual, opening up possibilities for discussions among experts without a quantitative background.

10.4 Inference using permutation tests

Note that when defining the quantity of interest, τ_t, we did not use an expectation, like in Abadie et al. (2010). This is because the synthetic control method is developed within a framework where we observe not a random sample of individuals from a super-population, but aggregated data. Therefore, the uncertainty does not come from sampling (or at least, it is negligible), but from the assignment of treatment to well-defined units. An example illustrating this point is Card (1990), which uses the *Mariel boatlift* as a natural experiment to measure the effect of a sudden and substantial flow of migrants on the wages and employment of less skilled native workers in the Miami labor market. Between April and October 1980, about 125,000 Cubans fled Fidel Castro and sought asylum in Florida, which suddenly increased Miami's workforce by 7%. Card uses individual-level data from the Current Population Survey (CPS) for Miami and four comparison cities (Atlanta, Los Angeles, Houston, and Tampa-St. Petersburg) to conduct a difference-in-differences analysis. Table 10.1 presents an abbreviated version of a table from the article:

Official statistics can provide us with unemployment rate number at the city level with lower standard errors. Anecdotally, the standard deviation for the estimation

Table 10.1 Difference-in-differences estimator for the unemployment rate

	Year		
	1979	1981	1981–1979
Miami	8.3 (1.7)	9.6 (1.8)	1.3 (2.5)
Comparison cities	10.3 (0.8)	12.6 (0.9)	2.3 (1.2)
Miami–Comparison cities	-2.0 (1.9)	-3.0 (2.0)	-1.0 (2.8)

Note: Based on Table 4 in Card (1990). African American workers. Standard errors in parentheses.

of the French unemployment rate is close to 0.2. The moral of the story is that if the aggregated data we are dealing with is expressed per capita, $Y_{i,t}^{obs}$ is probably already an average over a sufficiently large sample to apply the law of large numbers. For example, $Y_{i,t}^{obs} = \bar{U}_{i,t} \approx \mathbb{E}(U_{k,it})$ where $U_{k,it}$ is a Bernoulli variable equal to one when individual k is unemployed at time t in city i. For more information on this topic, see e.g., Abadie et al. (2020). This observation justifies the use of a different type of inference in the synthetic control methodology.

10.4.1 Permutation tests in a simple framework

In this section, we temporarily move away from the synthetic control framework to a cross-sectional data framework, in order to introduce what are called *exact Fisher p-values* that are used to conduct permutation tests (see also Chapter 5 in Imbens and Rubin, 2015). We consider a simple framework of a randomized experiment at a single date where we observe an i.i.d. sequence $(D_i, Y_i^{obs})_{i=1,\dots,n}$ with:

$$Y_i^{obs} = Y_i(D_i) = \begin{cases} Y_i(0) & \text{if } D_i = 0 \\ Y_i(1) & \text{if } D_i = 1 \end{cases}$$

$(Y_i(0), Y_i(1)) \perp\!\!\!\perp D_i$. The missing outcome is denoted by $Y_i^{mis} := Y_i(1 - D_i)$. Fisher's idea is to test the null hypothesis of a constant treatment effect for everyone. The null hypothesis can be written for a constant C as:

$$H_0(C) : \text{“}Y_i(1) = Y_i(0) + C,\ i = 1, \dots, n.\text{”}$$

This hypothesis should not be confused with a constant treatment effect *on average*, $n^{-1} \sum_{i=1}^{n} Y_i(1) - Y_i(0) = C$. It seems much stronger and logically implies a hypothesis about a constant average treatment effect. However, the paradox discussed in Ding (2017) shows that when the null hypothesis does not hold, there are cases where the Neymanian hypothesis of no average treatment effect is rejected while Fisher's strong null hypothesis is not, which contradicts the logical link between the two hypotheses. This surprising result can be explained by the lack of power of Fisher tests.

Under $H_0(C)$ it is possible to recover the outcome variable in the regime where the unit is not observed, simply by imputing the constant treatment effect: $Y_i^{mis} = Y_i^{obs} - (2D_i - 1)C$. In other words, under $H_0(C)$, we can solve the problem of missing variable through imputation. In the case where $C = 0$, this means that treatment assignment should not matter since the potential outcomes under both treatment regimes are the same. We construct an estimator of the treatment effect $\widehat{\tau}(\boldsymbol{D})$, which in practice depends on both the treatment assignment $\boldsymbol{D} = (D_1, \ldots, D_n)$ and the observed outcomes $\boldsymbol{Y} = (Y_1, \ldots, Y_n)$, but we only specify the dependence on the assignment for simplification. For example, $\widehat{\tau}(\boldsymbol{D})$ could be the difference in means of the outcome variable between treated and untreated units. Recall that a permutation π is a bijective function $\pi : \{1, \ldots, n\} \to \{1, \ldots, n\}$. Thanks to $H_0(C)$, we can compute any treatment effect statistic $\widehat{\tau}(\boldsymbol{D}_\pi)$ for the allocation $\boldsymbol{D}_\pi := (D_{\pi(1)}, \ldots, D_{\pi(n)})$ for any permutation $\pi \in \Pi$, the set of all permutations of the first n integers onto themselves. We denote by $\boldsymbol{D}^{obs} := (D_1, \ldots, D_n)$ the vector of observed assignments. The Fisher p-value is defined as follows:

$$p(C) := \frac{1}{|\Pi|} \sum_{\pi \in \Pi} \mathbf{1}\left\{\widehat{\tau}(\boldsymbol{D}_\pi) \geq \widehat{\tau}(\boldsymbol{D}^{obs})\right\}.$$

In practice, since Π can be very large, the distribution is approximated by Monte Carlo, using the following procedure:

1. For $b = 1, \ldots, B$, a new permutation of the treatment assignment $\boldsymbol{D}_b$ is drawn, and the statistic $\widehat{\tau}(\boldsymbol{D}_b)$ is computed using $H_0(C)$.
2. The Fisher p-value is approximated using:

$$\widehat{p}(C) := \frac{1}{B+1}\left(1 + \sum_{b=1}^{B} \mathbf{1}\left\{\widehat{\tau}(\boldsymbol{D}_b) \geq \widehat{\tau}(\boldsymbol{D}^{obs})\right\}\right).$$

3. The null hypothesis $H_0(C)$ is rejected if $\widehat{p}(C)$ is smaller than a predetermined threshold: the observed treatment allocation gives an effect that is unusually large compared to the randomized distribution. For $\alpha \in (0, 1)$, the test is:

$$\varphi_\alpha = \mathbf{1}\left\{\widehat{p}(C) \leq \alpha\right\}. \tag{10.5}$$

Lemma 10.1 (Test level). *Suppose that $\boldsymbol{D}^{obs} = (D_1, \ldots, D_n)$ is exchangeable with respect to Π under $H_0(C)$. Then, for $\alpha \in]0, 1[$, the test (10.5) is of level α, i.e., under $H_0(C)$:*

$$\mathbb{P}\left[p(C) \leq \alpha\right] \leq \alpha.$$

A vector of random variables (X_1, X_2) is said to be exchangeable if the distribution of (X_1, X_2) is the same as that of (X_2, X_1). A sufficient condition $\boldsymbol{D}^{obs} = (D_1, \ldots, D_n)$ to be exchangeable with respect to Π is if $D_1, \ldots, D_n$ are i.i.d. random variables. The proof of Lemma 10.1, in the appendix of this chapter, is inspired by Chernozhukov et al. (2021).

Let's illustrate this intuition with a simulation exercise. Let $\mathbb{P}(D = 1) = .2$ and let's draw a single sample of size $n = 200$ from $Y|D \sim \mathcal{N}(\tau_0 D, 1)$ for $\tau_0 \in \{0; 0.75\}$. We take the absolute difference between the estimator of the average treatment effect and C as the estimator:

$$\widehat{\tau} = \left| \frac{1}{n_1} \sum_{i:D_i=1} Y_i^{obs} - \frac{1}{n - n_1} \sum_{i:D_i=0} Y_i^{obs} - C \right|,$$

which is recomputed under a large number of random permutations π of $\mathbf{D}$ (while not permuting $\mathbf{Y}$).

Figure 10.1 represents the distribution of the previous estimator calculated from random permutations of the treatment allocation under the hypothesis of no effect ($C = 0$). The value of the estimator for the first allocation is represented by the dashed line. $H_0(0)$ is false in the left panel ($\tau_0 = 0.75$), and true in the right panel ($\tau_0 = 0$). In the first case, the observed statistic is in the tail of the distribution of estimations calculated under a random permutation. In this sense, the observed effect is abnormally large: the estimated effect is significant. In the second case, the observed effect is in the center of the distribution, which makes it non-significant. The p-values indicated under the graph quantify the conclusion associated with the Fisher tests.

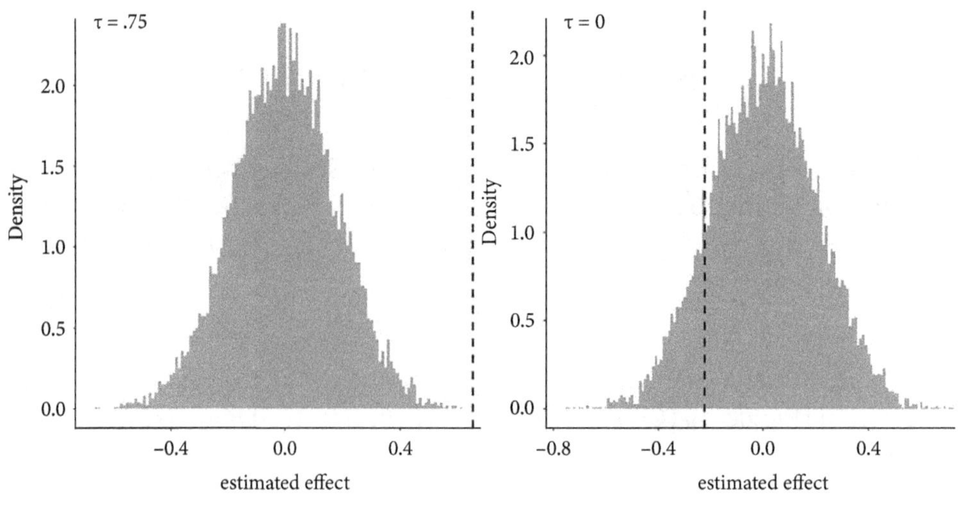

Figure 10.1 A simple Fisher test: $H_0 : C = 0$ false *vs.* $H_0 : C = 0$ true.

Note: histograms constructed from the recomputed estimator of random permutations of the treatment allocation. The dashed vertical line is the value of the estimator under the initial allocation. On the left, $\widehat{p} = 0.006$ ($\widehat{\tau} = 0.671$), on the right $\widehat{p} = 0.271$ ($\widehat{\tau} = -0.23$) for the null hypothesis of no treatment effect.

10.4.2 The confidence interval-test duality

From the tests presented in the previous section, we can construct confidence intervals by exploiting the duality between these two concepts. Most often, this duality is intuitively used to conclude the significance of an estimation through its confidence interval – i.e., does it contain the value zero? Here, we use it in the opposite direction. The intuition for constructing a confidence interval of level $1 - \alpha$ is as follows: perform the hypothesis test $H_0(C)$ at level $\alpha \in (0,1)$ and include in the confidence interval any value of C for which $H_0(C)$ is not rejected. More formally, the confidence interval will be defined as follows:

$$CI_{1-\alpha} = \{C \in \mathbb{R} \mid \widehat{p}(C) > \alpha\}.$$

We denote τ_0 as the true value of the treatment effect, we can calculate the probability that the interval obtained in this way indeed contains τ_0:

$$\mathbb{P}[CI_{1-\alpha} \ni \tau_0] = \mathbb{P}[\widehat{p}(\tau_0) > \alpha] = 1 - \mathbb{P}[\widehat{p}(\tau_0) \leq \alpha] \geq 1 - \alpha,$$

using Lemma 10.1. Thus, $CI_{1-\alpha}$ is indeed of level $1 - \alpha$.

Figure 10.2 plots the p-value as a function of C in the null hypothesis tested for the two cases $\tau_0 \in \{0, 0.75\}$. In the first case, $\tau_0 = 0.75$, the 95% confidence interval is approximately $[0.3, 1]$. In the second case, $\tau_0 = 0$, the 95% confidence interval is approximately $[-0.6, 0.25]$. We note that unlike asymptotic confidence intervals or intervals based on the normal distribution, these intervals are not symmetric around the estimated value. In practice, as we will see in the application presented below, for computational efficiency reasons, we may not necessarily plot the entire curve $C \to \widehat{p}(C)$, but rather numerically search for the solutions C^* of $\widehat{p}(C) = \alpha$.

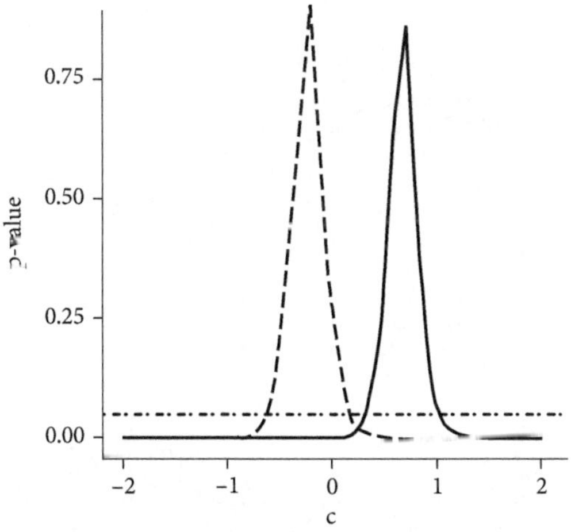

Figure 10.2 p-value as a function of the value C in the null hypothesis

Note: The solid line illustrates the first case $\tau = 0.75$, the dotted line the second case $\tau = 0$. The horizontal line has the equation $y = 0.05$.

10.5 Empirical application: tobacco control program

This section serves both as an illustration of the previously discussed concepts, as well as to detail the implementation of certain inference procedures.

In January 1989, the state of California enacted the "Proposition 99," one of the first large-scale tobacco control programs, which increased the cigarette tax by 25 cents per pack, allocated tax revenues to anti-smoking budgets, funded prevention campaigns, etc. What has been its effect on per capita tobacco consumption? This is the emblematic example used to illustrate the synthetic control method, where the goal is to create a synthetic California state by reweighting the states that did not modify their tobacco legislation. X_i measures the retail price of cigarettes, the logarithm of per capita income, the percentage of the population aged 15 to 24, beer consumption per capita (averages from 1980 to 1988), cigarette consumption from 1970 to 1974, 1980, and 1988. Further details of this application can be found in Abadie et al. (2010). Most of the tables and figures in this section are reproduced from the raw data of this article.

Figure 10.3 represents cigarette consumption in California and in 38 other states that did not modify their tobacco legislation. It is very clear that no common trend is observed.

Figure 10.4 compares the same data for California and its synthetic counterpart that did not implement the treatment. The synthetic unit is composed of Utah (34.3%), Nevada (23.6%), Montana (18.2%), Colorado (17.5%), and Connecticut (6.2%). And Table 10.2 compares the characteristics of California, its synthetic unit, and the other 38 states. The synthetic unit accurately replicates the behavior of California's tobacco consumption before the treatment. The treatment effect is given by the difference between the solid curve and the dotted curve. Proposition 99 led to a decrease in consumption estimated at approximately 25 packs per capita in 2000.

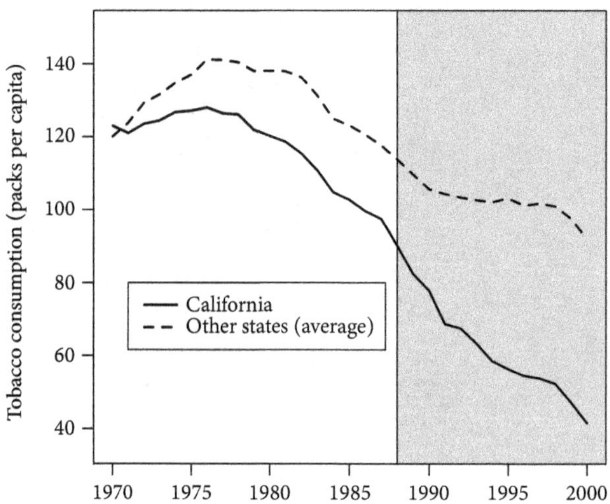

Figure 10.3 Proposition 99: California *vs.* rest of the United States.

Note: Based on the data from Abadie et al. (2010). The dotted line is a simple average of 38 states.

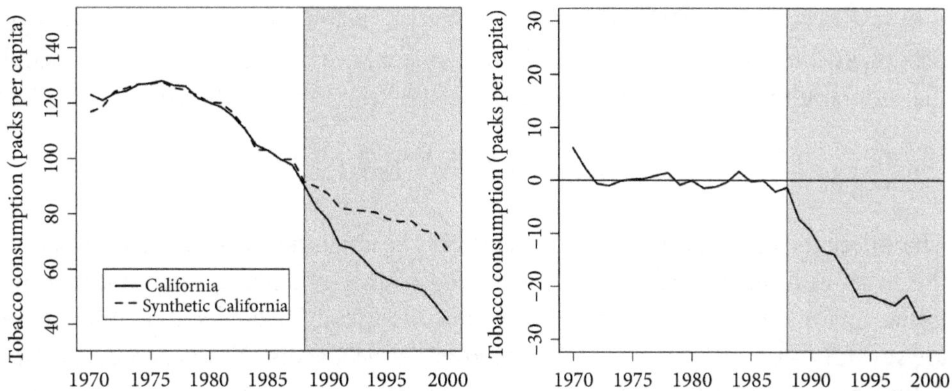

Figure 10.4 Proposition 99: California *vs.* synthetic California.

Note: Based on the data from Abadie et al. (2010). The graph on the right represents the treatment effect over time as the difference between the solid curve and the dotted curve in the left graph.

Table 10.2 Proposition 99: comparison of characteristics among California, synthetic unit, and other 38 states.

	California		Average of 38 other States
	Observed	Synthetic	
	(1)	(2)	(3)
GDP per capita (log)	10.1	9.9	9.8
Cigarette prices	89.4	89.3	87.3
Percentage of 15-24 year-olds	0.2	0.2	0.2
Beer consumption per capita	24.3	24.1	23.7
Cigarette consumption per capita, 1988	90.1	91.4	113.8
Cigarette consumption per capita, 1980	120.2	120.2	138.1
Cigarette consumption per capita, 1975	127.1	126.9	136.9

Remark 10.5 Sparsity of the solution

In most cases, n_0, the number of control units, is larger than p, the number of pre-treatment characteristics. As a consequence of this observation and the constrained optimization problem (10.3) s.t. (10.1) and (10.2), the obtained solution is often sparse, i.e., $\|\omega^*\|_0 \ll n_0$: only a small number of untreated units are used to produce the synthetic unit. This is the case in this example since only five states have a non-zero weight. Theorem 1 from Abadie and L'Hour (2021) shows that under weak regularity conditions, $\|\omega^*\|_0 \leq p + 1$.

We also show that a necessary condition for $\omega_i^* > 0$ to occur is that control unit i is connected to the treated unit in a specific tessellation of the data points defined by the columns of (X_1, X_c), called the Delaunay triangulation.

To evaluate the significance of this effect, we adapt the method proposed in Section 10.4 to the synthetic control framework, where there are multiple dates and therefore multiple outcome variables. We want to test the hypothesis:

$$H_0 : \text{“}Y_{1,t}(1) = Y_{1,t}(0), t = T_0 + 1, \ldots, T\text{”}.$$

The inference procedure consists of randomly reassigning the treatment to one of the 38 states and comparing it to the observed synthetic control estimator under the initial treatment assignment (i.e., California as the only treated state). Since there are several dates in this example, we need to define a statistic $\widehat{\tau}$ to aggregate them. A first possibility is to simply take the average of the squared prediction error (or mean squared prediction error, MSPE) for all dates after the treatment. Let $\mathcal{T}_1 = \{T_0 + 1, \ldots, T\}$, we have:

$$\frac{1}{|\mathcal{T}_1|} \sum_{t \in \mathcal{T}_1} \widehat{\tau}_t^2,$$

where $\widehat{\tau}_t = Y_{1,t}^{obs} - \sum_{j=2}^{n} \omega_j^* Y_{j,t}^{obs}$. In Abadie and L'Hour (2021), we suggest using the ratio between the average squared prediction error for post-treatment dates and the same average calculated for pre-treatment dates $\mathcal{T}_0 = \{1, \ldots, T_0\}$, in order to underweight the units that are less well reproduced during the pre-treatment period and overweight the others:

$$\frac{1}{|\mathcal{T}_1|} \sum_{t \in \mathcal{T}_1} \widehat{\tau}_t^2 \Big/ \frac{1}{|\mathcal{T}_0|} \sum_{t \in \mathcal{T}_0} \widehat{\tau}_t^2.$$

To what extent are these two statistics larger when calculated for the state of California, compared to these same statistics when we pretend that any other state is the treated state? Figure 10.5 shows the histogram of these two statistics. The calculation was performed as follows: for each of the 39 states (including California), we assign it the treatment (even if it is not California) and that the other 38 states do not receive it (even California can be considered as untreated in this case), we calculate the synthetic control weights, and then the two previous statistics. We obtain a p-value of 0.2 in the first case, and 0.03 in the second. We observe that California is the state for which the effect is the largest, when taking into account the quality of the pre-treatment fit.

Now we want to calculate a confidence interval for a given level $1 - \alpha$. Let's start with a simple approach to illustrate the implementation of this method. We will rely on a Fisher test of the null hypothesis for a constant treatment effect over time, of the form:

$$H_0(C) : \text{“}Y_{1,t}(1) = Y_{1,t}(0) + C, t = T_0 + 1, \ldots, T\text{”}.$$

The next step is to choose a test statistic that will be close to zero if $H_0(C)$ is true and will be "large" if $H_0(C)$ is false. Let's take the statistic of the ratio between the average post-treatment MSPE and the average pre-treatment MSPE:

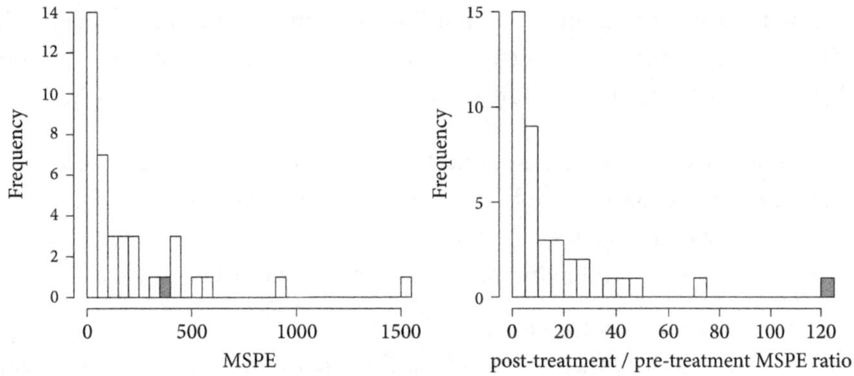

Figure 10.5 Proposition 99: permutation tests.
Note: Based on the source data from Abadie et al. (2010). Shaded value represents California.

$$\frac{1}{|\mathcal{T}_1|}\sum_{t\in\mathcal{T}_1}(\widehat{\tau}_t - C)^2 \Bigg/ \frac{1}{|\mathcal{T}_0|}\sum_{t\in\mathcal{T}_0}\widehat{\tau}_t^2.$$

Intuitively, this statistic should be small under $H_0(C)$ since the treatment effect should be equal to C, and diverge otherwise. This statistic can be computed under the observed treatment assignment (i.e., when California receives the treatment), as well as under any other desired configuration (i.e., by reassigning the treatment to another state). In the latter case, since we are under $H_0(C)$, the following adjustments must be made:

1. California, indexed by $i = 1$, sees its "placebo" tobacco consumption vary by C at each post-treatment date: $Y_{1,t}^{obs} - C$ for $t \in \mathcal{T}_1$ since under this hypothesis, it is considered untreated.
2. The state that suddenly becomes treated, indexed by $i = i^*$, sees its "placebo" tobacco consumption vary by C at each post-treatment date: ${Y_{i^*,t}}^{obs} + C$ for $t \in \mathcal{T}_1$.

Let $\widehat{S}_1, \ldots, \widehat{S}_{n_0+1}$ be the statistics computed under each possible reassignment of the treatment. The Fisher p value for the hypothesis $H_0(C)$ is then given by:

$$\widehat{p}(C) := \frac{1}{n_0+1}\sum_{i=1}^{n_0+1}\mathbf{1}\left\{\widehat{S}_i \geq \widehat{S}_1\right\},$$

where California is always indexed by $i = 1$. Finally, we want to compute the bounds $\widehat{C}_l$ and $\widehat{C}_u$ of the confidence interval at level $1 - \alpha$. In other words, we are looking for $[\widehat{C}_l, \widehat{C}_u]$ such that for any $C \in [\widehat{C}_l, \widehat{C}_u]$, $\widehat{p}(C) > \alpha$, and for any $C \notin [\widehat{C}_l, \widehat{C}_u]$, $\widehat{p}(C) \leq \alpha$. These bounds are computed using a dichotomy since this function does not have a simple analytical expression. Note that the solution is not unique because the p-value function is a priori piece-wise constant. We illustrate the implementation of this algorithm for computing the upper bound $\widehat{C}_u$:

1. We choose two initial values a and b such that $\widehat{p}(a) - \alpha > 0$ and $\widehat{p}(b) - \alpha < 0$. A crude approximation can be used for this initialization.
2. We choose a convergence tolerance $\epsilon > 0$.
3. We then repeat the following series of operations until $|b - a| < \epsilon$:
   (a) We compute $m = (a + b)/2$ and $\widehat{p}(m)$.
   (b) If $(\widehat{p}(b) - \alpha) \times (\widehat{p}(m) - \alpha) > 0$ (b and m are on the same side of the zero of the function $x \to \widehat{p}(x) - \alpha$), then we set $b = m$.
   (c) Otherwise, we set $a = m$.

The method for computing $\widehat{C}_l$ is the same. Figure 10.6 displays the 80% confidence interval based on this calculation method (dotted curves). It can be observed that because the policy effect takes time to spread, the treatment effect is not constant over time, rendering this approach inappropriate. The same method can be implemented by inverting the Fisher test for each date. In Figure 10.6, this interval is plotted as dashed lines.

Testing using conformal inference. Another way to test the hypothesis $H_0 : Y_{1,t}(1) = Y_{1,t}(0) + C_t, t{=}T_0 \;\; = \;\; 1, \ldots, T$ for a certain user-specified trajectory $(C_t)_{t=T_0+1,\ldots,T}$ is to compare the distribution of $(\widehat{u}_t)_{t=1,\ldots,T}$ before and after treatment, where $\widehat{u}_t$ is defined as:

$$\widehat{u}_t = \begin{cases} Y_{1,t}^{obs} - \sum_{i=2}^{n_0+1} \omega_i^* Y_{i,t}^{obs} & \text{if } t \leq T_0, \\ Y_{1,t}^{obs} - C_t - \sum_{i=2}^{n_0+1} \omega_i^* Y_{i,t}^{obs} & \text{if } t \geq T_0 + 1. \end{cases}$$

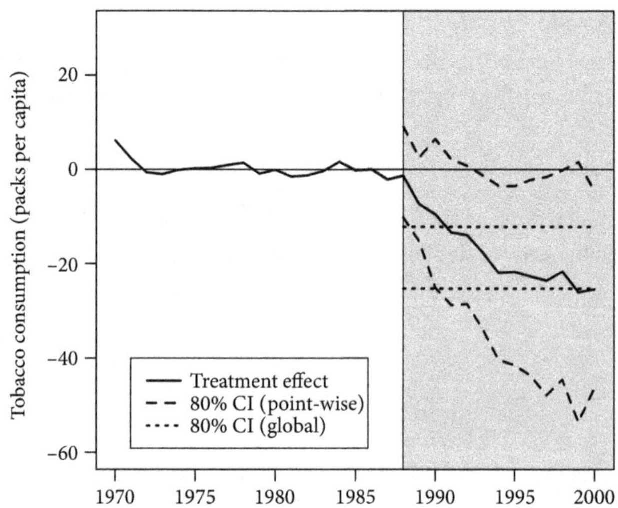

Figure 10.6 Proposition 99: Confidence intervals.

Note: CI means confidence interval.

Attention here, the synthetic control weights are directly computed under the null hypothesis. Next, we compute the statistic:

$$S(\hat{u}) = \frac{1}{\sqrt{T - T_0}} \left| \sum_{t=T_0+1}^{T} \hat{u}_t \right|.$$

under all permutations $\pi \in \Pi$ of $\{1, \ldots, T\}$ and compute the p-value:

$$\hat{p} = \frac{1}{|\Pi|} \sum_{\pi \in \Pi} \mathbf{1}\left\{S(\hat{u}_\pi) \geq S(\hat{u})\right\}.$$

The validity of this approach is developed in Chernozhukov et al. (2021). It is computationally attractive since the error terms are defined once and for all and do not need to be recomputed under each permutation.

10.6 Multiple treated units

So far, we have only considered cases with a single treated unit where we used the synthetic control method to create a single counterfactual. How does this method apply to a case with multiple treated units? Two potential solutions, each with their advantages and disadvantages, can be considered: (i) creating a synthetic unit for each treated unit and taking the average, or (ii) creating a synthetic unit for the average of the treated units.

Let's consider the first solution, which comes with a series of potential problems to solve. In particular, considering many treated units increases the probability that at least one of them falls within the convex hull defined by the untreated units, resulting in the synthetic control solution (10.3) not being unique. In Abadie and L'Hour (2021), we introduce a penalty term in (10.3) and calculate a synthetic unit for each treated unit (indexed by i here). Thus, if there are n_1 treated units, for each $i = 1, \ldots, n_1$, the synthetic control weights solve:

$$\omega_i^*(\lambda) = \arg\min_{\omega} \|X_i - X_c\omega\|_V^2 + \lambda \sum_{j=n_1+1}^{n_1+n_0} \omega_j \left\| X_i - X_j \right\|_V^2$$

subject to the constraints (10.1) and (10.2). $\lambda > 0$ is a tuning parameter (similar to the Lasso penalty). λ defines the trade-off between a good reproduction of the treated unit and the sum of the pairwise distance between the treated unit and each control unit. $\lambda \to 0$ represents the pure synthetic control case, while $\lambda \to \infty$ corresponds to the nearest neighbor pair matching case. *In fine*, we average the difference between the treated units and their respective synthetic units:

$$\hat{\tau}_t(\lambda) := \frac{1}{n_1} \sum_{i=1}^{n_1} \left[Y_{i,t}^{obs} - \sum_{j=n_1+1}^{n_0+n_1} \omega_{i,j}^*(\lambda) Y_{j,t}^{obs} \right].$$

The theory and methods for choosing λ are developed in Abadie and L'Hour (2021). The resulting estimator also reduces the risk of having a significant interpolation bias by excluding units that are very different from the treated unit in the synthetic unit.

On the other hand, Ben-Michael et al. (2021) propose a "partially pooled" synthetic control estimator:

$$\left(\omega_1^*(\nu), \ldots, \omega_{n_1}^*(\nu)\right) = \arg\min \frac{\nu}{2}\frac{1}{n_1}\sum_{i=1}^{n_1} \|X_i - X_c\omega_i\|_V^2 + \frac{1-\nu}{2}\frac{1}{p}\sum_{j=1}^{p}\left[\frac{1}{n_1}\sum_{i=1}^{n_1} X_{i,j} - X_{c,j}\omega_i\right]^2,$$

subject to the constraints (10.1) and (10.2) for $\nu \in [0,1]$. This estimator balances two objectives: accurately reproducing each treated unit individually (the first part, similar to the standard synthetic control method) and accurately reproducing the average of the treated units for each characteristic (the second part). The authors argue that constructing a synthetic unit for each treated unit separately and then taking the average can result in suboptimal fit of the average of the treated units and can lead to potential bias. They show that their estimator is a solution to this problem.

10.7 Summary

Key concepts

Synthetic control method, control units, common trend assumption, sparsity, permutation tests, Fisher's p-value, test inversion.

Additional references

The main articles that contributed to the development of this method are Abadie and Gardeazabal (2003), Abadie et al. (2010), and Abadie et al. (2015). The most emblematic one is Abadie et al. (2010), where the authors studied the effect of a large-scale anti-smoking program in California. We use their data in Section 10.5. Abadie (2021) describes the methodology for applying the synthetic control method. Doudchenko and Imbens (2016) establish the link between synthetic control, difference-in-differences, regression, and matching. It is also worth mentioning a video by Alberto Abadie on the subject: youtu.be/2jzL0DZfr_Y. Lastly, Volume 536 of the *Journal of the American Statistical Association* is a special issue on recent advances in synthetic control.

Code and data

R, STATA, and Matlab packages for using the synthetic control are available at web.stanford.edu/jhain/synthpage.html.

Questions

1. Given the configuration of Chapter 10, is the synthetic control estimator a consistent estimator of the treatment effect on the treated units? Explain why or why not.
2. Give three advantages of using the synthetic control method when appropriate. Briefly explain these advantages.
3. "The synthetic control estimator does not use the complete sample of control units." Explain and critique.
4. How can you use tests to construct confidence intervals?
5. You use an exact Fisher test to test the hypothesis of no treatment effect H_0: "$Y_i(1) = Y_i(0)$". The p-value you obtained is 0.02. The 0.9 confidence interval you obtain using the same methodology is $[-0.50, 0.36]$. Is this possible?
6. Consider the model: $Y_i = D_i\tau_0 + X_i'\beta_0 + \varepsilon_i$, where D_i is a binary variable and $\varepsilon_i \perp\!\!\!\perp (X_i, D_i)$. Describe a methodology based on Fisher tests to perform inference on τ_0.

10.8 Proofs and additional results

10.8.1 Proofs of the main results

Proof of Theorem 10.1 By using the factor model specification, for any $t = 1, \dots, T$:

$$
\begin{aligned}
\hat{\tau}_t =& Y_{1,t}(1) - Y_{1,t}(0) + \left[Y_{1,t}(0) - \sum_{i=2}^{n_0+1} \omega_i^* Y_{i,t}(0) \right] \\
=& \tau_t + \delta_t \left[1 - \sum_{i=2}^{n_0+1} \omega_i^* \right] + \left[Z_1 - \sum_{i=2}^{n_0+1} \omega_i^* Z_i \right]' \theta_t + \lambda_t' \left[\mu_1 - \sum_{i=2}^{n_0+1} \omega_i^* \mu_i \right] \\
&+ \left[\varepsilon_{1,t} - \sum_{i=2}^{n_0+1} \omega_i^* \varepsilon_{i,t} \right] \\
=& \tau_t + \lambda_t' \left[\mu_1 - \sum_{i=2}^{n_0+1} \omega_i^* \mu_i \right] + \left[\varepsilon_{1,t} - \sum_{i=2}^{n_0+1} \omega_i^* \varepsilon_{i,t} \right],
\end{aligned}
\tag{10.6}
$$

where the last line comes from (10.2) and the perfect matching of the synthetic unit, Assumption 10.2. Now, let's consider the pre-treatment results written in matrix notation. $\mathbf{Y}_\mathbf{i}^\mathbf{P}$ is the $T_0 \times 1$ vector of pre-treatment outcomes for unit i with the t-th element equal to $Y_{i,t}^{obs}$. The $T_0 \times 1$ vector of pre-treatment transitory shocks is $\varepsilon_\mathbf{i}^\mathbf{P}$. Notice that because $\mathbf{Y}_\mathbf{1}^\mathbf{P} = (Y_{1,t}(0))_{t=1,\ldots,T_0}$, following the same steps as above:

$$\mathbf{Y}_\mathbf{1}^\mathbf{P} - \sum_{i=2}^{n_0+1} \omega_i^* \mathbf{Y}_\mathbf{i}^\mathbf{P} = \lambda^\mathbf{P} \left[\mu_1 - \sum_{i=2}^{n_0+1} \omega_i^* \mu_i \right] + \left[\varepsilon_\mathbf{1}^\mathbf{P} - \sum_{i=2}^{n_0+1} \omega_i^* \varepsilon_\mathbf{i}^\mathbf{P} \right]. \tag{10.7}$$

From Equation (10.7), using Assumption 10.3:

$$\begin{aligned}\left[\mu_1 - \sum_{i=2}^{n_0+1} \omega_i^* \mu_i \right] &= \left(\lambda^{\mathbf{P}\prime}\lambda^\mathbf{P}\right)^{-1} \lambda^{\mathbf{P}\prime} \left[\mathbf{Y}_\mathbf{1}^\mathbf{P} - \sum_{i=2}^{n_0+1} \omega_i^* \mathbf{Y}_\mathbf{i}^\mathbf{P} \right] \\ &\quad - \left(\lambda^{\mathbf{P}\prime}\lambda^\mathbf{P}\right)^{-1} \lambda^{\mathbf{P}\prime} \left[\varepsilon_\mathbf{1}^\mathbf{P} - \sum_{i=2}^{n_0+1} \omega_i^* \varepsilon_\mathbf{i}^\mathbf{P} \right].\end{aligned} \tag{10.8}$$

The above Equation (10.8) helps to understand the nature of the synthetic control methodology: the quality of the approximation of the factor loading coefficients of the treated unit, μ_1, by the synthetic unit depends on the distance between the pre-treatment results of the treated unit and those of the synthetic unit. This observation argues for the inclusion of pre-treatment outcomes in the program (10.3), and constitutes the crucial point of the theorem. Furthermore, given that Assumption 10.2 holds, the first term of Equation (10.8) disappears and we have a good bias decomposition for $t > T_0$ by inserting Equation (10.8) into Equation (10.6):

$$\begin{aligned}\widehat{\tau}_t - \tau_t &= \underbrace{\lambda_t' \left(\lambda^{\mathbf{P}\prime}\lambda^\mathbf{P}\right)^{-1} \lambda^{\mathbf{P}\prime} \sum_{i=2}^{n_0+1} \omega_i^* \varepsilon_\mathbf{i}^\mathbf{P}}_{:=R_{1,t}} - \underbrace{\lambda_t' \left(\lambda^{\mathbf{P}\prime}\lambda^\mathbf{P}\right)^{-1} \lambda^{\mathbf{P}\prime} \varepsilon_\mathbf{1}^\mathbf{P}}_{:=R_{2,t}} \\ &\quad + \underbrace{\left[\varepsilon_{1,t} - \sum_{i=2}^{n_0+1} \omega_i^* \varepsilon_{i,t} \right]}_{:=R_{3,t}}.\end{aligned}$$

When $t > T_0$, $R_{2,t}$ and $R_{3,t}$ have mean zero thanks to Assumption 10.1. This is not the case for $R_{1,t}$ as there is no reason to think that $\varepsilon_{i,t}$ and ω_i^* are independent for $t \leq T_0$ since ω_i^* depends on $\mathbf{Y}_\mathbf{1}^\mathbf{P}, \ldots, \mathbf{Y}_{\mathbf{n_0+1}}^\mathbf{P}$, and therefore on $\varepsilon_\mathbf{1}^\mathbf{P}, \ldots, \varepsilon_{\mathbf{n_0+1}}^\mathbf{P}$. We can rewrite it as:

$$R_{1,t} = \sum_{i=2}^{n_0+1} \omega_i^* \lambda_t' \left(\lambda^{\mathbf{P}\prime}\lambda^\mathbf{P}\right)^{-1} \lambda^{\mathbf{P}\prime} \varepsilon_\mathbf{i}^\mathbf{P} = \sum_{i=2}^{n_0+1} \omega_i^* \sum_{s=1}^{T_0} \lambda_t' \left(\sum_{t=1}^{T_0} \lambda_t \lambda_t' \right)^{-1} \lambda_s \varepsilon_{i,s}.$$

By Cauchy–Schwarz inequality, since $\left(\sum_{t=1}^{T_0}\lambda_t\lambda_t'\right)^{-1}$ is symmetric and positive definite, and by using Assumption 10.3:

$$\left(\lambda_t'\left(\sum_{t=1}^{T_0}\lambda_t\lambda_t'\right)^{-1}\lambda_s\right)^2 \leq \left(\lambda_t'\left(\sum_{t=1}^{T_0}\lambda_t\lambda_t'\right)^{-1}\lambda_t\right)\left(\lambda_s'\left(\sum_{t=1}^{T_0}\lambda_t\lambda_t'\right)^{-1}\lambda_s\right)$$
$$\leq \left(\frac{F\bar{\lambda}^2}{T_0 c_\xi}\right)^2.$$

Let $\tilde{\varepsilon}_i := \sum_{s=1}^{T_0}\lambda_t'\left(\sum_{t=1}^{T_0}\lambda_t\lambda_t'\right)^{-1}\lambda_s\varepsilon_{i,s}$. Using Assumption 10.1 and Holder's inequality:

$$|R_{1,t}| \leq \sum_{i=2}^{n_0+1}\omega_i^*|\tilde{\varepsilon}_i| \leq \left(\sum_{i=2}^{n_0+1}\omega_i^*|\tilde{\varepsilon}_i|^m\right)^{1/m} \leq \left(\sum_{i=2}^{n_0+1}|\tilde{\varepsilon}_i|^m\right)^{1/m}.$$

According to Holder's inequality, we also have:

$$\mathbb{E}\left(\sum_{i=2}^{n_0+1}\omega_i^*|\tilde{\varepsilon}_i|\right) \leq \left(\mathbb{E}\left[\sum_{i=2}^{n_0+1}|\tilde{\varepsilon}_i|^m\right]\right)^{1/m}. \tag{10.9}$$

And thanks to Rosenthal's inequality (Lemma 10.2), for a certain constant $C(m)$ defined in the statement of the inequality:

$$\mathbb{E}|\tilde{\varepsilon}_i|^m \leq C(m)\left(\frac{F\bar{\lambda}^2}{T_0 c_\xi}\right)^m \max\left(\sum_{t=1}^{T_0}\mathbb{E}|\varepsilon_{j,t}|^m, \left(\sum_{t=1}^{T_0}\mathbb{E}|\varepsilon_{j,t}|^2\right)^{m/2}\right).$$

According to the equation above and (10.9), and using Assumption 10.1:

$$\mathbb{E}|R_{1,t}| \leq C(m)^{1/m}\left(\frac{F\bar{\lambda}^2}{c_\xi}\right)n_0^{1/m}\max\left(\frac{(\mathbb{E}|\varepsilon_{i,t}|^m)^{1/m}}{T_0^{1-1/m}}, \frac{\sigma}{\sqrt{T_0}}\right).$$

According to the decomposition above and Jensen's inequality:

$$|\mathbb{E}\hat{\tau}_t - \tau_t| \leq \mathbb{E}|R_{1,t}| \leq C(m)^{1/m}\left(\frac{F\bar{\lambda}^2}{c_\xi}\right)n_0^{1/m}\max\left(\frac{(\mathbb{E}|\varepsilon_{i,t}|^m)^{1/m}}{T_0^{1-1/m}}, \frac{\sigma}{\sqrt{T_0}}\right).$$

□

Proof of Lemma 10.1 Let $\{\widehat{\theta}^{(i)}\}_{i=1}^{|\Pi|}$ be a non-decreasing rearrangement of $\{\widehat{\theta}(\boldsymbol{D}_\pi): \pi \in \Pi\}$. We have:

$$\mathbf{1}\{p(C) \leq \alpha\} = \mathbf{1}\left\{\widehat{\theta}(\boldsymbol{D}^{obs}) > \widehat{\theta}^{(k)}\right\},$$

for $k = \lceil (1-\alpha) \times |\Pi| \rceil$. Since Π forms a group, the randomization-invariant quantiles are the same:

$$\widehat{\theta}(\boldsymbol{D}_\pi)^{(k)} = \widehat{\theta}^{(k)}, \text{ for all } \pi \in \Pi,$$

thus:

$$\sum_{\pi \in \Pi} \mathbf{1}\left\{\widehat{\theta}(\boldsymbol{D}_\pi) > \widehat{\theta}(\boldsymbol{D}_\pi)^{(k)}\right\} = \sum_{\pi \in \Pi} \mathbf{1}\left\{\widehat{\theta}(\boldsymbol{D}^{obs}) > \widehat{\theta}^{(k)}\right\} \leq \alpha|\Pi|.$$

By exchangeability and for any $\pi \in \Pi$, $\mathbf{1}\left\{\widehat{\theta}(\boldsymbol{D}^{obs}) > \widehat{\theta}^{(k)}\right\}$ is distributed as $\mathbf{1}\left\{\widehat{\theta}(\boldsymbol{D}_\pi) > \widehat{\theta}(\boldsymbol{D}_\pi)^{(k)}\right\}$. Thus, we have:

$$\begin{aligned}\alpha &\geq \frac{1}{|\Pi|} \sum_{\pi \in \Pi} \mathbf{1}\left\{\widehat{\theta}(\boldsymbol{D}_\pi) > \widehat{\theta}(\boldsymbol{D}_\pi)^{(k)}\right\} \\ &= \mathbb{E}\left[\mathbf{1}\left\{\widehat{\theta}(\boldsymbol{D}^{obs}) > \widehat{\theta}^{(k)}\right\}\right] = \mathbb{E}[\mathbf{1}\{p(C) \leq \alpha\}].\end{aligned}$$

□

10.8.2 Additional Results

Lemma 10.2 (Rosenthal's inequality). *Let $\xi_1, \ldots, \xi_n$ be n independent random variables with zero mean, $\mathbb{E}|\xi_i|^m < \infty$ for some even integer $m > 2$, and let $S_n = \sum_{i=1}^n \xi_i$. Then:*

$$\mathbb{E}|S_n|^m \leq C(m) \max\left(\sum_{i=1}^n \mathbb{E}|\xi_i|^m, \left[\sum_{i=1}^n \mathbb{E}|\xi_i|^2\right]^{m/2}\right),$$

where $C(m) := \mathbb{E}(X-1)^m$ with $X \sim \mathcal{P}(1)$.

Proof of Lemma 10.2 see Ibragimov and Sharakhmetov (2002). □

Chapter 11
Forecasting in high-dimension

Real-time adjustment of economic and monetary policies requires the most reliable information possible on current and future economic conditions. However, most economic series are published with a lag of a few weeks (e.g., inflation, corporate orders), or even a few months (e.g., GDP, household consumption). Assessing real-time economic conditions, known as *nowcasting* (see, e.g., Giannone et al., 2008), and more generally forecasting at different horizons, are therefore important tasks where it is interesting not to restrict a priori the different sources of information that one may want to use. Moreover, these different real-time information, whether conventional (e.g., employment, unemployment, income, trade, consumption) or not (e.g., newspaper articles, maritime traffic, bank transactions, Google trends, etc.), are often published at different frequencies: daily (information flow, stock prices), weekly (unemployment benefit updates), monthly (inflation), depending on the variable to be predicted. The latter is often published at a lower frequency, quarterly like GDP or unemployment according to the International Labor Office (ILO). It should also be noted that in general, the higher the quality of the data, the less frequent or fast it is to calculate.

The most representative example of nowcasting is the prediction of the US GDP by the New York Central Bank, which, until September 2021, published its forecasts every Friday at 11:15 AM (more details in Bok et al., 2018). The central bank's forecasts are available on their website newyorkfed.org/research/policy/nowcast. These forecasts were suspended due to the "uncertainty surrounding the pandemic and the resulting data volatility." These forecasts are based on a factor model using 37 traditional economic variables. It is legitimate to wonder whether the high-dimensional methods developed in the second part of this book could extract useful information for short-term forecasting, using other sources of information such as textual data (Bybee et al., 2020, considers 180 thematic sections of the Wall Street Journal), satellite data (see, e.g., Moriwaki, 2019, for unemployment forecasting), or search engine data (see, e.g., Ferrara and Simoni, 2022). The fact that we often have only a limited time horizon with macroeconomic variables to predict naturally plunges us into the context of high dimension.

However, using the selection methods from the second part requires adapting them to the structure of time series data. The first fundamental characteristic is that we can no longer assume independence of observations. Economic and financial time series are also known to have fat-tailed distributions, whereas the methods

Machine Learning for Econometrics. Christophe Gaillac and Jérémy L'Hour, Oxford University Press.
 DOI: 10.1093/9780198918868.003.0011

from the second part assumed normality or exponential tails. We must also take into account the fact that the series are not sampled at the same frequency (we say they are not *aligned*). Finally, these different explanatory variables often have a "structure," i.e., they are related to different themes: macroeconomics, different sectors of activity, financial variables, news, etc., and we would like to be able to incorporate knowledge of this structure into the selection process.

In this chapter, we will first extend the methods from the second part in Section 11.1 to take into account these specificities. We will then present in Section 11.2 the limits of these methods, along two main directions. The first one is the criticism of the sparsity assumption and the second one is the criticism of linearity. Lastly, an important motivation for these methods is to allow for inference and thus to test statistically whether certain variables do contain useful information for prediction, which is described in Section 11.3. These sections are all associated with empirical illustrations.

11.1 Regression in high-dimension for forecasting

11.1.1 Time series in high-dimension

Several works propose extensions of high-dimensional tools from the second part of this book to time series, within a frequentist framework (see, e.g., Alquier and Doukhan, 2011; Basu and Michailidis, 2015; Kock and Callot, 2015; Uematsu and Tanaka, 2019; Babii et al., 2019; Ferrara and Simoni, 2022; Chernozhukov et al., 2021; Babii et al., 2022) and a Bayesian framework (see, e.g., De Mol et al., 2008; Mogliani and Simoni, 2021). In this section, we will mainly follow the approach developed in Chernozhukov et al. (2021), close to the formalization of the second part, and in Babii et al. (2019, 2022), which consider series sampled at different frequencies (MIxed frequency DAta Sampling, MIDAS for short) and other types of dependencies.

11.1.2 Model and estimator

Consider a forecasting horizon $h = 0, 1, 2, \dots,$ where $h = 0$ corresponds to nowcasting. Consider also the following forecasting model:

$$Y_{t+h} = X_t'\beta_0 + \varepsilon_t, \quad \mathbb{E}(\varepsilon_t X_t) = 0, \; t = 1, \dots, T, \tag{11.1}$$

where $X_t \in \mathbb{R}^p$, with p potentially larger than n. The vector X_t can contain past values of Y_t and transformations of the initial explanatory variables (see remark below). In the rest of this chapter, we consider real-time forecasting by setting $h = 0$ to simplify.

The methods developed in Section 4 can also be generalized to a system of regressions of this type, see Chernozhukov et al. (2021); Kock et al. (2024). To simplify, we assume here exact sparsity, meaning that the number of non-zero coefficients of β_0 is bounded by s:

$$\|\beta_0\|_0 \leq s \ll n. \tag{11.2}$$

As in the second part, we use a penalized ℓ^1-norm estimator for β^0:

$$\widehat{\beta} = \underset{\beta \in \mathbb{R}^p}{\operatorname{argmin}} \quad \frac{1}{T}\sum_{t=1}^{T}(Y_t - X_t'\beta)^2 + \frac{\lambda}{T}\sum_{k=1}^{p}|\beta_k|\widehat{\gamma}_k, \tag{11.3}$$

where λ is a fixed parameter below and $\widehat{\gamma}_k$ are estimators of the *ideal* penalties γ_k^0 that we now describe. Define the variable:

$$S_k = \frac{1}{\sqrt{T}}\sum_{t=1}^{T}\varepsilon_t X_{k,\,t},$$

where $\varepsilon_t = Y_t - X_t'\beta_0$ is not directly observed. As a result, the ideal parameter and penalties, respectively λ^0 and γ_k^0, are defined by: $\lambda^0 = Q(1-\alpha)$, where Q denotes the quantile of $2c\sqrt{T}\max_{1\leq k\leq p}|S_k/\gamma_k^0|$ and γ_k^0 is the long-run variance of S_k, that is:

$$\gamma_k^0 = \sqrt{\sum_{l=-\infty}^{\infty}\mathbb{E}(X_{k,\,t}\varepsilon_t X_{k,\,t-l}\varepsilon_{t-l})}.$$

These estimators $\widehat{\gamma}_k$ are selected in a similar way to Chapter 7, either by cross-validation (see Section 5.3 or, more adapted to this context, in Babii et al., 2019, 2022). The additional difficulty compared to Chapter 7 is that here we need to take into account the time dependence in the estimation of these penalties. Chernozhukov et al. (2021) propose a two-step procedure using block bootstrap:

1. Obtain a very preliminary estimator $\check{\beta}$ of β_0 using (11.3), where the parameter is based on the Gaussian approximation $\lambda = 2c'\sqrt{T}\Phi^{-1}(1-\alpha'/(2p))$, with $c' = 0.5$ and $\alpha' = 0.1$, and the penalties are, for example, taken to be uniform $\check{\gamma}_k = 1$. Then, preliminary estimators of the errors are formed $\check{\varepsilon}_t = Y_t - X_t'\check{\beta}$.
2. Obtain a second preliminary estimator $\widetilde{\beta}$ of β^0 using (11.3), where the parameter λ is still based on the Gaussian approximation and, at this step, the penalties are adapted using the Newey–West estimator:

$$\widehat{\gamma}_k = \sum_{l=-h_T}^{h_T} k\left(\frac{l}{h_T}\right)\mathrm{Cov}(X_{k,t}\check{\varepsilon}_t, X_{k,t-l}\check{\varepsilon}_{t-l}),$$

where $k(z) = (1 - |z|)1\{|z| \leq 1\}$ and $h_T \to \infty$ is a cut-off parameter (for example $h_T = 1.3T^{1/2}$, see Lazarus et al., 2018).

3. Update the error estimators $\widetilde{\varepsilon}_k = Y_t - X'_t\widetilde{\beta}$ and recalculate $\widetilde{\gamma}_k$ using $\widetilde{\varepsilon}_k$. Divide $\{\widetilde{\varepsilon}_k\}$ into l_T blocks of b_T observations, then choose:

$$\lambda = 2c\sqrt{T}q^{[B]}_{1-\alpha}, \tag{11.4}$$

where $q^{[B]}_{1-\alpha}$ is the $1 - \alpha$ quantile of $\max_{1\leq k\leq p} |Z^{[B]}_k / \widetilde{\gamma}_k|$,

$$Z^{[B]}_k = \frac{1}{\sqrt{T}} \sum_{i=1}^{l_T} e_i \sum_{l=(i-1)b_T+1}^{ib_T} \widetilde{\varepsilon}_l X_{k,l},$$

and $e_i \sim \mathcal{N}(0, 1)$ i.i.d.

This bootstrap-based approach (11.4) can also be used in the i.i.d setting, e.g., see Belloni et al. (2018); Lederer and Vogt (2021) for related theoretical results and Chetverikov (2024) for a survey. The advantage of this selection method is that, unlike the one based on Equation (7.2), it is not conservative under some regularity conditions.

11.1.3 Mixed data sampling regression models (MIDAS)

The more realistic cases encountered in practice, including time series sampled at different frequencies and satisfying an autoregressive model (ARDL-MIDAS type, see, e.g., Ghysels et al., 2005, 2007), can be expressed in the form of the model (11.1). Consider the following equation:

$$Y_t = \mu + \sum_{j=1}^{J} \rho_j Y_{t-j} + \sum_{k=1}^{p} \frac{1}{m_k} \sum_{j=1}^{m_k} \beta_{k,j} X_{t-(j-1)/m_k,k} + \varepsilon_t, \tag{11.5}$$

where for all $k \in \{1, \ldots, p\}$, the variables $X_{t,k}$ are sampled at frequencies m_k higher than that of the variable to be predicted Y_t (e.g., quarterly for GDP), leading to the series

$$(X_{t-(j-1)/m_k,k})_{j=1,\ldots,m_k,\ t=1,\ldots,T}.$$

Figure 11.1 illustrates a possible case where one may wonder if, in order to predict Y_t based on the past of X_t, which is sampled at a higher frequency, one can avoid using all the available values of X_t between $t - 1$ and t, or if a combination of these can be used. The MIDAS approach thus consists of reducing the dimension of the problem by moving from the estimation of β_k of dimension m_k to the estimation of

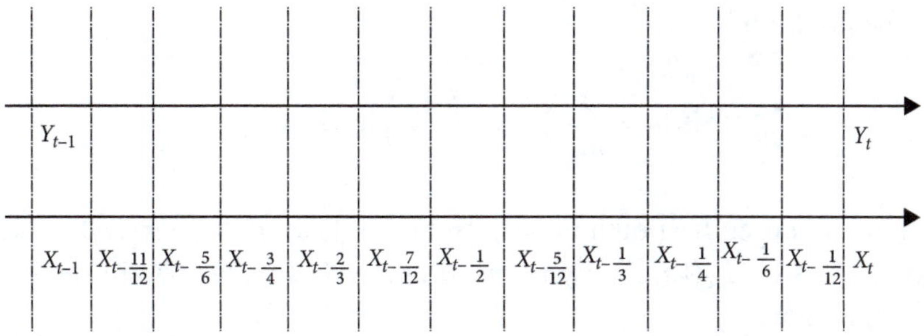

Figure 11.1 Illustration of two time series sampled at different frequencies: Y_t annually and X_t monthly

$\widetilde{\beta}_k$ of dimension $L < m_k$. To do this, a weighting function $\omega : [0,1] \times \mathbb{R}^L \to \mathbb{R}$ is considered to manage the different samplings:

$$\frac{1}{m_k}\sum_{j=1}^{m_k} \beta_{k,j} X_{t-(j-1)/m_k,k} = \frac{1}{m_k}\sum_{j=1}^{m_k} \omega\left(\frac{j-1}{m_k}, \widetilde{\beta}_k\right) X_{t-(j-1)/m_k,k}.$$

The standard approach (Ghysels et al. 2007) consists of using the specification

$$\omega\left(\frac{j-1}{m_k}, \widetilde{\beta}_k\right) = \frac{e^{\widetilde{\beta}_1 j + \widetilde{\beta}_2 j^2 + \dots + \widetilde{\beta}_l j^L}}{\sum_{j=1}^{m_k} e^{\widetilde{\beta}_1 j + \widetilde{\beta}_2 j^2 + \dots + \widetilde{\beta}_l j^L}},$$

called *exponential Almon lags*, where Almon polynomials are referring to $\{1, k, k^2, \dots\}$ in time series.

A more recent approach, with many advantages in terms of computation time, consists of using an approximation of this function $t \in [0,1] \mapsto \omega(t, \widetilde{\beta}_k)$ by a decomposition on a collection of functions called a *dictionary* $\{w_l(\cdot) : l = 1, \dots, L\}$. Evaluated at $(j-1)/m_k, j = 1 \dots, m_k$, we have

$$\omega\left(\frac{j-1}{m_k}, \widetilde{\beta}_k\right) \simeq \sum_{l=1}^{L} w_l\left(\frac{j-1}{m_k}\right) \widetilde{\beta}_{k,l},$$

which leads to the representation:

$$\begin{aligned}
\frac{1}{m_k}\sum_{j=1}^{m_k} \beta_{k,j} X_{t-(j-1)/m_k,k} &\simeq \frac{1}{m_k}\sum_{j=1}^{m_k}\sum_{l=1}^{L} w_l\left(\frac{j-1}{m_k}\right) \widetilde{\beta}_{k,l} X_{t-(j-1)/m_k,k} \\
&= \sum_{l=1}^{L} \widetilde{\beta}_{k,l}\left(\frac{1}{m_k}\sum_{j=1}^{m_k} w_l\left(\frac{j-1}{m_k}\right) X_{t-(j-1)/m_k,k}\right) \\
&= \widetilde{\beta}'_{k,.} Z_{t,k,.},
\end{aligned}$$

using the notation

$$Z_{t,k,l} = \frac{1}{m_k} \sum_{j=1}^{m_k} w_l \left(\frac{j-1}{m_k} \right) X_{t-(j-1)/m_k,k}.$$

For example, Legendre polynomials can be used as a dictionary, which form an orthogonal basis for $L_2([0,1])$. By reinjecting into (11.5), we obtain the following linear formulation:

$$Y_t = (\mu, Y_{t-1}, \ldots, Y_{t-J}, Z'_{t,1,\cdot}, \ldots, Z'_{t,p,\cdot})(1, \rho_1, \ldots, \rho_J, \widetilde{\beta}'_{1,\cdot}, \ldots, \widetilde{\beta}'_{p,\cdot})' + \varepsilon_t. \tag{11.6}$$

By putting this in matrix form, we then reduce it to a model similar to (11.1) and thus to an estimator of the form (11.3).

In some practical cases, the model is associated with a certain structure of predictive variables, which is interesting to include in the penalized estimation procedure. One might want to both select the groups of variables that are most relevant for prediction, and also, within these groups, select the important ones. The coefficients ρ and $\beta_{k,\cdot}$ in the linear formulation (11.6) of the MIDAS model (11.5) being of different natures, there naturally exists a group structure. Therefore, Babii et al. (2019, 2022) estimate the parameters of the model formulation (11.6) using the sparse-group Lasso, introduced by Lounici et al. (2011), which consists of using, instead of the ℓ_1 norm in (11.3), a mixed norm penalization:

$$\Omega_\gamma(\beta) = \gamma \|\beta\|_1 + (1-\gamma)\|\beta\|_{2,1}, \tag{11.7}$$

where $\gamma \in [0,1]$ is a weight indexing the compromise between the ℓ_1 norm and the group norm $\|\beta\|_{2,1} = \sum_{g \in \mathcal{G}} \|\beta_g\|_2$ where the group structure $\mathcal{G}$ is a partition of $\{1, \ldots, p\}$ for $\beta \in \mathbb{R}^p$. For example, certain macroeconomic, financial, or textual variables, as in the application in Section 11.2.4, may be highly correlated, and one would like to introduce this information in the penalization.

11.1.4 Asymptotic properties

In order to establish the asymptotic properties of the estimator (11.3), we need to specify the dependence structure of the observations in the model (11.1). Here, we present the results with the dependence structure introduced in Wu (2005); Wu and Wu (2016); Zhang and Wu (2017), which consider that the variables and errors have a functional representation depending on independent innovations. We refer to Section 11.1.5 describing how to use the notion of *mixing* in our context to describe dependence see Doukhan (2012).

Assumption 11.1 (Dependence structure) *For all $k = 1, \dots, p$, we assume that $X_{k,t}$ and ε_t are stationary processes with representations:*

$$X_{k,t} = g_k(\dots, \xi_{-1}, \xi_0, \xi_1, \dots, \xi_{t-1}, \xi_t)$$
$$\varepsilon_t = h(\dots, \eta_{-1}, \eta_0, \eta_1, \dots, \eta_{t-1}, \eta_t),$$

where ξ_t, η_t are i.i.d. innovations and g_k, h are functions measurable with respect to the filtration generated by $(\dots, \eta_{-1}, \xi_{-1}, \eta_0, \xi_0, \eta_0, \dots, \xi_{t-1}, \eta_{t-1}, \xi_t, \eta_t)$.

The notion of dependence in Assumption 11.1 is quite intuitive and easy to use. To obtain asymptotic results, we also need to introduce characteristics quantifying the importance of the dependence of the processes $(X_{k,.})$, $(\varepsilon_.)$, and $(X_{k,.}\varepsilon_.)$. Define the following quantities, considering an i.i.d. copy ξ_0^* of ξ_0 and denoting by $X^*_{k,t} = g_k(\dots, \xi_0^*, \dots, \xi_{t-1}, \xi_t)$ the process where ξ_0^* replaces ξ_0:

1. $\theta_{q,k,t} := \mathbb{E}(|X_{k,t} - X^*_{k,t}|^q)^{1/q}$ for $q > 0$, is a measure of dependence of ξ_0 on $X_{k,t}$, with cumulative effect measured by $\Theta_{m,q,k} = \sum_{t=m}^{\infty} \theta_{q,k,t}$;
2. the adjusted dependence measure $\|X_{k,\cdot}\|_{q,\zeta} = \sup_{m\geq 0}(m+1)^{\zeta}\Theta_{m,q,k}$, with $\zeta > 0$.

We introduce the same quantities for $(\varepsilon_.)$ and $(X_{k,.}\varepsilon_.)$.

Assumption 11.2 (Dependence structure, continued) *We have the moment conditions:*

$$\|\varepsilon\|_{q,\zeta} < \infty \text{ and, for all } k = 1, \dots, p, \ \|X_{k,\cdot}\|_{q,\zeta} < \infty, \ q \geq 8.$$

The largest value of ζ such that Assumption 11.2 is satisfied characterizes the dependence of the process. Large classes of usual processes, for example AR(1) with an absolute value of the coefficient less than 1 or certain ARCH(1) processes, satisfy these conditions (see Appendix C.2 in Chernozhukov et al., 2021). Finally, we make the following assumption, which is a variant of the restricted eigenvalue Assumption 4.4.

Assumption 11.3 (Restricted eigenvalue, variant) *Let $\bar{c} \geq 1$, with high probability we have:*

$$\kappa(\bar{c}) = \min_{\beta \in C[S,\bar{c}]} \frac{\sqrt{s}\|X'\beta\|_2}{\|\beta\|_1} > 0,$$

where $C[S, \bar{c}]$ is defined in (4.4), $S = \{k : \beta_k^0 \neq 0\}$ is the set of non-zero coefficients, $s = |S|$ is the number of non-zero coefficients.

Under Assumptions 11.1, 11.3, and the sparsity assumption 11.2, it follows from a direct modification of the proof of Lemma 7.1 in the second part (see also Theorem

1 in Belloni and Chernozhukov (2013)), that if

$$\frac{\lambda}{T} \geq 2c \max_{1\leq k\leq p} \left| \frac{S_k/\sqrt{T}}{\gamma_k^0} \right|, \tag{11.8}$$

with $c > 1, \bar{c} = (c+1)/(c-1)$, then

$$\left\| \hat{\beta} - \beta_0 \right\|_1 \leq \left(\frac{(1+2\bar{c})(1+1/c)s}{\kappa(2\bar{c})\kappa(\bar{c})} \max_{1\leq k\leq p} \gamma_k^0 \right) \frac{\lambda}{T}. \tag{11.9}$$

Note that the concentration inequality (7.6) used in the case of i.i.d. observations to conclude Theorem 7.1, by ensuring that event (11.8) occurs with high probability, must be adapted to the non-i.i.d. case of this chapter. We present this inequality here, and then we discuss the different regimes of convergence rates it induces. These regimes depend on the tails of the distribution and the magnitude of the dependence.

Theorem 11.1 ((Fuk–Nagaev Inequality, Theorem 2 in Wu and Wu, 2016 or Theorem 5 in Chernozhukov et al., 2021)) *Under Assumptions 11.1 and 11.2:*

$$P\left(2c\sqrt{T} \max_{1\leq k\leq p} \left| \frac{S_k}{\gamma_k^0} \right| \geq r \right)$$
$$\leq \sum_{k=1}^{p} \left(\frac{C_0 \|X_{k,\cdot}\varepsilon_\cdot\|_{q,\zeta}^q}{(\gamma_k^0)^q} \frac{\omega_T T}{r^q} + C_1 \exp\left(\frac{-C_2 r^2}{T(\|X_{k,\cdot}\varepsilon_\cdot\|_{2,\zeta}^2/(\gamma_k^0)^2)} \right) \right),$$

where $\omega_T = 1$ if $\zeta > 1/2 - 1/q$ (weak dependence) and $\omega_T = T^{q/2-1-\zeta q}$ otherwise (strong dependence).

This inequality, which extends the Fuk–Nagaev inequality, along with (11.9) and λ as the $1-\alpha$ quantile of the distribution of $2c\sqrt{n}\max_{1\leq k\leq p}|S_k/\gamma_k^0|$, allows to prove the convergence rate:

$$\left\| \hat{\beta} - \beta^0 \right\|_1 \leq C_3 \max_{1\leq k\leq p} \max \left(\underbrace{\sqrt{\frac{s^2 \log(p/\alpha)}{T}}}_{\text{exponential term}} \|X_{k,\cdot}\varepsilon_\cdot\|_{2,\zeta}, \underbrace{\left(\frac{p\omega_T}{\alpha T^{q-1}} \right)^{1/q}}_{\text{polynomial term}} \|X_{k,\cdot}\varepsilon_\cdot\|_{q,\zeta} \right)$$

where C_3 is a constant independent of T. In this rate, there is a term allowing the dimension p to grow exponentially with the number of observations T, and a polynomial term. Thus, when the latter dominates the former, we cannot allow the number of variables p to grow exponentially with T as in the results of the second part. If the dependence terms $\|X_{k,\cdot}\varepsilon_\cdot\|_{2,\zeta}$ and $\|X_{k,\cdot}\varepsilon_\cdot\|_{q,\zeta}$ are bounded (see Chernozhukov et al., 2021, for examples), we can allow p to grow at a rate of T^κ, where κ is typically decreasing in the persistence of the process and the thickness of the tails of the distribution.

11.1.5 Another dependence assumption: mixing

There are alternatives to the dependence Assumption 11.1. The concept of *mixing* relaxes the independence assumption by bounding the decay of correlations with the past and future of the process as a function of the time difference, see e.g., Doukhan (2012). Let $X = (X_t)_{t\in\mathbb{Z}}$ be a process, $P = (X_{t_1}, \ldots, X_{t_l})$, and $F = (X_{t_{l+1}}, \ldots, X_{t_m})$ represent a part of its past and future, respectively. The coefficient of *α-mixing* is defined as a function of the time difference $t_{l+1} - t_l \geq r$:

$$\alpha(r) = \sup_{P,F \text{ s.t. } t_{l+1}-t_l \geq r} \frac{1}{2} \sup_{\|f\|_\infty \leq 1,\ \|g\|_\infty \leq 1} |\mathrm{Cov}(f(P), g(F)|,$$

where $\|f\|_\infty$ is the sup norm of a function f. This captures the maximum covariance of functions from different parts of the past and future that are at least r units apart. The process is said to be strongly mixing if $\alpha(r) \to_{r\to\infty} 0$. This traditional notion of dependence of α-mixing (and also that of β-mixing) is not weak enough to encompass certain common cases. Andrews (1984) showed, in particular, that AR(1) processes are not α-mixing in general. An example of such a process is $X_t = (X_{t-1} + \xi_t)/2$, where ξ_t are i.i.d. random variables following a Bernoulli distribution with parameter 1/2.

The τ-mixing processes are introduced in Dedecker and Prieur (2005) to have a notion of dependence weaker than that of the α- and β-mixing processes, while still allowing for asymptotic results. For a stationary process $\xi_t \in \mathbb{R}$ with a past $\mathcal{P}_t$, we define:

$$\tau(r) = \sup_{j\geq 1} \frac{1}{j} \sup_{t+r\leq t_1 < \cdots < t_j} \tau(\mathcal{P}_t, (\xi_{t_1}, \ldots, \xi_{t_j})),$$

where $\tau(\mathcal{P}_t, \zeta) = \mathbb{E}\left|\sup_{f\in \mathrm{Lip}_1} |\mathbb{E}(f(\zeta)|\mathcal{P}_t) - \mathbb{E}(f(\zeta))|\right|$ and Lip_1 is the set of 1-Lipschitz functions on $\mathbb{R}$. The process is said to be τ-mixing if $\tau(r) \to_{r\to\infty} 0$. Babii et al. (2019) use this notion and provide a Fuk-Nagaev type inequality under bounded moments assumptions and a decay rate of $\tau(r)$. This inequality also includes the same polynomial and exponential regimes as in Theorem 11.1.

11.2 Limitations and other methods

11.2.1 Critical approach of the sparsity hypothesis

Methods for inference in high-dimensional settings can be broadly divided into two types. The first type is based on the sparsity hypothesis, which assumes a priori that only a small number of variables among all regressors are useful for prediction. The second type, known as *dense* methods, such as factor models, recognize that all variables potentially have explanatory power, but rely on dimension reduction techniques to extract maximum information. This raises critical questions about the empirical relevance of imposing the sparsity hypothesis when using the first type of methods: it may seem natural in some cases, but it is not the general framework.

Several recent papers have raised some concerns with the sparsity assumptions and the relative *fragility* in some contexts of sparsity-based methods see, e.g., Giannone et al. (2021); Wüthrich and Zhu (2023); Kolesár et al. (2023). Among other things, sparsity-based estimators lack invariance to some normalizations, such as the choice of baseline category with categorical controls, and in relatively low-dimensional contexts where p is large but $p < n$, this assumption is rejected in applications where it seems justified see Kolesár et al. (2023). Moreover, since it is necessary for estimation, if the model is misspecified in the sense that this assumption does not hold, it is generally difficult to refute it without additional restrictions within the framework we have described so far, leading to the *illusion of sparsity* as described in Giannone et al. (2021).

More specifically, Giannone et al. (2021) propose to introduce a model that can indicate whether the economic problem can be considered *sparse* rather than *dense*, i.e., probably characterized by a small number of explanatory variables. To this end, they consider a linear model to predict the variable y_t:

$$y_t = v_t'\phi + x_t'\beta + \varepsilon_t,$$

where the error term is assumed to be i.i.d. distributed according to a normal distribution $\mathcal{N}(0, \sigma^2)$, and v_t and x_t are regressors of respective dimensions k and l with $k \gg l$, and normalized variance of 1. The two types of regressors have a different status: the variables v_t are those that the researcher always wants to include, while some of the components of x_t may have zero coefficients. The idea is then to impose a Bayesian a priori (see, e.g., Robert et al., 2007) on the coefficients of x_t, allowing them to be degenerate to a Dirac at 0 with a certain probability (referred to as a *spike-and-slab* a priori). This allows for sparsity but does not impose it in the initial prior. More specifically, for every $i = 1, \dots, k$:

$$p(\sigma^2) \sim 1/\sigma^2, \quad \phi \sim \text{Non-informative Prior},$$

$$\beta_i | \sigma^2, \gamma^2, q \sim \begin{cases} \mathcal{N}(0, \sigma^2\gamma^2) & \text{with probability } q \\ \text{Dirac at } 0 & \text{with probability } 1 - q. \end{cases}$$

The important point to note about this a priori is that the coefficients β are equal to zero with a probability of $1 - q$ and have a normal distribution otherwise. The hyperparameter γ^2 controls the variance of this Gaussian distribution and allows for parameter shrinkage without forcing them to be zero. They also consider an a priori on the parameters $q \sim \text{Beta}(1, 1)$ and γ^2, defined through a non-informative prior on the

$$R^2(\gamma^2, q) = \frac{qk\gamma^2 v_x}{qk\gamma^2 v_x + 1} \sim \text{Beta}(1, 1),$$

where $v_x = 1$ is the variance of the regressors, and R^2 is the proportion of the variance of y_t explained by $x'_t\beta$ compared to the error. The limitation of the above approach is that this parametric model may have very poor performance if it is misspecified, for example, if the non-zero coefficients β are not normally distributed. By taking this limitation into account, we can interpret the results of this model as an example of an a priori distribution on coefficients that leads to a non-sparse a posteriori.

With the help of simulations, whether consistent or not with the Gaussian framework presented above, Giannone et al. (2021) show that in cases where the data generation process is not parsimonious, the Lasso overestimates the degree of sparsity by forcing too many coefficients to be zero. On the contrary, their model is robust to this deviation and allows for a better approximation of the true level of sparsity. The authors then study six different economic datasets. The assumption of sparsity seem rarely justified there: the distribution of q is not, in all cases except one, concentrated at 0. Moreover, the identity of the non-zero coefficients is quite uncertain. These results illustrate the importance, in a prediction context, of questioning and justifying the use of a model that imposes that only a small number of variables have explanatory power.

11.2.2 A mixed approach: FARM

Fan et al. (2023) introduce a regression model that combines both sparse and dense components using latent factors (see also respectively Fan et al., 2023; Beyhum and Striaukas, 2023, for a similar model in the context of panel data and with mixed-frequency data), thus addressing the criticism from the previous section. We assume that we observe an i.i.d. sample $(x_t, Y_t)_{t=1}^n$ from (x, Y) satisfying a *factor augmented sparse linear regression model* (FARM) composed of:

1. A factor model for the regressors x_t:

$$x_t = Bf_t + v_t, \tag{11.10}$$

   where B is a weighting matrix for the factors of size $p \times r$, f_t is a factor vector of size $r \times 1$ formed from $x_t \in \mathbb{R}^p$, and p is potentially high dimensional.
2. A main equation involving the residuals v_t from the factor model, which have high dimension p, and the latent factors f_t:

$$Y_t = f'_t\gamma^* + v'_t\beta^* + \varepsilon_t, \tag{11.11}$$

   with $\gamma^* \in \mathbb{R}^r$ and $\beta^* \in \mathbb{R}^p$.

The model (11.10)–(11.11) encompasses the *factor augmented regression* presented in (2.21) when $\beta^* = 0$. By rewriting (11.11) as $Y_t = f_t'\varphi^* + x_t'\beta^* + \varepsilon_t$ with $\varphi^* = \gamma^* - B'\beta^* \in \mathbb{R}^r$, we obtain

$$Y_t = f_t'\varphi^* + x_t'\beta^* + \varepsilon_t. \tag{11.12}$$

This shows that it is also a more general case of regression where sparsity is imposed ($\varphi^* = 0$). The advantage of this approach is that it addresses one of the criticisms raised in the previous section, as it includes a dense component, allowing for a test of whether both components are useful for prediction. Fan et al. (2023) develop a test for the adequacy of the sparse model in comparison to factor-augmented sparse alternatives via

$$H_0 : \beta^* = 0 \quad \text{vs.} \quad H_1 : \beta^* \neq 0,$$

based on a *desparsification* of the Lasso presented in Section 7.3. They also develop a test of the adequacy factor regression model in comparison to factor-augmented sparse regression alternatives via: Beyhum and Striaukas (2024) also propose a bootstrap test of this hypothesis which does not require tuning parameters and is implemented in the R package FAS. On some empirical examples using the Federal Reserve Bank of New York (FRED) data described in Section 11.2.4, they reject the adequacy of the classical factor regression model. This suggest that the sparse part captures, on top of the dense one, some useful information structure allowing to improve the prediction of Y_t.

$$H_0 : \varphi^* = 0 \quad \text{vs.} \quad H_1 : \varphi^* \neq 0 \text{ is sparse.}$$

We rewrite the model (11.10)–(11.11) in matrix form:

$$\boldsymbol{X} = \boldsymbol{F}\boldsymbol{B}' + \boldsymbol{V} \tag{11.13}$$

$$Y = \boldsymbol{F}\gamma^* + \boldsymbol{V}\beta^* + \mathcal{E}, \tag{11.14}$$

where $\boldsymbol{X} = (x_1, \ldots, x_n)'$, $\boldsymbol{F} = (f_1, \ldots, f_n)'$, $\boldsymbol{V} = (v_1, \ldots, v_n)'$, $Y = (Y_1, \ldots, Y_n)'$, and $\mathcal{E} = (\varepsilon_1, \ldots, \varepsilon_n)'$. Fan et al. (2023) suggest the following procedure:

1. By imposing identification constraints presented in Section 2.6, we estimate the factors by

$$(\hat{\boldsymbol{F}}, \hat{\boldsymbol{B}}) = \underset{\boldsymbol{F}\in\mathbb{R}^{n\times r},\, \boldsymbol{B}\in\mathbb{R}^{d\times r}}{\operatorname{argmin}} \left\| \boldsymbol{X} - \boldsymbol{F}\boldsymbol{B}' \right\|_{\mathbb{F}}^2,$$

subject to the constraint that $\boldsymbol{F}'\boldsymbol{F}/n = \boldsymbol{I}_r$ and $\boldsymbol{B}'\boldsymbol{B}$ is diagonal.

2. The regularized Lasso estimator of β^*, γ^* is then obtained by

$$(\hat{\beta}, \hat{\gamma}) = \operatorname{argmin}\left\{ \frac{1}{2n} \left\| Y - \hat{\boldsymbol{V}}\beta - \hat{\boldsymbol{F}}\gamma \right\|_2^2 + \lambda \|\beta\|_1 \right\},$$

where only the components of β are penalized. Thus, by least squares,

$$\hat{\gamma} = (\hat{\boldsymbol{F}}'\hat{\boldsymbol{F}})^{-1}\hat{\boldsymbol{F}}'Y = \frac{1}{n}\hat{\boldsymbol{F}}'Y,$$

and $\hat{\beta}$ is obtained by using a Lasso regression of $\tilde{Y} = (\boldsymbol{I} - \hat{\boldsymbol{P}})Y$ on $\hat{\boldsymbol{V}}$, where $\hat{\boldsymbol{P}} = \hat{\boldsymbol{F}}\hat{\boldsymbol{F}}'/n$ is the projector onto the subspace spanned by the columns of $\hat{\boldsymbol{F}}$.

Under classical assumptions allowing for asymptotic analysis of factor models, see Section 2.6, and of the Lasso, Fan et al. (2023) show the consistency of $\hat{\gamma}$ and $\hat{\beta}$.

11.2.3 Nonlinearity

Remark 11.1 Use of nonlinear ML methods

Another limitation of the models discussed in this chapter is that even though we can introduce a large number of non-linear transformations of the regressors, these models are linear in the parameters, while there are potentially many sources of nonlinearity that can enter the modeling of variables such as GDP, inflation, interest rates, or unemployment. Taking these into account using machine learning remains the main motivation for using these tools in the field of macroeconomic forecasting (e.g., Masini et al., 2021; Goulet-Coulombe et al., 2022; Medeiros, 2022).

In certain contexts such as inflation modeling (see Medeiros et al., 2021), machine learning methods like random forests can outperform classical methods. However, despite theoretical progress in the i.i.d. case (Section 8.3.9) and for dependent data (Davis and Nielsen, 2020), theoretical understanding of these tools and the conditions under which they can outperform classical methods in the latter case remains limited. Kock and Teräsvirta (2016) also highlight the difficulties associated with using neural networks to predict price indices and unemployment: predictions are highly sensitive to hyperparameters and the definition of the estimation window. They show that it is difficult to obtain clear and consistent conclusions regarding the contexts in which they yield better results than traditional methods (i.e., a linear autoregressive model with recursive forecasts).

11.2.4 Application: nowcasting of the US GDP

For our application, we use the classic dataset from the FRED, which provides a set of macroeconomic and financial series of interest (see McCracken and Ng, 2016, for more details). The objective is to predict the GDP using this data, as well as series derived from the processing of the *Wall Street Journal*. We use a simplified approach in terms of the number of variables, but we refer to Babii et al. (2022) for more details

Table 11.1 Performance measures on the test sample for different prediction methods.

	AR(1)	Gauss-Lasso	Boot-Lasso	Sg-Lasso, without text	Sg-Lasso
Mean squared error	5.115	4.110	3.999	3.626	3.558
Gain relative to AR(1)(%)		19.6	21.8	29.1	30.4

on this application. Specifically, we use three financial indicators and their lags (the Chicago Fed National Activity Index, the growth of non-farm payrolls, and the Aruoba-Diebold-Scotti Business Conditions Index), which are monthly indicators, therefore at a higher frequency than the GDP that we aim to predict. We use the previous nine months for each explanatory variable considered, and the previous four quarters for the GDP. We also consider textual data produced by Bybee et al. (2020). These are series quantifying the attention given to certain topics in the *Wall Street Journal*. They are derived from a topic analysis of the data, based on a latent Dirichlet allocation (LDA) model that will be presented in Section 12.4.3 of the section on textual processing (see also the detailed results on www.structureofnews.com). We use four monthly lags of each of the eighty-eight selected textual series, which have the advantage of being available at the time of GDP prediction (and the sliding window estimation technique for these series avoids any problem of future information bias).

In the end, the model we consider is therefore an ARDL-MIDAS type model like the one in Equation (11.5) from the note above. The training window spans from Q1 1990 to Q1 2002 (49 quarters) and we evaluate the performance on Q2 2002 to Q3 2019. We compare several models here:

1. A simple AR(1) model, which serves as our reference (labeled "AR(1)");
2. A sparse-group-Lasso MIDAS model, as described in the note above and based on the R package **midasml**, where we impose a group structure for each different economic or textual variable (thus encompassing the different lags); the parameters are selected through cross-validation (labeled "Sg-lasso");
3. A Lasso-MIDAS model like the one presented in Section 11.1.2, where we consider two choices of regularization parameters: either based on the Gaussian approximation (labeled "Gauss-lasso"), or based on block bootstrap (labeled "Boot-lasso"). A version is available in the R package **tsapp**.

Figure 1 and Table 2 present the out-of-sample estimation results, where it can be observed that high-dimensional methods perform better than the AR(1) benchmark. The sparse-group-Lasso without text data also yields better results than Lasso with block-bootstrap penalty, which is very close to the penalty chosen by Gaussian approximation (not shown in the figure for this reason). This may be because the penalty provides additional information, specifically about the data structure.

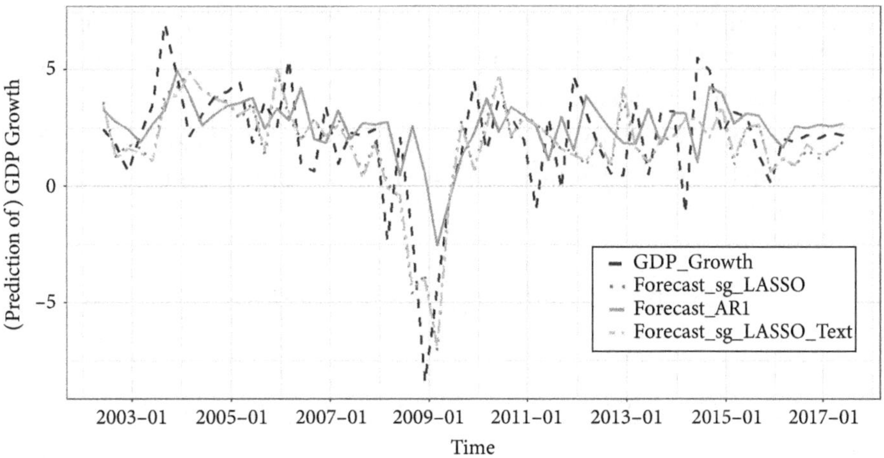

Figure 11.2 Nowcasting of the US GDP using financial, macroeconomic, and textual data.

The parameter γ of the penalty Ω_γ for the sparse-group-Lasso was chosen as fixed, but the performance can still be improved by choosing it through cross-validation, as in Babii et al. (2022). However, the gains from using text data, in addition to financial and macroeconomic data, appear to be relatively small in this case. For a more precise statistical comparison and a more thorough analysis of the gains of using text data in the nowcasting context, we refer to Babii et al. (2022).

11.3 Testing Granger causality

Forecasting time series using statistical learning is not the only task of interest when working with such data. Another common statistical task is to *test* hypotheses, as in the previous empirical application where we aim to identify significant variables. To do so, we will use an adaptation of the central limit theorem to establish simultaneous confidence regions for *groups of coefficients* estimated by Lasso. Section 11.3.1 extends the results described in Section 7.3 to the case of time series. As mentioned in the second part, given the estimation of other high-dimensional nuisance components, we need to employ an orthogonalization procedure to hope to be robust to the regularization bias that arises from selection.

11.3.1 Joint inference on a group of coefficients with time series

This section complements Section 7.3 of this book by presenting the adaptations to be made when dealing with non-i.i.d. data. Consider again the context of Section 11.1.2 and the model (11.1), still with $h = 0$. The objective here is to perform simultaneous inference for a group of coefficients $G \subseteq \{1,\dots,p\}$ of coefficients $\beta_{0,G} = \{\beta_{0,j}, j \in G\}$. The estimation method for the inverse of $\mathbf{\Sigma}$, denoted by $\widehat{\mathbf{\Theta}}$, proposed by Meinshausen and Bühlmann (2006) and described in Section 7.3 can be directly adapted. Similarly, the bias-corrected estimator of $\beta_{0,G}$ is $\check{\beta}_G = \widehat{\beta}_G + B_G$, where the initial estimator $\widehat{\beta}$ is the sparse-group Lasso introduced in Section 11.1.2:

$$\widehat{\beta} = \arg\min_{\beta \in \mathbb{R}^p} \frac{1}{T}\sum_{i=1}^{T}(Y_t - X_t'\beta)^2 + \lambda\Omega_\gamma(\beta),$$

where the penalty Ω_γ is defined in (11.7) and the bias correction is:

$$B_G = \widehat{\mathbf{\Theta}}_G\left(\frac{1}{T}\sum_{t=1}^{T} X_t(Y_t - X_t'\widehat{\beta})\right), \tag{11.15}$$

where $\mathbf{\Theta}_G$ is the submatrix of $\mathbf{\Theta}$ corresponding to the coefficients in group G.

Under stationary assumptions, restrictions on dependence (τ-mixing, see the remark in Section 11.1.4), as well as moment conditions (allowing for heavy tails), and for an increasing number of regressors ($s^2 \log(p)^2/T \to 0$), Babii et al. (2019) then show that the bias-corrected sparse-group Lasso estimator $\widehat{\beta}_G$ is asymptotically Gaussian, for any group $G \subseteq \{1,\dots,p\}$,

$$\sqrt{T}\left(\check{\beta}_G - \beta_{0,G}\right) \xrightarrow{d} \mathcal{N}(0, \Xi_G), \tag{11.16}$$

where Ξ_G is the long-term variance $\Xi_G = \lim_{T\to\infty} \mathrm{Var}\left(\frac{1}{\sqrt{T}}\sum_{t=1}^{T} \varepsilon_t \mathbf{\Theta}_G X_t\right)$ and $\mathbf{\Theta}_G$ is the submatrix of $\mathbf{\Theta}$ corresponding to the coefficients in group G.

11.3.2 Granger causality tests in high-dimension

As a reminder, the *Granger causality* concept, introduced by Granger (1969) and Sims (1972), is a property that characterizes the fact that one variable helps predict another, even after taking into account its entire past and the rest of the available information. This notion is statistical because it is related to the predictive ability of a variable and generally does not allow for rigorous counterfactual situations (Pearl, 2000). Therefore, it is a weaker notion than the causality defined in terms of the treatment effect, used in the second and third parts of this book.

More specifically, let's consider three time series $W_t := (Y_t, X_t, Z_t)$, and denote by $PL(Y_{t+1}|(W_t)_{t\in\mathbb{R}})$ the linear projection of Y_{t+1} onto $(W_t)_{t\in\mathbb{R}}$, the set of information available at time t. We say that $(Z_t)_{t\in\mathbb{R}}$ does not cause $(Y_t)_{t\in\mathbb{R}}$ in the sense of Granger if

$$PL(Y_{t+1}|(W_t)_{t\in\mathbb{R}}) = PL(Y_{t+1}|(Y_t)_{t\in\mathbb{R}}, (X_t)_{t\in\mathbb{R}}).$$

More stringent forms of this definition can also be defined in terms of conditional expectations or distributions. For instance, considering the linear projection:

$$Y_{t+1} = \alpha_0 + \sum_{j=0}^{K} \beta_j Z_{t-j} + \underbrace{\sum_{j=0}^{\infty} \gamma_j X_{t-j} + \sum_{j=0}^{\infty} \delta_j Y_{t-j}}_{\text{Controls for "all information available at t"}} + \varepsilon_{t+1}, \tag{11.17}$$

an implication of the non-Granger causality is

$$H_0 : \beta_j = 0 \; \forall j \in \{0, \ldots, K\}, \quad H_1 : \exists j \in \{0, \ldots, K\}, \; \beta_j \neq 0. \tag{11.18}$$

This implication can be tested. Note that, in (11.17), the number of control variables is generally of high dimension. When past available information is limited, a Granger causality test is performed through a Wald test or an F-test, where the F-statistic associated with $\beta_0 = \cdots = \beta_K = 0$ is calculated.

With the result of asymptotic normality (11.16) (also see Sections 4.2 and 5.6 in Chernozhukov et al., 2021), we can test Granger causality, including a large number of explanatory variables. Consider the model:

$$Y_{t+1} = \sum_{j=0}^{K} \beta_j Z_{t-j} + \sum_{j=K+1}^{p} \beta_j W_j + \varepsilon_{t+1}, \tag{11.19}$$

where W is a vector of size $p - K$ including a constant and the past of control variables X and Y, and ε_{t+1} is an innovation independent of W_j and the past of Z_t. In this framework, with $G = \{0, \ldots, K\}$, we want to test if $(Z_t, \ldots, Z_{t-K})$ provides useful information to predict Y_{t+1} that is not contained in W. This is equivalent to testing (11.18). Under the assumptions that lead to (11.16), the asymptotic distribution of the Wald statistic is known:

$$\mathcal{W}_T := T\left(\widehat{\beta}_G + B_G - \beta_{0,G}\right)' \widehat{\Xi}_G^{-1} \left(\widehat{\beta}_G + B_G - \beta_{0,G}\right) \xrightarrow{d} \chi^2_{|G|},$$

where $\chi^2_{|G|}$ follows a χ^2 distribution with $|G| = K + 1$ degrees of freedom and $\widehat{\Xi}_G$ is a consistent estimator robust to heteroscedasticity and autocorrelation (HAC) of the long-term variance Ξ_G (see the adaptation of Newey et al., 1987; Andrews, 1991 by Babii et al., 2019, in the high-dimensional context and Lasso estimation of the residuals). The test is then rejected at the level α when the statistic $\mathcal{W}_T$ is strictly greater than the $1 - \alpha$ quantile of the $\chi^2_{|G|}$ distribution.

Chernozhukov et al. (2021) propose a method to make inference about a group of coefficients in the time series framework introduced in Section 11.1.1. They use a double selection estimation procedure, similar to the one described in the second part for the i.i.d. case. The main modification to note is the use of a block bootstrap. The test performed here can also be done using their approach.

11.3.3 Application: text and GDP prediction

We continue using the context of the application from the previous Section 11.2.4, in order to perform the Granger test for the use of the textual variables in the prediction. We use the R package `midasml` to estimate Ξ_G and B_G. In the case of "sparse-group Lasso with text" from Section 11.2.4, we focus on the explanatory power of coefficients belonging to categories related to finance, growth, and crisis (see the details of these categories according to the codifications from www.structureofnews.com in Table 11.2). Table 11.2 presents the test results when considering the explanatory power of these groups of variables taken together or separately. In all cases, the test is not rejected at the 5% significance level. The variables that seem to have the most explanatory potential are the variables related to finance, which makes sense given the importance of the 2008 financial crisis in the period considered. This tends to confirm that in this context, the information provided by the text for prediction is weak. We refer to Babii et al. (2019) for a similar application on news and on the VIX stock index (indicator of S&P 500 volatility, the main US stock index) where, on the contrary, they show that news related to the financial crisis seems to have an impact on the VIX, in terms of Granger causality.

Table 11.2 Granger test results

Category	All	Finance group	Growth group	Crisis group
Statistic	6.711	5.442	0.985	1.111
5% critical value	16.91	7.814	5.991	5.991
p-value	0.667	0.142	0.611	0.573

Note: The test is not rejected at the 5% significance level for any of the tested news categories. The "Finance" group contains news related to *Profits, M.A, Savings-loans*, the "Growth" group contains *Economic.growth, Revenue.growth*, and the "Crisis" group contains *Financial.crisis, Recession*, according to the codifications from www.structureofnews.com.

11.4 Summary

Key concepts

Nowcasting, high dimension, mixed frequency data sampling (MIDAS), block bootstrap, sparse-group Lasso, mixing, Fuk–Nagaev inequality, sparse methods, dense methods, factor augmented sparse linear regression model (FARM), Granger causality, Lasso desparsification.

Additional references

We briefly discussed non-linear methods and we refer to Masini et al. (2021); Medeiros (2022); Babii et al. (2023) for more comprehensive treatments of these methods, which are very similar to the presentation of these tools in the i.i.d. framework of our introductory Chapter 2, except for the choice of the estimation window for the partitioning between training and evaluation samples, which must be well adapted to the structure of the time series data. Except for Section 11.2.1, we developed a purely frequentist approach. We recommend reading De Mol et al. (2008), Mogliani and Simoni (2021) for a Bayesian approach.

Code and data

The code `Nowcasting_application.R` used for the applications of this section is available on the course's GitHub. It uses the textual processing of the journals `Monthly_Topic_Attention_(Theta).csv` available at www.structureofnews.com and performed by Bybee et al. (2020). The R package `midasml` allows for the implementation of the MIDAS methods from Section 11.1.2 and is also useful for implementing the Granger causality test. The R package `tsapp` contains a direct implementation of the block bootstrap (labeled "boot-Lasso") mentioned in Section 11.1.2.

Questions

1. What are the peculiarities of macroeconomic and financial time series that require adaptation of the theoretical Lasso results developed in the previous sections?
2. Provide the interpretation of the mixed-norm penalization of the sparse-group Lasso.
3. Why is a bias correction needed for making inference on a group of parameters using the Lasso?
4. What is the risk of using a sparse method? Explain how the FARM approach addresses this problem.

PART V
TEXTUAL DATA

Chapter 12
Working with text data

Natural language processing (NLP) encompasses the set of concepts and algorithms that allow for the automatic processing of human language. "Natural" refers to the opposition between computer languages, such as C++, Python, etc., which are devoid of any semantic ambiguity, and human languages, for which words are often polysemous and whose meaning varies greatly depending on the context. This book focuses solely on the written form of language, excluding its oral counterpart (referred to as automatic speech recognition, ASR), which is more complex and currently less used in the economic literature. It is important to note at the outset that NLP extends beyond the realms of statistics and econometrics. Recent breakthroughs, exemplified by the enthusiastic response and concerns arising from ChatGPT, should be integrated into the toolkit of empirical economists A multitude of relevant economic data is only available in the form of strings of characters: newspaper articles, central bank speeches, stock analyst reports, political statements, social network comments, death reports, marketing messages extolling the merits of a product, etc. Whether it is the leveraging search engines queries to make economic forecasts (e.g., Ferrara and Simoni, 2019; Ke et al., 2019), measuring racial hatred (e.g., Stephens-Davidowitz, 2014), encoding textual information to capture qualitative information about a product or service (e.g., Hoberg and Phillips, 2016; Bajari et al., 2021), capturing cultural stereotypes (e.g., Kozlowski et al., 2019), etc. Textual data represents an untapped goldmine underutilized by empirical economists.

With the exception of the simplest applications, a sufficiently rich processing of textual data requires manipulating high-dimensional mathematical objects, and therefore using appropriate tools, such as those seen in Chapter 4. For example, if we take a message of T words constructed from a dictionary of W unique words, then the unique vector representation of a given message lies in a space of dimension W^T. This often implies pre-processing the document corpus to reduce the dimensionality of the problem, in particular by removing stopwords, lemmatizing, or stemming. However, even after this step, the problem at hand often remains high-dimensional, and the methods used must deal with this specificity.

Furthermore, if we consider, for example, a simple vector representation of a ten-word sentence written in a language using a vocabulary of W words (where W is much larger than ten, e.g., the English language has tens of thousands of words), we end up with a vector of size W filled with zeros except at the positions of the words present in the sentence – this is what is called the one-hot vector representation.

Machine Learning for Econometrics. Christophe Gaillac and Jérémy L'Hour, Oxford University Press.
 DOI: 10.1093/9780198918868.003.0012

We therefore have a very sparse feature vector. On the one hand, most modern machine learning algorithms perform better with dense vectors. And on the other hand, this representation is insufficient because it will not be able to capture the semantic similarity between two sentences using synonymous terms. This is why natural language processing relies largely on the concept of word embeddings, that is, a condensed mathematical representation of each word reflecting the structure of language.

This part of the book is divided into three chapters. Chapter 12 provides a general introduction to the processing of text, showing how to handle this unstructured data in order to connect, as much as possible, to standard statistical techniques. It also presents basic language models. Chapter 13 introduces the distributed representation of words, leading to meaningful lexical embeddings that reflect the structure of language. Finally, Chapter 14 addresses modern language models.

The guiding thread of this division into three chapters is the complexity increase of the language model underlying the adopted approaches. In other words, we start from a very basic representation of words and progress towards a representation that imitates the structure of language. Thus, the first chapter makes use of tools mainly based on word frequency. This is "NLP 1.0" if you will: a low-tech and somewhat outdated approach, but that can work well depending on the application and does not require large computing resources. The second chapter introduces the concept of lexical embeddings, allowing for the reflection of linguistic notions through simple mathematical operations. Dating back to the early 2010s, this technology takes the context into account, but in a fixed way: although the representation of a word has been learned in-context, it does not change with the sentence a word is in. The last chapter finally presents modern language models, a technology that emerged roughly after the famous "Attention is all you need" paper (Vaswani et al., 2017) and where lexical embeddings fully change as the context surrounding the usage of a word changes.

This chapter combines two objectives. The first consists of introducing the methodological tools necessary to convert character strings into numerical data in order to enable the use of standard statistical and econometric tools such as linear regression. The second is to introduce rudimentary language models.

12.1 Basic concepts and roadmap

Language processing encompasses a variety of tasks such as language modeling, morphosyntactic tagging, information extraction, text generation, named entity recognition, etc. In this text, we will limit ourselves to introducing the basic building blocks and exploring how text data can be exploited through standard statistical methods.

12.1.1 Definitions

For this chapter and the next two, the following concepts will be key:

- A *word n-gram* is a sequence of n words. For example, the sentence "The dog is eating a bone" is made up of the *unigrams* {*the, dog, is, eating, a, bone*}, the *bigrams* {*the dog, dog is, is eating, eating a, a bone*}, etc.
- A *character n-gram* is a sequence of n characters. Thus, the word "eating" is made up of the *bigrams* {*ea, at, ti, in, ng*}, the *trigrams* {*eat, ati, tin, ing*}, etc.
- A *token*, denoted as w, is the basic semantic unit. It is defined as an element of a dictionary $\mathcal{W}$, which is a set of size $W := |\mathcal{W}|$. A token can be indexed either directly as $w \in \mathcal{W}$ or via its position in $\mathcal{W}$, $w \in \{1, \ldots, W\}$, interchangeably. The token is not defined a priori but depends on the task. Note that, in a basic sense, a token can be a word but also a word n-gram or a character n-gram.
- A *document* is a sequence of T tokens, denoted as:

$$(w_1, \ldots, w_{t-1}, w_t, w_{t+1}, \ldots, w_T),$$

  where w_t is the t-th token in the sequence. Depending on the application, a document can be a sentence, a paragraph, a newspaper article, a tweet, a book, etc.
- A *corpus* is a collection of D documents. This is our dataset.

12.1.2 Road-map for leveraging text data

Most econometric applications involving analysis of text data can be divided into three main steps using the terminology inspired by Gentzkow et al. (2019). Let's assume we have a corpus of D documents and a vocabulary of W terms.

1. **Numerical representation of raw text.** This first step simply involves transforming a document to an array of numbers. This array can be the result of a one-to-one mapping between tokens and integers while preserving the order as what is done with modern tokenization (see Chapter 14), or can use less sophisticated, *bag of words*, approaches that do not preserve the order. An example of the latter and a traditionally used representation is the *document-term matrix*, which takes the form of a matrix that counts the number of occurrences of token w in document i. As such, it is of dimension equal to the number of documents by the number of relevant terms ($D \times W$) and is generally very sparse, because each document only spans a small portion of the vocabulary.
2. **Information retrieval.** This step can be seen as either a compression step, or a selection step. Still using the example of the document-term matrix, it is

often assumed that such a matrix can be well approximated by a low-rank representation and so that its dimension can be reduced using a singular value decomposition. Another approach, still in the bag-of-word domain, relies on using a distributed representation of words and averaging the representation of every token from the document (see Chapter 13). For simpler applications, this step is optional or can be limited to selecting columns of the document-term matrix. For example, when conducting financial sentiment analysis, a popular choice is to use the lexicon established by Loughran and McDonald (2011), which contains terms with positive and negative connotations. During this step, there is always a trade-off between maximizing information and minimizing noise.

3. **Causal or predictive analysis**. This is a final regression or classification step that is made possible once the numerical features have been extracted from the text. This task consists in estimating a quantity of interest that depends on the distribution of a certain target or outcome variable conditionally on the features.

The information retrieval step is crucial for the interpretability of causal analysis. For example, consider the case where one wants to understand how a job applicant's CV influences their return to employment, i.e., their probability of finding a job within a six-month window (the outcome variable). Since each CV is unique, we cannot directly estimate the effect of an individual biography. The econometrician could define a coding function that maps the text representation to the latent space in many ways. This mapping could be learned automatically from textual data, by searching for the presence or absence of the word "plumber" or a group of words or phrases indicating a person has this type of training. Another possibility is to group individuals with substitutable skills, for example, by defining clusters of similar CVs. This learning phase and the structure given by the researcher to the text representation must be carefully adapted based on its final use in subsequent analysis.

Finally, note that this three-step methodology constitutes what we call "NLP 1.0" for the purpose of this book. At present, and since the late 2010s, "off-the-shelf" approaches, such as those popularized by the `transformers` library from HuggingFace, are available and generally consist of two steps: (i) a *tokenization* step, which is more or less equivalent to step 1 above, in addition to the normalization step that we will study in the next section, but preserves the sequential aspect of the text, and (ii) an *inference* step, which encompasses steps 2 and 3 and involves processing the tokenized sequence through a neural network consisting of millions or even billions of parameters to extract a relevant and contextualized numerical representation (equivalent to step 2) or directly a numerical value reflecting a task of interest (here, we directly skip to step 3). For each of these two steps, we distinguish a *learning* phase that allows us to learn the model parameters using suitable data (vocabulary for the tokenizer, parameters for the neural network), and a *prediction* phase that uses these algorithms. This modern approach will be introduced in Chapter 14.

12.2 NLP 1.0: text-processing tools to build tabular data

12.2.1 Pre-processing

Let's focus on the concrete definition of the basic semantic unit for a text analysis task, that is, the definition of the *token*. The purpose of this data processing phase is to transform a document into a list of tokens relevant for analysis, through several steps:

1. **Normalization**: this step aims to format the character strings composing the documents, by encoding them in a relevant format such as UTF-8. This step can also force the words to be lowercase in order to avoid duplicating tokens. In the case of texts from social networks, for example, it may be interesting to remove accents if it is suspected that the users of the network have not systematically made use of them.
2. **Tokenization**: each character string is divided into relevant individual elements that will constitute the dictionary. This is when the nature of the tokens to be used is decided. It can be decided to consider only words, or word bi-grams, tri-grams, etc., or even character n-grams. Punctuation and numbers can be kept if they are meaningful for the application, or they can be eliminated. If the documents come from the internet, such as tweets, it may be interesting to keep emojis. When considering n-grams with $n > 1$, certain n-grams that do not have much meaning can also be eliminated (see Section 12.2.2). This step is largely automated, without necessarily requiring a token to define an intelligible semantic unit as we will see in Chapter 14.
3. **Stop-word removal**: *stop-words* are words that do not have a meaning by themselves, such as articles or prepositions. It is generally decided to remove them.
4. **Stemming and lemmatization**:
   - **Stemming**: this step consists of pruning a word to obtain its stem, by removing the suffixes or prefixes. For example, the term "*careless*" has the stem word "*care*." In English, a standard stemming algorithm is the *Porter stemmer*.
   - **Lemmatization**: this step consists of finding the *lemma* of a word. When it is a noun, it involves returning to its singular form from its plural form, or changing from a feminine form to a masculine form. When it is a verb, it involves returning to the infinitive form. This step is similar to stemming, but it is a more complex operation as it involves more abstract linguistic notions and the techniques used are more difficult to implement.

These four steps define a *bottom-up* approach seeking to prune the vocabulary. An alternative approach can be based on starting with a well-defined list of terms and trying to detect them in the corpus. But even in the context of such an approach, it may be beneficial to perform stemming or lemmatization to improve recall.

Remark 12.1 Regular expressions

The steps previously described are automated in standard NLP libraries such as `nltk` or `spaCy`. However, we cannot forget to mention *regular expressions*. A regular expression is a string that can make use of special characters called *quantifiers* to describe a string pattern according to a specific syntax. For example, the regular expression `som*` will refer to words such as "some" or "something" but not "lonesome" or "smile" since the quantifier $*$ designates zero, one, or more arbitrary characters. Regular expressions often prove useful, for example, for identifying quantities, volumes, or prices in a document.

This tool is beyond the scope of this book. However, Chapter 2 of Jurafsky and Martin (2019) discusses regular expressions in details.

Let's take an example: "Of all the ways to eat eggs, my favorite is the most fussy: devilled, the art of scooping out hard-boiled eggs and re-stuffing them with a jazzed-up yolk mixture."

The tokenization into unigrams shows that this sentence is composed of the following 28 unique tokens: "," "." ":" "a," "all," "and," "art," "devilled," "eat," "eggs," "favorite," "fussy," "hard-boiled," "is," "jazzed-up," "mixture," "most," "my," "of," "out," "re-stuffing," "scooping," "the," "them," "to," "ways," "with," "yolk."

After excluding stop-words using the `nltk` library, we are left with the list of the following 16 tokens: "," "." ":" "art," "devilled," "eat," "eggs," "favorite," "fussy," "hard-boiled," "jazzed-up," "mixture," "re-stuffing," "scooping," "ways," "yolk." Note that this operation keeps the punctuation, which may not be necessary. The list of stop-words is therefore arbitrary and should be reconsidered according to the application context. Let's remove them for the next step.

Passing through a stemmer gives the following list: "art," "devil," "eat," "egg," "favorit," "fussi," "hard-boil," "jazzed-up," "mixture," "re-stuff," "scoop," "way," "yolk." You can observe that plural forms have been reduced to singular, verbs to their stem, etc.

12.2.2 Selecting n-grams with mutual information

It is often necessary to prune the vocabulary, for example by removing stop-words, as mentioned in the previous section. However, this task is more delicate when it comes to selecting bi-grams. Let's take the example of the sentence "He lives in the city of New York." composed of the bi-grams: "he lives," "lives in," "in the," "the city,"

"city of," "of New," "New York." Intuitively, only the bi-gram "New York" deserves to be kept as it refers to a city name, whereas the other bi-grams do not a priori provide more information than the constituent unigrams.

To automatically detect bi-grams that have a meaning from the others, one can use the point-wise mutual information (PMI) defined between a target word w_t and a context word w_c by the following formula which will be computed over the entire corpus:

$$PMI(w_t, w_c) = \log_2\left(\frac{\widehat{P}(w_t, w_c)}{\widehat{P}(w_t)\widehat{P}(w_c)}\right).$$

The numerator gives the empirical probability of observing the word w_c in the context of the word w_t for a context defined either as a bi-gram, or as a window around the word w_t (Section 13.2), or as an entire document. The denominator gives this probability if we assumed that the occurrence of these two words was independent. Thus, a PMI value greater than zero indicates that the words w_t and w_c appear in the same context with a frequency higher than expected if we assumed it was purely random. In the context of the previous example, we may empirically find a high value for the mutual information between the words "New" and "York" leading to the retention of the bi-gram "New York." One can then set a threshold in order to retain only meaningful bi-grams.

Since for a given corpus, a majority of the words are never used in the same context, the value $\widehat{P}(w_t, w_c)$ can be equal to zero. To solve this problem, the negative values of the fraction can be replaced by zero:

$$PMI(w_t, w_c) = \max\left[\log_2\left(\frac{\widehat{P}(w_t, w_c)}{\widehat{P}(w_t)\widehat{P}(w_c)}\right), 0\right].$$

12.2.3 The document-term matrix

The *bag of words* representation is the simplest representation of a document. It assumes that the order of words does not matter and that a document is described by a vector of size equal to the vocabulary length, where each element counts the number of times the corresponding token appears in the document. For a corpus of D documents, with a vocabulary of size W, this results in a matrix $\mathbf{C}$ of dimension $D \times W$. This is the *document-term* matrix. In general, only a tiny fraction of the vocabulary words appear in a given document resulting in very sparse rows for the matrix $\mathbf{C}$. In this model, the row C_i represents document i so that $\mathbf{C} := (C_i')_{i=1,\dots,D}$. Obviously, the length of C_i depends on the definition of the vocabulary, and thus on the nature of the steps described in the previous section. Notice that normalizing the rows of the matrix by the sum of their elements, gives the term frequency of each token in a document, which we will denote $f_{i,t} := C_{i,t} / \|C_i\|_1$ below.

C can be built from raw counts, or by overweighting words that appear frequently in few documents and underweighting words that appear often in many documents. The former set of words contains some signal that can helps characterize documents well, while the second set contains words that have no discriminatory power. To implement this, a common transformation is the TF-IDF (term frequency-inverse document frequency) weighting. It gives importance to words that appear multiple times in few documents. The formula for token t in document i out of D documents is given by:

$$(tf - idf)_{i,t} = \underbrace{f_{i,t}}_{\text{Term Frequency}} \times \underbrace{\log\left(\frac{D}{\sum_{j=1}^{D} 1\{f_{j,t} > 0\}}\right)}_{\text{Inverse Document Frequency}},$$

$$f_{i,t} = \frac{\text{Number of times token } t \text{ appears in document } i}{\text{Number of tokens in document } i},$$

The term *IDF* is the logarithm of the inverse of the proportion of documents containing t, which will be low for a common word. For example, Cagé et al. (2019) adopt a TF-IDF approach to group documents by semantic similarity in order to study the online spread of information.

12.2.4 How to measure similarity?

Recall that for two real vectors of dimension p, x and y, the Euclidean distance is given by:

$$\|x - y\|_2 := \sqrt{\sum_{j=1}^{p}(x_j - y_j)^2},$$

while the cosine similarity is defined as:

$$\text{cossim}(x, y) := \frac{x'y}{\|x\|_2 \, \|y\|_2}.$$

Cosine similarity gives a value between -1 and 1. Vectors that are aligned have a value of 1. Opposite vectors have a value of -1. And orthogonal vectors have a value of 0. It can easily be transformed into a distance by taking $1 - \text{cossim}(x, y)$. Both the Euclidean and the cosine distances measure a degree of similarity, since they decrease as both vectors become more similar. Notice that in NLP in general, cosine similarity is the "distance"' of choice, as it cares more about alignment between vectors, tolerating differences in magnitudes.

In the context of the document-term matrix for example, where documents i and j are represented by vectors C_i and C_j, although the two documents could display the same distribution of word usage over the vocabulary, one may be much longer than the other, so that the Euclidean distance between two vectors may be large although the two documents are close. In the toy case where $C_j = \alpha C_i$ for some positive real number α, $\|C_i - C_j\|_2 = |1 - \alpha| \, \|C_i\|_2$, while $\text{cossim}(C_i, C_j) = 1$.

12.2.5 Textual regression

The previous method allows to build numerical features by converting a corpus of texts into a simple matrix representation such as $\mathbf{C}$ or its counterpart obtained from the TF-IDF transformation. Suppose there is an outcome Y_i associated with document i in the corpus. We may then want to explain these results by the content of this document. To do so, take the row C_i as features that summarize numerically this information:

$$Y_i = C_i' \beta_0 + \varepsilon_i.$$

Note that this is a high-dimensional regression problem since there are W explanatory variables and W is generally large. To estimate β_0, one can use penalized regression techniques, random forests, or neural networks (Chapter 2). Another approach consists in determining a priori the important terms with respect to the economic phenomenon being studied, either in an ad hoc manner, or by using a lexicon established in the literature, such as that of Loughran and McDonald (2011) for financial applications, for example.

Many empirical articles use such tools. For example, Hansen et al. (2019) use the content of the Bank of England's inflation report to assess the impact of the central bank's communication on financial markets. One could also use the information contained in companies' quarterly earnings call to explain the evolution of their stock prices (e.g., Isichenko, 2021). Another standard example is the prediction of stock returns using newspaper articles (e.g., Ke et al., 2019).

12.3 Empirical applications based on word frequency

This section presents two empirical social science applications that use textual data as described in the previous section.

12.3.1 Impact of racism on American elections

Stephens-Davidowitz (2014) asks the following question: "Does racism cause a significant loss of votes for a Black candidate in contemporary America?" He assesses racial animosity in a county based on the percentage of a popular search-engine queries that include a well-known racially connoted term. The intuition is that people tend to not reveal their true opinions when asked in surveys, and that search engine queries, made in privacy, more easily express socially taboo opinions. He shows that the rate of racially connoted queries is a negative and significant predictor of votes cast for Obama in 2008 and 2012, while controlling for Kerry's share of votes in 2004. The rate of racially connoted queries in county i is denoted as:

$$\text{Rate of connoted queries}_i = \left(\frac{\text{Queries including the term}}{\text{Total number of queries}}\right)_{i,\,2004\text{–}2007},$$

where the "term" in question is a well-known racist adjective. To test the impact of racism on the score of a Black candidate in presidential elections, the author regresses the difference between the share of votes for Barack Obama in 2008 and the share of 2004 votes for Democratic candidate John Kerry on this query rate. The estimated model is:

$$\begin{aligned}&(\%\text{Obama2008} - \%\text{Kerry2004})_i\\&= \text{Rate of connoted queries}_i \times \tau + X_i'\beta + \varepsilon_i,\end{aligned}$$

where X_i contains control variables and an intercept, and τ is the parameter of interest. The results are statistically significant and partially explain why candidate Obama received fewer votes in areas where the rate of racially connoted queries is highest, compared to another Democratic candidate. This racism is estimated to have cost the candidate Obama an average of four percentage points.

A limitation of this approach, called the *dictionary method*, is that it focuses solely on variation through a limited number of dimensions (here, a single term), while completely ignoring its context of use. In fact, racial slurs can undergo cultural re-appropriations, and their meaning can change depending on the context (e.g., in this application, a number of rappers re-appropriate the term in question, thus altering its significance). In a sense, this application requires very little knowledge of any NLP technique, but would potentially benefit from including queries for synonyms of the target query found in a data-driven way.

12.3.2 Definition of business sectors using company descriptions

Hoberg and Phillips (2016) exploit 10-K reports, which are annual mandatory descriptions of goods and services offered by publicly traded firms in the United States, to define a measure of similarity between them. The objective is to provide a data-driven definition of a market rather than an expert opinion-based one. The unit of observation (i, t) is the firm-year pair. The documents are individual 10-K forms, represented individually by a vector $C_i^t \in \mathbb{R}^{n_t}$ resulting from a processing method similar to those described in the previous section. The data contains 50,673 companies 10-K reports per year. They pay particular attention to proper nouns and limit the analysis to nouns and proper nouns that do not appear in more than 25% of all product descriptions. This leads to $n_{1996} = 61,146$ unique nouns and proper nouns in 1996 and $n_{2008} = 55,605$ in 2008. The data is available via the *edgar* and *edgarWebR* libraries in R, which provide access to the Edgar website of the Securities and Exchange Commission (SEC) where the legal descriptions of 10-K companies are stored.

A cosine similarity score per pair of firms i and j, $s_{ij}^t := \text{cossim}(C_i^t, C_j^t)$ for a year t measures the proximity of descriptions of goods and services offered by the two firms. The square matrix of these s_{ij}^t scores defines an *affinity matrix* that measures proximity links between firms.

Next, this affinity matrix is processed through a clustering algorithm to define sectors. The initial state assumes that each firm constitutes its own sector. The algorithm then groups the most similar firms into sectors one by one, using, when there are several firms in a sector, an average pairwise similarity of firms for all pairs of firms in sectors G_1 and G_2:

$$s_{G_1,G_2}^t = \frac{1}{|G_1||G_2|} \sum_{i \in G_1} \sum_{j \in G_2} s_{ij}^t.$$

The algorithm stops when the number of sectors reaches a predefined number.

The predicted sector membership of each firm-year pair allows to analyze the effect of shocks experienced by the military and software industries on supply chain links and competition between firms. The events of September 11, 2001 pushed firms to enter the buoyant military markets and pushed products from this industry towards "the collection of information off the battlefield" and "products for potential ground conflicts."

Note that two problems can arise when using cosine similarity computed from document-term matrix rows, which can lead to inaccurate similarity despite similar content: synonymy and polysemy. This problem cannot be solved without considering the context of the sentence or without using generative (i.e., structural) models to capture the text. Chapter 13 presents ways to deal with synonymous terms, and Chapter 14 presents ways to consider the context of a sentence.

12.4 Language modeling with latent variables

This section is an introduction to simple language models. The assumption of independence between each word in a document, known as the *unigram model*, described in Section 12.4.1, is the starting point for language modeling. We then introduce complexities one step at a time.

12.4.1 The unigram model

The unigram model is the simplest language model. It makes the convenient assumption that the probability of observing a given word does not depend on the surrounding words. As a result, the maximum likelihood estimator of this probability is given by the word frequency.

Start with a representation of a document of length T as a sequence of words $(W_1, \dots, W_T)$. The unigram model assumes independence between each word, such that the probability of observing a certain document $(w_1, \dots, w_T)$ is given by:

$$\mathbb{P}(W_1 = w_1, \dots, W_T = w_T) = \prod_{t=1}^{T} \mathbb{P}(W_t = w_t). \tag{12.1}$$

Let $\beta \in [0,1]^W$ denote $(\beta_w)_w := (\mathbb{P}(W_t = w))_w$, the probability that the word takes the value w. By definition, the sum of the elements of β is 1, since this vector defines a probability distribution on the vocabulary. The information contained in the data can be summarized by the row of the term-document matrix where we drop the document subscript, denoted $C = (C_w)_{w \in \mathcal{W}}$, and the likelihood factorized as:

$$\mathbb{P}(\beta | C) = \prod_{w \in \mathcal{W}} \beta_w^{C_w}.$$

Considering the log-likelihood and incorporating the constraints that β defines a probability distribution, the Lagrangian is given by:

$$\sum_{w \in \mathcal{W}} C_w \log(\beta_w) + \lambda \left(1 - \sum_{w \in \mathcal{W}} \beta_w \right),$$

where λ is the Lagrange multiplier. The first order conditions imply: $\beta_w = C_w / \lambda$, $\lambda = \sum_{w \in \mathcal{W}} C_w = T$, and therefore $\widehat{\beta}_w = C_w / T = f_w$. The maximum likelihood estimator associated with this model is simply the word frequency.

However, this model is simplistic, and a first way to relax the independence assumption is to assume conditional independence with respect to the topic of the document.

12.4.2 Unigram modeling with topic mixture

This next model adds a layer of complexity: the probability of a word appearing depends on the category to which the document belongs, or equivalently, on the topic of the document. This category is assumed to be chosen from an arbitrary number K of unobserved and mutually exclusive categories. This is a *mixture model with hidden variable*, where the hidden variable is the category.

Each document in the corpus is assumed to belong to one and only one unobserved latent category, denoted by $Z \in \{1, \ldots, K\}$. Consider the matrix parameter that column-wise stacks the probability vector of word appearance under each category $\boldsymbol{\beta} = (\beta_1, \ldots, \beta_K)$ such that $\boldsymbol{\beta}_{w,k} := \mathbb{P}(W_t = w|Z = k)$ is the probability that the t-th word, W_t, takes the value w given that the document belongs to category k. Let $\rho = (\mathbb{P}(Z = k))_{k=1,\ldots,K}$ the vector of marginal probabilities of category membership. Using Equation (12.1), we have:

$$\begin{aligned}
&\mathbb{P}(W_1 = w_1, \ldots, W_T = w_T|\boldsymbol{\beta}, \rho) \\
&= \sum_{k=1}^{K} \mathbb{P}(Z = k|\boldsymbol{\beta}, \rho) \prod_{t=1}^{T} \mathbb{P}(W_t = w_t|Z = k, \boldsymbol{\beta}, \rho),
\end{aligned}$$

and therefore, since the observations can also be summarized by the document-term matrix, the likelihood function is written:

$$\mathbb{P}(\boldsymbol{\beta}, \rho|C) = \sum_{k=1}^{K} \rho_k \prod_{w \in \mathcal{W}} \boldsymbol{\beta}_{w,k}^{C_w}.$$

Consequently, for a corpus of D documents indexed by the mute variable j, we have the following log-likelihood:

$$\sum_{j=1}^{D} \log\left(\sum_{k=1}^{K} \rho_k \prod_{w \in \mathcal{W}} \boldsymbol{\beta}_{w,k}^{C_{j,w}}\right) + \underbrace{\lambda_1 \left(1 - \sum_{k=1}^{K} \rho_k\right)}_{\text{1 constraint}} + \underbrace{\sum_{k=1}^{K} \lambda_{k+1}\left(1 - \sum_{w \in \mathcal{W}} \boldsymbol{\beta}_{w,k}\right)}_{\text{K constraints}}.$$

Unobservable latent categories make the likelihood intractable. The *expectation-maximization* (EM) algorithm is particularly well suited for the estimation of this type of models.

Remark 12.2 Estimation via the EM algorithm

The basic idea of the EM algorithm is that the log-likelihood function would be simplified if the latent variables $\{Z_j\}_{j=1,\ldots,D}$ were observed:

$$\begin{aligned}
&\ell_{\text{full}}\left(\boldsymbol{\beta}, \rho \middle| C, \{Z_j\}_{j=1,\ldots,D}\right) \\
&= \sum_{j=1}^{D} \sum_{k=1}^{K} 1\{Z_j = k\} \left(\log(\rho_k) + \sum_{w \in \mathcal{W}} C_{j,w} \log(\boldsymbol{\beta}_{w,k})\right).
\end{aligned}$$

Continued

Remark 12.2 *Continued*

Thus, when integrating over $\{Z_j\}_{j=1,\dots,D}$, the likelihood can be decomposed as:

$$
\begin{aligned}
&\ell(\boldsymbol{\beta}, \rho | \mathbf{C}) \\
&= \mathbb{E}_{\{Z_j\}_{j=1,\dots,D} | \mathbf{C}, \boldsymbol{\beta}, \rho}\left[\ell_{\text{full}}\left(\boldsymbol{\beta}, \rho \middle| \mathbf{C}, \{Z_j\}_{j=1,\dots,D}\right)\right] \\
&= \sum_{j=1}^{D} \sum_{k=1}^{K} \mathbb{E}_{Z_j | \mathbf{C}_j, \boldsymbol{\beta}, \rho}\left[1\{Z_j = k\}\right]\left(\log(\rho_k) + \sum_{w \in \mathcal{W}} \mathbf{C}_{j,w} \log(\boldsymbol{\beta}_{w,k})\right).
\end{aligned}
\tag{12.2}
$$

Then, the EM algorithm proceeds iteratively starting from initial values $(\boldsymbol{\beta}^{(0)}, \rho^{(0)})$, and then moves to the next step via:

$$
\begin{aligned}
&(\boldsymbol{\beta}^{(t+1)}, \rho^{(t+1)}) \\
&= \arg\max_{\boldsymbol{\beta}, \rho}\left\{\mathbb{E}_{\{Z_j\}_{j=1,\dots,D} | \mathbf{C}, \boldsymbol{\beta}^{(t)}, \rho^{(t)}}\left[\ell_{\text{full}}\left(\boldsymbol{\beta}, \rho \middle| \mathbf{C}, \{Z_j\}_{j=1,\dots,D}\right)\right]\right\}
\end{aligned}
\tag{12.3}
$$

It is guaranteed that each iteration increases the log-likelihood.

1. (**E step**) Compute the expectation (12.3) using (12.2) and

$$
\begin{aligned}
&\mathbb{E}_{Z_j | \mathbf{C}_j, \boldsymbol{\beta}, \rho}\left[1\{Z_j = k\}\right] \\
&= \mathbb{P}\left(Z_j = k | \mathbf{C}, \boldsymbol{\beta}, \rho\right) \\
&\propto \mathbb{P}\left(\mathbf{C} | Z_j = k, \boldsymbol{\beta}, \rho\right)\mathbb{P}\left(Z_j = k | \boldsymbol{\beta}, \rho\right) \quad \text{(Bayes rule)} \\
&= \left(\prod_{w \in \mathcal{W}} \boldsymbol{\beta}_{w,k}^{\mathbf{C}_{j,w}}\right)\rho_k.
\end{aligned}
$$

2. (**M step**) The first-order conditions for the following objective function:

$$
\begin{aligned}
&\sum_{j=1}^{D} \sum_{k=1}^{K} \left(\prod_{w \in \mathcal{W}} (\boldsymbol{\beta}_{w,k}^{(t)})^{\mathbf{C}_{j,w}}\right)\rho_k^{(t)}\left(\log(\rho_k) + \sum_{w \in \mathcal{W}} \mathbf{C}_{j,w} \log(\boldsymbol{\beta}_{w,k})\right) \\
&\quad + \lambda_1\left(1 - \sum_{w \in \mathcal{W}} \boldsymbol{\beta}_w\right) + \sum_{k=1}^{K} \lambda_{k+1}\left(1 - \sum_{w \in \mathcal{W}} \boldsymbol{\beta}_{w,k}\right),
\end{aligned}
$$

give the expressions for $\boldsymbol{\beta}_{w,k}^{(t+1)}, \rho_k^{(t+1)}$ in terms of $\mathbf{C}_{j,w}$ and $\widehat{C}_{j,k}^{(t)} := \left(\prod_{w \in \mathcal{W}} (\boldsymbol{\beta}_{w,k}^{(t)})^{\mathbf{C}_{j,w}}\right)\rho_k^{(t)}$.

The resulting topics can be interpreted *ex-post* by looking at words with higher or lower relative frequencies conditionally on each topic. It is also possible to compute the membership probability of a document in order to cluster the corpus.

12.4.3 Latent Dirichlet allocation

An extra relaxation of the independence assumption is to allow a document to be a mixture of several categories or "topics" that are not observed. Words are assumed to be drawn independently and conditionally on the topic. This is the principle of latent Dirichlet allocation (LDA) and its variants (e.g., correlated topic models). LDA is a mixed-membership model in which documents are represented as random mixtures over latent topics, each topic being characterized by a distribution over words. Each document has its own probability distribution over topics.

Remark 12.3 The Dirichlet probability distribution

Let us define the Dirichlet distribution, a key tool in this section. In Bayesian statistics, the posterior distribution, $\mathbb{P}(\boldsymbol{\beta}|\boldsymbol{C})$, is given by:

$$\mathbb{P}(\boldsymbol{\beta}|\boldsymbol{C}) = \frac{\mathbb{P}(\boldsymbol{C}|\boldsymbol{\beta})\,\mathbb{P}(\boldsymbol{\beta})}{\mathbb{P}(\boldsymbol{C})},$$

where $\mathbb{P}(\boldsymbol{C}|\boldsymbol{\beta})$ is the likelihood and $\mathbb{P}(\boldsymbol{\beta})$ is the prior distribution, determined by the researcher. A particularly useful prior distribution is a *conjugate prior*, which leads to a posterior distribution of the same family.

Here, we have a multinomial likelihood function for the word frequency in a document $\boldsymbol{C}$, given by:

$$\mathbb{P}(\boldsymbol{C}|\boldsymbol{\beta}) = \frac{\Gamma\left(\sum_{w\in\mathcal{W}} C_w + 1\right)}{\prod_{w\in\mathcal{W}} \Gamma(C_w + 1)} \prod_{w\in\mathcal{W}} \beta_w^{C_w},$$

where Γ is the Gamma function. The Dirichlet distribution, parameterized by $\alpha = (\alpha_w)_{w\in\mathcal{W}}$, is defined on the $(|\mathcal{W}| - 1)$-dimensional simplex (i.e., $\alpha \in \mathbb{R}_+^{|\mathcal{W}|}$, $\sum_{w\in\mathcal{W}} \alpha_w = 1$), and is characterized by:

$$\mathbb{P}(\boldsymbol{\beta}|\alpha) = \frac{\prod_{w\in\mathcal{W}} \Gamma(\alpha_w)}{\Gamma\left(\sum_{w\in\mathcal{W}} \alpha_w\right)} \prod_{w\in\mathcal{W}} \beta_w^{\alpha_w - 1}.$$

Thus, the posterior distribution is:

$$\mathbb{P}(\boldsymbol{\beta}|\boldsymbol{C}) \propto \prod_{w\in\mathcal{W}} \beta_w^{C_w + \alpha_w - 1},$$

Continued

Remark 12.3 *Continued*

which is also a Dirichlet distribution of parameters $(C_1 + \alpha_1, \ldots, C_W + \alpha_W)$. The mean and variance of a Dirichlet(α) distribution are given by:

$$\mathbb{E}\left[\boldsymbol{\beta}_w\right] = \frac{\alpha_v}{\overline{\alpha}}, \quad \mathbb{V}\left[\boldsymbol{\beta}_w\right] = \frac{\alpha_w(\overline{\alpha} - \alpha_w)}{\overline{\alpha}^2(\overline{\alpha} + 1)},$$

where $\overline{\alpha} = \sum_{w \in \mathcal{W}} \alpha_w$. Therefore, we have:

$$\mathbb{E}\left[\boldsymbol{\beta}_w | \boldsymbol{C}\right] = \frac{C_w + \alpha_w}{T + \overline{\alpha}}.$$

Compared to the maximum likelihood estimator $\widehat{\boldsymbol{\beta}}_w = C_w/T$, we can see that the parameter α tends to smooth cases with very low or zero frequency $\boldsymbol{C}_w$.

Let's describe the LDA models from Blei et al. (2003) and Blei and Lafferty (2009). The generative process for document j composed of T words abides by the following assumptions:

1. $T \sim$ Poisson(ξ);
2. $\rho \sim$ Dirichlet(α), $\rho, \alpha \in \mathbb{R}_+^{|\mathcal{W}|}$;
3. For each of the T words in the sequence $(W_1, \ldots, W_T)$:
   (a) Choose a topic $Z_t \sim$ Multinomial(ρ);
   (b) Choose a word w_t by drawing according to $\mathbb{P}(W_t = w_t | Z_t, \boldsymbol{\beta})$, according to a multinomial distribution conditioned on the topic Z_t and the parameter matrix $\boldsymbol{\beta}$ of dimension $|\mathcal{W}| \times K$.

Thus, conditionally on the total number of words used $T = \sum_{w \in \mathcal{W}} C_w$, the column of frequencies $\boldsymbol{C}$ (i.e., the row of the document-term matrix corresponding to this document) follows a multinomial distribution:

$$\boldsymbol{C} \sim \text{Multinomial}(\rho_1 \boldsymbol{\beta}_{\cdot,1} + \ldots + \rho_K \boldsymbol{\beta}_{\cdot,K}, T). \tag{12.4}$$

For document j, we have:

$$\mathbb{P}(W_t = w | \rho^j) = \sum_{k=1}^{K} \mathbb{P}(W_t = w | Z_t = k) \mathbb{P}_j(Z_t = k) = \sum_{k=1}^{K} \boldsymbol{\beta}_{w,k} \rho_k^j,$$

thus justifying the distribution (12.4). Our aim is to estimate the parameters $\boldsymbol{\beta}$ and α. The data generating process gives the following matrix factorizations, which allow for the interpretation of documents and topics:

$$\underbrace{C}_{\text{documents} \times \text{words } (D\times|W|)} \propto \underbrace{\begin{pmatrix} \rho^{1\prime} \\ \vdots \\ \rho^{D\prime} \end{pmatrix}}_{\text{documents } \times \text{topics } (D\times K)} \times \underbrace{\boldsymbol{\beta}'}_{\text{topics} \times \text{words } (K\times|W|)} .$$

For a document j, given the parameters ρ^j and α, the joint distribution of a mixture of topics, a set of K topics, and a sequence of T words is given by:

$$\mathbb{P}\left(\rho^j, \{w_t, z_t\}_{t=1,\ldots,T} | \alpha, \rho^j\right) = \mathbb{P}\left(\rho^j | \alpha\right) \prod_{t=1}^{T} \mathbb{P}\left(Z_t = z_t | \rho^j\right) \mathbb{P}\left(W_t = w_t | Z_t, \rho^j\right),$$

where $\mathbb{P}\left(Z_t = z_t | \rho^j\right) = \rho_k^j$ for k such that $Z_t = k$. By integrating with respect to the topic distribution and summing over all possible values of Z_t, we obtain:

$$\begin{aligned} &\mathbb{P}\left(W_1 = w_1, \ldots, W_T = w_T | \alpha, \rho^j\right) \\ &= \int \mathbb{P}\left(\rho^j | \alpha\right) \left(\prod_{t=1}^{T} \sum_{Z_t} \mathbb{P}\left(z_t | \rho^j\right) \mathbb{P}\left(W_t = w_t | Z_t, \rho^j\right) \right) d\rho^j. \end{aligned}$$

However, maximizing such likelihood is numerically complex, due to the products between ρ and $\boldsymbol{\beta}$. Common techniques for estimating these models involve Gibbs sampling and variational EM algorithms. The variational EM algorithm approximates the true posterior distribution with a simpler functional form that depends on a set of variational parameters. Then, it proceeds by optimizing the approximate posterior distribution with respect to the variational parameters so that it is "close" to the true posterior distribution.

Zhao et al. (2015) propose an approach to select the number of latent topics K in an LDA model. The idea is to select the number of topics such that the marginal gain in terms of perplexity (a concept from information theory similar to entropy) slows down.

12.5 Empirical applications

12.5.1 Monetary policy transparency

Hansen et al. (2017) study the impact of increased transparency in the decision-making process of central banks using an LDA model. They exploit the meetings of the US Federal Reserve Open Market Committee (FOMC), during which, eight times a year, the 19 members formulate the US monetary policy. The US Federal Reserve publishes full minutes of FOMC meetings, which can be analyzed to identify the topics of discussion.

Their research question is as follows: what are the effects of greater transparency towards citizens on internal deliberations? They use a natural experiment: FOMC meetings have been recorded on tape since the 1970s. However, initially, committee members believed that these tapes were subsequently erased. Then, in 1993, under pressure from the US Senate, Alan Greenspan discovered and revealed that, in fact, the tapes had been transcribed and kept in archives since the beginning.

After processing the minutes, the authors obtain $W = 8,615$ unique tokens, collectively used $2,715,586$ times, in $D = 46,169$ documents. They consider LDA models where $K = 50$ and $K = 70$. As a model validity test, the authors conduct a correlation study between the intensity of certain estimated topics and the occurrence of external events. For example, they examine the evolution of the number of words used associated with two pro-cyclical topics, defined by a decrease in their occurrence before each recession. In particular, they use the index developed by Baker et al. (2016) to measure the perception of economic policy uncertainty and expiring fiscal measures by economic agents. Topics estimated by the LDA can be represented and classified based on their correlation with this index, as well as the most representative associated words of these topics (see the example on articles from the *Wall Street Journal* in Section 11.1).

Finally, regarding the effect of transparency on deliberations, the authors examine in particular the herding (or anti-herding) behavior of FOMC members: they can choose to conform (or publicly deviate) from the chairman's opinion and choose to address a similar topic (or change the topic). For this purpose, they estimate the following linear model:

$$Y_{it} = \alpha_i + D_t \times \tau + X_t'\beta + \varepsilon_{it},$$

where α_i is a topic fixed-effects D_t is a binary variable representing the transparency regime and X_t are control variables of a macroeconomic nature. Y_{it} represents various measures of central bank communication based on topics, particularly a Herfindahl concentration index computed on the distribution of policy topics, the percentage of time spent on factual topics, the number of words from technical jargon, as well as the similarity between the topic distribution of a speaker and the FOMC average. Using a measure of similarity between the topics addressed by the chairman and the other members after and before 1993, they find significant evidence of conformist behavior of committee members relative to the chairman.

12.5.2 Political division

Gentzkow et al. (2019) use the US Congressional Record from the 43rd Congress to the 114th Congress to estimate the average ideological division in the Congress using a multinomial logit model.

The features representing session t are measured in a matrix $\mathbf{C}_t$ where the rows correspond to speakers and the columns to selected distinct bigrams. Therefore, an element C_{ijt} gives the number of times speaker i uttered phrase j in session t. They assume that, for speaker i from party P:

$$C_{it} \sim \text{Multinomial}\left(m_{it}, q_t^P(X_{it})\right),$$

and $q_t^P(X_{it}) \in]0,1[^W$ denote the vector of choice probabilities defined by:

$$q_{jt}^{P(i)}(X_{it}) = \frac{\exp(\alpha_{jt} + X_{it}'\gamma_{jt} + \varphi_{jt}1_{i\in R_t})}{\sum_k \exp(\alpha_{kt} + X_{it}'\gamma_{kt} + \varphi_{kt}1_{i\in R_t})},$$

α_{jt} is a scalar parameter capturing the baseline popularity of expression j in session t, γ_{jt} is a vector of dimension K capturing the effect of features X_{it} on the propensity to use expression j in session t, φ_{jt} is a scalar parameter capturing the effect of party affiliation on the propensity to use expression j in session t, $R_t = \{i : P(i) = R, m_{it} > 0\}$, and $D_t = \{i : P(i) = D, m_{it} > 0\}$. These variables measure the ideological content of the speech as the divergence between $q_t^R(X_{it})$ and $q_t^D(X_{it})$ through

$$\pi_t(X_{it}) = \frac{1}{2}q_t^R(X_{it})'\rho_t(X_{it}) + \frac{1}{2}q_t^D(X_{it})'(1 - \rho_t(X_{it})),$$

where

$$\rho_{jt}(X_{it}) = \frac{q_{jt}^R(X_{it})}{q_{jt}^R(X_{it}) + q_{jt}^D(X_{it})},$$

is the posterior belief that an observer with a neutral a priori would attribute to a speaker if they choose expression j in session t and have characteristics X_{it}. The estimation of the structural parameters is performed using a penalized estimator proposed by Taddy (2013). The resulting index shows that the average ideological division between Democrats and Republicans has significantly increased since the 1990s, compared to the evolution between 1870 and 1990, in the sense that they now speak different languages to a much larger extent than before.

Finally, Gentzkow and Shapiro (2010) estimate a structural demand model for newspapers using a new measure of media bias, which measures the similarity of a media's language to that of a Republican or Democratic member of Congress.

12.6 Summary

Key concepts

Natural language processing (NLP), word n-gram, character n-gram, token, tokenization, document, corpus, document-term matrix, stop-word, stemming, de-suffixing, lemmatization, regular expression, mutual information, TF-IDF, text regression, cosine distance, unigram model, EM algorithm, latent Dirichlet allocation (LDA).

Additional references

A very good general reference on natural language processing is Jurafsky and Martin (2019), available online.

In the economic literature, Bholat et al. (2015), Gentzkow et al. (2019), Ash and Hansen (2022), Stephen Hansen's conferences and lecture notes (sekhansen.github.io/teaching.html) and Elliott Ash's (elliottash.com/text_course) are excellent starting points.

Questions

1. Why does text data processing often require manipulating high-dimensional vectors?
2. Provide two concrete examples where the use of character n-grams is advantageous compared to using word n-grams only.
3. In your opinion, what are the advantages and limitations of modeling language through latent variables?
4. In early 2021, GameStop's soaring stock price made headlines, highlighting the activity of users on the Reddit forum `r/WallStreetBets`, a group of individual investors looking for stock tips. Suppose we have, on one hand, daily time series of stock prices for a given basket of stocks (observation unit: day × financial asset), and on the other hand, a collection of messages posted on this forum (observation unit: timestamped message). Propose a detailed empirical strategy to estimate the impact of this activity on the stock prices of these assets. You will start from explaining how to construct the relevant database and go up to describing the model you would like to estimate.

Chapter 13
Word embeddings

This chapter deals with the mathematical representation of words through vectors or *embeddings,* which are the basis of modern language models. This is not just any type of vector representation, but a *distributed representation* that serves several purposes. First, it reduces storage costs by distributing n objects across $p \ll n$ axes, instead of using n axes for n words (Section 13.1). Second, it helps tackle the curse of dimensionality, which makes it difficult to estimate the joint probability of word sequences (Bengio et al., 2000). Finally, it produces a vector space in which mathematical relationships have linguistic meaning (i.e., two words used in a similar context will be close to one another in this space).

This chapter starts by discussing the limits of the one-hot representation (Section 13.1) and continues with Section 13.2 that presents traditional approaches based on the factorization of the co-occurrence matrix. Section 13.3 constitutes the core of this chapter: it details the models that underlie the word embeddings commonly used today. Section 13.4 provides some guidelines on how to use embeddings for a classification task. Finally, we will explore how this idea of embeddings can be applied to other types of unstructured data (Section 13.5). This chapter relies on concepts related to neural networks, presented in Section 2.8.

In this chapter, a word is denoted by the symbol w, while a set of words (the vocabulary) is denoted by $\mathcal{W}$. x_w, x_i, or simply x when context is devoid of ambiguity denotes the vector representation of word $w \in \mathcal{W}$, which occupies position i in the vocabulary. This is a parameter vector that we seek to learn (estimate). Furthermore, a document consisting of T words is represented by a word sequence of length T, denoted by $(w_1, \ldots, w_T)$. From a statistical viewpoint, a document is therefore considered as a sequence of T discrete random variables, $(W_1, \ldots, W_T)$, each taking values in $\mathcal{W}$, of which $(w_1, \ldots, w_T)$ is a realization. Notice also that we take these word sequences as given and abstract from the data-cleaning steps described in Chapter 12. In this sense, while we use the term "word" in this chapter, it actually refers to a *token*.

13.1 Limitations of the one-hot representation

So far, we have considered a one-hot representation of words, also called *one-hot encoding*. That is, for a vocabulary, i.e., a set of words $\mathcal{W}$ of size W, each word is represented by a sparse vector of size W with one element equal to one and the rest

Machine Learning for Econometrics. Christophe Gaillac and Jérémy L'Hour, Oxford University Press.
 DOI: 10.1093/9780198918868.003.0013

of the elements equal to zero. For the word occupying position $i \in \{1, \dots, W\}$ in the vocabulary, we therefore have the following representation:

$$x = (x_j)_{j=1,\dots,W} = \begin{cases} 1 & \text{if } j = i, \\ 0 & \text{otherwise.} \end{cases}$$

First, this representation is inefficient since representing a document in this system requires a vector of dimension W (see Section 12.2.3). Similarly, each addition to the vocabulary results in an increase in the dimension of all vectors representing a document. In textual regressions of the type seen in Section 12.2.5, it quickly creates problems of dimensionality as each added word represents an additional coefficient to estimate. It is also limited by its inability to capture the semantic proximity of words. Indeed, for any two distinct words, x_1 and x_2, we necessarily have $\|x_1 - x_2\|_2 = \sqrt{2}$. All words are at the same distance from each other. The notion of distance, as measured by the Euclidean distance, when considering this representation, therefore does not carry any meaning. And this is not a problem caused by this distance, because if we consider the cosine similarity, we have the same result: $\text{cossim}(x_1, x_2) = 0$. This representation is therefore unable to account for the semantic proximity between words: there is no mathematical translation of synonym, antonym, lexical field, etc.

Finally, adequate language modeling – which often requires learning the joint probability of any sequence of words – without using a more sophisticated approach than one-hot encoding, suffers from the curse of dimensionality (Bengio et al., 2000).

13.2 Factorization of the co-occurrence matrix

Modern language models are based on the observation made by English linguist John Rupert Firth (1890–1960) that "*you shall know a word by the company it keeps.*" Therefore, the construction of word vectors relies on the idea that similar words, such as synonyms or words fulfilling the same function, are used in similar contexts. Consequently, similar words are often accompanied, in their usage, by a specific context defined as a shared subset of words. Analyzing these contexts enables us to generate lexical embeddings, which serve as mathematical representations of these words. In this vein, many traditional approaches relied on word counting, notably through the *co-occurrence matrix*, which we will present here.

13.2.1 Representation using the co-occurrence matrix

Let $\mathcal{W}$ be a vocabulary of W words, and let M be an integer, which we will call the *window size*. The *context* of a word in a sentence is defined as the set of $2M$ words consisting of the union of the M preceding words and the M following words. The context is truncated to avoid exceeding the sentence boundaries. Thus, the context of the first word in a sentence consists only of the M following words. A value of 4 or 5 for M is often used in practice. The co-occurrence matrix $\mathbf{F}$ is a square matrix of dimension W such that the element at the intersection of the i-th row and the j-th column counts the number of times the word w_j appears in the context of the word w_i. Thus, we are dealing with a high-dimensional sparse matrix, since a priori a given word is only used in a small number of contexts. We can still define a slightly more advanced representation of a word w_i than the *one-hot* representation seen in the previous section, simply by taking the row $x_i = (\mathbf{F}_{i,1}, \ldots, \mathbf{F}_{i,W})$ that corresponds to it in the co-occurrence matrix. In this case, for two words that share exactly the same context, we will have $\|x_1 - x_2\|_2 = 0$ or $x_1' x_2 / \|x_1\|_2 \|x_2\|_2 = 1$.

13.2.2 Dimension reduction through singular value decomposition

However, the raw vector representation obtained from the co-occurrence matrix still suffers from a dimensionality problem, as it has a size of W. We can then perform a *dimension reduction* step in order to obtain vectors of smaller size using the truncated singular value decomposition (SVD). This method aims to construct the best possible approximation of the initial vectors in a lower-dimensional space, by maximizing the amount of variation present in the initial data captured by this approximation (or equivalently: minimizing the noise from the initial data). From Section 2.2, we can set all but the p largest singular values of $\mathbf{F}$ to zero so as to obtain $\widehat{\mathbf{F}} = \sum_{j=1}^{p} s_j u_j v_j'$. Denote $\mathbf{U}$ the matrix of dimension $W \times p$ which j-th column is the vector u_j. We can then take the i-th row of the matrix $\mathbf{U}$ as the representation of the word w_i: $x_i = (\mathbf{U}_{i,1}, \ldots, \mathbf{U}_{i,p})$. This vector representation tends to exaggerate the closeness of words in the original representation $(\mathbf{F}_{i,1}, \ldots, \mathbf{F}_{i,W})$ by making similar words even more similar and dissimilar words more distinct.

This new representation obtained from the truncated SVD is what is called a *distributed representation* in computer science, as there is no longer a need for W dimensions to represent W words as in the one-hot encoding system. On the contrary, the W words are represented through their distribution on the p axes.

13.3 `word2vec` and self-supervised learning

13.3.1 Vector arithmetic

Before diving into how to build word embeddings using neural networks, let's take the output vectors of a popular language model, `fastText` (Mikolov et al., 2018), and illustrate the vector arithmetic obtained by these models. We will see that they lead to representations where word vectors are arranged based on their respective relationships and where vector arithmetic carries meaning. One famous application of this property is the *parallelogram model* for analogical reasoning (Rumelhart and

Abrahamson, 1973). Analogical reasoning consists in answering the question: what is the equivalent, for *c*, of *b* for *a*? For example, what is the equivalent, for *child*, of *king* for *man*? And in general, in properly trained word vector models, the nearest neighbor of the vector $x_{king} + x_{child} - x_{man}$ is x_{prince}, which is the correct answer.

Table 13.1 displays the results from a simple nearest-neighbor search of the closest capital among a pre-defined list for a few countries using cosine similarity. The model is able to find the correct answer. Figure 13.1 illustrates a two-dimensional

Table 13.1 Finding capitals for a given country.

France	Paris (.69)	Brussels (.52)
Spain	Madrid (.73)	Lisbon (.51)
Germany	Berlin (.70)	Vienna (.56)
Italy	Rome (.66)	Vienna (.45)
Portugal	Lisbon (.73)	Madrid (.54)
Denmark	Copenhagen (.73)	Stockholm (.59)
Austria	Vienna (.72)	Berlin (.46)
Belgium	Brussels (.68)	Paris (.47)
Sweden	Stockholm (.75)	Copenhagen (.57)
China	Beijing (.77)	Moscow (.42)
Russia	Moscow (.76)	Beijing (.44)

Note: Closest and second closest neighbors of a given country within a set of capitals. Cosine similarity in parentheses. Model is `fastText` (Mikolov et al., 2018).

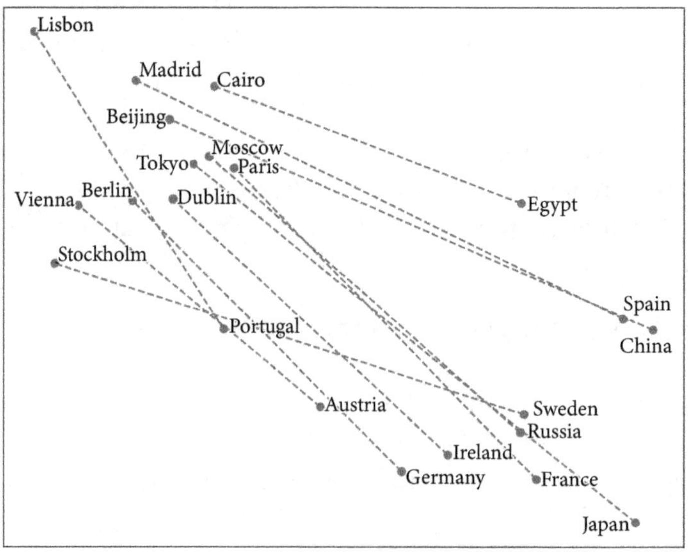

Figure 13.1 Two-dimensional vector representations of countries and their capitals.
Note: vectors derived from the `fastText` model in English Mikolov et al. (2018). Graph inspired by Mikolov et al. (2013).

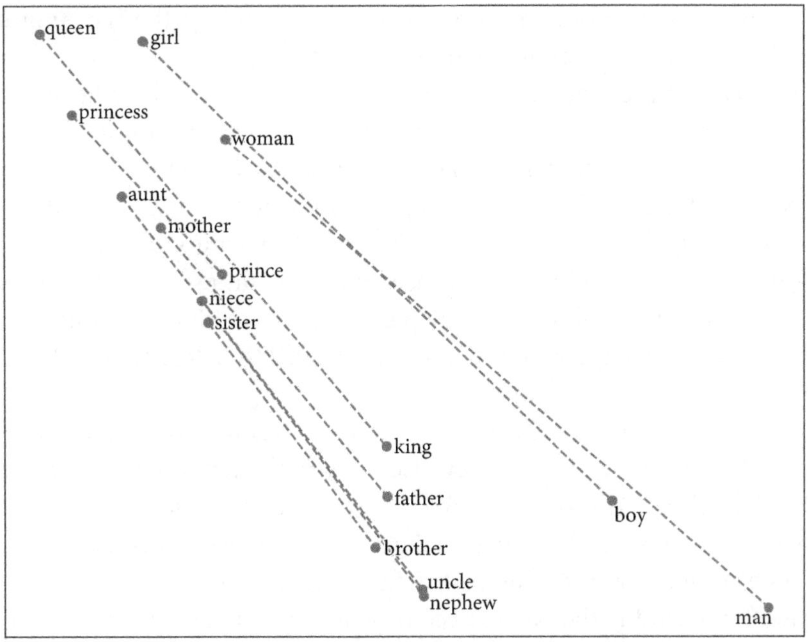

Figure 13.2 Vector representations of feminine and masculine word equivalents.
Note: vectors derived from the `fastText` model in English Mikolov et al. (2018), with dimension $p = 300$, and projected on the "masculine" and "feminine" vectors.

representation of vectors for some countries and their capitals, using pre-trained vectors from the `fastText` model for the English language.

First, it can be observed that the segments connecting the vector representation of a country to that of its capital tend to be parallel. One might imagine reconstructing the relationship between a country and its capital by taking the average of the difference between the vectors representing the country and its capital. It would then suffice to add this vector to that of a country and perform a nearest neighbor search in order to potentially find its capital. It can also be observed that the arrangement of the (country, capital) pairs in this space tends to partially reflect their geographical proximity. These two observations are even more remarkable considering that these vectors have been obtained without any form of supervision, that is, without the model having prior knowledge of the relationship between Paris and France.

Similarly, Figure 13.2 illustrates the relationship that exists, in this model, between a feminine word and its masculine equivalent.

13.3.2 Self-supervised learning

The three most popular word vector models are `word2vec` Mikolov et al. (2013), `GloVe` Pennington et al. (2014), and `fastText` Mikolov et al. (2018). The vector outputs of such models are able to represent words in a vector space of dimension

$p \ll W$, where the respective locations of words capture the meaning of their relationships as we have seen in the previous section.

Rather than compressing descriptive statistics as what was done through a truncated SVD of the co-occurence matrix, these specific word vector models allow for more sophisticated representations. They are trained using self-supervised learning (SSL). SSL tasks are auxiliary tasks specifically created to make a model learn its parameters, although the task in itself is not of primary importance. They convert an unsupervised problem into a supervised one by defining a specific loss. SSL is a more general concept than what we will present in this section and although we will also use SSL task in Chapter 14, the reader is referred to Balestriero et al. (2023) for an overview.

Two SSL tasks are used to learn word embeddings in the original `word2vec` article of Mikolov et al. (2013). They also require the definition of a context as a window of fixed size M around the word. Given a document with T tokens and a dictionary of length W, each word w_i in the dictionary is associated with two embeddings, both of dimension p. The first is the word vector x_i when it is the central word and the second is the context vector y_i when it is part of a context of a central word. The learning tasks aim to estimate both these vectors. The first learning strategy is called the *skip-gram* model and seeks to predict the context of a central word given its occurrence. The second learning strategy is called *continuous bag of words* (CBOW) and aims to predict the central word from its context. In both these strategies, the scalar product $y_i'x_j$ between two distinct word vectors plays a key role: the larger this value, the more likely it is that word i appears within the context of word j. Notice that the scalar product appears at the numerator of the cosine similarity.

13.3.3 Skip-gram

The objective is to learn the vector representations of words x_i that efficiently predict the words in a neighboring window using a maximum-likelihood approach (Section 2.4). Start from a sequence of T consecutive words and consider a sub-sequence of $2M + 1$ consecutive words:

$$w_{t-M}, \ldots, w_{t-1}, w_t, w_{t+1}, \ldots, w_{t+M},$$

where w_t is called the *central word* or *target word*. We aim to learn the word vectors $\{x_i\}_{i=1,\ldots,W}$ and the context vectors $\{y_i\}_{i=1,\ldots,W}$. To achieve this, we define a sequence of $2M + 1$ random variables, each taking a value in $\mathcal{W}$:

$$W_{t-M}, \ldots, W_{t-1}, W_t, W_{t+1}, \ldots, W_{t+M}.$$

Assume that the probability of observing the word w_{t+i} in the context of the target w_t is given by a softmax which allows to convert the scalar product $y_{t+i}'x_t$ encoding the similarity between two words into a probability:

$$\frac{\exp(y'_{t+i}x_t)}{\sum_{k=1}^{W}\exp\left(y'_k x_t\right)}.$$

To predict the whole context, assume that the joint probability is given by the product of the marginal probabilities, which arises from an implicit assumption of exchangeability between the context elements, $W_{t-M}, \ldots, W_{t-1}, W_{t+1}, \ldots, W_{t+M}$. The words order is not taken into account, which is a strong assumption that will be challenged in Chapter 14. Still, we can write the probability that the context is $w_{t-M}, \ldots, w_{t-1}, w_{t+1}, \ldots, w_{t+M}$ given the target word w_t as:

$$P(\{W_{t+i} = w_{t+i}\}_{-M\leq i\leq M, i\neq 0} \,|W_t = w_t) = \prod_{-M\leq i\leq M, j\neq 0} \frac{\exp(y'_{t+i}x_t)}{\sum_{k=1}^{W}\exp\left(y'_k x_t\right)}.$$

The log-likelihood computed over the entire sequence is therefore:

$$\frac{1}{T}\sum_{t=1}^{T}\sum_{-M\leq i\leq M, i\neq 0} y'_{t+i}x_t - \log\left(\sum_{k=1}^{W}\exp\left(y'_k x_t\right)\right), \tag{13.1}$$

and is to be maximized over both the target and context vectors. This amounts to maximizing the probability that a given word, among all other words in the vocabulary, appears in the context of the target word. In a nutshell, the skip-gram model seeks to maximize the similarity of word representations that occur in the same context.

13.3.4 Continuous bag of words

The *continuous bag of words* (CBOW) is also a model that aims to learn representation of words and their context. However, this time the problem is inverted, as the task consists of predicting the target word based on its context, by averaging the vectors of the words appearing in a fixed-size adjacent window. More precisely, we define $\bar{u}_t := \frac{1}{2M}\sum_{-M\leq i\leq M, j\neq 0} y_{t+i}$ as the average context vector. We can then formulate the probability of observing the target word given the context as a softmax:

$$P(W_t = w_t|\left\{W_{t+i} = w_{t+i}\right\}_{-M\leq i\leq M, i\neq 0}) = \frac{\exp(x'_t\bar{u}_t)}{\sum_{k=1}^{W}\exp\left(x'_k\bar{u}_t\right)}.$$

This leads to the following log-likelihood for the entire sequence:

$$\frac{1}{T}\sum_{t=1}^{T} x'_t\bar{u}_t - \log\left(\sum_{k=1}^{W}\exp\left(x'_k\bar{u}_t\right)\right). \tag{13.2}$$

We note that this representation also implies an assumption of word exchangeability, as the simple average does not take into account the order of word occurrence.

13.3.5 Computational considerations

These two models can be interpreted from the perspective of neural networks (Section 2.8), since each word corresponds to two layers of embeddings depending on whether the word is central or appears in the context, followed by simple operations (average, dot product, softmax, etc.) leading to the loss function. Therefore, it is possible to optimize it via stochastic gradient descent. However, it is worth noting that the denominator at each probability level is a sum over the size of the vocabulary, W. For example, in Equation (13.2), we have $\sum_{k=1}^{W} \exp\left(x_k' \bar{u}_t\right)$. This makes it a very expensive object to compute – not to mention its gradient – considering that a vocabulary generally consists of around 10^5 to 10^7 terms.

A first idea is to remove certain words from the vocabulary based on their frequency of occurrence, thus performing undersampling. Indeed, words such as articles (*the*, *a*, etc.) or prepositions (*in*, *where*, *about* etc.) do not carry very important informational content. Moreover, they appear in the context of almost every word. It is known that the frequency of word usage follows a power law, more precisely the Zipf's law, $\mathbb{P}(x) = x^{-(1+1/s)}$ where $s > 0$ and x is the frequency. Mikolov et al. (2013) therefore suggest removing certain words during the training phase, with the following probability for each word $\max(0, 1 - \sqrt{\delta/\text{freq}(w)})$, with $\delta \in [10^{-5}, 10^{-3}]$. This allows for significant undersampling of words with a frequency greater than δ.

One can also perform what is called *negative sampling* to reduce the computation time of the denominator. This strategy, although based on the *skip-gram* model, takes a different view of the problem to arrive at a simpler objective function. Instead of computing the probability over all possibilities, the problem is recasted as a classification problem by seeking to discriminate pairs (x, y) consisting of a target word and a context word. The idea is that for each pair observed in the training set, we draw a number B of pairs that never appear in the data. Let D be the binary random variable taking the value 1 if the pair (x, y) appears in the training data, and 0 otherwise. We seek to optimize the value of the vectors in order to maximize the probability $P[D = 1]$ for the pairs appearing in the training data, and to minimize it for the others (i.e., seek to maximize $P[D = 0]$ for the other B pairs). Assuming the following sigmoid form:

$$P[D = 1] = \frac{\exp(x'y)}{1 + \exp(x'y)}.$$

We then get, for each sequence of length T, the following objective function that we would like to maximize:

$$\frac{1}{T} \prod_{t=1}^{T} \left[\frac{\exp(y_0' x_t)}{1 + \exp(y_0' x_t)} \prod_{b=1}^{B} \frac{1}{1 + \exp(y_b' x_t)} \right],$$

where y_0 is a word appearing in the context of x_t, and $(y_b)_{b=1,\ldots,B}$ are randomly drawn words that do not appear in its context. To specify this function in the same format as before, by taking the log, we seek to minimize the negative log-likelihood:

$$\frac{1}{T}\sum_{t=1}^{T}\left[\log\left(1+\exp(-y_0'x_t)\right)+\sum_{b=1}^{B}\log\left(1+\exp(y_b'x_t)\right)\right].$$

We can then observe that this objective function is much simpler to compute, compared to the function in Equation (13.1), as there is no longer a need to compute a sum of W terms in the denominator. It should be noted that the same trick can be used for the model (13.2), simply by replacing y with $\bar{u}$. It is recommended to choose a value of B between 5 and 20 for a small dataset, while a value between 2 and 5 may be sufficient for a very rich dataset. Which distribution should be chosen for the random drawing of context words in order to create "fake" word pairs? Mikolov et al. (2013) propose sampling words with a probability proportional to their empirical frequency of appearance in the training corpus, raised to the power of 3/4. This power allows to enhance the frequency of very infrequent terms without excessively altering the frequency of very frequent terms.

Finally, note that we can make the simplifying assumption that $y_i = x_i$ for all $i \in \mathcal{W}$, which reduces the number of parameters to be estimated by half.

13.3.6 Choice of hyperparameters

Learning word embeddings requires making several prior choices, most notably the dimension of the latent space p and the size of the context window M.

Regarding the window size M, a larger window leads to training the model on more examples and may result in increased accuracy, but at the cost of longer training time. The same goes for the dimension p of the embedding space: the larger it is, the more likely it is to capture subtle relationships, but training time also increases. Generally, the value of p is chosen to be sufficiently small for dimensionality reduction to be significant, but still large enough as to capture subtitle relationships between words. There is a middle ground to be determined depending on the application. Most downloadable vectors found online have dimensions proportional to a hundred.

Rodriguez and Spirling (2022) explore these questions and suggest choosing a dimension p greater than 100 and a context window size greater than or equal to 5, while acknowledging that beyond $p > 300$ and $M > 6$, the improvement is only marginal. Moreover, the authors provide avenues for evaluating the performance of these models, such as using the embeddings derived from the model for a supervised task. Antoniak and Mimno (2018), on the other hand, show that, especially for moderate-sized corpora, cosine similarity between embeddings is not always stable across models. They suggest adopting a "bootstrap" approach where the documents in the corpus are sampled with replacement to train a model, and then the models trained on each sample are averaged to form a final model.

Another question is also whether to start the learning from scratch to obtain word embeddings that are very corpus-specific, or to fine-tuned pre-existing vectors to make them seem more adapted to a new corpus. We explore the pros and cons of each option in Chapter 14. Finally, like any neural network, one must also choose the learning rate, batch size, etc. We further develop these practical aspects in Section 2.8.

13.3.7 Empirical applications

Kozlowski et al. (2019) construct a lexical embedding model to describe the gender and social class dimensions of certain symbols or cultural activities. Using representations in a low-dimensional space constructed from books published in the United States between 1900 and 1999, they perform a longitudinal analysis of the co-evolution of gender and class associations in the United States during the twentieth century. Here, the gender representation is constructed as the average of the differences between the embeddings of the pairs (man, woman), (men, women), (he, she), (him, her), (male, female), (boy, girl), etc. Similarly, the class representation is constructed by calculating the average of the differences between the embeddings of the word pairs (rich, poor), (affluence, poverty), (expensive, inexpensive), (luxury, cheap), etc. The authors can then project the lexical embedding corresponding to a particular activity onto these two axes (gender and social class) and see how this activity is positioned in this language representation. Based on the figures presented in Kozlowski et al. (2019), it can be observed that softball and volleyball are very feminine activities, in contrast to baseball and boxing. In between, football (soccer) appears to be relatively neutral. The remarkable aspect of these results is that, once again, the model is learned completely unsupervised: the captured phenomena are solely based on published works.

To measure the sexist bias of American judges, Ash et al. (2021) construct lexical embeddings for each judge based on their opinions, and compute the cosine similarity between the vector representing the gender dimension and the vector representing the "career vs. family" dimension. They show that judges with a higher cosine similarity between these two vectors, indicating language that reflects a closer alignment with traditional male and female roles, also make decisions against women more regularly and show less consideration for their female colleagues. Similarly, Gennaro and Ash (2021) define embeddings for the emotional and rational dimensions of language based on averaging word lists associated with these concepts, and then estimate a propensity for emotional or rational appeals in political speeches to study their prevalence over time and with different speakers.

From `fastText` vectors it is possible to compute a gender axis and a social class axis, based on the words in Table 13.2. Words representing a specific activity or object are projected onto these two axes, as shown in Figure 13.3. Can you guess what each of the two axes represents? Overall the intuition seems respected.

Table 13.2 Words used to define the axes

Gender	Social class
man – woman	rich – poor
men – women	wealth – poverty
boy – girl	luxury – deprivation
boys – girls	expensive – cheap
he – she	abundance – need
him – her	opulence – destitution
masculine – feminine	prosperity – misery
male – female	profusion – lack
sister – brother	

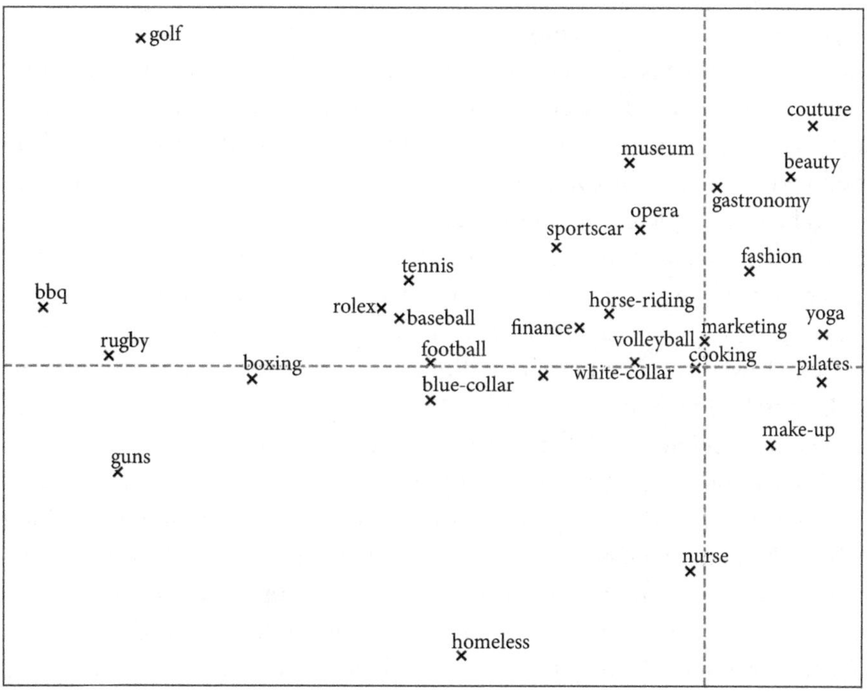

Figure 13.3 Projections of some terms along the gender and social class axes.

Note: Vectors from the `fastText` model in English (Mikolov et al., 2018) with dimension p = 300 are projected onto axes defined by the words in Table 13.2.

13.4 Classification using text embeddings

13.4.1 Potential applications

Classification tasks using textual data are ubiquitous. They may be of interest in their own right, but in the context of economic studies, they often constitute a preliminary data processing task, aiming to summarize information or classify documents, generally with the idea of creating new variables to be added to a regression model. The concepts seen previously such as lexical embeddings, in combination with the power of neural networks, offer a very effective tool for addressing this type of problem. It is generally easier to think of classification problems in this context, although this section also applies to "regression" problems (predicting a value rather than a category).

One standard classification task with textual data is known as *sentiment analysis*. Its aim is to classify a document as reflecting a positive or negative sentiment. A simple example is the categorization of a tweet as reflecting a positive or negative opinion on the stock price of a company, in order to automatically take a position in the market based on the overall sentiment expressed by users of this social network (e.g., Sul et al., 2016).

One may also want to use subjective measures of the quality of a good or a service in order to model demand by consumers. Indeed, traditionally in demand equations, it is known that price is an endogenous variable, particularly because certain characteristics such as brand image or "vibe" are difficult to objectively measure (see Chapter 6). Estimating these equations using OLS on tabular data suffers from an omitted variable bias. However, a certain amount of unstructured data such as text (e.g., product descriptions, user comments) or images contain important information taken into account in the consumer's purchasing decision. Imagine that we want to measure the factors influencing demand for restaurants. We can of course include objective factors such as location, average price, or the number of items on the menu. However, it is much more difficult to measure the quality of the dishes, the politeness of the staff, or the originality of the decor. If, on the other hand, we have customer reviews available on the internet, it is possible to use them to train a model reflecting the sentiment of a comment by classifying it as "neutral," "positive," or "negative," and then aggregate the sentiment of the comments at the level of each establishment. Generally, two scenarios arise: either the textual reviews are accompanied by a rating (in the form of stars, for example), in which case the data set is labeled, or this is not the case, and the examples generally need to be manually annotated to produce the necessary training data for the model. For example, Bana (2022) trains a language model to predict the salary associated with a job offer from its textual description. Note that for fairly standard tasks such as sentiment analysis, pre-trained and performant tools are readily available, especially via the Hugging-Face hub (huggingface.co/blog/sentiment-analysis-python). They generally do not require, or require very few, labeled examples to function well.

Another example is automatic coding, which aims to classify items into categories. It can be interesting to infer an individual's profession or socio-professional category from their declared occupation, code a firm's activity within a specific classification, or classify a product purchased in a supermarket according to a consumption function classification such as the Classification of Individual Consumption by Purpose (COICOP), used for the calculation of the consumer price index by Eurostat.

Conceptually, the task is clear: for each observation described by a string of characters, it is a matter of assigning it to one of the predefined categories. For this type of problem, we assume the existence of a fixed number of categories in the target classification, with this number generally ranging from two to several hundreds. We will see a simple architecture to address this problem, while Chapter 14 gives the tools to pursue a more complex approach.

13.4.2 Bag-of-word architecture

Suppose that we observe a string of arbitrary length s describing an observation (e.g., a profession, a product, a company, a newspaper article) that we want to classify into $K \geq 2$ classes. The classification task consists of constructing a function $s \mapsto \mu^{classif}(s)$ that takes a string s as input and outputs either an integer $k \in \{1, \ldots, K\}$ designating one of the categories in the classification, or a K-dimensional vector giving the probability of belonging to each of the K categories. Note that if we estimate the probability of belonging to each of the K categories, it is easy to derive a classifier by simply taking the category associated with the highest probability (the *argmax*). The following paragraphs describe a very simple procedure for constructing such a function, similar to the one used by the supervised module in `fastText` (Bojanowski et al., 2016). The next section will provide elements to make this function more complex, potentially increasing its ability to capture fine relationships in the data and capture the polysemy of certain words.

The first step is to transform the string s into appropriate numerical features, that is, to apply the steps described in Section 12.2.1. Particularly for automatic coding tasks where short string sequences are available, one may want to consider not only word n-grams as tokens but also character n-grams. Indeed, this allows the algorithm to be robust to typing or spelling mistakes, as two string sequences that only differ by a few characters will share a high proportion of their character n-grams. This may also be useful for capturing similarities between a term and its abbreviation. At the end of this step, the string s is generally transformed into a list of indices, which, for each token present in the string, gives the corresponding index in a token dictionary. Suppose, for example, that the string s contains T tokens; we then obtain a list $[w_1, \ldots, w_T]$. Note that different strings of characters will generally result in lists of different lengths. For this tokenization step, there also exists data-driven tokenizers, as we will describe in Chapter 14.

The second step is to transform each index in this list into an arbitrary dimensional lexical embedding p representing the tokens it refers to. Let $[x_1, \ldots, x_T]$ be the list of embeddings corresponding to each token in the string. A simple solution to represent the embedding of the complete string of characters is to aggregate the embeddings of each token by taking their average:

$$X := \frac{1}{T}\sum_{t=1}^{T} x_t.$$

However, one can also consider more complex aggregation systems, using weights that could be learned. For example, Arora et al. (2017) suggest taking a weighted average of the embeddings of the tokens contained in a sentence (where the word frequency appears in the denominator), then subtracting the projection of this average onto the first eigenspace of the matrix whose columns are these averages for the sentences in the training set. This amounts to subtracting the first mode (the first principal component), which can be interpreted as the syntax of the language and is common to all the textual sequences.

How to choose the embeddings to represent each token? Usually, two strategies, which are not mutually exclusive, are distinguished: either pre-trained embeddings available on the web can be used, through language models such as GloVe (Pennington et al., 2014) or fastText (Bojanowski et al., 2016), or randomly initialized vectors can be used and treated as trainable parameters. Note that when pre-trained vectors are used, one can choose to make them "trainable" during the learning phase in order to make their representations better adapted to the final classification task. Thus, at the end of this step, a string is represented by a set of p abstract explanatory variables X that will be used to predict the category to which the string belongs.

Finally, the goal is to go from the representation X to a probability vector. For this purpose, the most straightforward strategy is to pass through a softmax output layer, such that the probability of belonging to category k is given by:

$$\frac{\exp(X'\beta_k)}{\sum_{j=1}^{K} \exp(X'\beta_j)}.$$

This way, the probabilities sum to one. This output layer is natural for problems in which an observation is associated with only one of the categories. In other tasks, one may want to associate multiple categories to a given observation, a practice known as *multiple tagging*. In this case, we prefer an output layer of the one-vs-all type, giving the probability of belonging to category k as follows:

$$\frac{\exp(X'\beta_k)}{1 + \exp(X'\beta_k)}.$$

In this case, we consider that the item is in each of the categories for which the membership probability exceeds 50%, or any other threshold determined empirically in order to optimize the trade-off between precision and recall.

In a nutshell, the function $\mu^{classif}(.)$ depends on two types of parameters that we will seek to learn by optimizing the prediction: the lexical embeddings of arbitrary dimension p, $x_1, \ldots, x_W$ where W is the size of the token vocabulary, on the one hand, and the parameters that weight the features for classification $\beta_1, \ldots, \beta_K$ on the other hand.

Once the input-output relationship is established, an appropriate loss function needs to be chosen to guide the learning process. Suppose we have the true label $D \in \{1, \ldots, K\}$ and it is unique. For a standard classification problem, the natural loss is the cross-entropy, which corresponds to the negative log-likelihood. Thus, for an individual observation, i.e., for a character string s and a label D, or rather for a pair (X, D) where X is the lexical embedding corresponding to s, the loss function to minimize is given by:

$$\log\left(\sum_{k=1}^{K} \exp\left(X'\beta_k\right)\right) - \sum_{k=1}^{K} \mathbf{1}\{D = k\}X'\beta_k.$$

Then, the tools seen in Chapter 2 can be used to train the network.

13.4.3 Other applications

In general, the applications of word embeddings derived from models such as `word2vec` are too vast to be covered exhaustively. However, we can mention a few potential applications:

- Concept detection via automatic lexical field search: when we want to detect the mention of a concept in a document (e.g., inflation in a central banker's speech, computer skills in a CV), a simple way to proceed is to search for words belonging to a pre-determined list. However, this technique suffers from low recall because it can only detect documents mentioning exactly these terms. It may be interesting to enrich this "source" list of words with words drawn from their closest neighbors defined according to the `word2vec` embeddings and a given distance. Thus, Gennaro and Ash (2021) use this technique to refine the lists of terms that materialize the concepts of "emotion" and "rationality" in political speeches.
- Document representation and clustering: a simple way to represent a document is to take the average of the embeddings of the tokens that compose it. It is then possible to look for "clusters" in order to group similar documents. For example, Demszky et al. (2019) apply this approach to millions of tweets associated with mass shootings in the United States to analyze how these events are perceived by individuals based on their position on the political spectrum. This strategy is an alternative to latent topic modeling, discussed in Section 12.4.
- More generally, these vector models outperform previous vector representations for most supervised tasks (e.g., named entity recognition, sentiment analysis) and allow, for example, the automatic identification of "narratives,"

which are coherent interpretations of series of events or facts, by revealing a logical structure between each element that composes them (e.g., Ash et al., 2021).

13.5 Going further: representation of unstructured data

The fundamental idea behind embeddings is to assume that an object can be represented by its context (i.e., a set of other objects observed at the same time and related to the target object). This involves modeling an observation conditionally on neighboring observations by vectors in a space, where mathematical operations encode proximity relationships. This concept is applied not only in natural language processing but also in processing unstructured data like images. This section explores the potential applications of embeddings in empirical economics through examples. Rudolph et al. (2016) develop a general approach to define embeddings for a wide variety of types of data.

13.5.1 Encoding textual or visual information

Traditionally, when studying consumer behavior, economists only had access to tabular data about a product, such as its price, brand, color, dimensions, and a few other relevant characteristics. Such data is sufficient to capture differences between fairly homogeneous products, such as tulips or laundry detergent. However, a number of characteristics of consumer goods are not objectively measurable, such as the design or the quality of finishes, making these structured data insufficient to fully characterize certain heterogeneous products like automobiles, handbags, or watches. However, these characteristics are relevant to consumer preferences and the cost function of the producing firm, and thus necessary for studying demand. Traditionally, instrumental variable strategies were implemented. For instance, the model proposed by Berry et al. (1995) cleverly uses the unobserved random variable ζ_j that is correlated with price to capture unobservable factors of the product in Equation (6.13).

Nevertheless, modern techniques in language processing and computer vision make it possible to capture more of this information that is observable to the consumer but not easily to the economist. Thus, Bajari et al. (2021) use both a language model and a vision model to encode certain unstructured data from the product's presentation on Amazon.com, such as the image, title, or product description. These models are trained on classical tasks in computer-assisted vision (e.g., image categorization) and natural language processing (e.g., word prediction). Once these models are trained, the penultimate layer of the neural network is isolated to allow for the encoding of textual or visual information in a way that makes it usable in standard econometric models. The authors choose to encode this information into a vector of dimension 5120. It is worth noting that this approach is similar to the strategy implemented in siamese networks that will be discussed in Section 14.4.

13.5.2 Embeddings for consumer goods

In a very ingenious paper, Ruiz et al. (2020) apply the concept of embedding not to texts or images as is typically done in machine learning, but directly to consumer goods, by modeling consumers' preferences for baskets of goods when they go shopping at the supermarket. Here, the structure of the latent space reflects the co-purchase relationships between goods and allows for the definition of economic properties such as substitutability and complementarity. More directly, the authors model, for a consumer, the conditional probability of buying item W_{t+1}, given that they already have items $W_1, \ldots, W_t$ in their basket. In this definition, a dummy item for the "checkout" is also used, which represents the end of the shopping session and the checkout process, and is necessarily placed last in the basket of goods. In this case, the parameter of interest is the moderate-dimensional embedding x that represents an item available in the supermarket.

For a user represented by preferences θ, who already has the t goods represented by embeddings $x_1, \ldots, x_t$ in their basket, the probability of them buying the $t+1$-th good is given by a soft-max function computed over all goods not yet added to the basket:

$$P(W_{t+1} = w_{t+1} | \{W_i = w_i\}_{i=1,,\ldots,t}) = \frac{\exp\left(\theta' x_{t+1} + y'_{t+1} \frac{1}{t} \sum_{i=1}^{t} x_i\right)}{\sum_{c>t} \exp\left(\theta' x_c + y'_c \frac{1}{t} \sum_{i=1}^{t} x_i\right)},$$

with y_{t+1} an embedding defining the effect of interaction with items already purchased, similar to the context vectors in the skip-gram (13.1) and CBOW (13.2) models. The term $\theta' x_c + y'_c \frac{1}{t} \sum_{i=1}^{t} x_i$ can be interpreted as the utility of product c given that products $1, \ldots, t$ are in the consumer's basket. This formulation is compatible with the framework of utility maximization, as the product that provides the greatest utility is the one with the highest probability of being in the consumer's basket in the next step.

When the terms $y'_i x_j$ and $y'_j x_i$ are positive, it means that the presence of item i (e.g., slices of ham) in the basket increases the probability of item j (e.g., a baguette) being purchased in the next step, and vice versa, indicating that they are *complementary*. Hence a measure of complementarity between i and j is given by the formula:

$$\frac{y'_i x_j + y'_j x_i}{2}.$$

Measuring the *substitutability* between two products is difficult because the large number of available goods in a store means that most pairs of items are never found together in a consumer's basket. The authors therefore define the concept of *exchangeability*, which allows for measuring the degree of similarity in the interaction between two items and the rest of the products. They assume that when two products are exchangeable without being complementary, they are substitutes (e.g., buying slices of ham, regardless of the brand, should have the same impact on the probability of buying a baguette, but should not increase the probability of buying slices of ham of another brand).

The model developed by Ruiz et al. (2020) is actually more complex and allows for the fact that we do not observe the order in which goods are being placed in the basket. The source code, directly optimized to run on a GPU, is available online at github.com/franrruiz/shopper-src and includes some simulated data. Kumar et al. (2020) propose a conceptually similar approach but using different tools. The main point to remember is that embeddings can find relevant applications for exploring typically economic questions.

13.6 Summary

Key concepts

Word embedding, one-hot representation, co-occurrence matrix, (truncated) singular value decomposition (SVD), word2vec, skip-gram, continuous bag of words (CBOW), negative sampling, embeddings for unstructured data.

Additional references

Chapter 6 of Jurafsky and Martin (2019) deals with word embeddings.

Code and data

Pre-trained word vectors are available online for GloVe (nlp.stanford.edu/projects/glove) and fastText (fasttext.cc).

Questions

1. Compute the cosine similarity for two distinct words represented in one-hot encoding.

2. Why is one-hot encoding not able to capture the semantic proximity between words?
3. What is a word embedding? How can it be used in the context of text data classification?
4. Propose a simple alternative to one-hot encoding to efficiently represent words.
5. What is a co-occurrence matrix and how can it be used to represent words?
6. How is the continuous bag-of-words (CBOW) language model different from the skip-gram model?
7. What are the advantages and limitations of skip-gram and CBOW language models?
8. For a properly trained word embedding model, in your opinion, what should be the nearest neighbor to the resulting vector from the operation $x_{cow} - x_{female} + x_{\text{male}}$?
9. How can the use of subjective quality measures help model consumer demand? Propose two possible approaches for modeling prices based on comments left on products.
10. How could the bag-of-words approach be marginally modified to take into account the word order in a string? What is its limitation?

Chapter 14
Modern language models

Modern language models are artificial intelligence systems designed to process textual data. For the purpose of this chapter, we will define them as pre-trained deep neural networks that make use of special layers known as *transformer blocks* in order to model the structure of the language. These models share two characteristics: they are very large and they are trained on an enormous amount of data. Indeed, they contain anywhere from a few tens of millions of parameters to a few hundreds of billions for the larger ones (the so-called *large language models*, LLMs). Additionally, they are typically trained on vast amounts of data collected from the internet to perform a simple task such as predicting the next word in a sequence of text. This simple task transfers very well to more specific NLP tasks. Contrary to what we have seen in previous chapters, these models take the actual context of a sentence into account, making them very flexible and powerful.

These models gained significant attention and traction after the famous "Attention is all you need" paper by Vaswani et al. (2017). One of the most notable milestones in the development of modern language models is the introduction of architectures like the OpenAI's Generative Pre-trained Transformer (GPT) series, starting with `GPT-1` (Radford et al., 2018) These models demonstrated unprecedented capabilities in natural language understanding and generation by leveraging transformer architectures and large-scale pre-training on massive text corpora.

The architecture of these models relies on and expands the concept of embeddings seen in Chapter 13. However, because these models stem from a computer science literature that directly models the language in a realistic fashion, they are general-purpose and rely less the tailor-made processing of text that we have seen in Chapter 12 (e.g., lemmatization, stemming) although some form of text normalization is always necessary. Instead, a first key ingredient is the *tokenizer* that cuts a sequence of text into chunks that will be fed to the model. The difference with the older NLP technology is that the way to cut the text sequences is learned directly from the data.

This chapter studies the two components of any such language model: the tokenizer, which converts a string into a sequence of integers (Section 14.1) and the neural network that processes such sequences (14.2). The third section discusses how to train and use these models (14.3). Because it is the workhorse model for many applications and larger models are mostly a scale-up from it, `BERT` (Devlin et al., 2019) is presented in detail. Finally, Section 14.4 illustrates how these models

Machine Learning for Econometrics. Christophe Gaillac and Jérémy L'Hour, Oxford University Press.
 DOI: 10.1093/9780198918868.003.0014

can be leveraged to learn text embeddings with another self-supervised technique, known as *distance learning*.

14.1 Tokenizers

A *tokenizer* is an algorithm that transforms a piece of text into a sequence of integers, so it can be used as input in a language model, or more generally in any computerized statistical model. In this context, *encoding* refers to the process of going from text to integers, and *decoding* to the reverse process that goes from a sequence of integers to the original text. This process can be seen as a special type of data compression. As is the case for any such algorithm, it can be *lossless* when encoding and then decoding a piece of text outputs the same exact piece of text, or *lossy* if this is not the case.

Chapters 12 and 13 relied on defining tokens as words (i.e., strings separated by white spaces), with three possible extra ingredients: (i) adding word *n*-grams, (ii) adding character *n*-grams that span words, and (iii) pruning the vocabulary by removing stop words, lemmatizing and stemming. This approach can be perfectly suited to certain NLP tasks, but is hand crafted and leaves room for better text compression, as will be illustrated in this section.

14.1.1 Character-level tokenization

The priority when defining a tokenizer is to choose the level at which the tokenization operates. The simplest tokenizer one can think of is a character-level tokenizer where each single character, including numbers, punctuation, and emojis, is mapped to an arbitrary integer. A piece of text is then converted by looking up the corresponding integer for each character. In Python, it can be easily coded as building a dictionary and a function that will look up the characters:

```
# Get the list of all the unique characters appearing in
  the training set.
# train_text is a string containing the corpus.
chars = sorted(list(set(train_text)))

# Define the encoder
ch2idx = {ch: i for i, ch in enumerate(chars)}
encode = lambda x: [ch2idx.get(i, 0) for i in x]

# Define the decoder
idx2ch = {i: ch for i, ch in enumerate(chars)}
decode = lambda x: ''.join([idx2ch[i] for i in x])
```

It's good to define an *out-of-vocabulary* token that get assigned when the algorithm stumble upon an unknown character – it is 0 in the above code. Notice that this tokenizer will be lossy if the text used to define the mapping that goes from character to integer does not contain all the possible characters. The likeliness of such a corner case depends on the application, but will happen in particular if the test data is not properly cleaned to use the same characters as the train data.

The character-level tokenizer presents the advantage that the resulting vocabulary will be very short. Moreover, if all possible characters are included, out-of-vocabulary errors cannot occur, making tokenization lossless. The tokenizer can adapt to never-seen-before words at test time. However, it does not compress the text, as a string will have the same length whether it is tokenized or not. This results in longer training and inference times, particularly affecting transformer models (see Section 14.2 below), as longer input sequences increase the context size and the number of operations required. Intuitively, this is because self-attention complexity increases with the squared sequence length since a similarity measure has to be computed for each possible couple of elements in the sequence, through the inner product of some embeddings.

14.1.2 Word-level tokenization

At the other end of the spectrum, we can define tokens at the word level. It makes sense from a human point of view: we assemble words to produce meaningful sentences. For that, we could adapt the previous code and simply break the text on white spaces. In Python:

```
# Get the list of all the unique words appearing in the training set.
words = sorted(list(set(train_text.split())))

# Define the encoder
w2idx = {w: i for i, w in enumerate(words)}
encode = lambda x: [w2idx.get(i, 0) for i in x.split()]

# Define the decoder by analogy from previous code box,
# using 'words' instead of 'chars'.
```

However, it is wasteful to represent *dog* and *dogs* by two different tokens. It means that the vocabulary would have to contain the plural form of every possible word. Instead, a better encoding of *dogs* would leverage the token *dog* and the token *-s* to signify a plural form. Similarly, it would make sense to have *ice cream* in addition to *ice* and *cream* in the vocabulary, since this represents a frequently used concept. As a consequence, one would like tokens to contain a combination of words, n-grams of words, and n-grams of characters.

That being said, word-level tokenization can still be relevant depending on the application and doesn't have to rely on a simple rule like white-space splitting. Indeed, a tokenizer can be defined *ex-ante*, using a known lexicon. For example, Loughran and McDonald (2011) established a lexicon of positively and negatively connoted words with the purpose of analyzing the sentiment of financial documents. In a very narrow sense, this lexicon defines a tokenizer, albeit very lossy.

It also risks missing important synonyms not included in the vocabulary. But it may be enough if the application has a very specific set of words that capture the object of study. These so-called *vocabulary methods* can either depend on a given lexicon, or require to define an application-specific one, in a data-driven fashion. Moreover, modern algorithms can still use simple rules like white-space splitting in a preprocessing step called *pre-tokenization.*

14.1.3 Sub-word tokenization

Fortunately, modern tokenizers operate at the sub-word level and are *trained* rather than defined *ex-ante.* During this training process, the vocabulary of tokens is created. For sophisticated algorithms, automatic merging rules are implemented, where a longer token might represent part of a sequence of text instead of using two shorter tokens. This is particularly useful when the goal of the tokenizer is to efficiently represent and process language data.

There are currently three popular algorithms for training a tokenizer: byte-pair encoding (BPE), WordPiece, and Unigram. Their definitions and implementation details can be found in the HuggingFace course online (HuggingFace, 2022).

To illustrate how they operate, let's explain how the BPE algorithm works. First proposed by Gage (1994), BPE has been modified by Sennrich et al. (2016) to operate at the character level. It requires the specification of a single hyperparameter: the vocabulary size. The vocabulary is initialized by including all single characters. Strings are represented by sequences of characters, exactly like in Section 14.1.1. At this initial point, a token is exactly one character. Then, the most frequent pair of tokens is merged into a new token that results from the concatenation of these two tokens. The new token is added to the vocabulary. This step is iterated for as long as the vocabulary contains fewer elements than specified beforehand. The algorithm quickly merges common character sequences like *t*, *h*, and *e* to form *the*, aiming to recover common words while avoiding their plural forms or typos. BPE tokenization is used for example in `roberta` (Liu et al., 2019) and `GPT-2` (Radford et al., 2019).

The WordPiece algorithm (Schuster and Nakajima, 2012; Song et al., 2021) operates similarly to BPE. However, it doesn't merge pairs solely based on frequency; instead, it considers the frequency of the pair divided by the product of the frequencies of each pair constituent. WordPiece tokenization is used for the training of `BERT` (Devlin et al., 2019).

The Unigram algorithm (Kudo, 2018) works in the opposite direction by starting with a vocabulary containing all the possible sub-word units and iteratively removing the token pairs that have the least probability of occurring in a Unigram model. For more on the history of the concept of *token*, the reader is referred to Mielke et al. (2021).

14.1.4 Practical considerations when training a tokenizer

In modern tokenizers, since the vocabulary is defined in a completely data-driven fashion, the key parameter to choose is its size. First of all, a multiple of 64 is advised for optimizing training and inference performance. As stated by Andrej Karpathy in a celebrated tweet regarding a simplified version of `GPT`: "*The most dramatic optimization to nanoGPT so far (≈25% speedup) is to simply increase vocab size from 50257 to 50304 (nearest multiple of 64). This calculates added useless dimensions but goes down a different kernel path with much higher occupancy.*"

As far as choosing the right multiple of 64, this is an empirical exercise: too large and useless tokens will be added, too small and there are some opportunities for more efficient compression that is lost. Indeed, the trade-off here is always between memory and compression, since a larger vocabulary will allow to compress the text more and to obtain shorter tokenized sequences, but at the price of increasing the number of parameters in the language model and hence the memory requirement when loading it. A good exercise is to look at the last added tokens during the training process: if they look like very uncommon terms, compound words, words with typos, plural forms etc. it might be a sign that the vocabulary size is too large. Training a tokenizer is fairly quick, so one can proceed by trial and error.

Besides this important parameter, training a custom tokenizer can reveal itself a thorny endeavor. First of all: the role of spaces. Indeed, assuming we want to achieve lossless compression, one has to decide how to encode spaces, and it would not make sense to encode each space by itself since this would be by far the most frequently used token is the text. This will create two issues. First, the encoded sequence will be approximately twice as long. Second, because language models ultimately perform a complex classification task, encoding spaces as single tokens will create a large imbalance in probabilities that will bias the language modeling problem: assuming a word contains on average 1.5 tokens, if the classifier always guesses a space, it will be correct roughly 40% of the times. In tokenizers like the one used by `GPT-2` (Radford et al., 2019), the choice is made to encode the word with its preceding space if there is one. For words at the beginning of a sentence, there is no space before, meaning some token can exist in two versions in the vocabulary: with and without a preceding space. Then there are a few other choices that can make a difference: should the tokenizer break down numbers to encode each digit separately as is done for `StarCoder` (Li et al., 2023), a software development assistant, and `BloombergGPT` (Wu et al., 2023), a large language model developed for finance? Should some tokens like entities (e.g., companies, individual names) be masked?

Finally, before tokenizing the text, a light cleaning step is highly recommended, as we have mentioned in Section 12.2.1. This process takes the form of a pipeline combining several steps such as removing extra white spaces, Unicode normalization, lower casing, removing accents, etc.

14.2 Building BERT

This section introduces the transformer architecture in a formal way, with the goal of explaining the intuition behind it and underlining the important hyperparameters. One of the most well-known variants of language models using the transformer architecture of Vaswani et al. (2017) is BERT (Devlin et al., 2019). Although it has been surpassed by larger and better models, this is still a useful baseline to study and consider in practice, especially since it is at a scale where one can train it from scratch for under $100 (Izsak et al., 2021; Portes et al., 2023).

14.2.1 Context matters

The issue with embeddings produced by models such as word2vec (Section 13.3) is that they do not change based on the context of a sentence. There is a simple one-to-one mapping between a dictionary of tokens and a set of numerical vectors. While this may be sufficient for many simple applications, language does not operate in such a straightforward manner. Words are polysemous, and their meaning changes depending on the context. For example, the word *mouse* can either mean a small animal that is covered in fur and has a long thin tail, or a small device that is moved by hand across a surface to control the movement of the cursor on a computer screen. Representing it with one single vector, devoid of any context, cannot do it justice. Pronouns are place-holder words referring to different entities based on the reality that the text is describing: *he*, *she* or *it* need to be defined within context. For example, in the sentence "the cat ran after the mouse as it escaped," it is obvious that "it" refers to the mouse. Ideally, we would like to have a contextual representation of "it" that is close to the representation of "mouse" since it designates the same entity. This representation of "it" should also be different from the one in this sentence: "the ECB is ready to do whatever it takes to preserve the euro. And believe me, it will be enough."

Fortunately, modern language models are very good at in-context representation, thanks to the self-attention mechanism.

14.2.2 Self-attention

The idea of self-attention (Vaswani et al., 2017) is to build a contextual representation of a token by computing a convex combination of its context, with weights depending on how much tokens interact with each other. We will be careful in keeping track of the dimensions of all the objects, as they are key to understand how all the pieces work together.

Consider a sequence of T tokens: $w_1, \ldots, w_T$, each associated with their initial embeddings of dimension h: $x_1, \ldots, x_T$. We call "context" the whole sequence of tokens. Starting from the output of the self-attention layer, we will transform x_t into an in-context representation for token w_t which is a convex combination of the *value embeddings* of the other tokens:

$$\sum_{s=1}^{T} \alpha_{t,s} v_s,$$

where $\alpha_{t,s}$ (the *attention score*) is a positive number that quantifies how much token w_t interacts with the token w_s, and v_s is a vector of dimension p that represents the so-called *value* of token w_s. Notice that unlike the `word2vec` model described in the previous chapter, each element of the context is weighted by a coefficient vector that depends on the element t – in the `word2vec` models, each element of the context had the same weight. In other words, the attention given to each element of the context is not constant. Now let's see how these quantities are computed.

In the self-attention layer, each token w_t is represented by three distinct embeddings of dimension p stemming from a linear transformation of the initial embedding x_t: the query, the key, and the value. The first embedding is called the query and is defined as $q_t := M_Q x_t$ for a $p \times h$ matrix M_Q – it represents the token when it is looking to interact with its context. The second embedding is called the key and is defined as $k_t := M_k x_t$ for a $p \times h$ matrix M_K – it represents the token as part of the context. The inner product $q_t' k_s$ quantifies the strength of the interaction between token t and token s, just as the numerator in the formula of the cosine similarity. The higher the inner product, the more w_s is a key element to define the representation of w_t. Because we want to normalize it to be between 0 and 1 so it defines a weight, the so-called *attention score* makes use of a soft-max:

$$\alpha_{t,s} := \frac{\exp\left(q_t' k_s / \sqrt{p}\right)}{\sum_{i=1}^{T} \exp\left(q_t' k_i / \sqrt{p}\right)}, \tag{14.1}$$

and it is easy to see that summing $\alpha_{t,s}$ across the second index gives 1. Dividing by $\sqrt{p}$ prevents the value of the inner product from exploding when p is large. The third embedding is called the value and is defined as $v_t := M_V x_t$ for a $p \times h$ matrix M_V – it represents the token value. As stated at the beginning of this section, the self-attention value for element t is finally given by the convex combination of its context values:

$$\text{Self-Attention}(q_t, K, V) := \sum_{s=1}^{T} \alpha_{t,s} v_s = \sum_{s=1}^{T} \frac{\exp\left(q_t' k_s / \sqrt{p}\right)}{\sum_{i=1}^{T} \exp\left(q_t' k_i / \sqrt{p}\right)} v_s,$$

where the capital letter K and V denote the matrix of (row-wise) stacked keys and values, $K := (k_1', \ldots, k_T')'$ and $V := (v_1', \ldots, v_T')'$. This layer reflects the context carried by token t by extracting a signal computed from its interaction with the whole context. This value, Self-Attention(q_t, K, V), sometimes called *attention head*, defines a contextualized embedding.

In practice, neural networks rarely use a single self-attention layer, but concatenate multiple attention heads with their own parameters into a single vector of dimension

p multiplied by the number of heads, further linearly transformed using a square weight matrix and a constant vector. Going forward, we will call MultiHeadSelf-Attention such layer. In general, h the dimension of the initial embedding vectors is set to equate the size of the multi-head self-attention output, i.e., it is equal to the number of heads times p. In the original base `BERT` model (Devlin et al., 2019), there are 12 attention heads, $p = 64$ and $h = 12 \times 64 = 768$.

Remark 14.1 Taking token position into account

This presentation of the self-attention mechanism has been silent on the way to take the token order within the sequence into account. In practice, this is done through *positional embeddings*, where each token position $1, \ldots, T$ is associated to a particular embedding $p_1, \ldots, p_T$ that depends only on the position. Then, initial token embeddings $x_1, \ldots, x_T$ and positional embeddings are summed and used as inputs into the first self-attention layer. Notice that the use of positional embeddings forces the model to set a maximum context length T^{max}, because at inference, processing sequences longer than T^{max} would require knowledge of positional embeddings for positions above T^{max}, which have not been learned during training.

So far, we have not explained how the parameters governing the self-attention mechanism are estimated – we will do so in Section 14.3. But we hope that when trained properly they will yield a high attention score value $\alpha_{t,s}$ between "mouse" and "it" in the sentence "the cat ran after the mouse as it escaped."

The attention score (14.1) defines a *bidirectional* attention, in the sense that a given token representation can be defined by previous tokens, as much as next tokens. This layer is used in *encoders*, neural networks that aim at representing sequences of tokens without text generation in mind. It is possible to consider instead a *causal* attention mechanism by masking the words coming later in the sequence:

$$\text{Causal Self-Attention}(q_t, K, V) := \sum_{s=1}^{t-1} \frac{\exp\left(q_t' k_s / \sqrt{p}\right)}{\sum_{i=1}^{t-1} \exp\left(q_t' k_i / \sqrt{p}\right)} v_s.$$

This layer is used in *decoders* or *generative language models*, neural networks that aim at representing sequences of tokens with the idea of predicting the next token.

14.2.3 Transformer layer

A *transformer* block defined in Vaswani et al. (2017) consists in the composition of multiple steps around the self-attention layer, mainly as a way to facilitate training and prevent the vanishing gradient problem.

Let us first introduce the additional layers. The first layer is called *layer normalization* (Ba et al., 2016) and ensures that outputs from intermediate layers are properly scaled to zero mean and unit variance to avoid numerical issues during training. For a given vector x of dimension h and trainable parameters β and γ, *layer normalization* operates the following transformation:

$$\text{LayerNorm}(x) := \beta + \gamma \frac{x - h^{-1} \sum_{j=1}^{h} x_j}{\sqrt{h^{-1} \sum_{j=1}^{h} (x_j - h^{-1} \sum_{k=1}^{h} x_k)^2}}.$$

When applied to a matrix, for example on the output of a self-attention layer for all the tokens in a sequence (a matrix of dimension $T \times h$), the LayerNorm operates row-wise, normalizing the embedding of each token so its elements have zero mean and unit variance when computed across each row.

The second additional layer is a simple feed-forward layer with an activation function in the middle. This layer transforms an input vector x of dimension h, in the following fashion:

$$\text{FeedForward}(x) := W_2 \text{GeLU}(W_1 x + b_1) + b_2,$$

where W_1 is a $\ell \times h$ matrix, b_1 is a vector of dimension ℓ, W_2 is a $h \times \ell$ matrix, b_2 is a vector of dimension h and $\text{GeLU}(x) := x\Phi(x)$ operating element-wise. ℓ is the hidden dimension of this layer, usually set as multiple of h. $\ell := 4h$ in Vaswani et al. (2017) or in Devlin et al. (2019). When applied to a matrix, it operates row-wise.

We have now all the elements to define a transformer block, starting from the initial $T \times h$ embedding matrix $X := (x_1', \ldots, x_T')'$ as input, where h is assumed to be a multiple of the number of heads. Note that this process is iterative:

1. Compute the output of the MultiHeadSelf-Attention, by computing the queries, keys and values corresponding to each head, from the embedding matrix X.
2. Compute $\tilde{X} = \text{LayerNorm}(X + \text{MultiHeadSelf-Attention}(X))$.
3. Compute $Y = \text{LayerNorm}(\tilde{X} + \text{FeedFoward}(\tilde{X}))$.

The order and exact definition of each step within the transformer block have changed slightly over the years. We presented here the original version, but a more commonly used version is called the *pre-normed* version where the layer normalization steps come before the self-attention and feed-forward layers.

This output matrix of dimension $T \times h$, let's call it Transformer(X), defines a contextualized embedding that can be used as input for any NLP task. Indeed, at the end of the computation, the embedding representing a particular token has been mixed with all the other tokens in a non-linear fashion. The upside of this machinery is that the token representation now takes into consideration its context. The downside is that this representation depends heavily on the sequence of which it is a part, so a given token is now uniquely mapped to a single embedding. This representation is sometimes called *hidden state* in transformer models.

14.2.4 The anatomy of BERT

The original base BERT model uses embeddings of dimension $h = 768$ and stacks 12 transformer layers of 12 heads on top of each other for a total of 110 million parameters, the output of the previous layer serving as the input of the next layer. A larger model, known as BERT-large, stacks 24 such layers of 16 heads and uses an embedding dimension of size 1024 for a total of 340 million parameters. This set of layers constitutes what is referred to as the *body* of the model, which is non-specific. Figure 14.1 represents a sentence as it is processed through the body of BERT.

Then, a task-specific *model head* is added on top of it to perform the desired predictive task. There are different possible model heads depending on the task at hand. For example, if the goal is to perform a classification task with K classes, the output of the last layer of the body will be transformed linearly using a matrix of dimension $K \times h$ and then normalized using a soft-max to output a probability vector. Since the output of the body is a $T \times h$ matrix, in practice people either take the

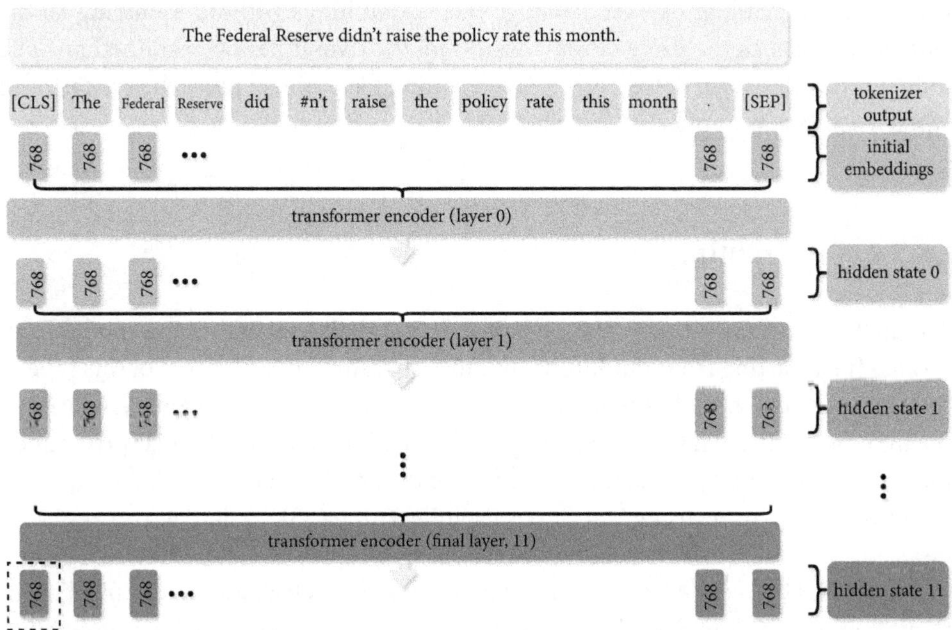

Figure 14.1 The body of BERT.

Note: The embedding at the bottom left, corresponding to the final layer representation of the [CLS] token is usually used as a feature summarizing the text sequence in subsequent tasks.

embedding corresponding to the first token of the sequence, or average across all the tokens of the sequence.

LLMs such as `GPT-3` (Brown et al., 2020), `PaLM` (Chowdhery et al., 2022), `GPT-4` (OpenAI, 2023), `Llama2` (Touvron et al., 2023), `Mistral` (Jiang et al., 2023), etc. all use an architecture that stacks transformer layers, with a few tricks here and there. The only difference is a larger scale, going up to several hundred billion parameters. Training these models is made possible using vast amounts of data and computer clusters gathering about 6–10 thousands of GPUs, for a total training cost around a few millions dollars.

The literature using transformer-type architectures is often difficult to access for novices and not so explicit about implementation details so that it is generally necessary to read the source code to know exactly what is being done. Nevertheless, Phuong and Hutter (2022) give the necessary details and provides clear pseudocode to reproduce this type of networks. We can also signal this great tutorial video by Andrej Karpathy: www.youtube.com/watch?v=kCc8FmEb1nY.

14.3 Training `BERT`

Training a modern language model such as `BERT` from scratch requires a substantial volume of data and computational resources, typically requiring at least 2 to 4 GPUs. Fortunately, pre-trained models are accessible online, relieving the burden of training, and enabling users to leverage their capabilities without incurring all the associated costs, at the price of not controlling the data it has been trained on. The following sections will delve into various training tasks and explore the scenarios in which each task is applicable (Figure 14.2).

14.3.1 Pre-training

The first type of training is called *pre-training* and aims at training a model from scratch (i.e., starting from randomly initialized parameters). The goal of this type of training is for the model to acquire knowledge about the structure and semantics of the human language that can then be specialized to a given task. Popular pre-trained models available on the HuggingFace hub are trained in such a way.

Pre-training is done using Self-Supervised Learning (SSL, Balestriero et al., 2023) tasks, see section 13.3 for a precise definition.

A first SSL task is called *masked token prediction*. In such a task, tokens from input sequences are randomly masked using a special *mask* token with a fixed probability and the goal is to predict the original token using all the other tokens of the sequence. Often, tokens are also swapped with any other token from the vocabulary at random to add noise to the sequence and robustify training. Ultimately, this task is a simple

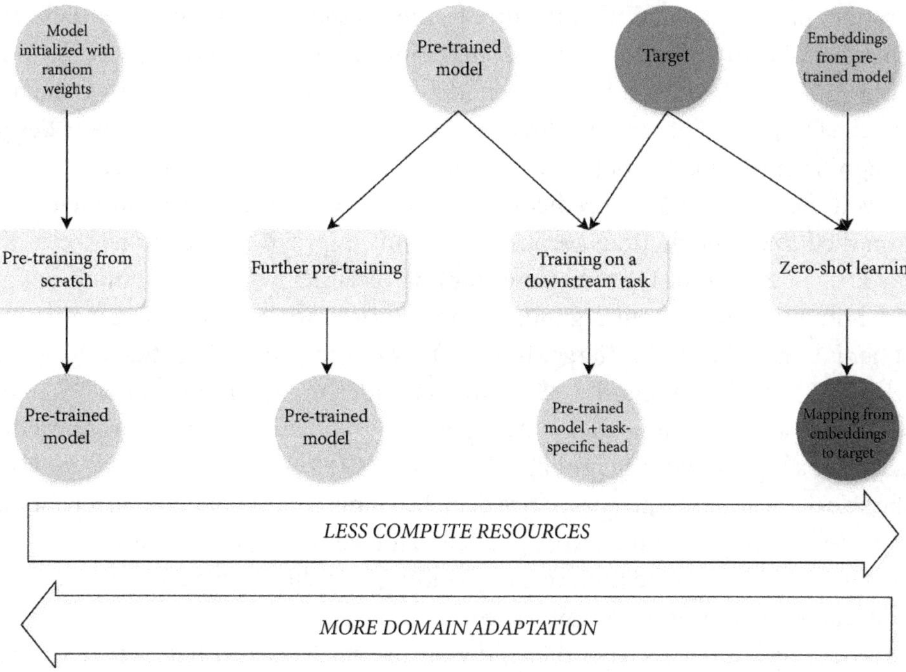

Figure 14.2 Types of training tasks for language models

classification task over the whole vocabulary. In practice, a good masking probability is about 15 %, but Portes et al. (2023) suggest that using 30 % makes training converge faster.

A second SSL task is called *next token prediction* or *text generation*. The goal is simply to predict the next token in a sequence using all the preceding tokens, using a causal attention mechanism (see section 14.2). Models pre-trained on this task are called *decoder-only* and are the basis for text generation models such as the GPT family.

A third type of SSL task is called *next sentence prediction* and was used in the original `BERT` model. In this task, for a given sentence either the following sentence in the document (50 % of the time) or a randomly sampled sentence (the other 50 % of the time) is added to form a pair. In the first case, the pair is labeled as "true" since the two sentences follow each other, or "false" in the other case. Then the model is trained to classify pairs of sentences as either following each other or not. For this purpose, tokenizers add beginning-of-sequence (BOS) and end-of-sequence (EOS) special tokens around the sentence with the idea that these tokens will capture its general context. Specifically, Devlin et al. (2019) use the symbol `[CLS]` as the BOS token, consider its embedding as the aggregate sequence representation and feed it to the classification head to complete the task.

Pre-training a model is costly and requires a large dataset. For example, `BERT` has been trained on 3.3 billion tokens. Fortunately, a large literature has studied ways to speed up model pre-training while keeping the costs under control by playing on model parameters and architecture, training tasks, training hyper-parameters such as batch size or learning rate, float precision etc. Some improvements play only on the computing side and leave the model and training tasks unchanged such as using the DeepSpeed library (Rasley et al., 2020). However, leveraging model design can significantly enhance both training and inference processes. Liu et al. (2019) removed the next sentence prediction used by Devlin et al. (2019) to focus only on masked token prediction, because it did not improve the performance of the model. Izsak et al. (2021) studies the training of `BERT` with a computing budget of 24 hours under different regimes of model size (larger is better), learning rate (higher is better), batch size (larger is better), warm-up (shorter is better), etc. Portes et al. (2023) propose a specific `BERT` model under the name `MosaicBERT` that implements a few training tricks. Wettig et al. (2023) suggests that larger models should use a higher masking probability of about 40 %. Another source of speed-up is the size of the input sequences: since deep learning libraries operate on tensors, all sequences within a batch have to be padded to the same length. Grouping sequences by similar lengths to avoid unnecessary padding or reducing the context size of the model can greatly improve training speed.

Pre-training a model is a good idea if your use case deals with data that are very specific and unlikely to have been seen by models available online, for example, if you are building a model in a specific language or on a proprietary dataset that is very different from commonly available corpora. Be aware that your dataset should be large enough to fuel the model pre-training. Notice also that pre-training a model is absolutely necessary if you have trained a new tokenizer. Indeed, the vocabulary has changed and words might not be tokenized in the same fashion as with a pre-existing tokenizer. Another way to say it is that you cannot just train a tokenizer and plug it into an existing neural network since the mapping from vocabulary to integers has changed.

14.3.2 Fine-tuning

Fine-tuning a model is a form of transfer learning where the training starts from parameters that have been optimized on another corpus. It can be done in two ways: either continue pre-training it on a new corpus, or directly train it to complete a task of particular interest.

Further pre-training on a different corpus

Extra pre-training on a different corpus happens exactly as pre-training from scratch, but from a model that has already been pre-trained. The amount of training contained in the model checkpoint can be a considerable saving on training time as the model no longer needs to start from randomly initialized weights. It had presumably already encoded common statistical patterns that occur in written language. For example, Dai et al. (2022) provide evidence that pre-trained `BERT` encodes syntactic dependencies. The downside of this approach is the need to reuse the same tokenizer, which might not be adapted to the new corpus. For example, if the tokenizer takes casing into account while it should not matter for the application, it is important to question whether the model is appropriate or if the text should be normalized.

Training on a downstream task

Training on a downstream task consists of taking a pre-trained model and adding a task-specific head on top of it. The nature of the head will depend on the task: for example, a classification task will use a linear layer and a soft-max to represent a probability distribution over the outcome possible values. The established convention consists of taking the hidden state of the `[CLS]` token from the last layer of a popular pre-trained model to represent a sequence and feed it to the head of the model as a *feature* for a prediction task. Nevertheless, some approaches take the average of the hidden states of the tokens that make up the sequence, especially for *question answering* tasks. Finally, some articles such as Rogers et al. (2021) suggest that the middle layers of the model are more transferable, i.e., they have a better performance on a new classification task, as they are less specific to the tasks that have been used to pre-train large language models.

Notice that training on a downstream task can be quite fast if one decides to *freeze* some layers of the model. Typically in such exercises, only the last third of layers (the ones closer to the prediction layer) and the model head are modified during training, while the other layers are kept intact. This means the amount of computations is greatly reduced.

14.3.3 Zero-shot learning

Language models as feature encoders

Finally, a simple, computationally inexpensive alternative to neural network training, called *zero-shot learning*, is to use pre-trained embeddings as *features* in a simple linear or logistic regression model. The idea is to process the textual inputs with the language model to obtain the embeddings resulting from the `[CLS]` token of the last layer and estimate a simple linear model based on them. Compared to the bag-of-words approach for textual regression (Section 12.2.5), the dimension is often reduced since the number of parameters to estimate goes from a few thousands (usually one per word) to a number equal to the size of the output embeddings of a model. Generally speaking, this strategy makes it possible to achieve decent results, without paying the costs of training a model. This zero-shot learning approach can at least provide an initial baseline estimate before developing more complex approaches.

To echo Chapter 4, it is worth noting that the sparsity assumption on these embeddings is generally not verified, which prevents the use of techniques that rely on sparsity such as the Lasso. OpenAI points out on its blog that: "*we observed that generally the embedding representation is very rich and information dense. For example, reducing the dimensionality of the inputs using SVD or PCA, even by 10%, generally results in worse downstream performance on specific tasks.*" (platform.openai.com/docs/guides/embeddings/use-cases)

Should you train your own language model?

Since the publication of Vaswani et al. (2017), marking the beginning of the intensive use of transformer-type architectures, progress in NLP has been disarmingly fast and made easily accessible to the public, notably via the Hugging-Face hub. On the other hand, the cost of training models at the state of the art is too high to be borne by a single individual. This begs the question: do we necessarily have to re-train models? Can't we just use them without specific training?

It is a question whose precise answer obviously depends on the context, but we can give some food for thought. First of all, if the data to be analyzed is very different from those on which the available models were trained (e.g., different languages, very specific lexical field), then it may be necessary to train your own model. Second, for most standard tasks (e.g., sentiment analysis, translation, named-entities recognition), efficient models already exist so it is often not necessary to re-train models.

Finally, most state-of-the-art LLMs are simply too complex and costly to train. Even the inference step can be costly to run on a personal computer, although this state of affair is rapidly evolving thanks to libraries such as `ollama`. Zhao et al. (2023) provide a detailed survey of these new models that have quickly captured public attention, especially following the online release of `ChatGPT`.

Table 14.1 summarizes this section.

Table 14.1 Comparison of training approaches

Approach	Can use a new tokenizer	Modifies model weights	Domain-specificity	Speed
pre-training from scratch	yes	yes	highest	slowest
further pre-training	no	yes	high	moderate
training on a downstream task	no	yes	moderate	moderate
zero-shot learning	no	no	no	fastest

Remark 14.2 Using LLMs as assistants

With the release of `ChatGPT`, it has been increasingly common to interact with generative models and LLMs in particular through so-called *prompts*, short textual instructions of the task the model is to perform. Although they do not require any quantitative skill, crafting a good prompt that will make the model perform the exact task the user has in mind is a form of art and requires working by trial and error. This technology opens up new avenues for research as it lowers the cost of access to artificial intelligence, which can be used to perform standard tasks (e.g., sentiment analysis of documents, machine translation, entity recognition) or more tailored tasks (e.g., document parsing, summarization). Depending of the number of documents to process, using a closed-source API (e.g., OpenAI) or open-source local models (e.g., through ollama) can be relatively cheap. However, inference time can be prohibitive. Moreover, the inherent randomness in generative models' response creates difficulties for reproducible research. Generative AI and prompt-engineering are beyond the scope of this textbook, but a good starting point is lilianweng.github.io/posts/2023-03-15-prompt-engineering/.

14.4 Application: matching via Siamese neural networks

14.4.1 Description of the problem

The previous section was covering the training of language models in generic terms. This next section describes a specific example of a *matching* task that can be useful for the empirical economist. Imagine two different text sequences describing the same entity and one would like to design a system that is able to correctly match the two pieces of text together. For example, one may want to match an individual's statements about their employer in the census to the description of that employer in the SIRENE directory (the French national system for the identification and directory of companies and their establishments), or similar products described in different ways in two databases, one providing for example the daily quantities sold, the other providing the characteristics of the product. Another application is to identify that a newspaper article provides information about a specific company.

How does this problem differ from a traditional classification task? First, the number of possible matches is vast and not limited to a reasonable number of alternatives. On the contrary, millions of possibilities may exist. Additionally, these possibilities appear and disappear over time. Take the example of associating an individual with the establishment employing them on a given date: on one hand, the French economic fabric consists of more than eight million businesses and, on the other hand, it evolves at every point in time due to the creation and destruction of companies.

It would therefore be futile to try to train an algorithm that outputs the identifier of a company from a fixed collection of them, as it would quickly become obsolete.

The idea here is to adopt a flexible approach, allowing us to learn a relevant distance to match objects together. This is referred to as *distance learning* or *metric learning*. These techniques have been successfully used in tasks such as facial recognition (e.g., Schroff et al., 2015) and question answering. More generally, the strategy we will describe can be applied to the representation of any set of objects containing unstructured data (e.g., text, image) on which we measure a certain notion of similarity (e.g., belonging to the same category or to the same basket of goods, describing the same individual or company, associated as the result of a matching mechanism such as the labor market).

14.4.2 General strategy

The idea is to estimate a function $m(.,.)$ that gives a distance between two inputs in such a way that this distance is small if the pair of inputs is indeed concordant, and it is large if the pair of inputs is discordant. Let s_1 and s_2 be two inputs corresponding to two strings whose compatibility we want to study. The idea is to learn a projection function μ^{proj} into $\mathbb{R}^p$ and to define a distance measure d on $\mathbb{R}^p$, in order to compute:

$$m(s_1, s_2) = d(\mu^{proj}(s_1), \mu^{proj}(s_2)).$$

Once these elements are fixed, the closest item t among the collection of items $\{t_1, \dots, t_n\}$ to the item s is defined as:

$$\widehat{t} = \underset{t \in \{t_1, \dots, t_n\}}{\arg\min}\, d(\mu^{proj}(s), \mu^{proj}(t)).$$

Since the function μ^{proj} is the same for both inputs and it is estimated by a neural network, we refer to it as a *Siamese network*. Note that once this model is trained, it may be interesting to store the representations $t_1, \dots, t_n$ in a database in order to avoid recalculating them on the fly each time a new query is submitted to the system.

Remark 14.3 Levenshtein distance

The idea of being able to evaluate the similarity between two strings is not new. One of the standard distances defined directly on the space of strings, the edit distance, proposed by Levenshtein (1966), counts the minimal number of basic operations (addition or deletion of a character) necessary to go from one string to another. The lower this number – called the edit distance or Levenshtein distance – the more similar the two strings are. A substitution counts double since it consists of a deletion followed by an addition.

For example, the Levenshtein distance between HOUSE and HOME is three, since starting from the word HOUSE we need to delete the letters U and S, and add the latter M to get to the word HOME. Moreover, this is the shortest way to go from one to the other.

This distance can be interesting in certain contexts, however, it remains superficial in the sense that it is not able to bring together two synonyms with distant spellings.

How do we choose the functions d and μ^{proj}? Regarding the distance d, a common choice is the cosine similarity, which measures a similarity coefficient between two vectors. This measure takes its values between -1 and 1, with a value close to 1 indicating aligned vectors. Compared to the Euclidean norm, it tolerates differences in magnitude but will consider "close" two vectors that have the same direction, see Section 12.2.4 for a discussion. Translated in terms of distance, this measure gives:

$$d(x, y) = 1 - \frac{x'y}{\|x\|_2 \, \|y\|_2}. \tag{14.2}$$

A good choice for μ^{proj} is a pre-trained neural network that uses the transformers architecture such as BERT as we have seen in Section 14.2. Here, the idea if simply to add a "model head" that averages the output embeddings of the body across the sequence and produce a unique vector that takes real values in a space of reasonable dimension. The question arises as to the dimension of this final representation. Generally, a dimension lower than 30 is too low to capture the complexity of the structure of the space. However, going too far (400 or more) can considerably lengthen the training of the network and also not yield good performance because the information is scattered. There is a middle ground to determine depending on the application: the more heterogeneous the data, the more complexification of the space is needed.

Only the function μ^{proj} depends on unknown parameters, so the focus of training the model will be on learning a representation $\mu^{proj}(s)$ of an input s that will allow bringing concordant pairs closer and separating discordant pairs. Notice that this model can be fully trained from scratch, fine-tuned on this matching task, partially trained (training only the layers close to the output), or implemented in a zero-shot learning fashion as we have described in Section 14.3.

14.4.3 Loss functions

Now that we have described the general strategy, we need to implement it by defining a loss function so that the model can learn from the data. Fortunately, the literature has identified several loss functions that fit within this framework. Notice that the choice of loss function also dictates how to structure the data for training the model.

Let's start with the simplest one, which is called the *contrastive loss*. To compute it, we are given a triplet (s_1, s_2, D) with s_1 and s_2 two inputs, and D a binary variable that takes the value 1 if the inputs are concordant, and 0 if the inputs are discordant. Let M be a positive real number called the margin. The contrastive loss is given by:

$$Dd(x_1, x_2)^2 + (1 - D)\max(0, M - d(x_1, x_2))^2,$$

where $x_i := \mu^{proj}(s_i)$, $i = 1, 2$. The intuition is as follows: for a pair of concordant inputs ($D = 1$), we will modify the projection in the direction of minimizing the distance between these inputs, while for a pair of discordant inputs ($D = 0$), we will modify the projection in order to maximize the distance between the inputs, as long as it is currently below the margin M. The existence of this margin prevents us from excessively trying to separate representations that are already sufficiently distant. In general, a value chosen for M is 1. Indeed, if we take the loss based on cosine similarity (14.2), whose values range from 0 to 2, we can see that a loss of 1 corresponds to a cosine similarity of 0, i.e., orthogonality between the two vectors. The idea in this case is to seek to make the cosine similarity between the representations of two discordant character strings less than or equal to zero, without aiming to minimize it at all costs into negative values.

Note that the contrastive loss considers only two inputs, excluding all others. This can lead to side effects, in the sense that modifying the projection of these inputs to the target space can have unexpected consequences on the projection of other inputs and result in an overall degradation of the model's performance. To remedy this problem, one possibility is to use the triplet margin loss, which takes as input a triplet (s_A, s_+, s_-) with s_A being a given input (the *anchor*), s_+ being a positive input such that the pair (s_A, s_+) consists of concordant items, and s_- being a negative input such that the pair (s_A, s_-) consists of discordant items. The loss is defined as follows:

$$\max(d(X_A, x_+) - d(x_A, x_-) + M, 0),$$

where $x_A := \mu^{proj}(s_A)$, $x_+ := \mu^{proj}(s_+)$, and $x_- := \mu^{proj}(s_-)$. In other words, this loss seeks to impose the following inequality for each triplet of the described form:

$$d(x_A, x_+) + M \leq d(x_A, x_-).$$

The distance from the anchor to the negative example must be greater than the distance from the anchor to the positive example with a margin of at least M. For triplets where the difference between the distance to the negative example and the distance to the positive example is less than a threshold $M > 0$, we will seek to modify the projection μ^{proj} in order to bring the representation of the anchor closer to that of the positive example and move it away from that of the negative example.

Generalizations of these losses exist, such as the quadruplet margin loss (Chen et al., 2017) or the multi-class N-pair loss (Sohn, 2016). Other strategies of this kind, borrowing from the SSL approach, can be interesting (Balestriero et al., 2023).

14.4.4 Model evaluation

The loss functions presented in the previous section are useful for training and selecting models. However, they are too abstract and do not allow humans to simply evaluate their quality. To address this, we propose two evaluation methods.

The first consists in calculating the *top-k accuracy*. For a given input, we look for its k nearest neighbors and determine if a matching observation is among them. The top-k accuracy is then given by the empirical probability of forming a matching pair when associating the input with one of its k nearest neighbors. The drawback of this strategy is that it is resource intensive, as each input must be passed through the network to retrieve the vector representations, and then compute pairwise distances, resulting in a complexity of $\mathcal{O}(n^2)$ for n inputs. Note that optimized algorithms exist for calculating nearest neighbors when working with dense vectors (e.g., Matsui et al., 2018).

To avoid this computational cost, another approach is to set up an exercise called *N-way one-shot learning*. The idea is to provide an answer to the following question: for a given input, among a collection of $N+1$ other inputs, where only one is a match, in what proportion of cases can the model correctly reconstruct the pair?

In the $N = 2$ case, for a given input, the model simply needs to choose the example that matches among the two. Random chance gives a theoretical success probability of 50%. Therefore, we want a model that discriminates significantly better than random chance among the presented examples. Logically, this score should decrease with the number of incorrect inputs N, as it gives more opportunities for the model to make mistakes. The theoretical success probability by randomly selecting an example is then $1/(N + 1)$. The idea is to randomly generate a large number of exercises of this type and take the average result of each exercise to evaluate the model's ability to discriminate objects and reconstruct pairs.

In both cases (top-k accuracy and one-shot learning), the resulting measure is directly interpretable by humans, as it gives the probability that the model correctly discriminates.

14.4.5 Training tips

The following tools can serve as anchor points for making progress specifically when training such models:

- **Transfer learning.** When training neural networks, transfer learning is always welcome as it allows to build on models that have been proved to work. In this case, the `sentence-transformers` library in Python (Reimers and Gurevych, 2019) offers the tools and pre-trained models to create embeddings of sentences with the explicit purpose of performing semantic similarity tasks.
- **Increase the number of negative examples.** In general, transitioning to triplet margin loss or quadruplet margin loss, compared to the standard contrastive

loss, provides significant performance gains. The idea is as follows: the standard contrastive loss aims to move a pair of inputs apart or closer together without considering the rest of the inputs. By performing this operation, it is possible that it inadvertently modifies the space and brings closer or moves apart two items that should not be. Triplet or quadruplet losses limit this side effect. Some articles even present 50 negative pairs per anchor. While not going that far, using 10 examples can be advantageous. Similarly using large batches helps avoid this side effect.

- **Modify the computation of the "top k" by using new distances.** Notice that the concept of a "nearest neighbor" is not reciprocal: one vector can be the nearest neighbor to another without the reverse being true. In practice, some vectors may be found in the neighborhood of others with a very high probability, while others may be completely isolated and therefore never considered. To address this issue, Conneau et al. (2017) introduce the *cross-domain similarity local scaling*, which penalizes "hubs" (concentrations of points) and alleviates the penalty on "anti-hubs" (isolated points). The idea is to better separate the regions where certain observations concentrate, while leaving the sparse regions unchanged. This modification can be made even without retraining the model, simply during the evaluation phase.
- **Building a classifier to initialize the first layers.** Training Siamese neural networks is a self-supervised learning technique. Nevertheless, supervised learning generally works better. The idea, then, is to initialize the first layers of the Siamese network by training a binary classifier on a concatenated sequence $[(s_A, s_+, 1), (s_A, s_-, 0), \dots]$ with the same network architecture, adding a layer that uses the final embeddings to extract a similarity probability – i.e. $\exp(x_A' x_+)/(1 + \exp(x_A' x_+))$. This system can be called the "slow system" since if it were used to decide on a match, all candidate pairs would have to be processed for each input. It could be used after a "fast system" (our method so far): the latter obtains the top k nearest neighbors for a candidate item; they are then presented to this classifier, and the accuracy of the "top k" is computed based on the resulting score.
- **Hard-mining.** The technique of "hard-mining" or "try-hard loss" consists of selecting particularly difficult negative examples to distinguish from positive examples. The idea is to guide the learning of the network in order to better discriminate ambiguous cases. This involves defining a specific way to load the data in batches, which can be time consuming for training, but there are solutions to optimize this step (see next point).
- **Efficient search for similar vectors.** The FAISS library (github.com/facebookresearch/faiss) allows for optimized search for nearest neighbors when dealing with high-dimensional vectors, which is useful for inference. The basic idea of FAISS is to perform clustering of the vector space to optimize the search: this reduces the complexity from $\mathcal{O}(n)$ to $\mathcal{O}(\sqrt{n})$ since, for a query, instead of evaluating the distance to each vector in the database, we first evaluate the distance to the centroids of each cluster, and then the distance to

each point in the nearest cluster. It can be shown that the number of clusters that minimizes the average number of operations is $K = \sqrt{n}$. Several functions are implemented on GPU, which is computationally advantageous.

14.5 Summary

Key concepts

Tokenizers, byte-pair encoding (BPE), self-attention mechanism, `BERT`, self-supervised learning, pre-training, zero-shot learning, Siamese neural networks, distance learning, Levenshtein distance, cosine similarity, contrastive loss, triplet margin loss, top-k accuracy, one-shot learning, large language models (LLMs).

Additional references

The self-attention mechanism and, more generally, transformer layers are described in detail in Chapter 9 of Jurafsky and Martin (2019). An excellent tutorial for understanding transformers in practice can be found on YouTube at youtube.com/watch?v=kCc8FmEb1nY. The book Godbole et al. (2023) offers an in-depth discussion. In general, the online course "Full-stack deep learning" (fullstackdeeplearning.com) is a comprehensive and highly practical reference for implementing machine learning systems beyond textual applications.

Code and data

It is now easy to download pre-trained language models for various tasks such as named entity recognition, text generation, sentiment analysis, topic classification, or automatic translation, notably through the `transformers` package maintained by HuggingFace, available at huggingface.co/transformers/. In this regard, Tunstall et al. (2022) is an excellent practical guide that contains mainly code that can be easily modified. The associated Python notebooks can be found here: github.com/nlp-with-transformers/notebooks.

Questions

1. Explain the self-attention mechanism without any equation.
2. What distinguishes data matching from a typical classification task? Describe a method for implementing a matching system.
3. How is the contrastive loss used to model pairs of concordant and discordant inputs?

14.6 Appendix: Siamese networks beyond text data

To put distance learning into perspective, this appendix goes beyond textual data to show how this self-supervised learning task can help build features from unstructured data.

14.6.1 Vector representation of job offers

Using the principle of Siamese networks, Schmitt et al. (2017) train a model to project job offer descriptions into a 200-dimensional vector space, using data collected from recruitment agencies on the internet. The strategy is identical to that of Section 14.4, with a distance given by 1 minus the cosine similarity, and a contrastive loss function. The observed similarity between two offers is given by a binary variable that equals 1 if at least one candidate clicked on both job offers, and 0 otherwise (i.e., no candidate was interested in both offers at the same time).

This approach is astute because it allows the exploitation of job seekers' revealed preferences and their subjective evaluation of the similarity between two offers, in order to construct embeddings that go beyond their textual content. Indeed, it is possible that two offers require similar skills but are formulated with different vocabulary (e.g., because they come from companies operating in different sectors), which limits the scope of a purely textual analysis.

The authors note that the contrastive loss function used to train the model can pose a problem by inadvertently creating transitivity: they observe that two job offers will be close in the target space if they have been seen by job seekers who have also viewed the same third offer, even though these two offers have never interested the same job seeker. This flaw could be corrected by using a triplet margin loss.

14.6.2 Differentiation in the font market

Han et al. (2021) study the impact of the 2014 acquisition of FontFont by its competitor Monotype on the diversity of products offered in the font market. Fonts are purely visual products, so their characteristics are completely unstructured and difficult to measure, while consumers weigh aesthetic differences to make their purchase decision. To capture this, the authors use Siamese neural networks with a triplet margin loss to encode the visual characteristics of fonts into dense vectors of dimension 128. The strategy used is exactly the one described in Section 14.4. Once the model is trained, each font i is projected into this 128-dimensional space via the representation x_i. Two measures of font differentiation are used. The first measure is the Euclidean distance to the mean:

$$\|x_i - \bar{x}\|_2 ,$$

with $\bar{x} = \sum_{i=1}^{n} x_i/n$, measuring the average representation of the n fonts available on the market. The second measure is defined as:

$$-\sum_{j \neq i} \frac{1}{\|x_i - x_j\|_2}.$$

In both cases, these measures tend to have high values when font i is highly differentiated from competing fonts. These two measures are then aggregated by date and by firm, to compute an index of product diversity offered by each firm over time. Finally, the authors use a strategy based on the construction of a synthetic control to compare the impact of the merger (see Chapter 10). They show that the merger has led to increased diversification in the font market.

PART VI
EXERCISES

Chapter 15
Exercises

This chapter proposes exercises inspired from exams given at ENSAE Paris. Elements of correction are available in the associated GitHub repository, github.com/jeremylhour/ml4econometrics.

15.1 Regression as a weighting estimator

This problem mainly relies on Chapters 3 and 10.

The aim of this exercise is to show that regression adjustment for estimating the treatment effect is equivalent to using a weighted average of the control group's outcomes to construct the counterfactual. We observe an i.i.d. sample of the vector (Y_i^{obs}, D_i, X_i) for $i = 1, \dots, n$. Y_i^{obs} is the outcome variable whose value depends on the treatment status of unit i. If unit i is treated ($D_i = 1$), then $Y_i^{obs} = Y_{1i}$. If unit i is not treated ($D_i = 0$), then $Y_i^{obs} = Y_{0i}$. X_i is a vector of covariates of dimension p which includes an intercept. The index i is dropped when unnecessary. Let $\pi := \mathbb{P}(D = 1)$. The quantity of interest is the average treatment effect on the treated (ATT) defined by:

$$\tau^{ATT} = \mathbb{E}\left[Y_1 - Y_0 | D = 1\right].$$

In many applications, the ATT is estimated by considering an estimator of the following form:

$$\tau^{ATT} = \mathbb{E}\left[Y^{obs} | D = 1\right] - \mathbb{E}\left[W_0 Y^{obs} | D = 0\right].$$

where W_0 is a random variable depending on both X and D. Suppose the untreated outcome follows a linear model: $Y_0 = X'\beta_0 + \varepsilon$ with $(D, X) \perp\!\!\!\perp \varepsilon$ and $\mathbb{E}\varepsilon = 0$. We assume that $\mathbb{E}\left[(1 - D)XX'\right]$ is non-singular.

The Oaxaca–Blinder procedure estimates the ATT in two steps. The first step consists in estimating β_0. The second step consists in estimating the ATT as a simple average of the residuals computed on the treated group as $\widehat{\varepsilon}_i = Y_i^{obs} - X_i'\widehat{\beta}$, for i such that $D_i = 1$.

Machine Learning for Econometrics. Christophe Gaillac and Jérémy L'Hour, Oxford University Press.
 DOI: 10.1093/9780198918868.003.0015

1. Show that $\mathbb{E}\left[Y_1 - Y_0 | D = 1\right] = \mathbb{E}\left[Y^{obs} | D = 1\right] - \mathbb{E}\left[X | D = 1\right]' \beta_0$.
2. Let $\beta_0 = \arg\min_{\beta \in \mathbb{R}^p} \mathbb{E}\left[(1 - D)(Y^{obs} - X'\beta)^2\right]$. Express β_0 as a function of certain moments. What is its empirical counterpart? What regression would you use to estimate β_0?
3. Show that in this case $W_0 = \mathbb{E}\left[X | D = 1\right]' \mathbb{E}\left[XX' | D = 0\right]^{-1} X$.
4. Show that this weight satisfies:

$$\mathbb{E}[X|D = 1] = \mathbb{E}[W_0 X | D = 0].$$

   Interpret this condition.

5. Based on the previous questions, propose an estimator of the ATT of the form:

$$\widehat{\tau}^{OB} := \frac{1}{n_1} \sum_{i:D_i=1} Y_i^{obs} - \sum_{i:D_i=0} \omega_i Y_i^{obs}.$$

   Give the expression of the weights for this case. Do the weights ω_i sum up to one?

6. Compare with the synthetic control estimator.

15.2 Orthogonal score for treatment effect on treated

This problem mainly relies on Chapters 2, 3, 4, and 5.

Consider an i.i.d. sample of the random vector $W_i = (Y_i^{obs}, D_i, X_i')'$ for $i = 1, \ldots, n$. Y_i^{obs} is the outcome variable whose value depends on whether unit i was treated or not. If unit i was treated ($D_i = 1$), then $Y_i^{obs} = Y_{1i}$. If unit i was not treated ($D_i = 0$), then $Y_i^{obs} = Y_{0i}$. X_i is a covariate vector of dimension $p_X > 1$ which includes an intercept. The index i is omitted when superfluous. The quantity of interest is the average treatment effect on the treated, defined as follows:

$$\tau_0 = \mathbb{E}\left[Y_1 - Y_0 | D = 1\right]. \tag{15.1}$$

Let $\pi = \mathbb{P}(D = 1)$ and the propensity score $p(X) = \mathbb{P}(D = 1|X)$. We make the following two assumptions. The conditional independence assumption:

$$Y_0 \perp\!\!\!\perp D | X, \tag{15.2}$$

and the common support assumption:

$$0 < p(X) < 1. \tag{15.3}$$

1. (a) Let:

$$m(W_i, \tau, p) = \left(D_i - \frac{p(X_i)}{1 - p(X_i)}(1 - D_i)\right) Y_i^{obs} - D_i\tau.$$

Verify that $\mathbb{E}[m(W_i, p, \tau_0)] = 0$.

(b) Suppose we have an estimation of the propensity score $\widehat{p}$. Propose an estimator $\widehat{\tau}$ for τ_0.

2. (a) Suppose the propensity score is given by a Logit, i.e., $p(X) = [1 + \exp(-X'\beta_0)]^{-1}$. The moment condition from question 1 is denoted by $m(W_i, \tau, \beta)$ from now on. Compute $\mathbb{E}\left[\partial_\beta m(W_i, \tau_0, \beta_0)\right]$.

(b) Consider the small dimension case where p_X, the dimension of X, is small and constant for any sample size. What is the most efficient method to estimate β_0? Give the formula of the corresponding estimator. Will the resulting estimator of τ_0, $\widehat{\tau}$, be asymptotically normal?

(c) Let's consider a high-dimensional case where β_0 is estimated using:

$$\min_{\beta \in \mathbb{R}^{p_X}} -\left[\frac{1}{n}\sum_{i=1}^{n} D_i X_i'\beta - \log\left(1 + \exp(X_i'\beta)\right)\right] + \lambda \|\beta\|_1,$$

where $\lambda > 0$ is a tuning parameter. What would you call such a method? Will the estimator of τ_0 be asymptotically normal in this case?

3. Suppose the outcome of no treatment is given by $Y_0 = X'\gamma_0 + \varepsilon$ with $\varepsilon \perp\!\!\!\perp X$ and $\mathbb{E}\varepsilon = 0$.

(a) Show that $\mathbb{E}\left[DX(Y_0 - X'\gamma_0)\right] = 0$.

(b) Suggest an orthogonal moment condition ψ. Prove that it is orthogonal.

4. Based on the previous questions, provide an estimator $\check{\tau}$ of τ_0 that is asymptotically normal even in the high-dimensional case. What theorem are you using?

15.3 Voting model

This problem mainly relies on Chapters 2, 6 and 8.

Consider the following utility model of an individual i in electoral district t who chooses between two parties L and R:

$$U_{L,i,t} = g(X_t'\beta_0) + \tau_0 D_t + \xi_{L,t} + \varepsilon_{i,t,L}, \tag{15.4}$$
$$\mathbb{E}\left[\varepsilon_{i,t,L}\right] = 0,\ \xi_{L,t} \perp\!\!\!\perp (X_t, Z_t),\ \text{ and } \mathbb{E}\left[\xi_{L,t}^2 | X_t\right] = \sigma^2,$$

$U_{R,i,t} = 0$. $X_t \in \mathbb{R}^{p_X}$ is a random vector measuring the characteristics of the party's candidate in district t, D_t is the amount of party's advertising expenditure in district

t, $\xi_{L,t}$ is an unobserved shock specific to the district (e.g., candidate's reputation), and $\varepsilon_{i,t,L}$ is an unobserved idiosyncratic shock distributed with cdf $F_\varepsilon(t) = \left[1 + e^{-t}\right]^{-1}$. X_t is considered exogenous while D_t is endogenous, and Z_t is an instrumental variable. $g(\cdot)$ is an infinitely differentiable function on $\mathbb{R}$ of the index $X_t'\beta_0$.

For the first-stage equation, we assume:

$$D_t = f_0(X_t, Z_t) + u_t, \quad u_t \perp\!\!\!\perp (X_t, Z_t), \tag{FS}$$

where $f_0 \in \mathcal{F}_{p,q}$ and $\mathcal{F}_{p,q}$ is the class

$$\left\{ f : f(x,z) = \sum_{i=1}^{p} \gamma_{0,i} 1\{x \in C_{a_i,r}\} + \sum_{i=1}^{q} \delta_{0,i} 1\{z \in C_{b_i,r}\}, (a_i, b_i) \in \mathbb{R}^{dx+dz} \right\},$$

where $C_{a_i,r}$ and $C_{b_i,r}$ are hypercubes of dimensions $\mathbb{R}^{dx}$ and $\mathbb{R}^{dz}$, centered at $\{a_i\}$ and $\{b_i\}$, and with side lengths r.

We observe an i.i.d. sample of $(W_t)_{t=1}^n = (S_t, X_t, D_t, Z_t)_{t=1}^n$, among the n electoral districts, where $S_t \in (0,1)$ is the (observed) proportion of votes in favor of candidate L in district t.

A. Estimation of the first-stage equation

1. Suppose that $p < n$ and $q < n$ and that the true function f_0 has only a few zero coefficients $\{\gamma_{0,i}\}_{i=1}^p$ and $\{\delta_{0,i}\}_{i=1}^q$ in its decomposition. Propose a consistent and relevant estimator for the regression function $\mathbb{E}[D|X = x, Z = z]$. Can it be used when the assumption $p < n$ and $q < n$ is not satisfied? Explain.
2. Now suppose that $p > n$ and $q > n$, and also the sparsity of the coefficients $\{\gamma_{0,i}\}_{i=1}^p$ and $\{\delta_{0,i}\}_{i=1}^q$ in the decomposition of f_0. Give a consistent and relevant estimator for the regression function $\mathbb{E}[D|X = x, Z = z]$, as well as the estimation equation.

B. Estimation of τ_0

3. Write down the estimating equation, starting from (15.4), and using the dependent variable $\tilde{S}_t := \ln(S_t/(1 - S_t))$.
4. Find two functions Q_1 and Q_2 such that

$$m(W_t, \eta, \tau_0) = \left(\tilde{S}_t - Q_1(\eta, Y_t, D_t, X_t)\right) Q_2(\eta, Z_t, X_t),$$

where η is a nuisance parameter to be defined, such that:

$$\mathbb{E}\left[m(W_t, \eta, \tau_0)\right] = 0 \tag{15.5}$$

$$\mathbb{E}\left[\partial_\eta m(W_t, \eta, \tau)\right] = 0, \forall \tau \in \Theta, \tag{15.6}$$

where Θ is a compact neighborhood of τ_0. Similar to the corresponding chapter, we need to use (15.4), (FS), as well as an additional linear equation of your choice specifying the correlation structure between instruments and regressors.

5. Give the conditions on the function g under which the estimator $\widehat{\tau}$ defined by (15.5) is asymptotically Gaussian, using only a theorem from the course.

15.4 Gender wage gap

This exercise primarily relies on knowledge from Chapters 2, 4, 5, and 8.

We are interested in measuring the wage gap between genders, defined as the relative difference in earnings that appears between men and women when controlling for observable characteristics. Consider an i.i.d. sample of the random vector $(\ln W_i, F_i, X_i)_{i=1,...,n}$ where $\ln W_i$ is the natural logarithm of weekly wage, F_i is an indicator variable equal to 1 if individual i is female and 0 otherwise, X_i is a vector of observed characteristics of dimension p which can be (very) large.

1. Interpret the quantity

$$\mathbb{E}[\ln W_i|X_i, F_i = 1] - \mathbb{E}[\ln W_i|X_i, F_i = 0].$$

2. Consider the model:

$$\ln W_i = \alpha + \theta F_i + X_i'\beta + \varepsilon_i, \text{ where } \mathbb{E}[\varepsilon_i|X_i, F_i] = 0 \text{ and } \|\beta\|_0 \leq s \ll p. \quad (15.7)$$

   (a) Given the problem at hand, what can be included in X_i?
   (b) Provide a (simple) consistent estimator of θ in the case where p is a small integer (e.g. $p = 6$), as $n \to \infty$.
   (c) Is it still a consistent estimator if $p > n$ and/or $p \to \infty$? Propose a consistent estimator in the case you answered no to the previous question.
   (d) Show that $\mathbb{E}[\ln W_i|X_i, F_i = 1] - \mathbb{E}[\ln W_i|X_i, F_i = 0] = \theta$. Do you think this is a reasonable assumption?

3. To further analyze the situation, consider the model

$$\ln W_i = \alpha + \theta(Z_i)F_i + X_i'\beta + \varepsilon_i \quad (15.8)$$

where $\mathbb{E}[\varepsilon_i|X_i, F_i] = 0$, $\|\beta\|_0 \leq s \ll p$, and $\theta(Z_i)$ measures an effect that depends on certain covariates $Z_i \subset X_i$. Specifically, we assume that

$$\theta(z) = \sum_{k=1}^{K} \theta_k z_k.$$

   (a) << *The model (15.8) allows us to study a heterogeneous wage gap* >>. What can we think about this? Justify (a formula or two would be welcome).
   (b) Rewrite the model (15.8) as a linear regression model. What are the corresponding normal equations?

(c) Assuming that $p > n$ and $p \to \infty$, but K and s are small integers, how could you consistently estimate $(\theta_1, \ldots, \theta_K)$? Explicitly write an immunized moment condition ψ for $(\theta_1, \ldots, \theta_K)$ and add the necessary assumptions.

4. The table in Appendix A is extracted from Bach et al. (2018). It displays estimates of $(\theta_1, \ldots, \theta_K)$ based on the model (15.8) obtained from the method in Question 3, using a sample of US college graduates. Interpret three rows of your choice.
5. Based on this table, what do you think is the main problem for making inference in this context?
6. Another way to model the heterogeneity of the wage gap is by using causal random forests. In the following question, assume that $(X_i)_{i=1}^n$ are i.i.d. and uniformly distributed $X_i \sim U([0,1]^p)$. Then, at a certain point x in the support of X_i, we define the causal random forest as follows

$$\widehat{\mu}(x; X_1, \ldots, X_n) = \binom{n}{s}^{-1} \sum_{1 \leq i_1 < \cdots < i_s \leq n} T(x; X_{i_1}, \ldots, X_{i_s}),$$

where

$$T(x; X_{i_1}, \ldots, X_{i_s}) = \sum_{i \in \{i_1, \ldots, i_s\}} \alpha_i(x) \ln W_i, \quad \alpha_i(x) = \frac{1\{X_i \in L(x)\}}{s|L(x)|},$$

$L(x)$ are the leaves of tree T, $|L(x)|$ is their Lebesgue measure, and $s \in [n/2, n)$ is the fixed size of the subsamples. Assuming that the regression function $\mu : x \to \mathbb{E}[\ln W_i | X_i = x]$ is Lipschitz with constant C and that the construction of the leaves L is independent of the sample $(X_i)_{i=1}^n$, prove the following inequality

$$|\mathbb{E}[\hat{\mu}(x; X_1, \ldots, X_n)] - \mu(x)| \leq C \,\mathrm{Diam}(L(x)), \tag{15.9}$$

where $\mathrm{Diam}(L(x))$ is the diameter of the leaf containing v.

7. Explain, based on (15.9), what high-level condition we can apply to $\mathrm{Diam}(L(x))$ to obtain consistency. Do standard random forests satisfy this condition and why? How is this implemented in practice in the causal random forest by Athey and Wager?
8. For any given ML proxy, we form five groups G_k, for $k \in \{1, \ldots, 5\}$, among the population based on the predicted outcome $T(X_i)$, using splits I_k based on the quantiles

$$I_k := [l_{k-1}, l_k], \text{ where} l_k = F_{T(X_i)}^{-1}\left(\frac{k}{5}\right),$$

and $F_{T(X_i)}^{-1}$ is the quantile function of $T(X_i)$. Using Figure 15.1 and Table 15.2, provide your interpretation of wage gap heterogeneity and compare it with the interpretation provided in Question 4 based on the tables in the appendix.

Explicitly describe the differences regarding the nature of the parameter of interest and their consequences in interpretation.

9. *(Bonus)* We want to take into account selection effects in labor market participation. Explain how it can be modeled and provide a potential estimation procedure if the selection equation depends on a set of unknown high-dimensional variables, but is a priori sparse.

Heterogeneity of the gender wage gap, Appendix A, Q4–5

Table 15.1 Reproduction of Table 4 from Bach et al. (2018)

Variable	Estimate	p-value
Intercept	−0.0463	0.9070
Marital status		
Married, spouse present	−0.1096	0.0000
Married, spouse absent	−0.0737	0.0010
Separated	−0.0575	0.0030
Divorced	−0.0571	0.0000
Widowed	−0.0536	0.0700
English language proficiency		
Does not speak English	0.0550	0.1600
Yes, speaks very well	0.0111	0.9200
Yes, speaks well	0.0172	0.8850
Yes, but not well	0.0303	0.3400
Ethnicity and nationality		
Black/African American	0.0789	0.0000
Chinese	0.0819	0.0100
Other Asian or Pacific Islander	0.0716	0.0000
Hispanic	0.0115	0.9200
Veteran status		
Veteran	0.0429	0.0140
Industry		
AGRI	−0.0419	0.8540
MINING	−0.0656	0.8540
CONSTR	−0.0511	0.1330
MANUF	−0.0283	0.4020
TRANS	−0.0535	0.0030
RETAIL	−0.0444	0.0150
FINANCE	−0.0493	0.0180
BUISREPSERV	−0.0433	0.0640
PERSON	−0.0384	0.3860
ENTER	−0.0281	0.9200
PROFE	−0.0742	0.0000
ADMIN	−0.0527	0.0140
MILIT	0.1145	0.2650

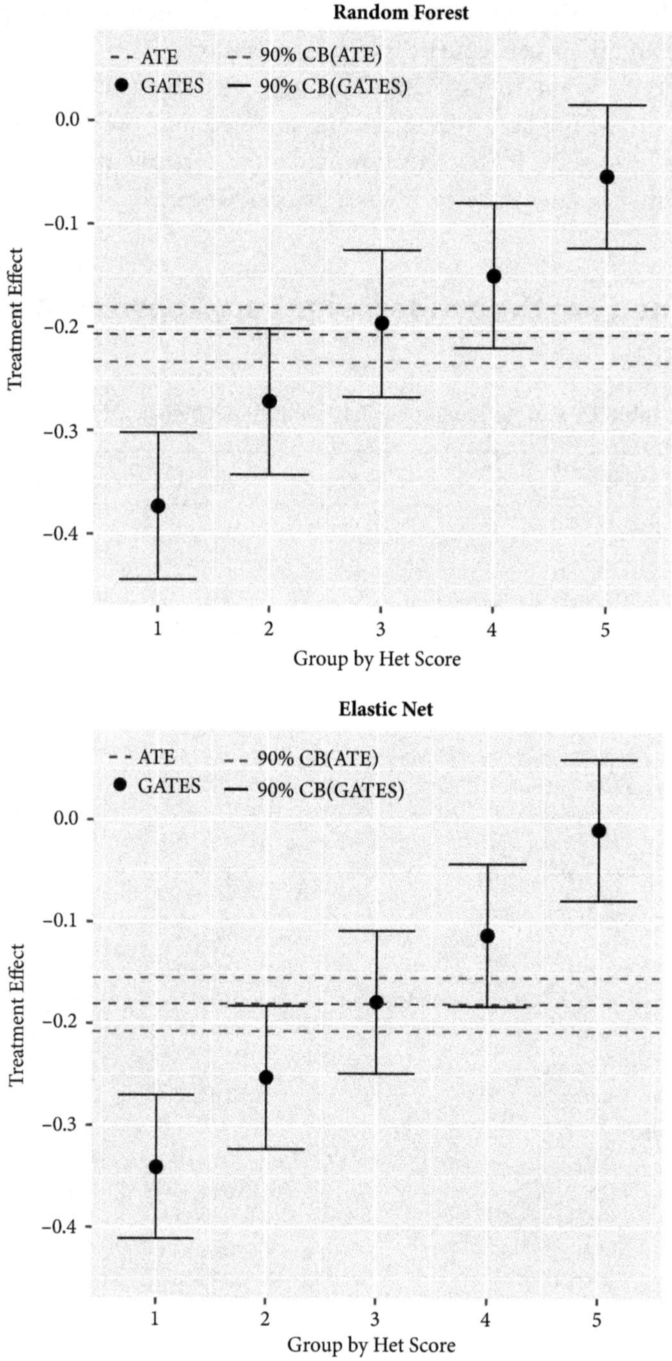

Figure 15.1 Estimated GATES (sorted group average treatment effect).

Note: In black are the 90% robust confidence intervals for the two best ML methods used, based on 100 splits.

Table 15.2 Performance measures for GATES and best linear predictor.

	Elastic Net	Boosting	Nnet	Random forest
$\hat{\bar{\Lambda}}$	0.046	0.040	0.043	0.055
$\hat{\Lambda}$	0.120	0.104	0.108	0.109

Note: For the four ML methods used on log wages, based on 100 splits.

Table 15.3 Estimation of constant β_1 and slope β_2 of the best linear predictor.

	Random forest	Random forest	Elastic net	Elastic net
	β_1	β_2	β_1	β_2
Log wage	−0.207	0.810	−0.181	0.686
90 % CI	(−0.234; −0.181)	(0.609; 1.010)	(−0.208; −0.155)	(0.538; 0.838)

Note: For the two best methods based on 100 splits using the Λ-based selection procedure: random forest and elastic net.

Heterogeneity of the gender wage gap, Appendix B, Q8–10

Let

$$\hat{\Lambda} = \left|\hat{\beta}_2\right|^2 \widehat{\text{Var}}\,(T(X))$$

and

$$\hat{\bar{\Lambda}} = \sum_{k=1}^{K} \hat{\gamma}_k^2 \mathbb{P}\,(T(X) \in I_k)\,,$$

where $\hat{\beta}_2$ is the estimator of the slope of the best linear predictor and $\hat{\gamma}_k$ is the estimator of the average treatment effect of sorted group averages (GATES). For any given ML proxy, we form five groups G_k, for $k \in \{1, \ldots, 5\}$, from the population based on the predicted outcome $T(X_i)$ using the splits I_k based on the quantiles $I_k := [l_{k-1}, l_k]$ where $l_k = F^{-1}_{T(X_i)}(k/5)$, and $F^{-1}_{T(X_i)}$ is the quantile function of $T(X_i)$.

15.5 Drought and incentives for water conservation

This exercise primarily relies on knowledge covered in Chapters 4 and 8.

During a drought in the Southeastern United States in 2007, brochures encouraging water conservation were randomly mailed to 35,000 out of the region's 106,000

Table 15.4 Estimated average characteristics for the least and most affected $\mathbb{E}[X_k|G_5]$ and .$\mathbb{E}[X_k|G_1]$

	Random forest			Elastic net		
	Least affected	Most affected	Difference	Least affected	Most affected	Difference
Log wage						
Age	31.47	34.36	−2.826	31.49	33.54	−2.044
	(31.21; 31.73)	(34.10; 34.62)	(−3.196; −2.456)	(31.22; 31.75)	(33.27; 33.81)	(−2.427; −1.660)
No. children < 19	0.263	0.831	−0.566	0.237	0.814	−0.586
	(0.238; 0.287)	(0.807; 0.856)	(−0.602; −0.530)	(0.212; 0.262)	(0.790; 0.838)	(−0.621; −0.551)
Experience	9.060	14.70	−5.634	9.238	14.06	−4.771
	(8.793; 9.328)	(14.43; 14.96)	(−6.004; −5.258)	(8.948; 9.528)	(13.78; 14.34)	(−5.185; −4.358)

Note: Based on 100 splits for the two variables age (Age), number of children under 19 (No. children < 19), and years of work experience (Experience) with 90% robust confidence intervals for the ML methods used. "Least affected" corresponds to group G_1 ("Most affected" corresponds to G_5).

households. The variable of interest is water consumption during the summer of 2007 (after the pro-social campaign), measured in thousands of gallons. The objective is to study whether there is heterogeneity in the treatment effect, and if this effect is more significant on households that (i) vote more often and (ii) are considered Democrats or Republicans.

D is a dummy variable that takes the value 1 if the household received a water conservation message and 0 otherwise. Recall that Y_1 and Y_0 represent the two random variables representing potential water consumption between June and September 2007 with and without treatment, respectively. $Y = Y_0 + D(Y_1 - Y_0)$ represents the observed water consumption. X represents a set of characteristics such as past water consumption, an indicator of voter registration, whether the property is rented or owned, the age and value of the property, the age of the owner, etc. All variables are measured at the household level.

$p(X)$ denotes the probability of treatment, and we use the notation $w(X) := 1/(p(X)(1 - p(X)))$.

In order to estimate the relevant effects, we implement the *generic machine learning* methodology. For all reported results, 30 different data divisions between a main sample and an auxiliary sample are considered.

1. $T(X)$ denotes the generic machine learning resulting from a given algorithm, that is, the prediction of the conditional average treatment effect, $\tau(X)$, for a household with characteristics X. Consider the following regression on the main sample:

$$w(X)(D - p(X))Y = \beta_1 + \beta_2(T(X) - \mathbb{E}[T(X)]) + \varepsilon. \tag{15.10}$$

   (a) In this regression, what does β_1 represent?
   (b) In this regression, what does β_2 represent? Explain how it can help address the question of heterogeneity of the treatment effect.

   For Questions 2 to 5, your answers should be supported by statistics (p-values, etc.) whenever possible.

2. We train four different algorithms: an elastic net, a gradient boosting machine, a neural network, and a random forest. Table 15.5 presents the statistics $\Lambda = |\widehat{\beta}_2|^2\widehat{V}(T(X))$, where $\widehat{\beta}_2$ was estimated from the regression above, for each algorithm.
   (a) Explain how and why the statistic Λ can help choose the best out of the four algorithms.
   (b) According to Table 15.5, which algorithm is the best?

3. Table 15.6 presents the results (estimator, 90% confidence interval, and p-values) of the regression from Question 1 for the two best algorithms.
   (a) Does the treatment have an effect?
   (b) Is this effect heterogeneous?
4. For a given ML proxy and $k = 1, \dots, 5$, we define group

$$G_k = \mathbf{1}\{\ell_{k-1} \leq T(X) < \ell_k\}$$

using quantiles $-\infty = \ell_0 \leq \ell_1 \leq \cdots \leq \ell_5 = +\infty$ such that the population is divided into five groups of 20% based on a ranking of households using the ML predictor. If a household has $G_1 = 1$, it is considered as being among the "most affected." If a household has $G_5 = 1$, it is considered as being among the "least affected." Table 15.7 reports the treatment effect estimates for the least and most affected populations, as well as their difference.
   (a) Write down the regression equation that yielded these results. Explain how it was estimated.
   (b) Does the treatment have an effect on each household?
   (c) Is there a difference in the treatment effect between the most and least affected households?
5. We want to see if the most and least affected households have different characteristics in order to answer the initial question. Table 15.8 reports the result.
   (a) How was this table obtained?
   (b) Are households that participate more often in elections more likely to respond to water-saving incentives?
   (c) Are households that vote more often for Democratic or Republican candidates more likely to respond to water-saving incentives?

We now focus on estimating the conditional average treatment effect (CATE) function:

$$\tau(x) = \mathbb{E}[Y_1 - Y_0|X = x] = \mu_1(x) - \mu_0(x),$$

where $\mu_j(x) = \mathbb{E}[Y_j|X = x]$, $j = 0, 1$.

6. Let's assume the following model for $j = 0, 1$,

$$Y_j = X'\alpha_j + \varepsilon_j, \; \mathbb{E}[\varepsilon_j|X] = 0,$$

where X has a large dimension (dimension $p >> n$, the number of observations). Give the formula for the Lasso estimators of α_1 and α_0. Propose an estimator for the CATE based on these estimators. Justify intuitively why, in practice, it does not have good properties.

7. What is the "solution" that has been proposed to address this problem, when $p < n$, in the causal random forest (CRF hereafter) estimator?
8. We consider the model of this randomized controlled trial (RCT), in which treatment allocation is random, $D \perp\!\!\!\perp X$, and

$$Y = X'\gamma + D\tau(X) + \varepsilon, \quad \varepsilon \perp\!\!\!\perp (D, X), \tag{15.11}$$

where $\tau(X)$ is assumed to be linear in X, which has a large dimension. We base our estimator for τ on

$$\begin{aligned}(\widehat{\beta}, \widehat{\delta}) \\ = \underset{\beta,\delta}{\operatorname{argmin}} \left\{ \frac{1}{n} \sum_{i=1}^{n} \left(Y_i - X_i'\beta - (D_i - \mathbb{E}[D_i])X_i'\delta\right)^2 + \lambda_\beta \|\beta\|_1 + \lambda_\delta \|\delta\|_1 \right\}.\end{aligned} \tag{15.12}$$

Identify γ and τ in terms of β and δ and give the estimator of τ based on $(\widehat{\beta}, \widehat{\delta})$. Write down the moment estimation equations that we use in (15.12).
9. What is β called in (15.12)? In the context of a RCT, is the estimator based on (15.12) immunized? Prove it.
10. Justify intuitively why such an estimator solves the problem mentioned in Questions 6 and 7.
11. Give a context in which this CATE estimator is more appropriate than the CRF estimator and another context in which the CRF is more suitable.
12. Returning to the application, one problem is that randomization was done at the level of water meter routes and not at the household level. This could lead to selection bias as households in the same neighborhood (sharing a water meter route) may have similar water consumption behaviors and reactions to the treatment.

   We want to control for this using the following model

$$D = Z'\gamma + \zeta, \quad Z \perp\!\!\!\perp \zeta, \quad Z \perp\!\!\!\perp \varepsilon,$$

where Z are available auxiliary variables (e.g., median or mean income at the neighborhood level, median or mean water consumption, occupancy rate of owner-occupied houses, etc.) and ε is the residual in (15.11). Write down how you would modify (15.12) to account for this so that your estimator is immune. Show this last point.

Drought and water conservation incentives, appendix

Table 15.5 Ranking of algorithms – Λ.

Λ	Elastic Net	Gradient boosting Machine	Neural Network	Random Forest
Water Cons. (Q3 2007)	1.137	1.165	1.000	0.933

Table 15.6 Regression results.

	Algorithm 1		Algorithm 2	
	β_1	β_2	β_1	β_2
Water Cons. (Q3 2017)	−0.952 (−1.278; −0.631) [0.000]	0.116 (0.068; 0.167) [0.000]	−0.902 (−1.233; −0.576) [0.000]	0.058 (−0.031, 0.146) [0.441]

Table 15.7 Group treatment effect.

	Algorithm 1			Algorithm 2		
	Less affected	More affected	Diff.	Less affected	More affected	Diff.
Water Cons. (Q3 2007)	−0.953 (−1.685; −0.217) [0.023]	−1.688 (−2.417; −0.960) [0.000]	0.700 (−0.302; 1.722) [0.342]	−0.707 (−1.459; 0.050) [0.135]	−1.483 (−2.235; −0.730) [0.000]	0.780 (−0.290; 1.858) [0.307]

Table 15.8 Average characteristics of groups.

	Algorithm 1			Algorithm 2		
	Less affected	More affected	Diff.	Less affected	More affected	Diff.
Frequency of voting	0.098 (0.096; 0.100) –	0.120 (0.118; 0.122) –	−0.017 (−0.020; −0.014) [0.000]	0.096 (0.094; 0.098) –	0.121 (0.119; 0.123) –	−0.024 (−0.027; −0.021) [0.000]
Democrat	0.166 (0.159; 0.174) –	0.204 (0.197; 0.212) –	−0.044 (−0.054; −0.033) [0.000]	0.147 (0.139; 0.154) –	0.242 (0.234; 0.249) –	−0.087 (−0.097; −0.077) [0.000]
Republican	0.408 (0.399; 0.418) –	0.448 (0.438; 0.458) –	−0.012 (−0.025; 0.001) [0.159]	0.409 (0.400; 0.419) –	0.390 (0.380; 0.399) –	0.008 (−0.006; 0.021) [0.531]

15.6 Synthetic control and regularization

This problem mainly relies on Chapters 2 and 10.

Consider a panel data framework where we observe an outcome $Y_{i,t}^{obs}$ for units $i = 1, \dots, N+1$ measured at dates $t = 1, \dots, T+1$. The matrix $(Y_{i,t}^{obs})_{i,t}$ is the only available data. Unit 1 is treated only at the last date $T+1$, but never before, so we observe the outcome without treatment as

$$Y_{1,t}^{obs} = Y_{1,t}(0)$$

for $t = 1, \dots, T$, and only at the last date, the outcome with treatment,

$$Y_{1,T+1}^{obs} = Y_{1,T+1}(1).$$

Units $1, \dots, N+1$ are never treated at any date, so for them, we always have $Y_{i,t}^{obs} = Y_{i,t}(0)$, which is the outcome without treatment. In short, we have the following missing variable model:

$$\boldsymbol{Y}(0) := \begin{pmatrix} ? & Y_{2,T+1}(0) & \cdots & Y_{N+1,T+1}(0) \\ Y_{1,T}(0) & Y_{2,T}(0) & \cdots & Y_{N+1,T}(0) \\ \vdots & \vdots & & \vdots \\ Y_{1,1}(0) & Y_{2,1}(0) & \cdots & Y_{N+1,1}(0) \end{pmatrix}.$$

We are interested in estimating the treatment effect for the first unit at the last date:

$$\theta = Y_{1,T+1}(1) - Y_{1,T+1}(0).$$

This problem discusses different strategies to estimate $Y_{1,T+1}(0)$ (and thus θ) using an estimator of the form:

$$\widehat{Y}_{1,T+1}(0) = \mu + \sum_{i=2}^{N+1} \omega_i Y_{i,T+1}^{obs},$$

with the parameters μ and $\boldsymbol{\omega} := (\omega_2, \dots, \omega_{N+1})$ estimated by solving the following program:

$$\underset{\mu,\boldsymbol{\omega}}{\arg\min} \sum_{t=1}^{T} \left(Y_{1,t}^{obs} - \mu - \sum_{i=2}^{N+1} \omega_i Y_{i,t}^{obs} \right)^2. \tag{15.13}$$

NB: No specific assumption is made regarding the dimensions N and T. These dimensions are to be discussed during the problem.

1. How can we justify the use of Equation (15.13) to estimate the parameters?
2. (a) Compute the parameters that solve equation (15.13). Under what condition(s) do they exist?

(b) Can we interpret the resulting value of $\boldsymbol{\omega}$? What does it represent?
(c) What problem(s) arise with the estimator of $Y_{1,T+1}(0)$?

3. For this question only, we add constraints to Equation (15.13) specifying that the elements of $\boldsymbol{\omega}$ must all be constant and their sum must be equal to one.
   (a) What is the value of $\boldsymbol{\omega}$ under this constraint?
   (b) Compute μ under this constraint.
   (c) Compute and explain the intuition behind the resulting estimator for θ. What is its name?
4. For this question only, we add three constraints to Equation (15.13): $\omega_i \geq 0$ for $i = 2, \ldots, N+1$, $\sum_{i=2}^{N+1} \omega_i = 1$, and $\mu = 0$.
   (a) Name this estimator and the advantages it offers compared to the estimator in Question 3.
   (b) Is the solution to Equation (15.13) under these constraints generally unique?
5. In Questions 3–4, we imposed several constraints on the parameters. Instead of that, in this question, we consider a modified version of Equation (15.13):

$$\underset{\mu,\boldsymbol{\omega}}{\arg\min} \sum_{t=1}^{T} \left(Y_{1,t}^{obs} - \mu - \sum_{i=2}^{N+1} \omega_i Y_{i,t}^{obs} \right)^2 + \lambda \left((1-\alpha) \left\| \boldsymbol{\omega} \right\|_2^2 + \alpha \left\| \boldsymbol{\omega} \right\|_1 \right),$$

   where $\alpha \in [0, 1]$ and $\lambda > 0$ are hyperparameters.
   (a) Explain how this modification allows overcoming the condition(s) found in Question 2(a).
   (b) Compute and describe the solution $\widehat{\boldsymbol{\omega}}$ when $\alpha = 0$.
   (c) Describe the solution $\widehat{\boldsymbol{\omega}}$ when $\alpha = 1$.
   (d) Propose a strategy for selecting the two hyperparameters α and λ.

Bibliography

Abadi, M., P. Barham, J. Chen, Z. Chen, A. Davis, J. Dean, M. Devin, S. Ghemawat, G. Irving, M. Isard, et al. (2016). Tensorflow: A system for large-scale machine learning. In *OSDI*, Volume 16, pp. 265–283.

Abadie, A. and M. D. Cattaneo (2018). Econometric methods for program evaluation. *Annual Review of Economics 10*(1), 465–503.

Abadie, A., and M. Kasy (2019, 12). Choosing among regularized estimators in empirical economics: the risk of machine learning. *The Review of Economics and Statistics 101*(5), 743–762.

Abadie, A., J. Angrist, and G. Imbens (2002). Instrumental variables estimates of the effect of subsidized training on the quantiles of trainee earnings. *Econometrica 70*(1), 91–117.

Abadie, A. (2021). Using synthetic controls: Feasibility, data requirements, and methodological aspects. *Journal of Economic Literature 59*(2), 391–425.

Abadie, A., S. Athey, G. W. Imbens, and J. M. Wooldridge (2020). Sampling-based versus design-based uncertainty in regression analysis. *Econometrica 88*(1), 265–296.

Abadie, A., A. Diamond, and J. Hainmueller (2010). Synthetic control methods for comparative case studies: Estimating the effect of california's tobacco control program. *Journal of the American Statistical Association 105*(490), 493–505.

Abadie, A., A. Diamond, and J. Hainmueller (2015). Comparative politics and the synthetic control method. *American Journal of Political Science 59*(2), 495–510.

Abadie, A., and J. Gardeazabal (2003, March). The economic costs of conflict: a case study of the Basque Country. *American Economic Review 93*(1), 113–132.

Abadie, A. and J. L'Hour (2021). A penalized synthetic control estimator for disaggregated data. *Journal of the American Statistical Association 116*(536), 1817–1834.

Acemoglu, D., S. Johnson, A. Kermani, J. Kwak, and T. Mitton (2016). The value of connections in turbulent times: Evidence from the United States. *Journal of Financial Economics 121*, 368–391.

Ahn, S. C. and A. R. Horenstein (2013). Eigenvalue ratio test for the number of factors. *Econometrica 81*(3), 1203–1227.

Allegretto, S., A. Dube, M. Reich, and B. Zipperer (2017). Credible research designs for minimum wage studies: A response to neumark, salas, and wascher. *ILR Review 70*(3), 559–592.

Alquier, P., E. Gautier, and G. Stoltz (2011). *Inverse Problems and High-Dimensional Estimation: Stats in the Château Summer School, August 31 - September 4, 2009.* Berlin, Heidelberg: Springer Berlin Heidelberg.

Alquier, P. and P. Doukhan (2011). Sparsity considerations for dependent variables. *Electronic Journal of Statistics 5*(none), 750–774.

Amemiya, T. (1974). The nonlinear two-stage least-squares estimator. *Journal of econometrics 2*(2), 105–110.

Andrews, D. W. (1984). Non-strong mixing autoregressive processes. *Journal of Applied Probability 21*(4), 930–934.

Andrews, D. W. (1991). Heteroskedasticity and autocorrelation consistent covariance matrix estimation. *Econometrica*, 817–858.

Angrist, J. and J.-S. Pischke (2009). *Mostly Harmless Econometrics: An Empiricist's Companion* (1st ed.). Princeton University Press.

Angrist, J. D. and J.-S. Pischke (2010, June). The credibility revolution in empirical economics: How better research design is taking the con out of econometrics. *Journal of Economic Perspectives 24*(2), 3–30.

Angrist, J. D. and B. Frandsen (2022). Machine labor. *Journal of Labor Economics 40*(S1), S97–S140.

Angrist, J. D. and A. B. Krueger (1991). Does compulsory school attendance affect schooling and earnings? *The Quarterly Journal of Economics 106*(4), 979–1014.

Antoniak, M., and D. Mimno (2018, 02). Evaluating the stability of embedding-based word similarities. *Transactions of the Association for Computational Linguistics 6*, 107–119.

Arora, S., Y. Liang, and T. Ma (2017). A simple but tough-to-beat baseline for sentence embeddings. In *ICLR.*

Ash, E. and S. Hansen (2022). Text algorithms in economics. *Annual Review of Economics forthcoming.*

Ash, E., D. L. Chen, and A. Ornaghi (2021). Gender Attitudes in the Judiciary: Evidence from U.S. Circuit Courts. CAGE Online Working Paper Series 462, Competitive Advantage in the Global Economy (CAGE).

Ash, E., G. Gauthier, and P. Widmer (2021, August). RELATIO: Text Semantics Capture Political and Economic Narratives. *arXiv e-prints, arXiv:2108.01720.*

Athey, S. and G. W. Imbens (2019). Machine learning methods that economists should know about. *Annual Review of Economics 11.*

Athey, S. (2017). Beyond prediction: Using big data for policy problems. *Science 355*(6324), 483–485.

Athey, S. and G. Imbens (2016). Recursive partitioning for heterogeneous causal effects. *Proceedings of the National Academy of Sciences 113*(27), 7353–7360.

Athey, S., J. Tibshirani, and S. Wager (2019, 04). Generalized random forests. *The Annals of Statistics 47*(2), 1148–1178.

Athey, S. and S. Wager (2019). Estimating treatment effects with causal forests: An application. *arXiv preprint arXiv:1902.07409.*

Athey, S. and S. Wager (2021). Policy learning with observational data. *Econometrica 89*(1), 133–161.

Athey, S. and G. W. Imbens (2017, May). The state of applied econometrics: Causality and policy evaluation. *Journal of Economic Perspectives 31*(2), 3–32.

Bühlmann, P. and B. Yu (2002). Analyzing bagging. *The Annals of Statistics 30*(4), 927–961.

Ba, J. L., J. R. Kiros, and G. E. Hinton (2016). Layer normalization. https://arxiv.org/abs/1607.06450.

Babii, A., E. Ghysels, and J. Striaukas (2019). High-dimensional granger causality tests with an application to vix and news. *arXiv preprint arXiv:1912.06307.*

Babii, A., R. T. Ball, E. Ghysels, and J. Striaukas (2023). Machine learning panel data regressions with heavy-tailed dependent data: Theory and application. *Journal of Econometrics. 237*(2), 105315.

Babii, A., E. Ghysels, and J. Striaukas (2022). Machine learning time series regressions with an application to nowcasting. *Journal of Business and Economic Statistics 40*(3), 1094–1106.

Babii, A., E. Ghysels, and J. Striaukas (2023). Econometrics of machine learning methods in economic forecasting. *arXiv preprint arXiv:2308.10993.*

Bach, P., V. Chernozhukov, and M. Spindler (2018). Valid simultaneous inference in high-dimensional settings (with the hdm package for r). *arXiv preprint arXiv:1809.04951.*

Bach, P., V. Chernozhukov, and M. Spindler (2018, December). Closing the U.S. gender wage gap requires understanding its heterogeneity. *arXiv e-prints, arXiv:1812.04345.*

Bai, J. (2003). Inferential theory for factor models of large dimensions. *Econometrica 71*(1), 135–171.

Bai, J. and S. Ng (2002). Determining the number of factors in approximate factor models. *Econometrica 70*(1), 191–221.

Bai, J. and S. Ng (2006). Confidence intervals for diffusion index forecasts and inference for factor-augmented regressions. *Econometrica 74*(4), 1133–1150.

Baiardi, A. and A. A. Naghi (2024). The value added of machine learning to causal inference: Evidence from revisited studies. *The Econometrics Journal*, utae004.

Bajari, P. L., Z. Cen, V. Chernozhukov, M. Manukonda, J. Wang, R. Huerta, J. Li, L. Leng, G. Monokroussos, S. Vijaykunar, and S. Wan (2021). Hedonic prices and quality adjusted price indices powered by ai. cemmap working paper CWP04/21, Centre for Microdata Methods and Practice (cemmap), London.

Baker, S. R., N. Bloom, and S. J. Davis (2016). Measuring Economic Policy Uncertainty. *The Quarterly Journal of Economics 131*(4), 1593–1636.

Balestriero, R., M. Ibrahim, V. Sobal, A. Morcos, S. Shekhar, T. Goldstein, F. Bordes, A. Bardes, G. Mialon, Y. Tian, A. Schwarzschild, A. G. Wilson, J. Geiping, Q. Garrido, P. Fernandez, A. Bar,

H. Pirsiavash, Y. LeCun, and M. Goldblum (2023, April). A Cookbook of Self-Supervised Learning. *arXiv e-prints*, arXiv:2304.12210.

Baltagi, B. H. (2005). *Econometric analysis of panel data.* (3rd ed.). New York: John Wiley & Sons Inc.

Bana, S. H. (2022, March). work2vec: Using language models to understand wage premia. Working paper, Stanford Digital Economy Lab.

Bartlett, P. L., M. I. Jordan, and J. D. McAuliffe (2006). Convexity, classification, and risk bounds. *Journal of the American Statistical Association 101*(473), 138–156.

Basu, S. and G. Michailidis (2015). Regularized estimation in sparse high-dimensional time series models. *The Annals of Statistics 43*(4), 1535–1567.

Beck, A. and M. Teboulle (2014). A fast dual proximal gradient algorithm for convex minimization and applications. *Operations Research Letters 42*(1), 1–6.

Belkin, M., D. Hsu, S. Ma, and S. Mandal (2019). Reconciling modern machine-learning practice and the classical bias–variance trade-off. *Proceedings of the National Academy of Sciences 116*(32), 15849–15854.

Belloni, A. and V. Chernozhukov (2013, 05). Least squares after model selection in high-dimensional sparse models. *Bernoulli 19*(2), 521–547.

Belloni, A., V. Chernozhukov, and C. Hansen (2014, Spring). High-dimensional methods and inference on structural and treatment effects. *Journal of Economic Perspectives 28*(2), 29–50.

Belloni, A., D. Chen, V. Chernozhukov, and C. Hansen (2012). Sparse models and methods for optimal instruments with an application to eminent domain. *Econometrica 80*(6), 2369–2429.

Belloni, A. and V. Chernozhukov (2011). *High Dimensional Sparse Econometric Models: An Introduction*, pp. 121–156. Springer Berlin Heidelberg.

Belloni, A., V. Chernozhukov, I. Fernández-Val, and C. Hansen (2017). Program evaluation and causal inference with high-dimensional data. *Econometrica 85*(1), 233–298.

Belloni, A., V. Chernozhukov, and C. Hansen (2010, December). LASSO Methods for Gaussian Instrumental Variables Models. *ArXiv e-prints.*

Belloni, A., V. Chernozhukov, C. Hansen, and W. Newey (2017). Simultaneous confidence intervals for high-dimensional linear models with many endogenous variables. *arXiv preprint arXiv:1712.08102.*

Belloni, A., V. Chernozhukov, D. Chetverikov, and C. Hansen (2018). High dimensional econometrics and regularized gmm. *arXiv:1806.01888, Contributed chapter for Handbook of Econometrics.*

Belloni, A., V. Chernozhukov, and C. Hansen (2014). High-dimensional methods and inference on structural and treatment effects. *The Journal of Economic Perspectives 28*(2), 29–50.

Belloni, A., V. Chernozhukov, C. Hansen, and D. Kozbur (2016). Inference in high-dimensional panel models with an application to gun control. *Journal of Business & Economic Statistics 34*(4), 590–605.

Belloni, A., V. Chernozhukov, and K. Kato (2015). Uniform post-selection inference for least absolute deviation regression and other z-estimation problems. *Biometrika 102*(1), 77–94.

Belloni, A. and V. Chernozhukov (2013). Least squares after model selection in high-dimensional sparse models. *Bernoulli 19*(2), 521–547.

Ben-Michael, E., A. Feller, and J. Rothstein (2021). The augmented synthetic control method. *Journal of the American Statistical Association 116*(536), 1789–1803.

Bengio, Y., R. Ducharme, and P. Vincent (2000). A neural probabilistic language model. In T. Leen, T. Dietterich, and V. Tresp (Eds.), *Advances in Neural Information Processing Systems*, Volume 13. MIT Press.

Berry, S., J. Levinsohn, and A. Pakes (1995). Automobile prices in market equilibrium. *Econometrica: Journal of the Econometric Society*, 841–890.

Berry, S. T. (1994). Estimating discrete-choice models of product differentiation. *The RAND Journal of Economics*, 242–262.

Beyhum, J. and J. Striaukas (2024). Factor-augmented sparse MIDAS regressions with an application to nowcasting. https://arxiv.org/abs/2306.13362.

Beyhum, J. and J. Striaukas (2024). Testing for sparse idiosyncratic components in factor-augmented regression models. *Journal of Econometrics 244*(1), 105845.

Bhattacharya, D. and P. Dupas (2012). Inferring welfare maximizing treatment assignment under budget constraints. *Journal of Econometrics 167*(1), 168–196.

Bholat, D. M., S. Hansen, P. M. Santos, and C. Schonhardt-Bailey (2015). Text mining for central banks. *Working Paper.*

Biau, G. and E. Scornet (2016). A random forest guided tour. *Test 25*(2), 197–227.

Bickel, P. J., Y. Ritov, and A. B. Tsybakov (2009, 08). Simultaneous analysis of lasso and dantzig selector. *Ann. Statist. 37*(4), 1705–1732.

Bléhaut, M., X. D'Haultfoeuille, J. L'Hour, and A. B. Tsybakov (2023). An alternative to synthetic control for models with many covariates under sparsity. In D. Belomestny, C. Butucea, E. Mammen, E. Moulines, M. Reiß, and V. V. Ulyanov (Eds.), *Foundations of Modern Statistics*, Cham, pp. 417–458. Springer International Publishing.

Blei, D. M. and J. D. Lafferty (2009). Topic models. *Text mining: classification, clustering, and applications 10*(71), 34.

Blei, D. M., A. Y. Ng, and M. I. Jordan (2003). Latent dirichlet allocation. *Journal of machine Learning research 3*(Jan), 993–1022.

Bohn, S., M. Lofstrom, and S. Raphael (2014). Did the 2007 legal Arizona workers act reduce the state's unauthorized immigrant population? *Review of Economics and Statistics 96*(2), 258–269.

Bojanowski, P., E. Grave, A. Joulin, and T. Mikolov (2016). Enriching word vectors with subword information. *arXiv preprint arXiv:1607.04606.*

Bok, B., D. Caratelli, D. Giannone, A. M. Sbordone, and A. Tambalotti (2018). Macroeconomic nowcasting and forecasting with big data. *Annual Review of Economics 10*, 615–643.

Bottou, L. (2010). Large-scale machine learning with stochastic gradient descent. In Y. Lechevallier and G. Saporta (Eds.), *Proceedings of COMPSTAT'2010*, Heidelberg, pp. 177–186. Physica-Verlag HD.

Breiman, L. (2001). Random forests. *Machine learning 45*(1), 5–32.

Breunig, C., E. Mammen, and A. Simoni (2020). Ill-posed estimation in high-dimensional models with instrumental variables. *Journal of Econometrics 219*(1), 171–200.

Brown, T., B. Mann, N. Ryder, M. Subbiah, J. D. Kaplan, P. Dhariwal, A. Neelakantan, P. Shyam, G. Sastry, A. Askell, S. Agarwal, A. Herbert-Voss, G. Krueger, T. Henighan, R. Child, A. Ramesh, D. Ziegler, J. Wu, C. Winter, C. Hesse, M. Chen, E. Sigler, M. Litwin, S. Gray, B. Chess, J. Clark, C. Berner, S. McCandlish, A. Radford, I. Sutskever, and D. Amodei (2020). Language models are few-shot learners. In H. Larochelle, M. Ranzato, R. Hadsell, M. Balcan, and H. Lin (Eds.), *Advances in Neural Information Processing Systems*, Volume 33, pp. 1877–1901. Curran Associates, Inc.

Bybee, L., B. T. Kelly, A. Manela, and D. Xiu (2020). The structure of economic news. Technical report, National Bureau of Economic Research.

Bühlmann, P. and S. Van de Geer (2011). *Statistics for High-Dimensional Data: Methods, Theory and Applications.* Springer-Verlag Berlin Heidelberg.

Cagé, J., N. Hervé, and M.-L. Viaud (2019, 12). The production of information in an online world. *The Review of Economic Studies 87*(5), 2126–2164.

Candes, E. and T. Tao (2007, 12). The dantzig selector: Statistical estimation when p is much larger than n. *Ann. Statist. 35*(6), 2313–2351.

Card, D. (1993, October). Using Geographic Variation in College Proximity to Estimate the Return to Schooling. NBER Working Papers 4483, National Bureau of Economic Research, Inc.

Card, D. (1990). The impact of the mariel boatlift on the miami labor market. *ILR Review 43*(2), 245–257.

Carrasco, M., J.-P. Florens, and E. Renault (2007). Linear inverse problems in structural econometrics estimation based on spectral decomposition and regularization. *Handbook of econometrics 6*, 5633–5751.

Carrasco, M. (2012). A regularization approach to the many instruments problem. *Journal of Econometrics 170*(2), 383–398.

Chamberlain, G. (1987). Asymptotic efficiency in estimation with conditional moment restrictions. *Journal of Econometrics 34*(3), 305–334.

Chatterjee, S. (2013, March). Assumptionless consistency of the Lasso. *ArXiv e-prints.*

Chen, W., X. Chen, J. Zhang, and K. Huang (2017). Beyond triplet loss: A deep quadruplet network for person re-identification. *2017 IEEE Conference on Computer Vision and Pattern Recognition (CVPR)*, 1320–1329.

Chernozhukov, V., M. Demirer, E. Duflo, and I. Fernandez-Val (2017). Generic machine learning inference on heterogenous treatment effects in randomized experiments. *arXiv preprint arXiv:1712.04802.*

Chernozhukov, V., C. Hansen, N. Kallus, M. Spindler, and V. Syrgkanis (2024). Applied causal inference powered by ML and AI. *rem 12*(1), 338.

Chernozhukov, V. and C. Hansen (2005). An iv model of quantile treatment effects. *Econometrica 73*(1), 245–261.

Chernozhukov, V., D. Chetverikov, M. Demirer, E. Duflo, C. Hansen, and W. Newey (2017, May). Double/debiased/neyman machine learning of treatment effects. *American Economic Review 107*(5), 261–65.

Chernozhukov, V., D. Chetverikov, M. Demirer, E. Duflo, C. Hansen, W. Newey, and J. Robins (2018). Double/debiased machine learning for treatment and structural parameters. *The Econometrics Journal 21*(1), C1–C68.

Chernozhukov, V., C. Hansen, and M. Spindler (2015a, May). Post-selection and post-regularization inference in linear models with many controls and instruments. *American Economic Review 105*(5), 486–90.

Chernozhukov, V., C. Hansen, and M. Spindler (2015b). Valid post-selection and post-regularization inference: An elementary, general approach. *Annu. Rev. Econ. 7*(1), 649–688.

Chernozhukov, V., W. K. Härdle, C. Huang, and W. Wang (2021). Lasso-driven inference in time and space. *The Annals of Statistics 49*(3), 1702–1735.

Chernozhukov, V., K. Wüthrich, and Y. Zhu (2021). An exact and robust conformal inference method for counterfactual and synthetic controls. *Journal of the American Statistical Association 116*(536), 1849–1864.

Chernozhuokov, V., D. Chetverikov, and K. Kato (2013). Gaussian approximations and multiplier bootstrap for maxima of sums of high-dimensional random vectors. *The Annals of Statistics,* December *41*(6), 2786–2819.

Chetverikov, D. N. and J. R.-V. Sørensen (2022). Analytic and bootstrap-after-cross-validation methods for selecting penalty parameters of high-dimensional m-estimators. Technical report, cemmap working paper.

Chetverikov, D. (2024). Tuning parameter selection in econometrics. *arXiv preprint arXiv:2405.03021.*

Chowdhery, A., S. Narang, J. Devlin, M. Bosma, G. Mishra, A. Roberts, P. Barham, H. W. Chung, C. Sutton, S. Gehrmann, P. Schuh, K. Shi, S. Tsvyashchenko, J. Maynez, A. Rao, P. Barnes, Y. Tay, N. Shazeer, V. Prabhakaran, E. Reif, N. Du, B. Hutchinson, R. Pope, J. Bradbury, J. Austin, M. Isard, G. Gur-Ari, P. Yin, T. Duke, A. Levskaya, S. Ghemawat, S. Dev, H. Michalewski, X. Garcia, V. Misra, K. Robinson, L. Fedus, D. Zhou, D. Ippolito, D. Luan, H. Lim, B. Zoph, A. Spiridonov, R. Sepassi, D. Dohan, S. Agrawal, M. Omernick, A. M. Dai, T. S. Pillai, M. Pellat, A. Lewkowycz, E. Moreira, R. Child, O. Polozov, K. Lee, Z. Zhou, X. Wang, B. Saeta, M. Diaz, O. Firat, M. Catasta, J. Wei, K. Meier-Hellstern, D. Eck, J. Dean, S. Petrov, and N. Fiedel (2022). Palm: Scaling language modeling with pathways.

Conneau, A., G. Lample, M. Ranzato, L. Denoyer, and H. Jégou (2017). Word translation without parallel data. *arXiv preprint arXiv:1710.04087.*

Cornwell, C. and W. N. Trumbull (1994). Estimating the economic model of crime with panel data. *The Review of economics and Statistics*, 360–366.

Crépon, B., E. Duflo, M. Gurgand, R. Rathelot, and P. Zamora (2013). Do labor market policies have displacement effects? Evidence from a clustered randomized experiment. *The Quarterly Journal of Economics 128*(2), 531–580.

Cunningham, S., and M. Shah (2017, 12). Decriminalizing indoor prostitution: Implications for sexual violence and public health. *The Review of Economic Studies 85*(3), 1683–1715.

Cybenko, G. (1989, December). Approximation by superpositions of a sigmoidal function. *Mathematics of Control, Signals, and Systems (MCSS) 2*(4), 303–314.

Dai, Y., M. de Kamps, and S. Sharoff (2022, June). BERTology for machine translation: What BERT knows about linguistic difficulties for translation. In N. Calzolari, F. Béchet, P. Blache, K. Choukri, C. Cieri, T. Declerck, S. Goggi, H. Isahara, B. Maegaard, J. Mariani, H. Mazo, J. Odijk, and S. Piperidis

(Eds.), *Proceedings of the Thirteenth Language Resources and Evaluation Conference*, Marseille, France, pp. 6674–6690. European Language Resources Association.

Darolles, S., Y. Fan, J.-P. Florens, and E. Renault (2011). Nonparametric instrumental regression. *Econometrica 79*(5), 1541–1565.

Davis, J. and S. B. Heller (2017). Using causal forests to predict treatment heterogeneity: An application to summer jobs. *American Economic Review 107*(5), 546–50.

Davis, J. M., and S. B. Heller (2020, 10). Rethinking the benefits of youth employment programs: The heterogeneous effects of summer jobs. *The Review of Economics and Statistics 102*(4), 664–677.

Davis, R. A. and M. S. Nielsen (2020). Modeling of time series using random forests: Theoretical developments. *Electronic Journal of Statistics 14*(2), 3644–3671.

De Mol, C., D. Giannone, and L. Reichlin (2008). Forecasting using a large number of predictors: Is bayesian shrinkage a valid alternative to principal components? *Journal of Econometrics 146*(2), 318–328.

Dedecker, J. and C. Prieur (2005). New dependence coefficients. examples and applications to statistics. *Probability Theory and Related Fields 132*(2), 203–236.

Demszky, D., N. Garg, R. Voigt, J. Zou, M. Gentzkow, J. Shapiro, and D. Jurafsky (2019, April). Analyzing Polarization in Social Media: Method and Application to Tweets on 21 Mass Shootings. *arXiv e-prints, arXiv:1904.01596.*

Devlin, J., M. Chang, K. Lee, and K. Toutanova (2019). BERT: pre-training of deep bidirectional transformers for language understanding. In J. Burstein, C. Doran, and T. Solorio (Eds.), *Proceedings of the 2019 Conference of the North American Chapter of the Association for Computational Linguistics: Human Language Technologies, NAACL-HLT 2019, Minneapolis, MN, USA, June 2-7, 2019, Volume 1 (Long and Short Papers)*, pp. 4171–4186. Association for Computational Linguistics.

Ding, P. (2017). A Paradox from Randomization-Based Causal Inference. *Statistical Science 32*(3), 331–345.

Doudchenko, N. and G. W. Imbens (2016). Balancing, regression, difference-in-differences and synthetic control methods: A synthesis. *NBER Working Papers 22791.*

Doukhan, P. (2012). *Mixing: properties and examples*, Volume 85. Springer Science & Business Media.

D'Haultfoeuille, X. (2011). On the completeness condition in nonparametric instrumental problems. *Econometric Theory 27*(3), 460–471.

Efron, B. (2014). Estimation and accuracy after model selection. *Journal of the American Statistical Association 109*(507), 991–1007.

Fan, J., C. Ma, and Y. Zhong (2021). A selective overview of deep learning. *Statistical Science 36*(2), 264–290.

Fan, J., Z. Lou, and M. Yu (2023). Are latent factor regression and sparse regression adequate? *Journal of the American Statistical Association*, 1–13.

Fan, J., R. P. Masini, and M. C. Medeiros (2023). Bridging factor and sparse models. *The Annals of Statistics 51*(4), 1692–1717.

Farrell, M. H., T. Liang, and S. Misra (2021). Deep neural networks for estimation and inference. *Econometrica 89*(1), 181–213.

Farrell, M. H. (2015). Robust inference on average treatment effects with possibly more covariates than observations. *Journal of Econometrics 189*(1), 1–23.

Feng, S. Y., V. Gangal, J. Wei, S. Chandar, S. Vosoughi, T. Mitamura, and E. H. Hovy (2021). A survey of data augmentation approaches for NLP. *CoRR abs/2105.03075.*

Ferman, B. and C. Pinto (2016). Revisiting the synthetic control estimator. *Working Paper.*

Ferrara, L. and A. Simoni (2019, February). When are Google data useful to nowcast GDP? An approach via pre-selection and shrinkage. Working Papers 2019-04, Center for Research in Economics and Statistics.

Ferrara, L., and A. Simoni (2022). When are Google data useful to nowcast gdp? *Journal of Business and Economic Statistics.*

Freedman, D. A. (2008). On regression adjustments to experimental data. *Advances in Applied Mathematics 40*(2), 180–193.

Fuller, W. A. (1977). Some properties of a modification of the limited information estimator. *Econometrica 45*(4), 939–953.

Gage, P. (1994). A new algorithm for data compression. *The C Users Journal archive 12*, 23–38.

Gaillac, C. and J. L'Hour (2023). *Machine Learning pour l'économétrie.* In *Economica.* (1st ed.).

Gautier, E. and C. Rose (2011). High-dimensional instrumental variables regression and confidence sets. *arXiv preprint arXiv:1105.2454.*

Gautier, E. and A. B. Tsybakov (2013). Pivotal estimation in high-dimensional regression via linear programming. In *Empirical inference.* New York, NY: Springer.

Gennaro, G. and E. Ash (2021, 12). Emotion and Reason in Political Language. *The Economic Journal 132*(643), 1037–1059.

Gentzkow, M., B. Kelly, and M. Taddy (2019, September). Text as data. *Journal of Economic Literature 57*(3), 535–74.

Gentzkow, M. and J. M. Shapiro (2010). What drives media slant? evidence from us daily newspapers. *Econometrica 78*(1), 35–71.

Gentzkow, M., J. M. Shapiro, and M. Taddy (2019). Measuring group differences in high-dimensional choices: Method and application to congressional speech. *Econometrica 87*(4), 1307–1340.

Ghysels, E., P. Santa-Clara, and R. Valkanov (2005). There is a risk-return trade-off after all. *Journal of Financial Economics 76*(3), 509–548.

Ghysels, E., A. Sinko, and R. Valkanov (2007). Midas regressions: Further results and new directions. *Econometric Reviews 26*(1), 53–90.

Giannone, D., M. Lenza, and G. E. Primiceri (2021). Economic predictions with big data: The illusion of sparsity. *Econometrica 89*(5), 2409–2437.

Giannone, D., L. Reichlin, and D. Small (2008). Nowcasting: The real-time informational content of macroeconomic data. *Journal of Monetary Economics 55*(4), 665–676.

Giraud, C. (2014). *Introduction to High-Dimensional Statistics* (1st ed.). New York, NY: Chapman and Hall.

Gobillon, L. and T. Magnac (2016). Regional policy evaluation: Interactive fixed effects and synthetic controls. *The Review of Economics and Statistics 98*(3), 535–551.

Godbole, V., G. E. Dahl, J. Gilmer, C. J. Shallue, and Z. Nado (2023). Deep learning tuning playbook. Version 1.0. https://github.com/google-research/tuning_playbook.

Goodfellow, I. J., Y. Bengio, and A. Courville (2016). *Deep Learning.* Cambridge, MA, USA: MIT Press. http://www.deeplearningbook.org.

Goulet-Coulombe, P., M. Leroux, D. Stevanovic, and S. Surprenant (2022). How is machine learning useful for macroeconomic forecasting? *Journal of Applied Econometrics 37*(5), 920–964.

Gourieroux, C., A. Monfort, and A. Trognon (1984). Pseudo maximum likelihood methods: Theory. *Econometrica 52*(3), 681–700.

Granger, C. W. (1969). Investigating causal relations by econometric models and cross-spectral methods. *Econometrica*, 424–438.

Grinsztajn, L., E. Oyallon, and G. Varoquaux (2022). Why do tree-based models still outperform deep learning on tabular data? *Thirty-sixth Conference on Neural Information Processing Systems Datasets and Benchmarks Track.* https://openreview.net/forum?id=Fp7__phQszn.

Hackmann, M. B., J. T. Kolstad, and A. E. Kowalski (2015). Adverse selection and an individual mandate: When theory meets practice. *American Economic Review 105*(3), 1030–1066.

Hahn, J. (1998). On the role of the propensity score in efficient semiparametric estimation of average treatment effects. *Econometrica 66*(2), 315–332.

Han, S., E. H. Schulman, K. Grauman, and S. Ramakrishnan (2021). Shapes as product differentiation: Neural network embedding in the analysis of markets for fonts. *arXiv preprint arXiv:2107.02739.*

Hansen, B. E. (2022). *Econometrics.* Princeton, NJ: Princeton University Press.

Hansen, S., M. McMahon, and A. Prat (2017). Transparency and deliberation within the fomc: a computational linguistics approach. *The Quarterly Journal of Economics 133*(2), 801–870.

Hansen, S., M. McMahon, and M. Tong (2019). The long-run information effect of central bank communication. *Journal of Monetary Economics 108*, 185–202.

Hartford, J., G. Lewis, K. Leyton-Brown, and M. Taddy (2017). Deep iv: A flexible approach for counterfactual prediction. In *International Conference on Machine Learning*, pp. 1414–1423. PMLR.

Hastie, T., R. Tibshirani, and J. Friedman (2009). *The Elements of Statistical Learning: Data mining, Inference and Prediction* (2nd ed.). New York, NY: Springer.

Hoberg, G. and G. Phillips (2016). Text-based network industries and endogenous product differentiation. *Journal of Political Economy 124*(5), 1423–1465.

Holland, P. W. (1986). Statistics and causal inference. *Journal of the American Statistical Association 81*(396), 945–960.

Hornik, K. (1991). Approximation capabilities of multilayer feedforward networks. *Neural Networks 4*(2), 251–257.

Hsu, Y.-C. (2017). Consistent tests for conditional treatment effects. *The Econometrics Journal 20*(1), 1–22.

HuggingFace (2022). The hugging face course, 2022. https://huggingface.co/course. [Online].

Hussam, R., N. Rigol, and B. N. Roth (2022). Targeting high ability entrepreneurs using community information: Mechanism design in the field. *American Economic Review 112*(3), 861–898.

Ibragimov, R. and S. Sharakhmetov (2002). The exact constant in the rosenthal inequality for random variables with mean zero. *Theory of Probability & Its Applications 46*(1), 127–132.

Imai, K. and M. Ratkovic (2014). Covariate balancing propensity score. *Journal of the Royal Statistical Society: Series B (Statistical Methodology) 76*(1), 243–263.

Imbens, G. W., and D. B. Rubin (2015, August). *Causal Inference for Statistics, Social, and Biomedical Sciences.* Cambridge Books. Cambridge University Press. Cambridge.

Imbens, G. W. and J. D. Angrist (1994). Identification and estimation of local average treatment effects. *Econometrica 62*(2), 467–475.

Isichenko, M. (2021). *Quantitative Portfolio Management: The Art and Science of Statistical Arbitrage.* Hoboken, NJ: Wiley.

Izsak, P., M. Berchansky, and O. Levy (2021). How to train BERT with an academic budget. *CoRR abs/2104.07705.*

Jiang, A. Q., A. Sablayrolles, A. Mensch, C. Bamford, D. S. Chaplot, D. de las Casas, F. Bressand, G. Lengyel, G. Lample, L. Saulnier, L. R. Lavaud, M.-A. Lachaux, P. Stock, T. L. Scao, T. Lavril, T. Wang, T. Lacroix, and W. E. Sayed (2023). Mistral 7b.

Jurafsky, D. and J. H. Martin (2019). *Speech and language processing: An introduction to natural language processing, computational linguistics, and speech recognition* (3rd ed.). Draft available at https://web.stanford.edu/ jurafsky/slp3/.

Künzel, S. R., J. S. Sekhon, P. J. Bickel, and B. Yu (2019). Metalearners for estimating heterogeneous treatment effects using machine learning. *Proceedings of the National Academy of Sciences 116*(10), 4156–4165.

Ke, Z. T., B. T. Kelly, and D. Xiu (2019, August). Predicting returns with text data. Working Paper 26186, National Bureau of Economic Research.

Kennedy, E. H. (2023). Towards optimal doubly robust estimation of heterogeneous causal effects. *Electronic Journal of Statistics17*(2), 3008–3049.

Kingma, D. P. and J. Ba (2015). Adam: A method for stochastic optimization. In Y. Bengio and Y. LeCun (Eds.), *3rd International Conference on Learning Representations, ICLR 2015, San Diego, CA, USA, May 7-9, 2015, Conference Track Proceedings.*

Kitagawa, T., S. Sakaguchi, and A. Tetenov (2021). Constrained classification and policy learning. *arXiv preprint arXiv:2106.12886.*

Kitagawa, T. and A. Tetenov (2018). Who should be treated? Empirical welfare maximization methods for treatment choice. *Econometrica 86*(2), 591–616.

Kleven, H. J., C. Landais, and E. Saez (2013). Taxation and international migration of superstars: Evidence from the european football market. *American Economic Review 103*(5), 1892–1924.

Kock, A. B., R. S. Pedersen, and J. R.-V. Sørensen (2024). Data-driven tuning parameter selection for high-dimensional vector autoregressions. *arXiv preprint arXiv:2403.06657.*

Kock, A. and T. Teräsvirta (2016). Forecasting macroeconomic variables using neural network models and three automated model selection techniques. *Econometric Reviews 35*(8-10), 1753–1779.

Kock, A. B. and L. Callot (2015). Oracle inequalities for high dimensional vector autoregressions. *Journal of Econometrics 186*(2), 325–344.

Kohavi, R. (1995). A study of cross-validation and bootstrap for accuracy estimation and model selection. In *Proceedings of the 14th International Joint Conference on Artificial Intelligence - Volume 2,* IJCAI'95, San Francisco, CA, USA, pp. 1137–1143. Morgan Kaufmann Publishers Inc.

Kolesár, M., U. K. Müller, and S. T. Roelsgaard (2023). The fragility of sparsity. *arXiv preprint arXiv:2311.02299.*

Kozlowski, A. C., M. Taddy, and J. A. Evans (2019). The geometry of culture: Analyzing the meanings of class through word embeddings. *American Sociological Review 84*(5), 905–949.

Kudo, T. (2018, July). Subword regularization: Improving neural network translation models with multiple subword candidates. In I. Gurevych and Y. Miyao (Eds.), *Proceedings of the 56th Annual Meeting of the Association for Computational Linguistics (Volume 1: Long Papers)*, Melbourne, Australia, pp. 66–75. Association for Computational Linguistics.

Kumar, M., D. Eckles, and S. Aral (2020, January). Scalable bundling via dense product embeddings. *arXiv e-prints, arXiv:2002.00100.*

L'Hour, J. (2020). L'économétrie en grande dimension. *Documents de Travail de l'Insee - INSEE Working Papers M2010*(01).

LaLonde, R. J. (1986). Evaluating the Econometric Evaluations of Training Programs with Experimental Data. *American Economic Review 76*(4), 604–20.

Lam, C. and Q. Yao (2012). Factor modeling for high-dimensional time series: inference for the number of factors. *The Annals of Statistics*, 694–726.

Lazarus, E., D. J. Lewis, J. H. Stock, and M. W. Watson (2018). Har inference: Recommendations for practice. *Journal of Business & Economic Statistics 36*(4), 541–559.

Leamer, E. E. (1983). Let's take the con out of econometrics. *The American Economic Review 73*(1), 31–43.

Lederer, J. and M. Vogt (2021). Estimating the lasso's effective noise. *Journal of Machine Learning Research 22*(276), 1–32.

Leeb, H. (2006). *The distribution of a linear predictor after model selection: Unconditional finite-sample distributions and asymptotic approximations*, Volume Number 49 of *Lecture Notes–Monograph Series*, pp. 291–311. Beachwood, Ohio, USA: Institute of Mathematical Statistics.

Leeb, H. and B. M. Pötscher (2005, 2). Model selection and inference: Facts and fiction. *Econometric Theory null*, 21–59.

Lei, J., M. G'Sell, A. Rinaldo, R. J. Tibshirani, and L. Wasserman (2017). Distribution-free predictive inference for regression. *Journal of the American Statistical Association.*

Levenshtein, V. I. (1966). Binary codes capable of correcting deletions, insertions and reversals. *Soviet Physics Doklady 10*(8), 707–710. Doklady Akademii Nauk SSSR, V163 No4 845-848 1965.

Li, R., L. B. Allal, Y. Zi, N. Muennighoff, D. Kocetkov, C. Mou, M. Marone, C. Akiki, J. Li, J. Chim, Q. Liu, E. Zheltonozhskii, T. Y. Zhuo, T. Wang, O. Dehaene, M. Davaadorj, J. Lamy-Poirier, J. Monteiro, O. Shliazhko, N. Gontier, N. Meade, A. Zebaze, M.-H. Yee, L. K. Umapathi, J. Zhu, B. Lipkin, M. Oblokulov, Z. Wang, R. Murthy, J. Stillerman, S. S. Patel, D. Abulkhanov, M. Zocca, M. Dey, Z. Zhang, N. Fahmy, U. Bhattacharyya, W. Yu, S. Singh, S. Luccioni, P. Villegas, M. Kunakov, F. Zhdanov, M. Romero, T. Lee, N. Timor, J. Ding, C. Schlesinger, H. Schoelkopf, J. Ebert, T. Dao, M. Mishra, A. Gu, J. Robinson, C. J. Anderson, B. Dolan-Gavitt, D. Contractor, S. Reddy, D. Fried, D. Bahdanau, Y. Jernite, C. M. Ferrandis, S. Hughes, T. Wolf, A. Guha, L. von Werra, and H. de Vries (2023). Starcoder: may the source be with you! cite arxiv:2305.06161.

Lin, W. (2013). Agnostic notes on regression adjustments to experimental data: Reexamining freedman's critique. *The Annals of Applied Statistics 7*(1), 295–318.

List, J. A., A. M. Shaikh, and Y. Xu (2016). Multiple hypothesis testing in experimental economics. Technical report, National Bureau of Economic Research.

Liu, Y., M. Ott, N. Goyal, J. Du, M. Joshi, D. Chen, O. Levy, M. Lewis, L. Zettlemoyer, and V. Stoyanov (2019). Roberta: A robustly optimized bert pretraining approach. *ArXiv abs/1907.11692.*

Loughran, T. and B. McDonald (2011). When is a liability not a liability? textual analysis, dictionaries, and 10-ks. *The Journal of Finance 66*(1), 35–65.

Lounici, K., M. Pontil, S. Van De Geer, and A. B. Tsybakov (2011). Oracle inequalities and optimal inference under group sparsity. *The Annals of Statistics 39*(4), 2164–2204.

Manski, C. F. (2004). Statistical treatment rules for heterogeneous populations. *Econometrica 72*(4), 1221–1246.

Masini, R. P., M. C. Medeiros, and E. F. Mendes (2021). Machine learning advances for time series forecasting. *Journal of Economic Surveys. 37*(1), 76–111

Matsui, Y., Y. Uchida, H. Jégou, and S. Satoh (2018). A survey of product quantization. *ITE Transactions on Media Technology and Applications 6*(1), 2–10.

Mbakop, E. and M. Tabord-Meehan (2021). Model selection for treatment choice: Penalized welfare maximization. *Econometrica 89*(2), 825–848.

McCracken, M. W. and S. Ng (2016). Fred-md: A monthly database for macroeconomic research. *Journal of Business & Economic Statistics 34*(4), 574–589.

Medeiros, M. C. (2022). Forecasting with machine learning methods. *in Econometrics with Machine Learning*, 111–149. New York, NY: Springer.

Medeiros, M. C., G. F. Vasconcelos, Á. Veiga, and E. Zilberman (2021). Forecasting inflation in a data-rich environment: the benefits of machine learning methods. *Journal of Business & Economic Statistics 39*(1), 98–119.

Meinshausen, N., and P. Bühlmann (2006). High-dimensional graphs and variable selection with the lasso. *The Annals of Statistics 34*(3), 1436–1462.

Meinshausen, N., L. Meier, and P. Bühlmann (2009). P-values for high-dimensional regression. *Journal of the American Statistical Association 104*(488), 1671–1681.

Mielke, S. J., Z. Alyafeai, E. Salesky, C. Raffel, M. Dey, M. Gallé, A. Raja, C. Si, W. Y. Lee, B. Sagot, and S. Tan (2021). Between words and characters: A brief history of open-vocabulary modeling and tokenization in nlp.

Mikolov, T., K. Chen, G. Corrado, and J. Dean (2013). Efficient estimation of word representations in vector space. *arXiv preprint arXiv:1301.3781.*

Mikolov, T., E. Grave, P. Bojanowski, C. Puhrsch, and A. Joulin (2018). Advances in pre-training distributed word representations. In *Proceedings of the International Conference on Language Resources and Evaluation (LREC 2018).*

Mikolov, T., I. Sutskever, K. Chen, G. S. Corrado, and J. Dean (2013). Distributed representations of words and phrases and their compositionality. In *Advances in neural information processing systems*, pp. 3111–3119. Red Hook, NY: Curran Associates, Inc.

Mogliani, M. and A. Simoni (2021). Bayesian midas penalized regressions: estimation, selection, and prediction. *Journal of Econometrics 222*(1), 833–860.

Moriwaki, D. (2019). Nowcasting unemployment rates with smartphone gps data. In *International Workshop on Multiple-Aspect Analysis of Semantic Trajectories*, pp. 21–33. New York, NY: Springer.

Nevo, A. (2001). Measuring market power in the ready-to-eat cereal industry. *Econometrica 69*(2), 307–342.

Newey, W. K., and D. McFadden (1994). Large sample estimation and hypothesis testing. *Handbook of Econometrics 4*, 2111–2245.

Newey, W. K. and J. L. Powell (2003). Instrumental variable estimation of nonparametric models. *Econometrica 71*(5), 1565–1578.

Newey, W. K. (1990). Efficient instrumental variables estimation of nonlinear models. *Econometrica, 58*(4) 809–837.

Newey, W. K., K. D. West, et al. (1987). A simple, positive semi-definite, heteroskedasticity and autocorrelation consistent covariance matrix. *Econometrica 55*(3), 703–708.

Nie, X. and S. Wager (2020, 09). Quasi-oracle estimation of heterogeneous treatment effects. *Biometrika 108*(2), 299–319.

Oliu-Barton, M., B. Pradelski, N. Woloszko, L. Guetta-Jeanreneaud, P. Aghion, P. Artus, A. Fontanet, P. Martin, and G. B. Wolff. (2022). The effect of covid certificates on vaccine uptake, health outcomes, and the economy. *Nature Communications 13*(3942).

Oliveira, R. (2013, December). The lower tail of random quadratic forms, with applications to ordinary least squares and restricted eigenvalue properties. *ArXiv e-prints.*

Olken, B. A. (2015, September). Promises and perils of pre-analysis plans. *Journal of Economic Perspectives 29*(3), 61–80.

OpenAI (2023). Gpt-4 technical report.

Paszke, A., S. Gross, F. Massa, A. Lerer, J. Bradbury, G. Chanan, T. Killeen, Z. Lin, N. Gimelshein, L. Antiga, A. Desmaison, A. Kopf, E. Yang, Z. DeVito, M. Raison, A. Tejani, S. Chilamkurthy, B. Steiner, L. Fang, J. Bai, and S. Chintala (2019). Pytorch: An imperative style, high-performance deep learning library. In *Advances in Neural Information Processing Systems 32*, pp. 8024–8035. New York, NY: Curran Associates, Inc.

Pearl, J. (2000). *Causality: Models, Reasoning, and Inference.* New York, NY: Cambridge University Press.

Pennington, J., R. Socher, and C. D. Manning (2014). Glove: Global vectors for word representation. In *Empirical Methods in Natural Language Processing (EMNLP)*, pp. 1532–1543.

Phuong, M. and M. Hutter (2022). Formal algorithms for transformers. https://arxiv.org/abs/2207.09238.

Portes, J., A. R. Trott, S. Havens, D. KING, A. Venigalla, M. Nadeem, N. Sardana, D. Khudia, and J. Frankle (2023). MosaicBERT: How to train BERT with a lunch money budget. In *Workshop on Efficient Systems for Foundation Models @ ICML2023.*

Powers, S., J. Qian, K. Jung, A. Schuler, N. H. Shah, T. Hastie, and R. Tibshirani (2017). Some methods for heterogeneous treatment effect estimation in high-dimensions. *arXiv preprint arXiv:1707.00102.*

Radford, A., K. Narasimhan, T. Salimans, and I. Sutskever (2018). Improving language understanding by generative pre-training. https://openai.com/research/language-unsupervised.

Radford, A., J. Wu, R. Child, D. Luan, D. Amodei, and I. Sutskever (2019). Language models are unsupervised multitask learners. *OpenAI.*

Rasley, J., S. Rajbhandari, O. Ruwase, and Y. He (2020). Deepspeed: System optimizations enable training deep learning models with over 100 billion parameters. In *Proceedings of the 26th ACM SIGKDD International Conference on Knowledge Discovery & Data Mining*, KDD '20, New York, NY, USA, pp. 3505–3506. Association for Computing Machinery.

Reimers, N. and I. Gurevych (2019, 11). Sentence-bert: Sentence embeddings using siamese bert-networks. In *Proceedings of the 2019 Conference on Empirical Methods in Natural Language Processing.* Association for Computational Linguistics.

Robert, C. P. et al. (2007). *The Bayesian choice: from decision-theoretic foundations to computational implementation*, Volume 2. New York, NY: Springer.

Robins, J. M., A. Rotnitzky, and L. P. Zhao (1994). Estimation of regression coefficients when some regressors are not always observed. *Journal of the American statistical Association 89*(427), 846–866.

Robinson, P. M. (1988). Root-n-consistent semiparametric regression. *Econometrica*, 931–954.

Rodriguez, P. L. and A. Spirling (2022). Word embeddings: What works, what doesn't, and how to tell the difference for applied research. *The Journal of Politics 84*, 101–115.

Rogers, A., O. Kovaleva, and A. Rumshisky (2021, 01). A Primer in BERTology: What We Know About How BERT Works. *Transactions of the Association for Computational Linguistics 8*, 842–866.

Rolnick, D. and M. Tegmark (2018). The power of deeper networks for expressing natural functions. In *International Conference on Learning Representations.*

Romano, J. P. and M. Wolf (2005). Stepwise multiple testing as formalized data snooping. *Econometrica 73*(4), 1237–1282.

Rosenbaum, P. R. and D. B. Rubin (1983). The central role of the propensity score in observational studies for causal effects. *Biometrika 70*(1), 41–55.

Rubin, D. B. (1974). Estimating causal effects of treatments in randomized and nonrandomized studies. *Journal of Educational Psychology 66*(5), 688.

Rudelson, M. and S. Zhou (2013, June). Reconstruction from anisotropic random measurements. *Information Theory, IEEE Transactions on 59*(6), 3434–3447.

Rudolph, M., F. Ruiz, S. Mandt, and D. Blei (2016). Exponential family embeddings. In D. Lee, M. Sugiyama, U. Luxburg, I. Guyon, and R. Garnett (Eds.), *Advances in Neural Information Processing Systems*, Volume 29. Curran Associates, Inc.

Ruiz, F. J. R., S. Athey, and D. M. Blei (2020). SHOPPER: A probabilistic model of consumer choice with substitutes and complements. *Ann. Appl. Statist. 14*(1), 1–27.

Rumelhart, D. E., G. E. Hinton, and R. J. Williams (1986). Learning Representations by Back-propagating Errors. *Nature 323*(6088), 533–536.

Rumelhart, D. and A. Abrahamson (1973). A model for analogical reasoning. *Cognitive Psychology 5*, 1–28.

Sala-I-Martin, X. X. (1997). I just ran two million regressions. *The American Economic Review 87*(2), 178–183.

Schmidt-Hieber, J. (2020). Nonparametric regression using deep neural networks with relu activation function. *Annals of Statistics 48*(4).

Schmitt, T., F. Gonard, P. Caillou, and M. Sebag (2017, November). Language Modelling for Collaborative Filtering: Application to Job Applicant Matching. In *ICTAI 2017 - 29th IEEE International Conference on Tools with Artificial Intelligence*, Boston, United States, pp. 1–8.

Schroff, F., D. Kalenichenko, and J. Philbin (2015). Facenet: A unified embedding for face recognition and clustering. In *CVPR*, pp. 815–823. IEEE Computer Society.

Schuster, M., and K. Nakajima (2012). Japanese and Korean voice search. In *ICASSP*, pp. 5149–5152. IEEE.

Sennrich, R., B. Haddow, and A. Birch (2016, August). Neural machine translation of rare words with subword units. In K. Erk and N. A. Smith (Eds.), *Proceedings of the 54th Annual Meeting of the Association for Computational Linguistics (Volume 1: Long Papers)*, Berlin, Germany, pp. 1715–1725. Association for Computational Linguistics.

Simonyan, K. and A. Zisserman (2015). Very deep convolutional networks for large-scale image recognition. In Y. Bengio and Y. LeCun (Eds.), *3rd International Conference on Learning Representations, ICLR 2015, San Diego, CA, USA, May 7–9, 2015, Conference Track Proceedings.*

Sims, C. A. (1972). Money, income, and causality. *The American Economic Review 62*(4), 540–552.

Sohn, K. (2016). Improved deep metric learning with multi-class n-pair loss objective. In D. Lee, M. Sugiyama, U. Luxburg, I. Guyon, and R. Garnett (Eds.), *Advances in Neural Information Processing Systems*, Volume 29. Curran Associates, Inc.

Song, X., A. Salcianu, Y. Song, D. Dopson, and D. Zhou (2021, November). Fast WordPiece tokenization. In *Proceedings of the 2021 Conference on Empirical Methods in Natural Language Processing*, Online and Punta Cana, Dominican Republic, pp. 2089–2103. Association for Computational Linguistics.

Stephens-Davidowitz, S. (2014). The cost of racial animus on a black candidate: Evidence using Google search data. *Journal of Public Economics 118*(C), 26–40.

Stock, J. H., and M. W. Watson (2002). Forecasting using principal components from a large number of predictors. *Journal of the American Statistical Association 97*(460), 1167–1179.

Stock, J. H. and M. W. Watson (2011). Dynamic factor models. In *Handbook on Economic Forecasting.* Oxford: Oxford University Press.

Stoye, J. (2009). Minimax regret treatment choice with finite samples. *Journal of Econometrics 151*(1), 70–81.

Stoye, J. (2012). Minimax regret treatment choice with covariates or with limited validity of experiments. *Journal of Econometrics 166*(1), 138–156.

Sul, H., A. Dennis, and L. Yuan (2016, 06). Trading on Twitter: Using social media sentiment to predict stock returns. *Decision Sciences 48*.

Sun, T., A. Gaut, S. Tang, Y. Huang, M. ElSherief, J. Zhao, D. Mirza, E. Belding, K.-W. Chang, and W. Y. Wang (2019, July). Mitigating gender bias in natural language processing: Literature review. In *Proceedings of the 57th Annual Meeting of the Association for Computational Linguistics*, Florence, Italy, pp. 1630–1640. Association for Computational Linguistics.

Szegedy, C., W. Liu, Y. Jia, P. Sermanet, S. Reed, D. Anguelov, D. Erhan, V. Vanhoucke, and A. Rabinovich (2015). Going deeper with convolutions. In *2015 IEEE Conference on Computer Vision and Pattern Recognition (CVPR)*, pp. 1–9.

Taddy, M. (2013). Multinomial inverse regression for text analysis. *Journal of the American Statistical Association 108*(503), 755–770.

Tibshirani, R. (1994). Regression shrinkage and selection via the lasso. *Journal of the Royal Statistical Society, Series B 58*, 267–288.

Touvron, H., L. Martin, K. Stone, P. Albert, A. Almahairi, Y. Babaei, N. Bashlykov, S. Batra, P. Bhargava, S. Bhosale, D. Bikel, L. Blecher, C. C. Ferrer, M. Chen, G. Cucurull, D. Esiobu, J. Fernandes, J. Fu, W. Fu, B. Fuller, C. Gao, V. Goswami, N. Goyal, A. Hartshorn, S. Hosseini, R. Hou, H. Inan, M. Kardas, V. Kerkez, M. Khabsa, I. Kloumann, A. Korenev, P. S. Koura, M.-A. Lachaux, T. Lavril, J. Lee, D. Liskovich, Y. Lu, Y. Mao, X. Martinet, T. Mihaylov, P. Mishra, I. Molybog, Y. Nie, A. Poulton,

J. Reizenstein, R. Rungta, K. Saladi, A. Schelten, R. Silva, E. M. Smith, R. Subramanian, X. E. Tan, B. Tang, R. Taylor, A. Williams, J. X. Kuan, P. Xu, Z. Yan, I. Zarov, Y. Zhang, A. Fan, M. Kambadur, S. Narang, A. Rodriguez, R. Stojnic, S. Ed unov, and T. Scialom (2023). Llama 2: Open foundation and fine-tuned chat models.

Tsybakov, A. B. (2009). *Introduction to nonparametric estimation.* New York, NY: Springer.

Tunstall, L., L. von Werra, and T. Wolf (2022). *Natural Language Processing with Transformers: Building Language Applications with Hugging Face.* Sebastopol, CA: O'Reilly Media.

Uematsu, Y. and S. Tanaka (2019). High-dimensional macroeconomic forecasting and variable selection via penalized regression. *The Econometrics Journal 22*(1), 34–56.

Van de Geer, S. A. (2008, 04). High-dimensional generalized linear models and the lasso. *Ann. Statist. 36*(2), 614–645.

Van der Vaart, A. W. (1998). *Asymptotic statistics.* Cambridge: Cambridge University Press.

Van der vaart, A. and J. Wellner (1996). *Weak Convergence and Empirical Processes: With Applications to Statistics.* Springer Series in Statistics. New York, NY: Springer.

Van de Geer, S., P. Bühlmann, Y. Ritov, and R. Dezeure (2014). On asymptotically optimal confidence regions and tests for high-dimensional models. *The Annals of Statistics 42*(3), 1166–1202.

Vapnik, V. (1998). *Statistical learning theory.* Wiley, New York.

Vaswani, A., N. Shazeer, N. Parmar, J. Uszkoreit, L. Jones, A. N. Gomez, L. u. Kaiser, and I. Polosukhin (2017). Attention is all you need. In I. Guyon, U. V. Luxburg, S. Bengio, H. Wallach, R. Fergus, S. Vishwanathan, and R. Garnett (Eds.), *Advances in Neural Information Processing Systems,* Volume 30. Curran Associates, Inc.

Vershynin, R. (2018). *High-Dimensional Probability: An Introduction with Applications in Data Science.* Number 47 in Cambridge Series in Statistical and Probabilistic Mathematics. Cambridge University Press.

Viviano, D. (2019). Policy targeting under network interference. *arXiv preprint arXiv:1906.10258.*

Viviano, D. and J. Bradic (2020). Fair policy targeting. *arXiv preprint arXiv:2005.12395.*

Wüthrich, K. and Y. Zhu (2023). Omitted variable bias of lasso-based inference methods: A finite sample analysis. *Review of Economics and Statistics 105*(4), 982–997.

Wager, S. and S. Athey (2017). Estimation and inference of heterogeneous treatment effects using random forests. *Journal of the American Statistical Association.*

Wager, S., T. Hastie, and B. Efron (2014). Confidence intervals for random forests: The jackknife and the infinitesimal jackknife. *The Journal of Machine Learning Research 15*(1), 1625–1651.

Wager, S. and G. Walther (2015, March). Adaptive Concentration of Regression Trees, with Application to Random Forests. *ArXiv e-prints.*

Wasserman, L. (2010). *All of statistics: A concise course in statistical inference.* New York: Springer.

Wettig, A., T. Gao, Z. Zhong, and D. Chen (2023, May). Should you mask 15% in masked language modeling? In A. Vlachos and I. Augenstein (Eds.), *Proceedings of the 17th Conference of the European Chapter of the Association for Computational Linguistics,* Dubrovnik, Croatia, pp. 2985–3000. Association for Computational Linguistics.

Wooldridge, J. M. (2002). *Econometric analysis of cross section and panel data.* Cambridge and London: MIT Press.

Wu, E. and J. A. Gagnon-Bartsch (2018). The loop estimator: Adjusting for covariates in randomized experiments. *Evaluation Review 42*(4), 458–488. PMID: 30442034.

Wu, W. B. (2005). Nonlinear system theory: Another look at dependence. *Proceedings of the National Academy of Sciences 102*(40), 14150–14154.

Wu, W.-B. and Y. N. Wu (2016). Performance bounds for parameter estimates of high-dimensional linear models with correlated errors. *Electronic Journal of Statistics 10*(1), 352–379.

Wu, S., O. Irsoy, S. Lu, V. Dabravolski, M. Dredze, S. Gehrmann, P. Kambadur, D. Rosenberg, and G. Mann (2023). Bloomberggpt: A large language model for finance.

Yang, Y. (2005). Can the strengths of aic and bic be shared? a conflict between model indentification and regression estimation. *Biometrika 92*(4), 937–950.

Zhang, C.-H. and S. S. Zhang (2014). Confidence intervals for low dimensional parameters in high dimensional linear models. *Journal of the Royal Statistical Society: Series B (Statistical Methodology) 76*(1), 217–242.

Zhang, T. (2004). Statistical behavior and consistency of classification methods based on convex risk minimization. *The Annals of Statistics 32*(1), 56–85.

Zhang, D. and W. B. Wu (2017). Gaussian approximation for high dimensional time series. *The Annals of Statistics 45*(5), 1895–1919.

Zhao, P. and B. Yu (2006, December). On model selection consistency of lasso. *J. Mach. Learn. Res. 7*, 2541–2563.

Zhao, W., J. Chen, R. Perkins, Z. Liu, W. Ge, Y. Ding, and W. Zou (2015, 09). A heuristic approach to determine an appropriate number of topics in topic modeling. *BMC Bioinformatics 16*, S8.

Zhao, W. X., K. Zhou, J. Li, T. Tang, X. Wang, Y. Hou, Y. Min, B. Zhang, J. Zhang, Z. Dong, Y. Du, C. Yang, Y. Chen, Z. Chen, J. Jiang, R. Ren, Y. Li, X. Tang, Z. Liu, P. Liu, J.-Y. Nie, and J.-R. Wen (2023). A survey of large language models.

Zhou, Z., S. Athey, and S. Wager (2018). Offline multi-action policy learning: Generalization and optimization. *arXiv preprint arXiv:1810.04778*.

Index

The locators followed by *f* and *t* indicates figures and tables.